Apple Training Series

Mac OS X Support Essentials Second Edition

Kevin M. White

Apple
Certified

Apple Training Series: Mac OS X Support Essentials, Second Edition
Kevin M. White
Copyright © 2008 by Apple Inc.

Published by Peachpit Press. For information on Peachpit Press books, contact:

Peachpit Press
1249 Eighth Street
Berkeley, CA 94710
510/524-2178
510/524-2221 (fax)

Find us on the Web at www.peachpit.com.
To report errors, please send a note to errata@peachpit.com.
Peachpit Press is a division of Pearson Education.

Project Editor: Rebecca Freed
Editor: Tracy Collins
Production Editor: Laurie Stewart, Happenstance Type-O-Rama
Copyeditor: Liz Welch
Tech Editor: Joel Rennich
Proofreader: Darren Meiss
Compositor: Chris Gillespie, Happenstance Type-O-Rama
Indexer: Karin Arrigoni
Cover design: Mimi Heft

ISBN 13: 978-0-321-48981-4
ISBN 10: 0-321-48981-0

9 8 7 6 5 4 3 2

Printed and bound in the United States of America

This book is dedicated in loving memory to Michael Reily White.

Acknowledgments In addition to the amazing staff at Apple and Peachpit who were instrumental in completing this work, I would also like to thank Schoun Regan, Mark Henderson, Chase Kelly, David Seebaldt, John Welch, Russ White, Shelley Watson, Duane Maas, and Doug Hanley. Finally, I could not have made this journey without the support of my family and wife, Michelle.

User Expe

Dashboard

Aqua

Appli on

Cocoa

Car

Graphics a

Q Core Audio Core In

Dar

Table of Contents

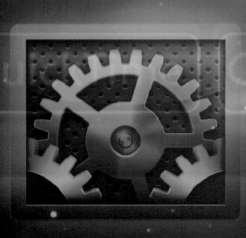

Getting Started

This manual is based on the same criteria used for Apple's official training course, Mac OS X Support Essentials v10.5, an in-depth exploration of troubleshooting on Mac OS X. It serves as a self-paced tour of the breadth of functionality of Mac OS X and the best methods for effectively supporting users of Mac OS X systems.

The primary goal is to prepare help desk specialists, technical coordinators, service technicians, system administrators, and others who support Macintosh users to knowledgeably address customer concerns and questions. This includes the ability to return a Mac OS X computer to normal operation using the proper utilities, resources, and troubleshooting techniques.

Whether you are an experienced system administrator or just want to dig deeper into Mac OS X 10.5, you'll learn in-depth technical information and procedures used by Apple-certified technicians to install, configure, maintain, and diagnose Macintosh computers running Mac OS X.

This manual assumes a basic level of familiarity with Mac OS X. Unless otherwise specified, all references to Mac OS X refer to Mac OS X 10.5.1, which was the most current version available at the time of writing. Due to subsequent upgrades, some screen shots, features, and procedures may be slightly different from those presented on these pages.

Learning Methodology

This manual is based on lectures and exercises provided to students attending Mac OS X Support Essentials v10.5, a three-day, hands-on course that provides an intense and in-depth exploration of how to troubleshoot on Mac OS X. For consistency, we follow the basic structure of the course material, but you may complete it at your own pace.

Each lesson is designed to help experienced users become experts who are able to support other Mac OS X users by:

▶ Providing *knowledge* of how Mac OS X works

▶ Showing how to use diagnostic and repair *tools*

▶ Explaining troubleshooting and repair *procedures*

For example, in Lesson 6, "Network Configuration and Troubleshooting," you'll learn basic networking concepts (knowledge). You'll acquire network configuration and trouble-shooting techniques using the Network preference and Network Utility (tools). And you'll explore methods for troubleshooting networking issues (procedures). In addition, each lesson includes troubleshooting techniques for dealing with common issues related to the topic of the lesson.

Each lesson focuses on a different aspect of Mac OS X:

▶ Lesson 1, "Installation and Initial Setup"—Preparing and partitioning the drive; installing Mac OS X; using the installer log files to verify a successful installation; configuring Mac OS X with the Setup Assistant; updating software with Software Update and Installer; learning tips and techniques for troubleshooting an installation problem.

▶ Lesson 2, "Users Accounts"—Creating and managing user and administrator accounts; locating directory attributes; implementing security; selecting passwords; managing the keychain; and FileVault.

▶ Lesson 3, "File Systems"—Identifying the file systems supported by Mac OS X; managing file and directory ownership and permissions; using Disk Utility; repairing files; using the command line for file management.

▶ Lesson 4, "Data Management and Backup"—Exploring the root volume, file system layout, preferences, frameworks, and file types unique to Mac OS X (i.e., resource forks and packages); using Spotlight, file archives, disk images; archiving and restoring data with Time Machine; managing backup data; accessing data outside of Time Machine.

▶ Lesson 5, "Applications and Boot Camp"—Understanding applications supported in Mac OS X, applications created with different developer APIs, the UNIX concept of a process, and the relationship of processes and applications; using tools to monitor and manage processes; setting application preferences; troubleshooting; using Boot Camp.

▶ Lesson 6, "Network Configuration"—Configuring basic networks; setting up TCP/IP networking, Ethernet, and AirPort; connecting multiple networks; using network locations; isolating and troubleshooting network elements.

▶ Lesson 7, "Accessing Network Services"—Connecting to common network resources; creating Network Users accounts with Directory Services; accessing AFP, SMB, SSH, FTP, and WebDAV connections; using Bonjour, NetBIOS, and the network browser; isolating client software issues from network issues.

▶ Lesson 8, "Providing Network Services"—Enabling network services on a Mac OS X client; setting up peer-to-peer collaboration, sharing files between Macs and Windows; sharing web documents; taking advantage of screen sharing; using firewalls; learning techniques to isolate server issues from client and network issues.

▶ Lesson 9, "Peripherals and Printing"—Connecting peripherals to a Macintosh; identifying cabling, connections, and device drivers for common peripherals; managing printers and print jobs; understanding printer PPDs and PDF workflow; learning techniques for isolating cabling, driver, or application issues.

▶ Lesson 10, "Startup Process"—Troubleshooting boot issues with a Macintosh at startup; understanding the phases of the startup process; identifying the active part of the system during each phase; exploring issues that can arise; launching processes automatically with the launchd and loginwindow startup items.

In an effort to be informative but not overwhelming, we also include an appendix of general Apple troubleshooting information. It may be valuable to you, but it's not essential for the coursework or certification.

Lesson Structure

Each lesson begins with an opening page that lists the learning goals for the lesson and an estimate of the time needed to complete the lesson. The explanatory material is augmented with hands-on exercises essential to developing your skills. For the most part, all you need to complete the exercises is a Macintosh computer running Mac OS X 10.5 or later. If you lack the equipment necessary to complete a given exercise, you are still encouraged to read the step-by-step instructions and examine the screen shots to understand the procedures demonstrated.

> **NOTE** ▶ Some of these exercises can be disruptive—for example, they may turn off network services temporarily—and some exercises, if performed incorrectly, could result in data loss or damage to system files. As such, it's recommended that you perform these exercises on a Macintosh that is not critical to your daily productivity. Apple Computer, Inc. and Peachpit Press are not responsible for any data loss or any damage to any equipment that occurs as a direct or indirect result of following the procedures described in this manual.

We refer to Apple Knowledge Base documents throughout the lessons, and close each lesson with a list of recommended documents related to the topic of the lesson. The Knowledge Base is a free online resource (http://www.apple.com/support) containing the very latest technical information on all of Apple's hardware and software products. We strongly encourage you to read the suggested documents and search the Knowledge Base for answers to any problems you encounter.

You'll also find "More Info" resources throughout the lessons, and summarized at the end of each lesson, that provide ancillary information. These resources are merely for your edification, and are not considered essential for the coursework or certification.

At the end of each lesson is a short "Lesson Review" that recaps the material you've learned. You can refer to various Apple resources, such as the Knowledge Base, as well as the lessons themselves, to help you answer these questions.

Apple Certification

After reading this manual, you may wish to take the Mac OS X Support Essentials v10.5 exam to earn the Apple Certified Support Professional 10.5 certification. This is the first level of Apple's certification programs for Mac OS X professionals:

▶ Apple Certified Support Professional 10.5 (ACSP)—Ideal for help desk personnel, service technicians, technical coordinators, and others who support Mac OS X customers over the phone or who perform Mac OS X troubleshooting and support in schools and businesses. This certification verifies an understanding of Mac OS X core functionality and an ability to configure key services, perform basic troubleshooting, and assist end users with essential Mac OS X capabilities. To receive this certification, you must pass the Mac OS X Support Essentials v10.5 certification exam. This manual is intended to provide you with the knowledge and skills to pass that exam.

> **NOTE** ▶ Although all of the questions in the Mac OS X Support Essentials v10.5 exam are based on material in this manual, simply reading it will not adequately prepare you for the exam. Apple recommends that before taking the exam, you spend time actually setting up, configuring, and troubleshooting Mac OS X. You should also download and review the Skills Assessment Guide, which lists the exam objectives, the total number of items, the number of items per section, the required score to pass, and how to register. A 10-item Sample Test is also available for download. Items on the Sample Test are similar in style to items on the certification exam, though they may vary in difficulty level. To download the Skills Assessment Guide and Sample Test, visit http://train.apple.com/certification/macosx

▶ Apple Certified Technical Coordinator 10.5 (ACTC)—This certification is intended for Mac OS X technical coordinators and entry-level system administrators tasked with maintaining a modest network of computers using Mac OS X Server. Since the ACTC certification addresses both the support of Mac OS X clients and the core functionality and use of Mac OS X Server, the learning curve is correspondingly longer and more intensive than that for the ACSP certification, which addresses solely Mac OS X client support. This certification is not intended for high-end system administrators or engineers, but may be an excellent step to take on an intended career path to system administration. This certification requires passing both the Mac OS X Support Essentials v10.5 and Mac OS X Server Essentials v10.5 exams.

▶ Apple Certified System Administrator 10.5 (ACSA)—This certification verifies an in-depth knowledge of Apple technical architecture and an ability to install and configure machines; architect and maintain networks; enable, customize, tune, and troubleshoot a wide range of services; and integrate Mac OS X, Mac OS X Server, and other Apple technologies within a multiplatform networked environment. The ACSA certification is intended for full-time professional system administrators and engineers who manage medium-to-large networks of systems in complex multiplatform deployments. This certification requires passing the Mac OS X Server Essentials v10.5, Directory Services v10.5, Deployment v10.5, and Advanced Administration v10.5 exams.

The Apple Certified Support Professional 10.5 certification can also be a step toward the Apple hardware service technician certifications. These certifications are ideal for people interested in becoming Macintosh repair technicians, but also worthwhile for help desk personnel at schools and businesses, and for Macintosh consultants and others needing an in-depth understanding of how Apple systems operate:

▶ Apple Certified Desktop Technician (ACDT)—This certification requires passing the Apple Desktop Service exam and a qualifying Mac OS X exam such as the Mac OS X Support Essentials v10.5 exam.

▶ Apple Certified Portable Technician (ACPT)—This certification requires passing the Apple Portable Service exam and a qualifying Mac OS X exam such as the Mac OS X Support Essentials v10.5 exam.

About the Apple Training Series

Apple Training Series: Mac OS X Support Essentials, Second Edition is part of the official training series for Apple products developed by experts in the field and certified by Apple. The lessons are designed to let you learn at your own pace. You can progress through the manual from beginning to end, or dive right into the lessons that interest you most.

For those who prefer to learn in an instructor-led setting, Apple also offers training courses at Apple Authorized Training Centers worldwide. These courses are taught by Apple certified trainers, and they balance concepts and lectures with hands-on labs and exercises. Apple Authorized Training Centers have been carefully selected and have met Apple's highest standards in all areas, including facilities, instructors, course delivery, and infrastructure. The goal of the program is to offer Apple customers, from beginners to the most seasoned professionals, the highest-quality training experience.

To find an Authorized Training Center near you, please visit http://train.apple.com.

1

Time   This lesson takes approximately 3 hours to complete.

Goals   Prepare a computer for installation of Mac OS X 10.5

Successfully install Mac OS X 10.5 software

Complete initial configuration of Mac OS X 10.5

Troubleshoot potential installation problems

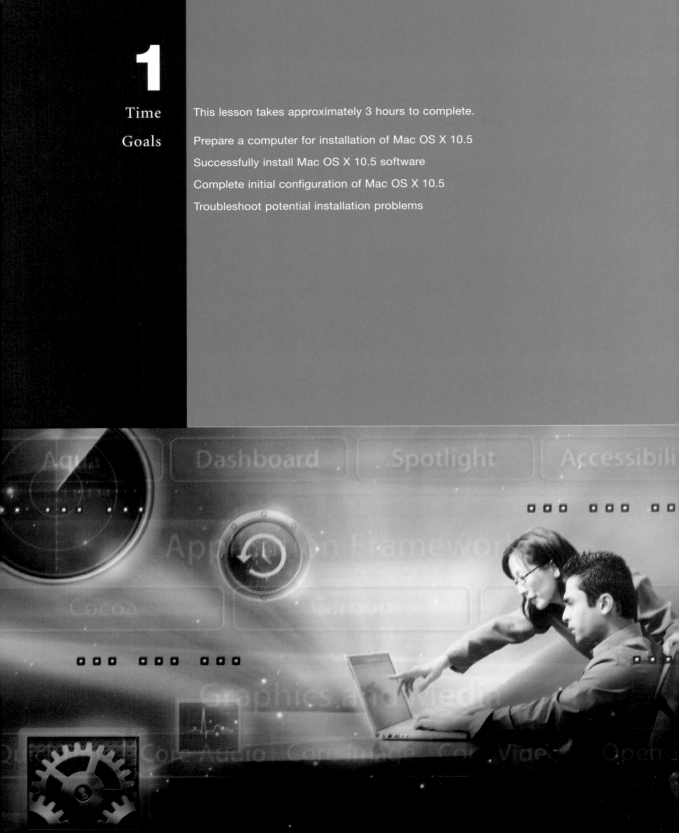

Lesson **1**
Installation and Initial Setup

Without software, a computer is nothing more than an expensive collection of sand, metals, and plastic. That's not to say that hardware doesn't matter. It would be foolish to ignore the exceptional quality and panache with which Apple creates its hardware. However, due to the homogenization of PC hardware, today's Macintosh uses many of the same parts found in lesser computers. So it's not the processor, nor storage, nor even the trend-setting design that alone set Apple's computers apart from the competition. The same thing that makes the Macintosh special is also responsible for elevating simple hardware to a functional computer. This, the true "soul" of a computer, is its operating system.

Every Macintosh computer had some version of Mac OS preinstalled when it was built. The particular version Mac OS X that ships with a computer is usually the latest available at the time it was introduced to market. Thus, the operating system on every Macintosh will at some point be outdated and require a newer version to take advantage of the latest features and bug fixes. This lesson starts with a brief introduction of Mac OS X 10.5, and then guides you through the installation and initial configuration processes, including troubleshooting any problems that may arise during these steps. Several of the operations that you will cover in this lesson involve significant changes, many of which are very difficult to reverse, if not completely irreversible. Therefore, if you plan on experimenting with the topics discussed in this lesson, it is advisable that you do so on a spare computer or external hard drive that does not contain critical data.

About Mac OS X 10.5

Mac OS X 10.5, also known by its development codename "Leopard," is the latest major revision of Apple's primary operating system. Since its introduction in 2001, Mac OS X has become an increasingly attractive alternative to more common operating systems due to its truly unique combination of innovative technologies. Mac OS X is the only operating system that combines a powerful open source UNIX foundation with a state-of-the-art user interface, including all the easy-to-use features for which Apple is known. Further, the Macintosh platform provides an exceptional development platform as evidenced by the large selection of high-quality, third-party software titles.

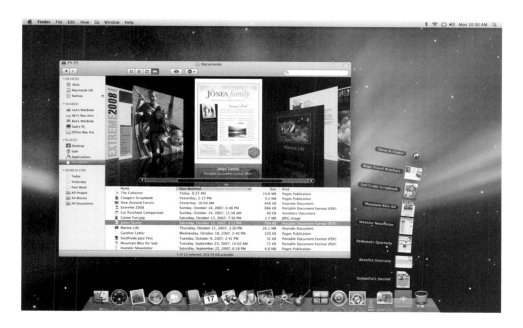

In addition to all the previous features found in older versions of Mac OS X, the latest version 10.5 adds a host of exciting new features that make life easier for everyone from casual users to experienced administrators. A redesigned user interface includes the Spaces multiple desktop manager and a completely new Finder with Cover Flow and Quick Look views for easier navigation. Nearly every included accessory application, including Mail, iCal, and Safari, boast significant new features. Other applications, like iChat and parental controls, have been updated with features that allow for simpler administration. Time Machine provides a revolutionary new backup and restoration mechanism that aids in data recovery. Finally, the most significant feature for anyone switching to Macintosh, Boot Camp allows any Intel-based Macintosh to run Windows XP or Windows Vista.

> **TIP** ▶ Apple's online Macintosh Products Guide is the definitive resource for finding hardware and software designed to work with the Macintosh: http://guide.apple.com/.

Integration Through Standards

Much of the success of Mac OS X can be attributed to Apple's copious use of industry-standard formats and open source software. The historic perception of the Macintosh platform being closed or proprietary is far removed from today's reality. Nearly every technology in Mac OS X is based on well-known standards. Adoption of common standards saves engineering time and allows for much smoother integration with other platforms. Even in the cases where Apple's developers had to engineer their own technology for a new feature, often Apple will release its details as a new standard. A fine example of this is the Bonjour network discovery protocol, which Apple pioneered and has maintained as an open standard for others to develop and use.

Some examples of common standards supported by Mac OS X are:

▶ Connectivity standards—Universal Serial Bus (USB), IEEE 1394 (FireWire), Bluetooth wireless, and the IEEE 802 family of Ethernet standards

▶ File system standards—UNIX File System (UFS), File Allocation Table (FAT32), New Technology File System (NTFS), Zettabyte File System (ZFS), ISO-9660 optical disc standard, Universal Disc Format (UDF)

▶ Network standards—Dynamic Host Configuration Protocol (DHCP), Domain Name Service (DNS), Hypertext Transfer Protocol (HTTP), Internet Message Access Protocol (IMAP), Simple Mail Transfer Protocol (SMTP), File Transfer Protocol (FTP), Network File System (NFS), and Server Message Block/Common Internet File System (SMB/CIFS)

▶ Application and development standards—Single UNIX Specification v3 (SUSv3), Portable Operating System Interface 1003.1 (POSIX), C and C++, Java, Ruby, Python, and Perl

▶ Document standards—ZIP file archives, Rich Text Format (RTF), Portable Document Format (PDF), Tagged Image File Format (TIFF), Portable Network Graphics (PNG), Advanced Audio Codec (AAC), and the Moving Picture Experts Group (MPEG) family of media standards

Layers of Mac OS X

In contrast to the apparent simplicity presented to the user on its surface, Mac OS X is a highly complicated operating system made up of hundreds of different processes and several hundred thousand files and folders. However, a bird's-eye view reveals that this operating system is made up of four primary components. Though covered briefly here, many of these concepts will be further discussed in Lesson 5, "Applications and Boot Camp."

Starting from the lowest levels of the system to the user interface, the four primary layers of Mac OS X are:

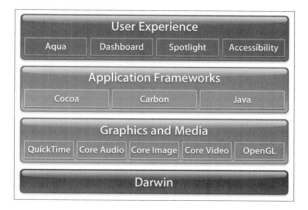

- ▶ Darwin—This is the open source UNIX core of Mac OS X. This lowest level of the system provides advanced functionality such as protected memory, preemptive multi-tasking, symmetric multiprocessing, a secure multiple user environment, and advanced multiple-link multihoming networking. Though based on the Mach microkernel and Berkeley Software Distribution (BSD) UNIX, Darwin has evolved into its own distinct version of UNIX. As of Mac OS X 10.5, Darwin is no longer simply "based on UNIX," but is now an Open Brand UNIX 03 Registered Product—meaning it boasts full compatibility with the Single UNIX Specification, Version 3 (SUSv3) and POSIX UNIX applications and utilities.

- ▶ Graphics and Media—Though close to the bottom, these technologies provide fundamental services that add tremendous value to the Apple user experience. Residing here are technologies such as OpenGL, OpenAL, Core Audio, Core Image, Core Video, Core Animation, Core Data, and QuickTime. These services allow developers to rapidly create advanced applications that require much less knowledge of complicated low-level code. Simply, Apple has done all the hard work commonly associated with creating an application that uses a graphical user interface, which allows developers to create higher-quality applications in less time.

▶ Application Frameworks—Here you find the primary development platforms that engineers use to create Macintosh applications. Cocoa is based on Objective-C and is the primary development platform for Mac OS X. Carbon, largely based on C and C++ code, is a development platform with roots in Mac OS 9 that allows developers to easily move their legacy code forward. Finally, Java is a highly portable development platform originally created by Sun Microsystems.

▶ User Experience—This is as deep as most users ever get with Mac OS X, and for good reason. This is where most users interact with the system and its applications. Technologies that really make the Macintosh platform stand out are on display at this level. The Aqua user interface, Spotlight search engine, and Dashboard widgets are present here. UNIX applications accessed via the command line and the X11 windowing environment can also be considered part of this level.

MORE INFO ▶ For more on Mac OS X system architecture, refer to Apple's own development resources: http://developer.apple.com/macosx/architecture/.

Installing Mac OS X 10.5

Apple is well known for designing every operation to be as easy as possible, and the installation process is an example of this. The installation process for Mac OS X is so well engineered that most users could easily complete it with no training. However, anyone tasked with supporting Mac OS X computers should be more familiar with all the necessary procedures to ensure a smooth installation.

New Macs usually come with a computer-specific release of Mac OS X that was engineered specifically for that model. This documentation assumes that you will be using a standard retail package of Mac OS X 10.5, so you may find that some details will vary if you are using a computer-specific install disc. For more information refer to Knowledge Base document 25784, "What's a 'computer-specific Mac OS X release'?"

Verifying Installation Requirements

It's important to understand the installation requirements for the copy of Mac OS X you plan to use and also the requirements of the particular Macintosh you intend to install it on. If you're not sure what the intended computers' specifications are, use the System Profiler application to view the computers' status. If the Macintosh is already running

Mac OS X, you can simply open System Profiler (in the /Applications/Utilities folder). Also, you can get to System Profiler by clicking About This Mac in the Apple menu, then clicking More Info. If you've booted from the Mac OS X Install DVD, the System Profiler is available from the Utilities menu. Within System Profiler, verify the computers' specifications by selecting and viewing the various content areas in the Hardware section.

Mac OS X 10.5 requires a Macintosh computer with:

▶ An Intel, PowerPC G5, or PowerPC G4 (867 MHz or faster) processor

▶ 512 MB of memory

▶ DVD drive for installation

▶ 9 GB of available disk space

▶ Some features require a compatible Internet service provider; fees may apply.

▶ Some features require Apple's .Mac service; fees apply.

> **MORE INFO** ▶ Some Mac OS X 10.5 features have additional requirements beyond these minimum system requirements. You can find out more about these feature-specific requirements at the Mac OS X 10.5 technical specifications website: http://www.apple.com/macosx/techspecs/.

As you can see from these requirements, Mac OS X generally supports hardware several years older than the latest version of the operating system. However, older versions of Mac OS X do not support hardware that is newer than when the operating system was released. In other words, you may come across a Macintosh that's newer than the Mac OS X installation disc you're trying to use. If this is the case, the installation disc will fail to boot or refuse to install the older operating system.

> **MORE INFO** ▶ For further information, refer to Knowledge Base document 25497, "Don't Install Older Versions of Mac OS than What Comes with Your Computer."

Preparing for Installation

While you could certainly jump right into the Mac OS X installation process without doing any preparation work, taking the time to complete some preliminary steps will greatly reduce your chances of experiencing installation problems or losing important data. There are four crucial steps you should take before any system installations:

1   Check for Firmware updates. Firmware is low-level software that facilitates the startup and management of system hardware. Though it's quite rare, Apple may release firmware updates that will be necessary for older Macintosh computers to operate properly with new system software. You can identify the Firmware version on a currently running Mac by opening /Applications/Utilities/System Profiler, or on a Mac booted from the Mac OS X Install DVD by choosing System Profiler from the Utilities menu. The default view for System Profiler will identify the Firmware version as the "Boot ROM Version." Additionally Intel-based Macintosh computers also use a "SMC Version" identifier.

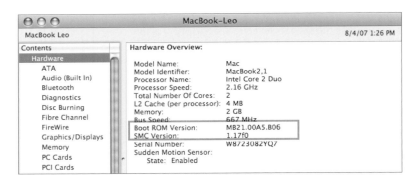

Once you have located your computer's Firmware version, you can determine if you have the latest updates by accessing Knowledge Base document 86117, "Mac OS X: Available Firmware Updates," for older PowerPC-based computers, or Knowledge Base document 303880, "Mac OS X: Firmware Updates for Intel-Based Macs."

If you determine that your Mac requires a Firmware update, you will need to find the appropriate update at the Apple Support Download website, http://www.apple.com/support/downloads/. Installing a Firmware update is very similar to a normal system software update in that it requires administrative user authorization and a reboot. However, most Firmware updates require that after the initial installation process, you must shut down and restart the computer, holding down the power button until you hear a long tone. This will initiate the remainder of the Firmware update process. Be sure to carefully read any instructions that come with a Firmware updater! Failure to properly update a Mac's Firmware could lead to hardware failure.

2   Verify application compatibility. When moving to a new operating system, many third-party applications may require updates to function properly. You can easily collect a list of installed applications on a currently running Mac by opening /Applications/Utilities/System Profiler. Once System Profiler has opened, you will need to verify that View > Full Profile is selected from the menu bar in order to reveal the Applications section in the Content list. Selecting Applications from the Content list will cause System Profiler to scan the current startup volume for all available applications.

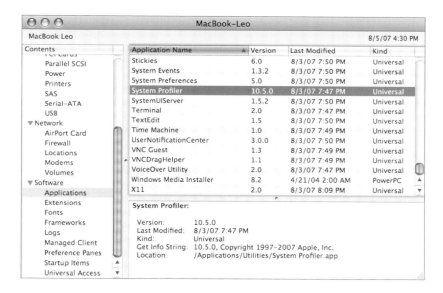

You don't have to worry about the applications installed as part of the operating system, as those will obviously be replaced when you run the new system installer. However, you will have to do your own research to determine if the installed third-party applications require updates. A good starting point is Apple's own Macintosh Products Guide, http://guide.apple.com/.

NOTE ▸ Using System Profiler while booted from the Mac OS X Install DVD will only show applications located on the DVD.

3   Back up vital files and folders. Experienced computer users should already know to keep current backups of their important files and folders. Having a current backup is even more important before making significant changes to the computer. Certainly,

installing a new operating system is a significant change, which if done improperly, could result in catastrophic data loss.

4   Document critical settings. Apple has designed Migration Assistant and the Installer to help ensure that previous settings are not lost when you are upgrading from an older version of Mac OS X. Nonetheless, some settings are so critical to your computer's function that you would be well served to document those settings should something go wrong.

Specifically, network settings are very critical and should be documented before a system upgrade is attempted. Network settings for all previous versions of Mac OS X can be located inside the Network preferences. System Preferences are easily accessed from the Apple menu. Avoid missing crucial settings by navigating through all the available network interfaces and configuration tabs.

TIP ▶ You can quickly document your settings by using the screen capture keyboard shortcut, Command-Shift-3, to create picture files of the dialogs onscreen.

Keeping Up to Date

The latest information regarding known issues at the time your installation disc was created can be found in the "Read Before You Install" document. This document is easy to find—it's the first icon at the very top when you're viewing the contents of the Mac OS X Install DVD in the Finder. When presented with any new software, you should always read this file, especially if you are replacing something as fundamental as the computer's operating system.

TIP ▶ You can also access the "Read Before You Install" documentation by clicking the "More Information" button on the Installer Welcome Screen.

For the most recent information regarding the installation process, your best source is the Apple Support page and Knowledge Base. A good place to start is the Leopard Support page at http://www.apple.com/support/leopard/. Any time you intend to install Mac OS X you should visit these resources to catch any recently discovered issues.

Starting the Installation Process

Though there are several ways to kick off the installation process for Mac OS X, they are all variations of methods to make the computer boot using the Mac OS X Install DVD. The following methods will all start the installation process:

▶ Insert the DVD in a currently running Mac and open the Install Mac OS X application from the DVD.

▶ Insert the DVD in a currently running Mac, and then select it as the startup destination using the Startup Disk preferences.

▶ Turn on the Mac while holding down the C key, and as soon as possible, insert the installation DVD and the computer will boot from it.

▶ Turn on the Mac while holding down the Option key, and as soon as possible, insert the disc. The computer will enter Startup Manager mode, where you'll use the cursor to select the installation DVD as the boot volume. If you have a tray-loading optical drive, you can open it with the keyboard Eject button after the Startup Manager appears.

The installation process involves a variety of choices up front, followed by the actual execution of the installation. This allows the user to spend just a few minutes choosing the installation options, and then leave the machine unattended while the time-consuming installation process completes. Here is an overview of the installation process:

1   Select your main language.

2   Continue through the Welcome screen.

3   Agree to the Apple Software License Agreement.

4   Select the installation destination.

5   Optionally select a different installation option to suit you needs.

6   Optionally customize the installed packages to suit your needs.

    Finally, the installation will execute, and the computer will eventually restart without any further user interaction.

Considering Partition Options

Before selecting a destination volume, you may want to pause and consider the various partition methodologies that are available as installable Mac OS X destinations. Most Macs have a single hard drive formatted as a single volume that defines the entire space on that hard drive. However, by repartitioning the hard drive you can choose to break up that single large volume into separate smaller discrete volumes. This allows you to treat a single physical storage device as multiple separate storage destinations.

Just as installing a new operating system will have long-lasting ramifications on how you use your computer, so does your choice in partition options. Thus, before you install a new operating system you should reconsider your partition methodology. The following lists present the pros and cons of various partition options. Though covered briefly here, many of these concepts will be further discussed in Lesson 3, "File Systems."

Single Partition

▶   Pros—Most drives are formatted with a single partition by default, so no changes are necessary and no data will be lost. Also, a single partition is the most efficient use of space on your drive, as you won't have wasted space due to having separate volumes.

▶   Cons—Having only a single partition severely limits administrative flexibility. Many maintenance and administrative tasks require multiple volumes, so you will have to use an additional physical storage device to accommodate those needs. Further, because system and user data are combined on a single drive, administration can be more difficult.

Multiple Partitions

▶   Pros—Multiple partitions allow you the flexibility to have multiple operating systems and multiple storage locations on one single device. Having multiple operating systems allows you to run different versions of Mac OS X from one drive, or create utility systems that can be used to repair the primary system. With multiple storage locations, it's much easier to replace a damaged operating system because all the user's data resides on another volume.

▶   Cons—You will have to repartition most drives in order to take advantage of multiple partitions, and in the process, completely erase the drive. Any future partition changes may also require that you completely lose all the data on the drive. Finally, multiple partitions can be very space inefficient if you don't plan carefully, as you may end up with underused volumes or volumes that ran out of space too soon.

Selecting the Destination

After you have passed the initial installation screens, you will be prompted to select the installation destination. Simply, this is the volume where Mac OS X will be installed. You may notice that the installer will not let you select certain volumes. This is because the installer has determined that your Mac cannot boot from that volume because:

▶   The device does not use the proper partition scheme for your Macintosh. PowerPC Macs use Apple Partition Map (APM) and Intel Macs use GUID Partition Table (GPT). You can resolve this issue by repartitioning the drive using Disk Utility.

▶   The volume is not formatted properly. Mac OS X 10.5 requires either Mac OS Extended (Journaled) or Mac OS Extended (Case-sensitive, Journaled). You can resolve this issue by reformatting the volume using Disk Utility.

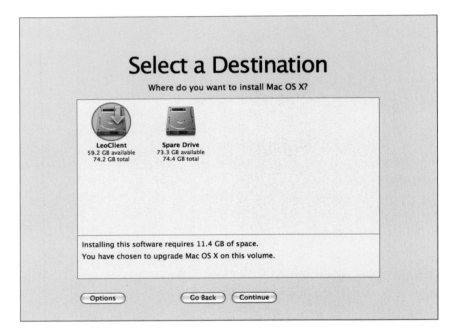

Reviewing Installation Options

When you select a destination volume, the installer will check to see if there is already another version of Mac OS X installed on the selected volume. It will automatically choose one of the following installation options for you based on the state of the selected volume:

▶   If no operating system is present on the selected volume, the installer will choose a full first-time installation.

▶   If there is a previous version of Mac OS X present on the selected volume, the installer will choose the Upgrade installation option.

▶   If there is a newer version of Mac OS X present on the selected volume, the installer will choose the Archive and Install option.

It is important that you understand the difference between these options because you may be better served by a different installation option. Any time an installable volume has been selected, you can click the Options button to bring up the installation options dialog to override the default action.

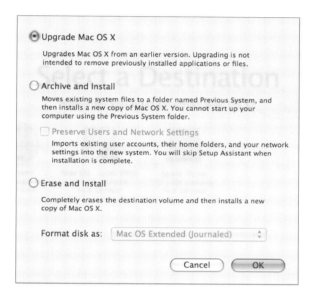

First-Time Installation

This will only be a choice if you have selected a volume with no operating system installed. With this option, Mac OS X will be installed in the free space on the drive. It will not erase any other files already on the volume.

Upgrade Installation

This will only be a choice if you have selected a volume with a previous version of Mac OS X installed. With this option Mac OS X will be installed by replacing any similar older files. It will not erase any nonsystem files already on the volume, so many of your previous configuration choices will remain intact. This type of installation will take longer than the other types, as the computer must examine every single file to determine whether it needs to be replaced. If you are attempting to resolve system issues by reinstalling the software, this is not the recommended approach.

Archive and Install

This will only be a choice if you have selected a volume that already has another version of Mac OS X installed. With this option, the installer will first move the previous system into a new folder called Previous System. It will then install a fresh copy of the entire operating system. Obviously, this option requires that you have enough available free space on the selected volume to accommodate an additional system installation. This is one of the preferred methods for reinstalling Mac OS X if you are trying to resolve system issues.

By default this option will also restore existing settings and user accounts after installing the new system. You can override this option by deselecting the Preserve Users and Network Settings checkbox. For more details regarding the files preserved during an Archive and Install, please refer to Knowledge Base document 107120, "Mac OS X: About the Archive and Install Feature."

Erase and Install

This option is always available regardless of the volume you select. With this option, the installer will reformat the selected volume before installing the new system. Obviously, reformatting the volume will effectively erase any previous data that was there, and everything on that volume will be lost. However, this will not affect any other volumes. This is also a preferred method to use when reinstalling Mac OS X to resolve system issues, though you may want to try the Archive and Install first as it does not erase the contents of the volume.

> **NOTE ▶** Using the Erase and Install option, you will only be allowed to reformat the volume using Mac OS Extended (Journaled) or Mac OS Extended (Case-sensitive, Journaled).

Selecting Package Options

The last choice you will make before the installation begins is determining which software packages are installed. The default, or "Easy Install" as it was known in earlier versions of Mac OS X, is to install all the packages that make up the complete system installation. Only the base Essential System Software package is required, so you can save a great deal of space by electing to not install various languages and printer drivers that you don't intend to use. The following is a brief description of each optional installation package to help you decide if they are required in your situation:

- ▶ Printer Drivers—This option will install printer drivers for many popular printers from a variety of printer manufacturers. Keep in mind that printer drivers for less-popular printers and printers released after Mac OS X 10.5 will not be included in this package. It's always best to check with the printer manufacturer for the latest drivers.

- ▶ Additional Fonts—This option will install high-quality non-Roman fonts to support writing in foreign languages. Non-Roman fonts use many special characters in their alphabets and can take up quite a bit of space.

- ▶ Language Translations—This option will install non-English versions of all the system resources. Mac OS X supports a variety of languages so this can take up quite a bit of storage space.

- ▶ X11—This option will install Apple's X11 windowing environment. X11 is a common graphical user interface platform for UNIX workstations. Apple's implementation of X11 is based on the popular open source XFree86 project. For more information about this, visit Apple's own X11 resource page, http://developer.apple.com/opensource/tools/X11.html.

You can override the default package installation options while at the Install Summary screen. Remember, you can always reinstall these optional packages at a later date should you need them.

To change your package installation options:

1 Click the Customize button to reveal the package selection dialog.

2 Select a package name to see more information about the package contents.

3 Click the small disclosure triangles on the left to reveal subpackages that make up a package group.

4 Deselect checkboxes next to the packages you do not wish to install.

5   Click Done when you have made your selections to dismiss the dialog, then click Install to complete the installation.

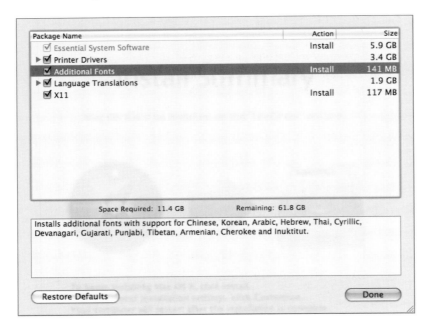

Configuring Mac OS X

If you are using a brand-new Mac for the very first time or you have just installed Mac OS X on a volume with no previous system, then you will be presented with the Setup Assistant. The Setup Assistant will guide you through the preliminary configuration setup required to use a new system. Any of the configurations made while using the Setup Assistant can be easily changed later by accessing the appropriate system preference.

First you will choose the primary language. This will ensure the appropriate language and dialect are used by the applications on your system. Then at the Setup Assistant Welcome screen, you'll need to choose a country or region to continue. This information is used to complete the registration process. At this point you will also select the primary keyboard layout.

TIP ▶ Both language and keyboard layout settings can be changed later from the International system preference.

NOTE ▶ If you pause for a few moments at the Startup Assistant Welcome screen, the VoiceOver Tutorial will begin. This is an optional tutorial that explains how to use the VoiceOver assistance technology designed for individuals who are visually impaired. VoiceOver will be further discussed in Lesson 5, "Applications and Boot Camp."

Migration Assistant

After you select the appropriate language, country or region, and keyboard layout, the Setup Assistant switches to the Migration Assistant. If you are migrating from a previous Mac or version of Mac OS X, the Migration Assistant is a huge time-saver. It enables you to easily transfer all the settings, user accounts, and data from another system to your new system. If you choose to transfer your previous settings with the Migration Assistant you will skip much of the remaining Setup Assistant configuration process. If you do not have a previous system to migrate from, then simply leave the default choice of "Do not transfer my information now" and click Continue to proceed through the rest of the Setup Assistant. However, if you wish to migrate from another Mac system.

1   At the Migration Assistant screen, select the radio button next to the appropriate location of your previous system. Your choices are:

▶   From another Mac—This option will instruct you on how to set up a FireWire connection between your new system and your previous Mac. Briefly, this involves connecting the two computers with a FireWire cable and then booting your previous Mac while holding down the T key. The Migration Assistant will then scan the targeted Mac for a previous system. Target Disk mode will be further discussed in Lesson 3, "File Systems."

▶   From another volume on this Mac—This option will scan all locally mounted volumes for a previous system. This includes drives connected via FireWire or USB but not mounted network volumes.

▶   From a Time Machine backup—This option will also scan all locally mounted volumes, but this time it will look for Time Machine archives.

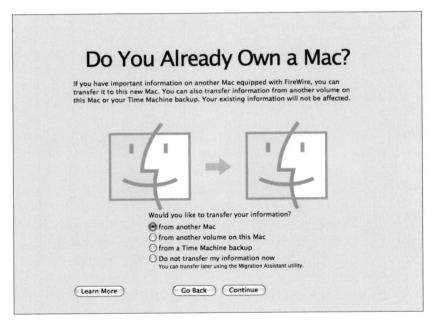

When the Migration Assistant finds a previous system volume or archive, it will scan the contents and present you with a list of available items to migrate. If the Migration Assistant discovers multiple system volumes or archives, you will need to select the specific system you wish to migrate from the Information pop-up menu.

2   From the items list, select the checkboxes next to items you want to migrate to the new system. The Migration Assistant will calculate the total size needed to migrate the selected items. Obviously, you will not be allowed to migrate more data than your new system can hold. The Migration Assistant can transfer the flowing items:

▶ User accounts, including home folders

▶ Network and system settings

▶ Applications not included with the operating system

▶ Other data from the selected system volume

▶ Other nonsystem locally mounted volumes

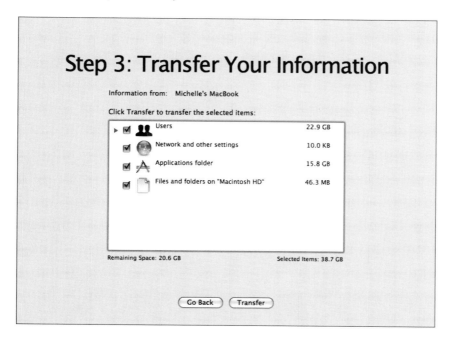

3   Click the Transfer button to start the transfer process. The more data you have selected to transfer, the longer the process will take. Mature systems with lots of data can take several hours to migrate.

TIP You can use the Migration Assistant at any time after the initial setup by opening /Applications/Utilities/Migration Assistant.

NOTE ▸ If multiple volumes are available on a system, you can choose to migrate that data as well. However, the migration process does not create new volumes on the new system; instead, it creates folders on the new system with the contents of the old volumes.

Setup Assistant

When you need to set up a new system from scratch, the Setup Assistant will guide you through the initial configuration procedure. Remember, many of the configurations made while using the Setup Assistant can be easily changed later by accessing the appropriate system preference. Without further ado, the Setup Assistant will walk you through the following initial settings.

Network Settings

At this point, the Setup Assistant wants to establish a connection to the Internet by configuring the Mac's network settings. It will first attempt to automatically detect the network settings via DHCP on an open Ethernet network. If it can't find an open network, you will see the network configuration screen. The assistant will try to figure out which type of network connection you need to set up first and present you with the appropriate configuration screen. If it makes a poor choice, you can simply click the Different Network Setup button and choose a different connection type to configure. Network configuration concepts will be further discussed in Lesson 7, "Accessing Network Services."

How Do You Connect?

Select how your computer connects to the Internet.

◉ AirPort wireless
○ Cable modem
○ DSL modem
○ Local network (Ethernet)
○ My computer does not connect to the Internet

(Go Back) (Continue)

Only one active network connection needs configuration to appease the Setup Assistant so it moves on with the setup. Alternately, you can also select the "My computer does not connect to the internet" radio button and the Setup Assistant will move on. However, if you decide to manually configure one of the network settings, your choices will vary depending on your Mac's hardware capabilities:

► Wired Ethernet—If you're connected to a wired Ethernet that does not have DHCP available, you will have to manually configure the settings here. This is primarily for users who require static manually configured network settings. You can also choose from Bootstrap Protocol (BOOTP), Point-to-Point Protocol Over Ethernet (PPPoE), and Dynamic Host Configuration Protocol (DHCP) with manual address Ethernet configurations.

► Wireless Ethernet—If wireless Ethernet networks are detected, you may automatically land at this configuration screen. Select a wireless network from the list and enter its password to connect. Or, you can specify a hidden wireless network by selecting Other Network from the list and entering both the network name and password.

► Telephone Modem—If you're stuck in the past and still use a directly connected analog phone line and modem to connect to the Internet, this dialog will let you enter your connection information here.

► Cable or DSL Modem—The configuration screen for these two selections is identical to the wired Ethernet configuration screen. This is because Mac OS X only supports connecting to cable or DSL modems via Ethernet.

Registration Process

The registration process, though not required, is an important part of the system setup. If you're connected to the Internet at this point, the registration process will send the registration information to Apple. You will also be able to create an Apple ID and .Mac account at this time if you do not already have either.

MORE INFO ▸ For more information about the Apple ID, the .Mac service, or the registration process, simply click the Learn More button. You can also visit the Apple ID FAQ page at http://myinfo.apple.com/html/en_US/faq.html, and the .Mac website, http://www.mac.com/.

If you do not want to complete the registration process during the initial setup, you can skip it now and complete it later by opening /System/Library/CoreServices/Setup Assistant or visiting http://www.apple.com/register/. You can cancel the registration process at any point by using the keyboard shortcut Command-Q, and then click the Skip button when the Cancel Registration dialog appears.

NOTE ▸ Attempting to use the Command-Q keyboard shortcut while viewing nonregistration screens during the Setup Assistant will not allow you to skip those screens. Instead, you will be forced to shut down or continue.

Otherwise, to complete the registration process:

1   First you are prompted for an Apple ID. An Apple ID is the login you will use for all Apple online services, including access to the Apple Support pages and the iTunes Store. A .Mac user account will also serve as a valid Apple ID. If you do not have an Apple ID, simply click the Continue button and one will be created for you later in the registration process based on information you will enter in the following steps.

2   If you are connected to the Internet and you entered your Apple ID, then the registration information page will automatically populate with your information. If not, you must enter a first name, last name, address, city, state, zip code, and phone number to continue.

3   You will need to complete one more information page regarding how you plan to use your Mac and if Apple can send you promotional email. You will not be able to continue unless you answer the two usage questions using the pop-up menus.

Initial Account Creation

The most important part of the setup process is the creation of the initial administrative user account. The account you create here will be the only administrative user account initially allowed to modify all system settings, including the creation of additional user accounts. Therefore, until you create additional administrative user accounts, it is important that you remember the authentication information for this first account. Though covered briefly here, user accounts will be further discussed in Lesson 2, "User Accounts."

To create the initial administrative user account:

1   Enter a long user name. This name can contain nearly any alphanumeric character.

2   Enter a short name. This name cannot contain any spaces, capitals, or special characters.

3   Enter the password twice (not three times) to verify it was typed correctly.

4   Only enter a password hint if you think you may forget this password. The password hint should not match your password.

5   Once you have double-checked your work, click the Continue button to create the new account.

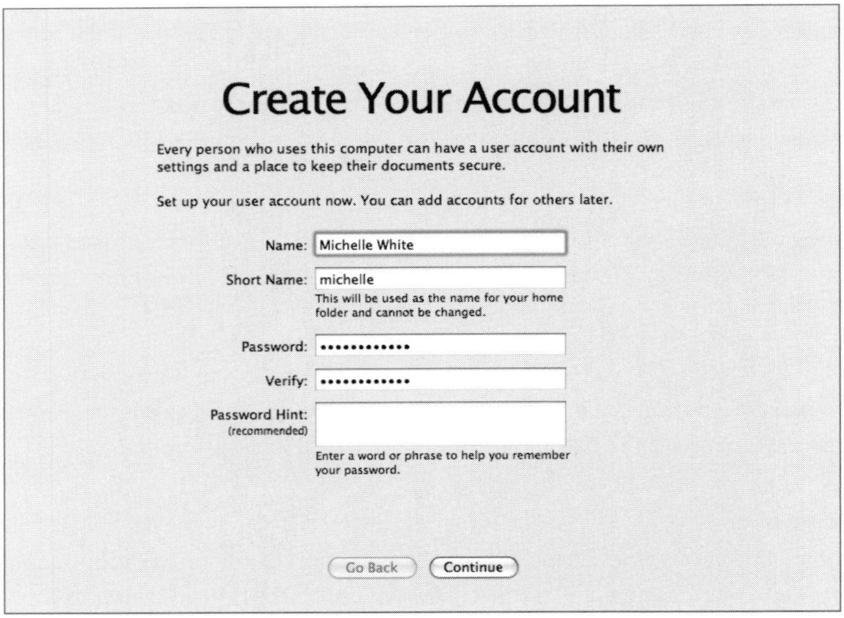

Create Your Account

Every person who uses this computer can have a user account with their own settings and a place to keep their documents secure.

Set up your user account now. You can add accounts for others later.

Name:	Michelle White
Short Name:	michelle
	This will be used as the name for your home folder and cannot be changed.
Password:	••••••••••••
Verify:	••••••••••••
Password Hint: (recommended)	
	Enter a word or phrase to help you remember your password.

(Go Back)   (Continue)

.Mac Account Creation

At this point in the Setup Assistant process, if you have successfully connected to the Internet and completed the registration process but you don't already have a .Mac account, the assistant will help you in acquiring one. Apple's .Mac service is an annual subscription-based Internet service that provides a variety of useful and fun features. If you're not convinced you need .Mac, you can still try it out for 60 days completely free of charge by completing the .Mac registration. Simply choose the appropriate .Mac account creation radio button, then click the Continue button. The following screen will allow you to enter your .Mac registration information and create the .Mac account.

If you do not want to sign up for .Mac during the initial setup, you can skip it now and complete it later by visiting an Apple retail store and purchasing a .Mac box, or by registering online at http://www.mac.com/. You can cancel the .Mac account creation process, or sign up for a free 60-day .Mac trial by selecting the "I don't want to purchase .Mac right now" radio button and then clicking the Continue button. The following screen will allow you to either sign up for a 60-day free trial or skip the .Mac account creation process altogether.

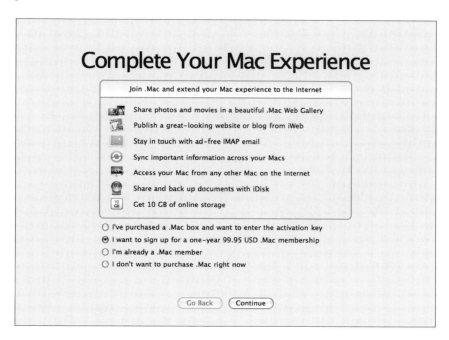

Date and Time

If you have fully completed the online registration process, you will now need to set the time zone, as this will be determined by your zip code. Further, if the Mac has successfully connected to the Internet during the installation process, you will not have to set the date and time, because the Mac will automatically synchronize via Apple's Network Time Protocol servers.

On the other hand, if it didn't complete the registration process or network setup, then you will need to set the Mac's date and time to complete the initial system setup. Remember, these settings can be changed later via the Date & Time preferences.

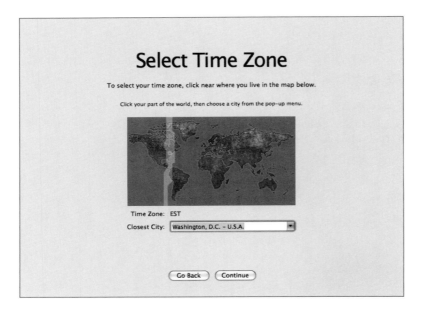

To set the date and time:

1   Click on the world map to select your time zone. You can further refine your time zone selection by choosing a city using the Closest City pop-up menu. Click the Continue button once you have chosen the most accurate time zone.

2   Set the date by clicking on the up/down arrows next to the date, or navigate and select the date using the calendar.

3   Set the time by clicking on the up/down arrows next to the time.

4   When you are done changing the date and time, click the Save button, and then click the Continue button to complete the Setup Assistant process.

System Preferences

The System Preferences application is the primary interface for adjusting user and system settings. (In other operating systems these settings would be accessed using Control Panels.) You will be using System Preferences quite frequently during these lessons and any time you are setting up a new Mac. The quickest access to System Preferences is via the Apple menu because it's almost always available from any application.

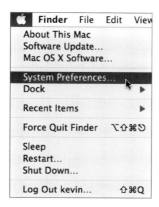

TIP ▶ The System Preferences application can also be found in the /Applications folder. You can use any shortcut method you like to access the System Preferences application, including placing it in the Dock and the Finder sidebar.

The first time you access System Preferences, you'll notice it is divided into four separate rows representing the four main categories of System Preferences: Personal, Hardware, Internet & Network, and System. Further, any third-party system preferences you install will appear automatically in a fifth row categorized as Others.

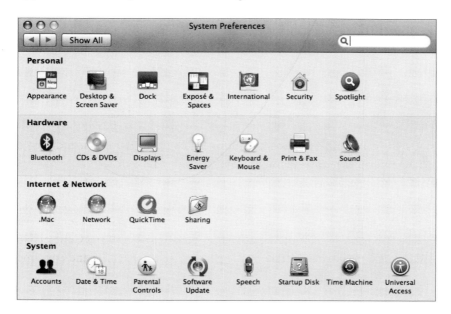

The categorization of the individual system preferences is deliberate:

▶ Personal—These system preferences will only affect settings for the active user account. In other words, for all of the system preferences in this category, each user has his own discrete settings.

▶ Hardware—These system preferences are specific to hardware settings. The Energy Saver and Print & Fax system preferences in this category can affect every user on the Mac, and thus they require administrative access to make changes.

▶ Internet & Network—These system preferences are specific to Internet and network settings. The Network and Sharing preferences in this category can affect every user on the Mac, and thus they require administrative access to make changes.

▶ System—These system preferences have a systemwide effect when changed. Consequently, all system preferences in this category, save for the Universal Access preferences, require administrative access.

▶ Others (optional)—There is no rhyme or reason to the classification of these preferences except that they are not part of the standard Mac OS X installation. The developer of a specific third-party system preference determines if their system preference requires administrative access.

Accessing an individual system preference is as simple as clicking once on its icon. Making changes to most system preferences are instantaneous and don't require you to click an Apply or OK button. Clicking the Show All button in the upper-left corner will return you to the view of all the system preferences.

If you're not sure where a specific feature setting is located inside the various system preferences, you can use the Spotlight search field in the upper-right corner to quickly locate the hidden setting.

You'll notice that some system preferences have a lock in the bottom-left corner. These system preferences can only be accessed by an administrative user account. If a system preference you need to access is locked from editing, simply click on the lock icon, and then authenticate as an administrative user to unlock it.

Software Update

Keeping current with software updates is an important part of maintaining a healthy Mac. Fortunately, Mac OS X includes an easy-to-use Software Update application that automatically checks Apple's servers via the Internet to make sure you're running the latest Apple software. Automatic Software Update checking is enabled the very first moment you start using your Mac. If an update is automatically detected, you will be presented with a Software Update dialog.

You will have three choices when presented with this dialog:

▶ Click the Show Details button to open the full Software Update so you can further inspect all the available updates.

▶ Click the Not Now button to dismiss the automatic update until the next scheduled update check.

▶ Click the Continue button, and then authenticate as an administrative user to have the updates download and install immediately.

NOTE ▶ An Internet connection is required to use Software Update for both auto-matic and manual updates. Also, the Software Update application checks only for updates of currently installed Apple software. Finally, some software updates require that you also agree to the Apple Software License Agreement.

You can also manually open the Software Update application to check for updates at any time via any of the following methods:

▶ Choose Software Update from the Apple menu.

▶ Click the Check Now button in the Software Update preferences.

▶ Click the Software Update button in the About This Mac dialog.

TIP ▶ The Software Update application can also be found in the /System/Library/ CoreServices folder. You can use any shortcut method you like to access the System Preferences application, including placing it in the Dock and the Finder sidebar.

When you choose to have Software Update install new software for you, it will first download the installation packages to your local Mac. After all the packages have been downloaded, it will install the new software one of two ways: if the new software does not require a restart for installation, then the software will automatically install without any further user interaction; however, if the new software requires a restart after the install process, then you will be prompted with a dialog featuring a Log Out and Install button. You can, of course, choose to install these updates later, but you will eventually have to restart to take advantage of the new software.

Advanced Software Update Features

Manually opening the Software Update application will reveal its full interactive interface. This will allow you individually inspect all the available Apple software updates. The information provided includes the update name, version, file size, and a detailed description. You will also be able to deselect updates that you do not wish to install right now.

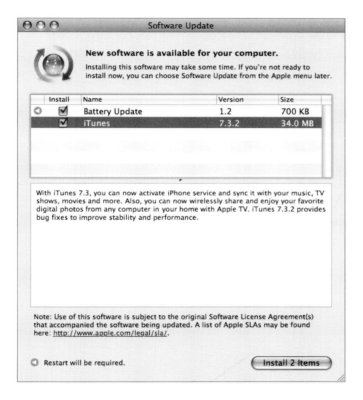

TIP If you don't want to be reminded of a particular update again, you can choose to ignore the update by selecting it from the list of available updates and then choosing Update > Ignore Update from the menu bar. You can bring back all ignored updates by choosing Software Update > Reset Ignored Updates from the menu bar.

Or, you can download available updates and save them to your local hard drive for use later. Administrators responsible for a large number of Macs will find this approach useful, as they can use a utility like Apple's Remote Desktop to easily manage the installation of a previously downloaded update on multiple computers.

To download and save a software update for future use:

1   Open the Software Update application. It will check for Apple software updates.

2   Select the software update, or hold down the Command key to select multiple software updates from the list of available updates.

3   From the Update menu, choose Download Only to download the update, or choose Install and Keep Package to download and immediately install the update.

4   Retrieve the software update packages from the current user's Downloads folder.

Software Update System Preferences
The Software Update preferences, accessed via the System Preferences application, enable you to adjust the schedule of automatic software updates and review previously installed updates.

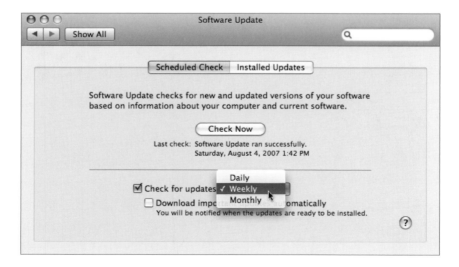

When the Scheduled Check tab is selected, you can:

▶   Click the Check Now button to manually open the Software Update application.

▶   Enable or disable automatic software updates by toggling the "Check for updates" checkbox.

▶   Adjust the frequency of automatic updates checks using the "Check for updates" pop-up menu.

▶   Enable or disable the automatic download of important Mac OS X system updates by toggling the "Download important updates automatically" checkbox. Primarily, important updates are defined as any security updates or bug fixes known to be serious threats to system stability.

    NOTE ▶ You will still need to authenticate as an administrative user to complete the installation of any automatically downloaded updates.

When you select the Installed Updates tab, you can investigate previously installed Apple software updates. You will be able to view the name, version, and date installed for any software update. Further, you can click the Open as Log File button to view the software update log from the Console application.

Information About Your Mac

Knowledge of your Mac's specifications is always important when installing new software, updating installed software, performing maintenance, or troubleshooting a problem. Your first stop to discovering a Mac's specifications is the About This Mac dialog. You can open this dialog at any point by choosing About This Mac from the Apple menu.

Initially, the About This Mac dialog will show you the Mac's system software version, processor type and speed, total system memory, and currently booted startup disk. You can also find the system build identifier and hardware serial number by repeatedly clicking the system version number directly below the bold "Mac OS X" text:

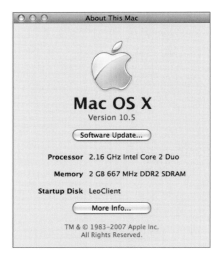

▶ System version number—This number represents the specific system software version currently installed on the Mac. The first digit, 10, obviously represents the tenth generation of the Mac operating system. The second digit, 5, represents the fifth major release of Mac OS X. The final digit represents an incremental update to the operating system. Incremental updates generally offer very few feature changes, but often represent a large number of bug fixes.

▶ System build number—This is an even more granular representation of the specific system software version currently installed on the Mac. Apple engineers create hundreds of different versions of each system software release as they refine the product. The build number is used to track this process. Also, you may find that the computer-specific builds of Mac OS X, which come preinstalled on new Mac hardware, will differ from the standard installation builds. This is an important detail to note if you are creating system images for mass distribution, as computer-specific builds of Mac OS X may not work on other types of Mac hardware.

▶ Hardware serial number—The hardware serial number is also located somewhere on the Mac's case. However, Apple has a tendency to choose form over function, so the serial number may be quite difficult to find. Like many other complicated products, the Mac's serial number is a unique number used to identify that particular Mac for maintenance and service issues.

NOTE ▶ Older Macs or Macs that have had their logic boards replaced may not properly display the serial number in the About This Mac dialog.

System Profiler

The system information on the About This Mac dialog is only the tip of the iceberg compared to the System Profiler application. From the About This Mac dialog, click the More Info button to open System Profiler.

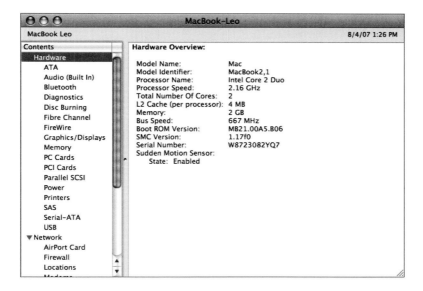

TIP ▶ The System Profiler application can also be found in the /Applications/Utilities folder. You can use any shortcut method you like to access the System Profiler application, including placing it in the Dock and the Finder sidebar.

You will be using System Profiler to locate critical system information in nearly every lesson throughout this book. Additionally, one of the most important uses of System Profiler is as a documentation tool. Any time you need to document the current state of a Mac, you can use System Profiler to create a detailed system report. To create this report while in System Profiler, simply choose Save from the File menu. Enter a name and destination for this report and be sure to choose an appropriate File Format option from the pop-up menu; then click the Save button.

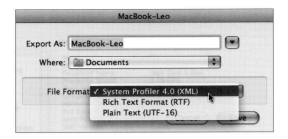

NOTE ► The XML code used by the default System Profiler file format is not easily legible when opened by standard text viewing applications. Applications that can understand Rich Text Format are common, and nearly every text reader understands plain text format.

Installer Application

A great feature of Mac OS X is the relative ease with which most new software is installed. In fact, many applications require only that the user copy a single application file to the local system drive. At the same time, more complicated software may require multiple resources placed at a variety of specific locations on your Mac. A prime example of a complicated software installation is any Mac OS X system software update.

The Installer application makes complicated application installations simple. Often, software developers will create an installer package with all the instructions necessary for the Installer application to set up the new software on your system. Though covered briefly here, packages will be further discussed in Lesson 4, "Data Management and Backup."

Double-clicking one of these software installer packages will open the Installer application and begin the installation process. Much like the Mac OS X installation process, the Installer application will guide you through the steps necessary to install or update software. This may include agreeing to software licenses, selecting a destination, selecting package options, and authenticating as an administrative user.

NOTE ► Third-party software developers may choose to use a proprietary non-Apple installer for their product. These installers will behave differently than the Apple Installer.

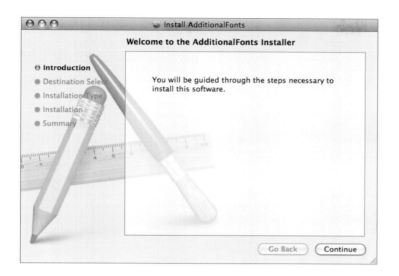

TIP ▶ Proceed with caution if an installer requires you to authenticate as an administrative user. These installers need administrative access so they can make changes to the system software.

Advanced Installer Features

If you're curious about what an installation package is actually doing to your Mac, you have two methods of finding out. First, you can view the Installer Log at any time while using the Installer application by choosing Window > Installer Log from the menu bar or using the Command-L keyboard shortcut.

The Installer Log is a live view of any progress or errors reported during the installation process. Once the installation is complete, you can save a text copy of the Installer Log by clicking the Save button in the toolbar or choosing File > Save from the menu bar.

If you want to inspect an installer package before it's installed, you can do that, too, but not with the Installer Log. After passing the initial installation welcome screens and agreeing to any software license agreements while using the Installer application, you can preview the list of files to be installed by choosing File > Show Items from the menu bar or using the Command-I keyboard shortcut.

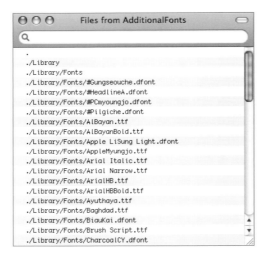

TIP ▶ Save time looking for what you need by using the Spotlight search field in the toolbar when examining the Installer Log or file list.

Mac OS X 10.5 Leopard introduced a few new significant Installer application features. For starters, users may now specify their home folder as the installation destination for applications that allow it. Apple has also introduced a dynamic installation package that will remain up to date as long as the Mac has Internet access. Network-based installation packages will automatically download the latest software from a vendor's servers during the installation process. Finally, Apple has increased the security and reliability of software installation packages by supporting signed packages. These packages contain special code used to validate the authenticity and completeness of the software during installation. This will make it nearly impossible for nefarious hackers to insert illegitimate files in trusted installation packages.

Installation Troubleshooting

Apple has worked hard to make the Mac OS X installation process as painless and reliable as possible. Yet, as with any complicated technology, problems may arise. This final part this lesson will cover installation troubleshooting techniques and installation utilities.

Methodology

Thoroughly verifying that your computer meets the requirements for Mac OS X 10.5 and completing the installation preparation steps outlined earlier in this lesson will go a long way toward preventing any serious problems. Should you still find yourself with installation problems, follow the techniques outlined in Knowledge Base document 106693, "Troubleshooting Mac OS X Installation from CD or DVD." In short, this document covers the following installation issues:

▶ Installer cannot start up from the installation disc.

▶ Installer cannot complete the computer check.

▶ Installer cannot complete the source disc check.

▶ Installer cannot complete the destination volume check.

▶ The installation process starts but does not complete and returns an error message.

▶ Problems occur after the installation completes.

▶ Installation is slow.

Two other Knowledge Base documents that will help you troubleshoot general installation issues are document 106692, "Mac OS X: Troubleshooting Installation and Software Updates," and document 106694, "Mac OS X: Troubleshooting the Mac OS X Installer."

Installer Log

The granddaddy of all troubleshooting resources for Mac OS X is the log file. Nearly every process writes entries in a log file, and the Installer is no different. The Installer Log contains progress and error entries for nearly every step of the installation process, including steps not shown by the standard interface. Information in the Installer Log will allow you to more precisely pinpoint problems or verify installation.

Any time during the installation process you can bring up the Installer Log by following these steps:

1   Choose Window > Installer Log from the menu bar or hold down the Command-L keyboard shortcut.

2   Choose Show All Logs from the Detail Levels pop-up menu to view the entire contents of the Installer Log.

3   Use the Spotlight search field in the toolbar to isolate specific entries in the Installer Log.

4   To save the Installer Log, choose File > Save from the menu bar or click the Save button in the toolbar.

You can leave the Installer Log window open during the entire installation process to monitor progress. You may find that, even during a successful installation, the Installer reports many warnings and errors. Many of these reported issues are benign, and you should only concern yourself with these issues if you are trying to isolate a showstopping problem. When the installation successfully completes, you should see summary entries in the Installer Log that look something like this:

    Aug 5 16:32:31 localhost OSInstaller[139]: Finalize disk "Vault mini 2"

    Aug 5 16:32:31 localhost OSInstaller[139]: Finalizing Disk for OS Install

    Aug 5 16:32:34 localhost installdb[522]: done. (0.206u + 0.081s)

    Aug 5 16:32:49 localhost OSInstaller[139]: Notifying system of updated components

    Aug 5 16:32:49 localhost OSInstaller[139]: TOTAL: Packages report 135563 files, 2712 actual files written

    Aug 5 16:32:50 localhost OSInstaller[139]: _installNextPackage of 0

    Aug 5 16:32:50 localhost OSInstaller[139]:

Aug 5 16:32:50 localhost OSInstaller[139]: **** Summary Information ****

Aug 5 16:32:50 localhost OSInstaller[139]: Operation Elapsed time

Aug 5 16:32:50 localhost OSInstaller[139]: ----------------------------

Aug 5 16:32:50 localhost OSInstaller[139]: script 23.55 seconds

Aug 5 16:32:50 localhost OSInstaller[139]: zero 0.03 seconds

Aug 5 16:32:50 localhost OSInstaller[139]: install 577.81 seconds

Aug 5 16:32:50 localhost OSInstaller[139]: validate 206.25 seconds

Aug 5 16:32:50 localhost OSInstaller[139]:   os 62.60 seconds

Aug 5 16:32:50 localhost OSInstaller[139]: extract 323.57 seconds

Aug 5 16:32:50 localhost OSInstaller[139]: receipt 0.00 seconds

Aug 5 16:32:50 localhost OSInstaller[139]: disk 18.01 seconds

Aug 5 16:32:50 localhost OSInstaller[139]: config 24.25 seconds

Aug 5 16:32:50 localhost OSInstaller[139]:

Aug 5 16:32:50 localhost OSInstaller[139]: Starting installation:

Aug 5 16:32:50 localhost OSInstaller[139]: Finalizing installation.

TIP ▶ The Mac will not automatically restart during the system installation process as long as the Installer Log window is the foremost window.

Installation Utilities

The Mac OS X Install DVD can be used to great effect as a troubleshooting resource. When you started up from this DVD, you may have already discovered the useful system administration and maintenance tools available from the Utilities menu. There are even a few indispensable utilities on this disc that you cannot find anywhere else in Mac OS X.

The utilities available on the Mac OS X Install DVD include:

▶ Startup Disk—This utility will allow you to select the default system startup disk. The default startup disk can be overridden using any of the alternate startup modes discussed in Lesson 10, "Startup Process."

▶ Reset Password—This utility will allow you to reset the password of any local user account, including the root user, on the selected system disk. Obviously, this is a dangerous utility that can lead to a serious security threat. Because of this, the Reset Password utility will not run if copied from the original media. You can find out more about the Reset Password utility in Lesson 2, "User Accounts."

▶ Firmware Password Utility—This utility will allow you to secure the Mac's startup process by disabling all alternate startup modes without a password. You can disable or enable this feature and define the required password. You can find out more about the Firmware Password utility in Lesson 2, "User Accounts."

▶ Disk Utility—You have already been introduced to this utility, which is responsible for all storage-related administration and maintenance. Disk Utility will be further discussed in Lesson 3, "File Systems."

▶ Terminal—This is your primary interface to the UNIX command-line environment of Mac OS X. Terminal will be further discussed in Lesson 3, "File Systems."

▶ System Profiler—You have already been introduced to this catchall utility for uncovering system specifications in the "Preparing for Installation" section of this lesson.

▶ Network Utility—This is the primary network and Internet troubleshooting utility in Mac OS X. Network Utility will be further discussed in Lesson 7, "Accessing Network Services."

▶ Restore System From Backup—You can use this utility to restore a full-system Time Machine archive from a locally connected volume to the target system disk. Time Machine will be further discussed in Lesson 4, "Data Management and Backup."

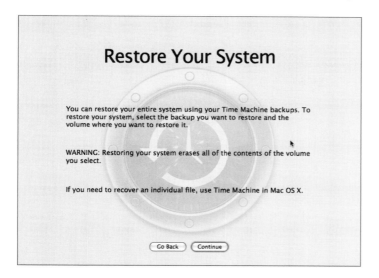

NOTE ▶ The utilities available from the Mac OS X Install DVD can certainly be used to compromise system security. Then again, any system where the default startup disk can be overridden during startup is wide open to compromise. Therefore, it is very important that you use the Firmware Password Utility to protect your secure systems from this attack vector.

Repair Permissions

One of the most common troubleshooting techniques for Mac OS X is to repair disk permissions. Many novice Mac administrators will use this technique every time they encounter any problem. The reality is that this process fixes only file permission issues specific to certain installed Apple software. Further, this process will not touch any incorrect permission settings on personal or user data. In other words, this process, though a good starting point for addressing application issues, will not fix every incorrect permission issues on a problematic Mac. Though covered briefly here, Disk Utility and file permissions will be further discussed in Lesson 3, "File Systems." For more information you can also refer to Knowledge Base document 25751, "About Disk Utility's repair disk permissions feature."

What You've Learned

▶ Mac OS X 10.5 requires a Macintosh computer with a PowerPC G4 (867 MHz or faster), G5, or Intel processor, a DVD drive, built-in FireWire, at least 512 MB of RAM, a display connected to a supported Apple-supplied video card, and at least 9 GB of available disk space.

▶ The Mac OS X Install DVD guides you through the system installation process.

▶ The Mac OS X Setup Assistant guides you through the initial configuration of your Mac system.

▶ The Migration Assistant can be used to easily transfer user accounts, settings, and data from a previous system.

▶ Apple provides updates to Mac OS X through the Software Update service. To ensure that your system is up-to-date, run Software Update on a regular basis.

▶ The Mac OS X Install DVD includes a variety of administration and troubleshooting utilities.

References

You can check for new and updated Knowledge Base documents at http://www.apple.com/support.

Apple Software Restore

61802, "How to restore your Apple software"

31086, "Apple software install and Apple software restore differences"

106941, "Mac OS X: How to back up and restore your files"

Firmware

303880, "Mac OS X: firmware updates for Intel-based Macs"

86117, "Mac OS X: Available Firmware Updates"

106482, "Setting up firmware password protection in Mac OS X 10.1 or later"

42642, "To continue booting, type 'mac-boot' and press return message"

58492, "Differences between the Mac OS ROM and bootROM"

60351, "Determining BootROM or firmware version"

Installation

25497, "Don't install older versions of Mac OS than what comes with your computer"

25404, "Mac OS X: How to reinstall a prior version"

75187, "Mac OS X: software installations require administrator password"

106163, "Mac OS X: system requirements"

106178, "Startup Manager: How to select a startup volume"

106235, "Mac OS X: Disk appears dimmed (or 'grayed out') in the installer"

106464, "Your Mac won't start up in Mac OS X"

106692, "Mac OS X: Troubleshooting installation and software updates"

106693, "Mac OS X: Troubleshooting installation from CD or DVD"

106694, "Mac OS X: Troubleshooting the Mac OS X Installer"

106695, "Troubleshooting Automatic Software Update in Mac OS X"

106704, "Mac OS X: Updating your software"

107120, "Mac OS X: About the Archive and Install feature"

306516, "Mac OS X 10.5 Leopard: Installing on a UFS-formatted volume"

306518, "Mac OS X 10.5 Leopard: Information to collect before an Erase and Install"

Miscellaneous

25784, "What's a 'Computer-Specific Mac OS X Release'?"

2238, "Resetting your Mac's PRAM and NVRAM"

86209, "Macintosh: Some computers only start up in Mac OS X"

107249, "Mac OS X: about File System Journaling"

25751, "About Disk Utility's Repair Disk Permissions feature"

URLs

Apple's product guide: http://guide.apple.com

Mac OS X system architecture overview: http://developer.apple.com/macosx/architecture/

Mac OS X 10.5 detailed technical specifications: http://www.apple.com/macosx/techspecs/

Apple's software downloads: http://www.apple.com/support/downloads/

Main Mac OS X 10.5 support website: http://www.apple.com/support/leopard/

Apple's X11 implementation: http://developer.apple.com/opensource/tools/X11.html

Apple ID FAQ: http://myinfo.apple.com/html/en_US/faq.html

.Mac Internet service: http://www.mac.com/

Apple product registration: http://www.apple.com/register/

Review Quiz

1. What are the minimum hardware requirements for installing Mac OS X 10.5?
2. What four preparation steps must you take before installing Mac OS X?
3. What are the advantages and disadvantages of using a single-partition drive with Mac OS X? How about a multiple-partition drive?
4. What are the differences between the various installation options available when installing Mac OS X?
5. Which packages are installed by default when installing Mac OS X?
6. How do the four System Preferences categories differ?
7. How do you ensure that you have the latest Apple software?
8. Where can you locate the system version number, build number, and serial number? What is the significance of these numbers?
9. What other utilities are available when booted from the Mac OS X Install DVD?

Answers

1. The minimum requirements are:
    ▶   An Intel, PowerPC G5, or PowerPC G4 (867 MHz or faster) processor
    ▶   512 MB of memory

    ►   DVD drive for installation

    ►   9 GB of available disk space

    ►   Some features require a compatible Internet service provider; fees may apply.

    ►   Some features require Apple's .Mac service; fees apply.

2. Check for firmware updates, verify application compatibility, back up vital files and folders, and document critical settings.

3. Single-partition drives are easier to set up initially, but they aren't as flexible for administration and maintenance. Multiple-partition drives require repartitioning during setup but provide several separate volumes, which can be used to segregate user data and host multiple operating systems.

4. A first-time installation is used when installing to a volume with no other version of Mac OS X. An update installation is used when updating a previous version of Mac OS X. An Archive and Install will set aside the previous system and install a new system while maintaining existing settings and user accounts. Finally, an Erase and Install will reformat the existing volume and install a fresh copy of Mac OS X.

5. All packages, including Printer Drivers, Additional Fonts, Language Translations, and X11, are installed by default.

6. Generally, Personal preferences affect only a single user, Hardware preferences adjust hardware and peripheral settings, Internet & Network preferences affect personal and system network settings, and System preferences affect all users and require administrative access.

7. The Software Update application will check for Apple software updates via the Internet. You can adjust automatic update settings or manually open the Software Update application from the Software Update preferences.

8. The system version, build number, and hardware serial number are located in the About This Mac dialog. The system version number defines the specific version of Mac OS X currently installed. The system build number is an even more specific identifier used primarily by developers. Finally, the hardware serial number is a unique number used to identify your specific Mac.

9. The Utilities menu when booted from the Mac OS X Install DVD includes Startup Disk, Reset Password, Firmware Password Utility, Disk Utility, Terminal, System Profiler, Network Utility, and Restore System From Backup.

2

Time   This lesson takes approximately 2 hours to complete.

Goals   Recognize various user account types and user attributes

Create and manage user accounts

Understand and implement user security techniques

Lesson **2**

User Accounts

One of the hallmarks of a modern operating system is support for multiple user accounts. Mac OS X 10.5 delivers in spades with a robust, secure, and highly polished multiple-user environment. Mac OS X's UNIX foundation is primarily responsible for providing such a sophisticated multiple-user environment. UNIX operating systems have a long history of providing such services. However, Apple has made many improvements by providing advanced user management features and streamlined administration tools, all with Apple's traditional ease of use.

In this lesson, you will explore the fundamental technologies that allow individuals to log in and use the Macintosh. Further, you will learn how to create and manage multiple user accounts on Mac OS X. Finally, you will learn account security and troubleshooting techniques.

Managing User Accounts

Mac users have been known to identify their beloved computer with a pet name; nevertheless, your Mac absolutely identifies you via a user account. With the exception of the rarely used single-user mode, you are required to log in with a user account to perform any task on the Mac. Even if the Mac is sitting at the login window and you haven't yet authenticated, the system is still utilizing a handful of system user accounts to maintain background services. Additionally, every single file and folder on your Mac's hard drive belongs to a user account. In short, every single item and process on your Mac belongs to some user account. Consequently, a thorough understanding of user accounts is necessary to effectively administer Mac OS X.

User Account Types

The vast majority of home Mac users are only aware of, and therefore only use, the account created when the Mac was initially set up with the Setup Assistant. Apple has engineered Mac OS X to appear as a single-user operating system by default. However, Mac OS X supports multiple simultaneous user accounts. Mac OS X also supports several types of user accounts to facilitate different levels of access. Essentially, you choose a specific account type to grant a defined level of access that best meets the user's requirements. User accounts are categorized into one of five types: standard users, administrative users, the guest user, sharing users, and the root user.

Standard Users

Ideally, standard is the account type most should use on a daily basis. Standard accounts are also commonly used when many users share a computer, as is the case with computer labs. This is because the standard account strikes the best balance between usability and security. Standard users have read access to most items, preferences, applications, and other users' Public and Sites folders. Yet, they are only allowed to make changes to personal preferences and items inside their own home folders. Essentially, standard users are not allowed to make changes to systemwide preferences, system files, or anything that might affect another user.

> **TIP** ▶ Standard users can be further restricted using parental controls. The account type Managed with Parental Controls is a standard account with Parental Controls turned on by default.

Administrative Users

Administrative users aren't much different from regular users, save for one important distinction: Administrative users are part of the "admin" group, and are essentially allowed full access to all applications, system preferences, and system files. By default, administrative users do not have access to protected system files or other users' files outside the Public and Sites folders. Despite this, administrative users can bypass these restrictions in both the graphical environment and on the command line if needed. For example, administrative users are allowed to update system software as long as they successfully authenticate when the installer application asks for authorization.

Because administrative access is required to make changes to the system, this is the default account type for the initial account created when the Mac is set up for the very first time with the Setup Assistant. Additional standard user accounts can be created for daily use, but the Mac should have access to at least one administrative account.

Guest User

Older versions of Mac OS X use only the guest account to facilitate file sharing by allowing nonauthenticated access to users' Public folders. Mac OS X 10.5 adds support for a full guest user. Once enabled, the guest user is similar to a nonadministrative account but without a password. Anyone with access to the Mac can use it to log in. However, when the user logs out, the guest user's home folder is deleted. This includes preference files, web browser history, or any other trace that the user might have left on the system. The next time someone logs in as a guest, a brand-new home folder is created for that user.

NOTE ► The guest user is enabled by default for file sharing access only.

Sharing Users

Mac OS X 10.5 also added support for special user accounts that only have access to shared files and folders. Sharing users have no home folder and cannot log in to the Mac's user interface or command line. Administrative users can create multiple shared users with unique names and passwords. Sharing users start out with access similar to that of the guest user, with access only to other users' Public folders. Administrative users can, however, define specific shared user access to any folder via the Sharing preference. File sharing will be further discussed in Lesson 7, "Accessing Network Services."

Root User

The root user account, also known as System Administrator, has unlimited access to everything on the Mac. In other words, the root user can read, write, and delete any file, can modify any setting, and can install any software. To help prevent abuse of this account, by default no one is allowed to log in as root, as a password hasn't been set for the root user. Since many system processes run as the root user, it needs to exist on the system; otherwise, Mac OS X wouldn't be able to boot. The root user will be covered in greater detail in "Account Security," later in this lesson.

User Account Attributes

Although the loginwindow process enables you to log in to the Macintosh environment, the DirectoryService background process is responsible for maintaining the account information. DirectoryService stores user account information in a series of XML-encoded files located in the /var/db/dslocal/nodes/Default/users folder. This folder is only readable by the System Administrator account, but if you were to directly inspect these files, you would discover that they are organized into lists of user attributes and their associated values. Each user has a variety of attributes used to define the account details. All of the attributes are important, but for the scope of this lesson you need only be familiar with the primary user account attributes:

▶ Name—This is the full name of the user. It can be quite long and contain nearly any character. You can also change it at any point.

▶ Short Name—This is the name used to uniquely identify the account. No other account on the system can have the same short name, and it cannot contain any special characters or spaces.

▶ User ID—This is a numeric attribute used to identify the account with file and folder permissions. This number is almost always unique to each account, though overlaps are possible. User accounts start at 501, while most system accounts are below 100.

▶ Unique User ID (UUID)—This alphanumeric attribute is generated by the computer during account creation and is unique in both space and time: No other user account will ever have the same UUID. It is used to reference the user's password, which is stored in a separate, more secure location. It is also used for group membership and some file permissions. The UUID is also called the Universally Unique ID.

▶ Group ID—This is a numeric attribute used to set the group membership when the user creates new files and folders. The default for most users is 20, which is the Group ID for the staff group. This means that, when you create a new file, it belongs to your user account and the staff group.

▶ Login Shell—This file path defines the default command-line shell used by the account. All users except for sharing users, who are not allowed to use the command line, have this set to /bin/bash by default.

▶ Home Directory—This file path defines the location of the user's home folder. All users except for sharing users, who do not have home folders, have this set to /Users/ <name>, where <name> is the short name of the account.

NOTE ▶ Account passwords are stored separately from the rest of the account attributes to enhance security. Password storage will be covered in greater detail in "Account Security," later in this lesson.

Creating a User Account

Now that you have a thorough understanding of all the user account types and attributes used in Mac OS X, it's time to get down to the relatively easy task of creating new user accounts.

To create new user accounts:

1 Open the Accounts preference by choosing Apple menu > System Preferences, then clicking the Accounts icon.

2 Click the lock icon in the bottom-left corner and authenticate as an administrative user to unlock the Accounts preference.

3   Click the plus button below the user list to reveal the account creation dialog.

4   Choose the appropriate account type from the New Account pop-up menu.

At a minimum, complete the Name and Short Name fields. A password is not required, but it's highly recommended that you choose a nontrivial password. Passwords and system security will be covered in "Account Security," later in this lesson.

Password hints are not required either, but you should enter a hint if you are forgetful of such things.

5   Finally, click the Create Account button to finish the job.

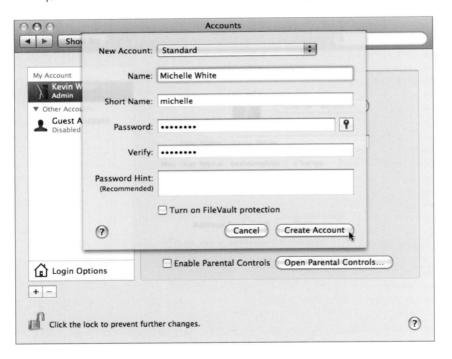

You can easily modify or add additional attributes at any time by simply selecting the account from the list in the Accounts preference. Additional configurable attributes include the user picture, .Mac account information, Address Book card, login items, and parental controls. You can also switch an account between standard and administrative at any time with this dialog.

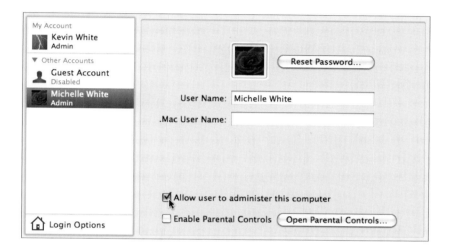

TIP ▶ The guest user account is also enabled and configured from the Accounts preference.

Login Items

Some users find it convenient to have their favorite files or applications open automatically as soon as they log in to the Mac. You can easily configure these automatic login items for your own account:

1   Open the Accounts preference and select your user account.

2   Click the Login Items tab.

3   Add login items either by clicking the plus button below the Login Items list to reveal a selection dialog or by simply dragging and dropping items from the Finder into the Login Items list.

4   You can delete login items by selecting them and then clicking the minus button.

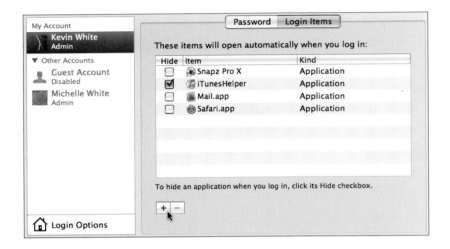

NOTE ▸ Even as an administrative user, you cannot configure login items for other user accounts unless you are currently logged in as that user.

TIP ▸ You can temporarily disable the login items from automatically opening by holding down the Shift key as you log in to the Mac.

Parental Controls

Mac OS X includes an extensive collection of user management options that enable you to further restrict what users can and cannot do. Apple puts these management features under the consumer-oriented parental controls moniker, but they are certainly still applicable in a business or institutional setting. As parental controls are designed to further limit standard user accounts, they cannot be applied to an administrative user.

Management options available via parental controls include the following:

▸ Use Simple Finder to simplify the Finder to show only the items most important to your managed user.

▸ Create a list that defines which applications a user is allowed to open. Users will not be allowed to open any application not specified in the list.

▸ Hide the user from profanity in the built-in Dictionary.

▶ Enable automatic Safari website filtering or manually manage a list of permitted websites.

▶ Limit Mail and iChat to allow exchanges only with approved addresses.

▶ Set weekday and weekend time usage limits.

▶ Maintain Safari, iChat, and application usage logs.

NOTE ▶ Many third-party applications will not honor parental controls' content filters and account limit settings.

To enable and configure parental controls:

1 Open the Accounts preference and authenticate as an administrative user to unlock its settings.

2 Select the user from the accounts list you wish to manage with parental controls.

3 Click the Enable Parental Controls checkbox and you will see the user's account type change from Standard to Managed in the accounts list.

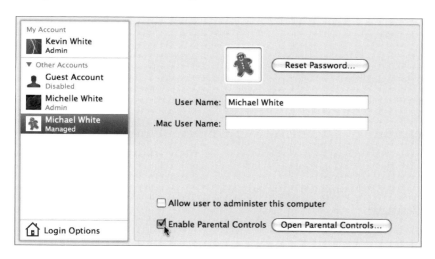

4 Click the Open Parental Controls button. You can also access parental controls directly from the main System Preferences window.

5 Select the user you wish to manage from the accounts list and use the tabs to navigate through all the options.

TIP ▶ Your Mac's Parental Controls preferences can be managed remotely by another Mac running Mac OS X 10.5. To enable this feature in the Parental Controls preferences, click the small gear icon at the bottom of the user list to reveal a pop-up menu allowing you to choose Allow Remote Setup. From another Mac on the local network, open the Parental Controls preferences and any Mac allowing this remote control will automatically appear in the user list. You will have to authenticate using an administrator account on the selected Mac to be granted Parental Controls preferences access.

Advanced Account Options

Further, you can access normally hidden attributes by right-clicking or Control-clicking on a user account to reveal the Advanced Options dialog. Although you are allowed to manually edit these attributes to make a desired change or fix a problem, you can just as easily break the account by entering improper information. For example, you can restore access to a user's home folder by correcting the Home Directory information, or you can accidentally prevent a user from accessing their home folder by mistyping this information.

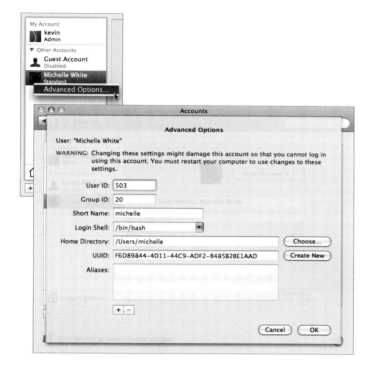

Group Accounts

A group account is nothing more than a list of user accounts. Groups are primarily used to allow greater control over file and folder access. Mac OS X uses several dozen built-in groups to facilitate secure system processes and sharing. For instance, all users are part of the staff group, administrative users are also part of the admin group, and the root user has its own group, known as wheel. Using groups to manage file sharing will be discussed in Lesson 7, "Accessing Network Services."

Creating new group accounts is similar to creating new user accounts:

1   Open the Accounts preference and authenticate as an administrative user to unlock its settings.

2   Click the plus button below the user list to reveal the account creation dialog.

3   Choose Group from the New Account pop-up menu.

4   Enter a group name and click the Create Group button.

5   Add user accounts to the group by selecting the appropriate checkboxes in the Membership list.

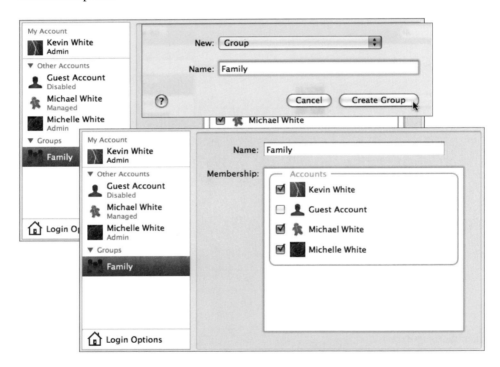

Login Window Options

The login window may look simple, but because it's the front door to your system, there are a variety of security options an administrator should be familiar with. Primarily, the options either provide higher security or greater accessibility. You can adjust the behavior of the login window from the Accounts preference by authenticating as an administrative user and then clicking the Login Options button.

Login window options include:

▶ Enable or disable automatic login as the Mac starts up. Obviously, you can only define one account for automatic login. The Automatic login option is turned on by default if the only account on the Mac is the initial administrative user.

▶ Choose whether the login window shows a list of available users or blank name and password fields. Not only is choosing to have name and password fields more secure, but it's also more appropriate for environments with network user accounts.

▶ Determine the availability of Restart, Sleep, and Shut Down buttons at the login window. Macs in environments that require security will not have these buttons available at the login window.

▶ Specify whether users can select a different keyboard input language at the login window.

▶ Determine whether the login window will show password hints after three bad password attempts. This may seem to be an insecure selection, but remember password hints are optional per user account.

▶ Enable users to take advantage of VoiceOver audible assistant technology at the login window.

▶ Enable fast user switching.

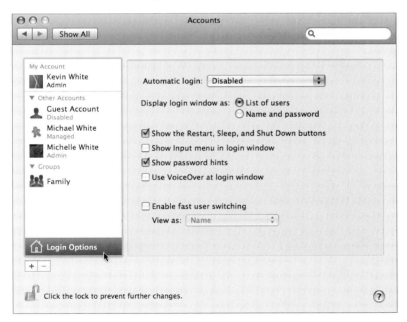

Fast User Switching

It's easy to imagine a situation when two users need to use a Mac at the same time. While it's not possible for two users to use the Mac's graphical interface at the same time, it is possible for multiple users to remain logged in to the Mac at the same time. Fast user switching enables you to quickly move between user accounts without logging out or quitting open applications. This allows users to keep their work open in the background while other users are logged in to the computer. A user can later return to his account instantly, right where he left off.

To enable fast user switching:

1   Open the Accounts preference and authenticate as an administrative user to unlock its settings.

2   Click the Login Options button below the user list.

3   Select the "Enable fast user switching" checkbox and continue through the Warning dialog.

4   Optionally you can choose a fast user switching menu style from the "View as" pop-up menu. You options are full name, short name, or a user silhouette icon.

5   The fast user switching menu item will appear on the far right next to the Spotlight search menu. From this menu you can switch to another user simply by choosing her name.

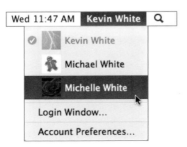

6   If the selected user account has a password, you will be presented with a Login Window dialog. You must authenticate as the selected user in order to switch to that account.

7   Once you're authenticated, the computer will switch to the other account, typically with a cube-spinning transition.

8   Click the fast user switching menu again, and you can verify that other user accounts are still active, as indicated by an orange checkbox next to their names. You can log in or return to any account, at any time, using this menu.

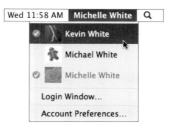

NOTE ▶ You may not be able to use fast user switching with network accounts. For more information, visit Knowledge Base document 25581, "Mac OS X 10.3 or Later: About Fast User Switching and Home Folders on Servers."

TIP ▶ You can move the "fast user switching" menu item, or any other menu item on the right side of the menu bar, by dragging the menu item while holding down the Command key.

Fast User Switching Issues

Apple has worked hard to make fast user switching a reliable feature. Many of the built-in Mac OS X applications are fast-user-switching savvy. For instance, when you switch between accounts, iTunes will automatically mute or unmute your music, iChat will toggle between available and away chat status, and Mail will continue to check for new messages in the background. However, there are some circumstances where you will experience resource contention when more than one user attempts to access an item.

Examples of fast user switching resource contention are:

▶   Document contention—These are cases where one user has a document open and remains logged in with fast user switching, often preventing other users from fully accessing the document. As an example, Microsoft Office will allow other users to open the document as read-only and will display an error dialog if the user tries to save changes. In more extreme examples, some applications will not allow other users to open the document at all.

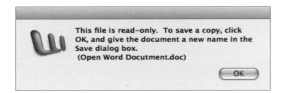

▶ Peripheral contention—Many peripherals can be accessed by only one user at a time. This becomes a fast user switching issue if a user leaves an application running that has attached itself to a peripheral. The peripheral will not become available to other applications until the original application is quit. Examples of this include video cameras, scanners, and audiovisual equipment.

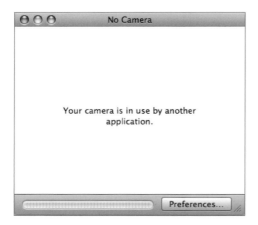

▶ Application contention—Some applications are designed in such a way that only one user can use the application at a time. If other users attempt to open these applications, they get an error dialog. Most of the applications that fall into this category are professional applications, which tend to be resource hogs, so it's advantageous to keep only one copy running at a time. Apple maintains a list of its own applications that share this limitation in Knowledge Base document 25619, "Mac OS X 10.3, 10.4: Some Applications Only Work in One Account at a Time."

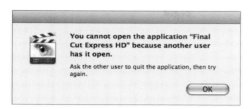

As you can see from the variety of error messages, fast user switching issues are not always consistently reported or readily apparent. There is no "fast user switching is causing a problem" dialog in Mac OS X. Still, if you are experiencing access errors to files, applications, or peripherals, your first step should be to check if any other users are still logged in. If so, you should have those other users log out and then reattempt access to the previously inaccessible items.

If you cannot log the other users out—perhaps because they are currently unavailable and you don't know their passwords—then your options are to force the other users' suspect applications to quit or to force the other users to log out by restarting the Mac. Changing a logged-in user's password isn't an option at this point because administrators cannot manage user accounts that are currently still logged in to the Mac. These accounts will be dimmed and not available in the Accounts preference. Thus, an administrator will have to force the other users' applications to quit or restart the Mac to free up any contested items or make any changes to the logged-in users. Neither option is ideal because forcing an application to quit with open files often results in data loss. Forcing an open application to quit will be covered in Lesson 5, "Applications and Boot Camp."

TIP ► If you have already set the master password, then you can reset a currently logged-in user's password from the login window using the master password. Setting the master password and resetting a user's password will be covered later in the "Passwords" section of this lesson.

Attempting to restart, though, will reveal another fast user switching issue: If any other users are still logged in, an administrator will have to force those users' open applications to quit in order to restart. The system makes it easy for an administrator to force the other users' applications to quit via an authenticated restart dialog, but once again this will very likely cause data loss to any open files.

Finally, there is one last security issue regarding fast user switching and volume access: Essentially, any volume directly connected to the Mac will be available to all users without restrictions. For example, if a user mounts a USB flash disk or FireWire hard drive, all other users will have unrestricted access to those volumes. This security risk, however, does not apply to network mounted volumes because those are protected by file system permissions.

User Home Folder

If you think of a user's account information as his mailing address, then you can think of his home folder as his house and its contents. The directions to his house are certainly important, but it's the stuff inside the house that's really valuable to the owner. The same is certainly true on the Mac. Aside from the primary account attributes, every other item that the user is likely to create or need is stored in that user's home folder. As mentioned earlier, the default location for a locally stored user home folder is /Users/<name>, where <name> is the short name of the account.

> **NOTE** ▶ Network user accounts often have home folders located on a shared server or possibly even a removable disk drive. Network user accounts are briefly covered in Lesson 7, "Accessing Network Services."

Traditional Mac users are notorious for putting personal files anywhere they like with little regard for order. Yet, with every revision of Mac OS X and its included applications, Apple has been coaxing its users into a tidier home folder arrangement. Though users can still create additional folders to store their items, most applications will suggest an appropriate default folder, while other applications won't even ask users and simply use the assigned default folder.

All the contents of the default folders inside a user's home folder are only viewable by the user, with the exception of the Public and Sites folders. Other users are allowed to view the contents of the Public and Sites folders, but they are not allowed to add items or make changes. There is a Drop Box folder inside the Public folder that others are allowed to put files into, but they still cannot see inside this folder. If a user puts other files and folders at the root level of her home folder, by default, other users will be able to view those items. Of course, you can change all of these defaults by adjusting file and folder access permissions as outlined in Lesson 4, "Data Management and Backup."

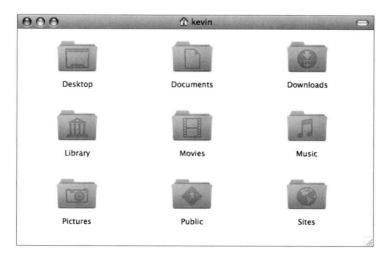

The default items in a Mac user's home folder are:

▶ Desktop—Many an old-school Mac user's files end up right here. This has been the traditional dumping ground for many users' files. Aside from being aesthetically unpleasing, there is no reason to stop users from keeping their items here and having a messy desktop.

▶ Documents—This is the default storage location for any document type that does not have a dedicated folder. Most famously, Microsoft Office prefers this folder as the default location for all its user documents. Certainly putting items here is the best alternative to cluttering up the desktop.

▶ Downloads—This new folder makes its premiere in Mac OS X 10.5 Leopard as part of another solution to prevent desktop clutter. This folder is the default location for all Internet applications to store downloaded files. Sequestering all Internet downloads to this folder also makes it much easier for virus and malware protection utilities to identify potentially harmful files.

▶ Library—Whether a user knows it or not, this is one of the most important folders on a Mac. Nearly all non-document-type resources end up in the user's Library folder. This includes, but certainly isn't limited to, user-specific preference files, fonts, contacts, keychains, mailboxes, favorites, screen savers, widgets, and countless other application resources.

▶ Movies—This is (obviously) the default location for movie files, and therefore is often preferred by applications such as iMovie, iDVD, and iTunes.

▶ Music—This is (obviously) the default location for music files, and therefore is often preferred by applications such as GarageBand, Logic, and iTunes.

▶ Pictures—This is (obviously) the default location for picture files, and therefore is often preferred by applications such as iPhoto, Aperture, and, once again, iTunes.

▶ Public—This is the default location for users to share files with others. Everyone who has access to a computer locally or via network file sharing can view the contents of this folder. There is a Drop Box folder inside this folder where others can place files that only the owner of the home folder can see.

▶ Sites—This is the default location for personal websites when Web Sharing is enabled. Outside of viewing these files through a web browser, only other local users can actually browse inside this folder.

Deleting a User Account

Deleting a user account on Mac OS X is even easer than creating one. To delete a user account, simply select it from the list of users in the Accounts preference, and then click the minus button at the bottom of the list. An administrator need only make one choice to delete a user account: what to do with the user's home folder.

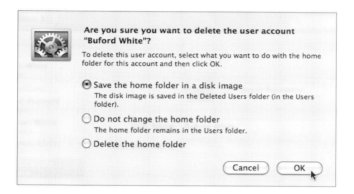

The administrator deleting the user account can choose one of three options:

▶ Save the home folder in a disk image—This option will create an archive of the user's home folder as a disk image file. The disk image file will be saved in the /Users/Deleted Users folder. Retaining the home folder as a disk image makes it easy to transport to other systems or import archived items to another user's home folder.

Keep in mind you must have enough free disk space available on the local system volume, essentially enough to duplicate the original home folder, in order to create the archive disk image. This process can also take quite a bit of time depending on the size of the user's home folder.

▶ Do not change the home folder—This will leave the user's folder unchanged save for its name. It will simply append "(Deleted)" to the home folder's name, letting you know the user account no longer exists. The deleted user's home folder will maintain the same access restrictions as a normal user home folder. Subsequently, even though this is a much quicker and more space-efficient method when compared to the archival option, you will have to manually adjust file ownership and permissions to access the items.

▶ Delete the home folder—This will delete the home folder contents immediately. The items will not be stored in a "Trash" folder before they are deleted, so they will not be recoverable using this method.

Restoring a Deleted User's Data

If you need to restore a deleted user's data to a new user account, it's a fairly simple process that can be done in the Finder:

1   If you haven't already created the new user account, do so first as outlined previously in this lesson. To make the restore process easier, it is best if the new user account is an administrator account.

Once the restore is complete, you can easily change the new user back to a standard account, but for now upgrade this user to an administrative user as outlined earlier.

2   Log in to the new user account.

3   Locate the deleted user's data for restoration and possibly change ownership and permissions.

Though covered briefly here, ownership and permissions will be further discussed in Lesson 4, "Data Management and Backup." At any rate, depending on your situation you will have to complete one of three following procedures:

▶   **If the deleted user's data is archived as a disk image.** Double-click on the deleted user's disk image file to mount its volume on the Mac. Locate the mounted disk image volume either on the desktop or in the Finder's sidebar. As you restore data to the local volume, the Finder will set the proper ownership on copied items.

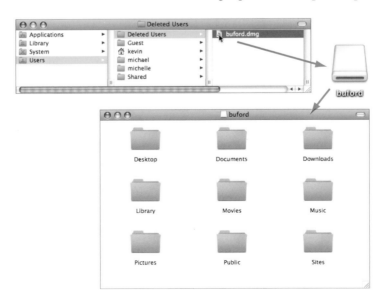

▶   **If the deleted user's data is stored normally on another nonsystem volume.** In the Finder, select the volume containing the deleted user's data and choose File > Get Info from the menu bar. In the Sharing & Permissions section of the Get Info dialog, select the "Ignore ownership on this volume" checkbox. As you restore data to the local volume, the Finder will set the proper ownership on copied items.

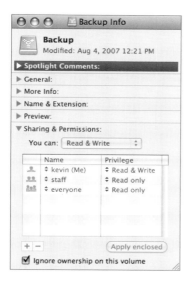

▶   **If the deleted user's data was from a previous user on the Mac but the data was never moved off the system volume or archived.** In this case the Finder will set the proper ownership and permissions, if you authenticate as an administrative user.

4   In the Finder, manually drag and drop all the items from the deleted user's home folder to the new user's home folder.

The Finder will not let you outright replace certain folders like Desktop and Library, so you will need to copy those folders' contents from the deleted user's home folder to the new one. You can quickly select all items in a folder using the Command-A keyboard shortcut.

5   Once all the home folder items have been restored, log out from the new user account.

6   If you need to change the new user account to a standard account, you can do that now.

7   Log in to the new user account and all the restored settings should take effect.

It would be wise to double-check important settings and application preferences before you erase the old user home folder.

Account Security

The primary purpose of a multiple-user operating system is to provide all users with a secure work environment. Mac OS X provides a relatively secure out-of-the box experience for most situations. Yet, there are some situations that call for greater security than the defaults afford. Thus, the remainder of this lesson will focus on the built-in advanced security features with Mac OS X, and how to best to manage and troubleshoot these features.

Account Vulnerabilities

As was discussed previously in this lesson, Mac OS X uses a variety of user account types: standard users, administrative users, the guest user, sharing users, and the root user. Apple has made available these different account types to allow greater flexibility for managing user access. Because each account type is designed to allow different levels of access, you should be aware of each account type's potential security risk.

Standard Users

This account type is very secure, assuming an appropriate password is set. This user is allowed to use nearly all the resources and features of the Mac, but they can't change anything that might affect another user. You can further restrict this account by using managed parental control settings, as discussed previously in this lesson.

Administrative Users

Because this is the initial account created when the Mac is set up for the very first time using the Setup Assistant, many use this as their primary account type. This is necessary and advantageous because it allows the user to literally change anything on the computer as is required for system management. The downside is that the user will be allowed to make changes or install software that can render the system insecure or unstable.

Additional administrative accounts can be used for daily use, but this isn't always the best idea, as all administrative accounts are created equal. In other words, all administrative accounts have the ability to make changes to anything on the system, including deleting or disabling other administrative accounts. Most significantly, though, any administrative user can enable the root account or change the root account password using the Directory Utility application located in the /Applications/Utilities folder. For this reason alone, you should seriously consider limiting the number of administrative user accounts on your Mac systems.

Guest User

Guest users are allowed, by default, to access your Mac via network file sharing without needing a password. Additionally, you can allow guests to log in to your Mac's graphical user interface without needing a password. Even though the guest home folder is deleted every time the guest logs out, the obvious security risk here is that literally anyone has access equivalent to that of a standard user account, including access to the Public, Drop Box, Sites, and Shared folders. This means they could execute some potentially nasty applications or fill your hard drive with unwanted files. The guest user can also restart or shut down your Mac, potentially allowing the guest user to compromise the system during startup.

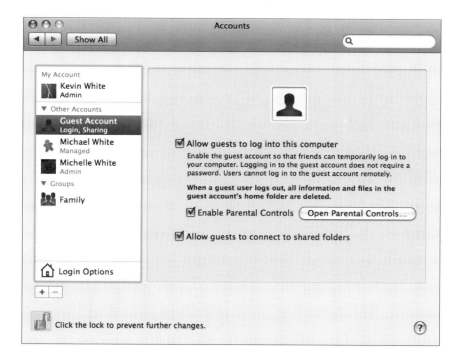

Fortunately, you can restrict the guest account using parental controls to prevent them from running unapproved applications or restarting the Mac. Additionally, you can change the access permissions on the Shared and Drop Box folders so the guest account is not allowed to copy any items to your hard drive. Changing file and folder permissions is covered in Lesson 4, "Data Management and Backup."

Sharing Users

Sharing users are by default allowed file sharing access to the Public and Drop Box folders, so, similar to the guest account, they can potentially fill your hard drive with unwanted files. On the other hand, shared users cannot log in to the Mac otherwise and they can be configured with a password, so using sharing users is generally much safer than using the guest account for file sharing. You can further control the sharing users' access to your files by adjusting file and folder permissions. Changing permissions is a two-way street, though, and you could accidentally give a sharing user too much access. Once again, changing file and folder permissions is covered in Lesson 4, "Data Management and Backup."

Root User

The root user account, also know as the System Administrator, is disabled by default on Mac OS X client, and for good reason: The root account has unlimited access to everything on the Mac, and root users can do anything they want with the system. The potential for nefarious activity is literally unlimited with root account access. Remember, though, it normally takes an administrative account to initially access the root account, so limiting administrative usage is the key to safeguarding the root account.

Passwords

Mac OS X relies on passwords as its primary method of verifying the user's authenticity. There are other more elaborate systems for proving a user's identity, such as biometric sensors and two-factor random key authentication, but these require special hardware. It's a pretty safe bet that every Mac is attached to an alphanumeric input device such as a keyboard, so passwords are still the most relevant security authentication method.

If you look closer at the security systems used by Mac OS X, you will discover that there are a variety of passwords at different levels used to secure the computer. Most users are only familiar with their account login password, but the Mac can also have a firmware password, a master password, many resource passwords, and several keychain passwords.

Each password type serves a specific purpose:

▶ Login password—Each user account has a variety of attributes that define the account. The login password is the attribute used to authenticate the account. For security reasons, a user's login password is stored in a separate file from the other account attributes. User account login passwords are stored as encrypted files in a folder that only the root user can access. These password files are located at /var/db/shadow/hash/ <UUID>, where <UUID> is the name of the password file that matches the Unique User ID attribute for the particular user account.

▶ Firmware password—The firmware password is used to protect the Mac during startup. Setting this password will prevent unauthorized users from using any startup-interrupt keyboard combinations. The password is saved to the Mac's firmware chip, so this password remains separate from the installed software.

You set the firmware password using a utility available when the Mac is booted from the Mac OS X Install DVD. If you require the highest level of security for your Mac, then you must set the firmware password, as any user with access to this DVD can set the password if it hasn't already been set. Once the firmware password is set, only an administrative user or a user who has physical access to the internal hardware can reset the password. For more information about the firmware password, reference Knowledge Base article 106482, "Setting up firmware password protection in Mac OS X 10.1 or later."

▶ Master password—The master password is used to reset standard, administrative, and FileVault user accounts if the user has forgotten his login password. Configuring and troubleshooting FileVault and the master password will be covered in greater detail in the "FileVault" section later in this lesson.

▶ Resource password—This is a generic term used to describe a password used by nearly any service that requires you to authenticate. Resource passwords include email, website, file server, application, and encrypted disk image passwords. Many resource passwords are automatically saved for the user by the keychain system.

▶ Keychain password—Mac OS X protects the user's important authentication assets, outside of the account login password, in encrypted keychain files. Keychain passwords are saved inside each keychain file and are not synchronized with the account login password. Configuring and troubleshooting the keychain security system will be covered in greater detail in the "Keychain" section later in this lesson.

Password Assistant

Regardless of how sophisticated a security system is, the protection it affords is only as strong as the password you choose. For this reason, Mac OS X includes a handy Password Assistant utility that will gauge the strength of your passwords or automatically create strong passwords for you. Any time you are creating or modifying a password that will grant access to a substantial resource, like a login or keychain password, you can use the Password Assistant.

To use the Password Assistant:

1   Open the Accounts preference and select your user account; then click the Change Password button.

2   Enter your current login password in the Old Password field.

You can reenter the same password in the New Password field if you just want to test its strength, or you can go ahead and create a new password.

3   Click the key icon next to the New Password field to open the Password Assistant.

The Quality bar in the Password Assistant dialog will instantly show the strength of your password. If your password is of low strength, the bar will be in shades of red to yellow, and you will be offered some tips as to why your password is a poor choice.

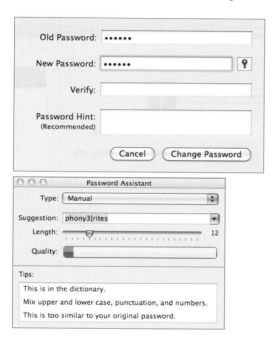

4   Try to find a stronger password by reentering it in the New Password field.

The Password Assistant will automatically gauge your password choices as you enter them. You know you have a strong password when the Quality bar starts turning green.

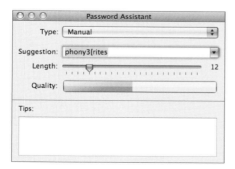

If you're having a hard time coming up with a good password, the Password Assistant will help you by automatically generating strong passwords. Choose a password type from the Type pop-up menu, and use the Length slider to adjust password length.

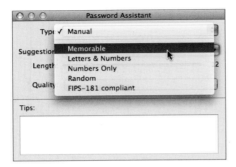

The Suggestion pop-up menu will show a variety of password options, or you can re-roll by choosing More Suggestions.

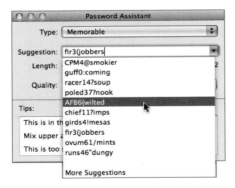

5   Once you have found a strong password with the Password Assistant, you will have to enter it in the New Password and Verify fields.

6   If you are indeed changing your account password, click the Change Password button to finish; otherwise click the Cancel button.

> **TIP** You can use the Password Assistant any time you see the small key icon next to a password field.

NOTE ► If your login password and keychain password are the same, when you change your password using the Accounts preference it will automatically change both passwords.

Keychain

Mac OS X features a very sophisticated system that automatically protects all your authentication assets in encrypted keychain files. Much like service workers might keep a keychain of all the keys needed during their workday, the Mac will keep all your resource passwords, certificates, keys, website forms, and even secure notes in a single secure location. Every time you allow the Mac to remember a password or any other potentially sensitive item, it will save it to your keychain. Only your account login password remains separate from all the other items saved to your keychain.

Because so many important items end up in keychain files, the keychain files themselves are encrypted with a strong algorithm: They are impenetrable unless you know the keychain password. In fact, if you forget a keychain's password, its contents are lost forever. Not even the software engineers at Apple can help you—the keychain system is *that* secure. Yet, probably the single best feature of the keychain system is that it's entirely automatic using the default settings. Most users will never know just how secure their saved passwords are because the system is so transparent.

Keychain Files

There are keychain files stored throughout the system for different users and resources:

► /Users/<username>/Library/Keychain/login.keychain—Every standard or administrative user is created with a single login keychain. As a default, the password for this keychain matches the user's account password, so this keychain is automatically unlocked and available when the user logs in. If the user's account password does not match the keychain's password, it will not automatically unlock during login.

Users can create additional keychains if they wish to segregate their authentication assets. For example, you can keep your default login.keychain for trivial items, and then create a more secure keychain that does not automatically unlock for more important items.

▶ /Library/Keychain/FileVaultMaster.keychain—This keychain contains the FileVault master password. Configuring and troubleshooting FileVault and the master password will be covered later in greater detail in the "FileVault" section.

▶ /Library/Keychain/System.keychain—This keychain maintains authentication assets that are non-user-specific. Examples of items stored here include AirPort wireless network passwords, 802.1X network passwords, and local Kerberos support items. Although all users benefit from this keychain, only administrative users can make changes to this keychain.

▶ /System/Library/Keychains/—You will find several keychain files in this folder that store root certificates used to help identify trusted network services. Once again, all users benefit from these keychains, but only administrative users can make changes to these keychains.

NOTE ▶ Some websites will remember your password inside a web cookie, so you might not see an entry in your keychain for every website password.

Keychain Access

The primary tool you will use to manage keychains is the Keychain Access application found in the /Applications/Utilities folder. With this application you can view and modify any keychain item including saved resource passwords, certificates, keys, website forms, and secure notes. You can also create and delete keychains, change keychain settings and passwords, and repair corrupted keychains.

To manage keychain items, including saved passwords:

1   As any user, open /Applications/Utilities/Keychain Access.

    The default view will show you the user's login.keychain.

2   To view all the keychains available to this user, choose View > Show Keychains from the menu bar.

3   Select a keychain from the Keychains list to reveal the items stored inside the keychain.

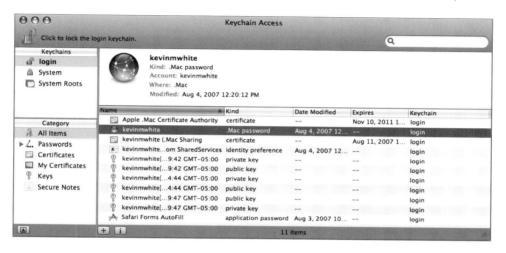

4   Double-click a keychain item to view its attributes.

5   If the item is a password, you can reveal the saved password by selecting the "Show password" checkbox.

6   When prompted, enter the keychain password once more, and then click the Allow
button to reveal the saved password. It is not advisable to click the Always Allow button.

Once you have authenticated, you can change any attribute in the keychain item dialog.

7   When you have finished making changes, click the Save button.

8   Click the Access Control tab in the keychain item's attributes dialog to adjust application access for the selected item.

> **TIP** ▶ To easily search through all the keychain items, use the Categories views to
> the left or the Spotlight search in the top-right corner of the toolbar.

> **TIP** ▶ The safest place to store secure notes on your Mac is keychains. In Keychain
> Access, you can create a new secure note by choosing File > New Secure Note Item
> from the menu bar.

To manage keychains, including resetting keychain passwords:

1   As any user, open /Applications/Utilities/Keychain Access and change the view to
show all keychains by choosing View > Show Keychains from the menu bar.

2   To create a new keychain, choose File > New Keychain from the menu bar. Next, enter
a name and location for the new keychain. The default location is the Keychains folder
inside your home folder. Finish by entering a nontrivial password that is six characters or longer for the new keychain and click the OK button.

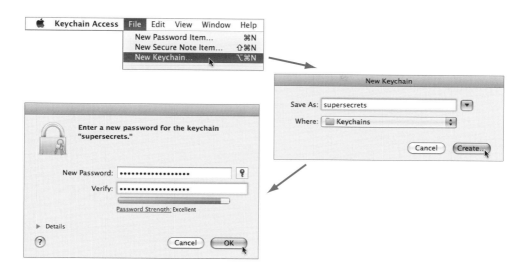

3   To change a keychain's settings, first select it from the list, and then choose Edit > Change Settings for Keychain from the menu bar. You will be able to change automatic keychain locking settings and enable .Mac synchronization. Finish by clicking the Save button.

4   To change a keychain's password, first select it from the list, and then choose Edit > Change Password for Keychain from the menu bar. You will have to enter the keychain's current password first. Finish by entering a nontrivial password that is six characters or longer and click the OK button.

5   To delete a keychain, select it from the list and choose File > Delete Keychain from the menu bar. When the Delete Keychain dialog appears, click the Delete References button to simply ignore the keychain or click the Delete References & Files button to completely erase the keychain.

> **TIP** ► You can move keychain items between keychains by dragging and dropping an item from one keychain to another.

> **TIP** ► For quick access to your keychains and other security features, you can enable the security menu item by choosing Keychain Access > Preferences from the menu bar. Then select the Show Status in Menu Bar checkbox to reveal the security menu item, as indicated by a small key icon on the right side of the menu bar.

To repair your keychains:

1   As any user, open /Applications/Utilities/Keychain Access and change the view to show all keychains by choosing View > Show Keychains from the menu bar.

2   If the troublesome keychain is not already in your keychain list, choose File > Add Keychain from the menu bar and you will be able to browse for it.

3   You need to unlock all the keychains you wish to check. Simply select the keychain from the list, then choose File > Unlock Keychain from the menu bar and enter the keychain's password.

4   Choose Keychain Access > Keychain First Aid from the menu bar.

5   You will have to enter your password once more, and then choose the Verify or Repair radio button and click the Start button.

A log will show the keychain verification or repair process.

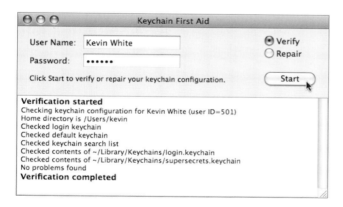

Security System Preference

In addition to specific user security settings, such as account passwords and keychain items, there are systemwide security preferences that affect all users on the Mac. Many of these security options are disabled by default because the average Mac user would probably consider them inconveniences. However, if your environment requires greater security, these additional security features are indispensable. Open the Security preference and authenticate as an administrative user to unlock the system security settings.

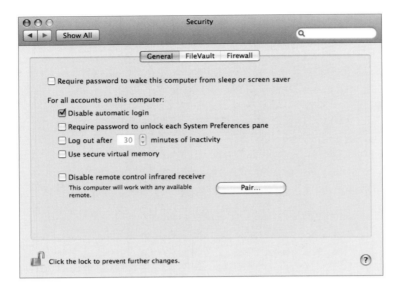

From the Security preference you can:

▶ Choose to require a password to wake the computer from sleep or screen saver mode. Both standard and administrative users can do this.

▶ Disable automatic login for all accounts.

▶ Require administrative authentication for all lockable system preferences every single time. This way, if a logged-in administrative user leaves her Mac temporarily unattended, anonymous users cannot make any changes to system preferences.

▶ Automatically log out accounts after a certain amount of inactivity. Keep in mind that enabling this option has the potential to cause data loss because the user's open files will not be saved if a forced logout occurs.

▶ Enable the use of secure virtual memory. All virtual memory will be encrypted by the system. This is an important feature for maximum security as passwords and other sensitive data are often temporarily stored in memory.

▶ Disable the built-in infrared Apple remote sensor on equipped Mac models. Unless the Mac has been paired to a specific Apple remote, any Apple remote will be able to affect the Mac.

▶ Enable and configure FileVault settings. FileVault will be covered next in this lesson.

▶ Enable and configure network Firewall settings. The network Firewall will be discussed in Lesson 8, "Providing Network Services."

NOTE ► Any administrative account can authenticate and unlock the Mac from sleep or screen saver modes, even if their account is not currently logged in. This means an administrative user could be granted access to another user's logged-in account.

FileVault

For the ultimate in account security, Mac OS X includes the FileVault service, which will maintain a user's home folder inside an encrypted disk image. It takes only a few moments for an administrator to initially prepare the Mac for FileVault service by setting a master password. As you'll see later, the master password is used to reset standard, administrative, and FileVault user accounts should a user forget his login password.

Once the master password has been set, it is easy for users to enable FileVault protection for their home folder. Though initially it may take a while to copy all the user's items into an encrypted disk image, once that is done FileVault protection will remain nearly transparent to the user. When a FileVault user logs in, the system will automatically unlock the encrypted disk image that contains her home folder items and make it available only to that user account. The moment a FileVault user logs out, the system will lock the encrypted disk image so no one else has access to it.

To set the master password and enable FileVault for a user:

1   Log out all other active user accounts, and then log in as the user for whom you're going to enable FileVault protection.

2   Open the Security preference and authenticate as an administrative user to unlock its settings; then click the FileVault tab.

3   If the master password has not been set, click the Set Master Password button. Otherwise, skip to step 6.

    When setting the master password, it's strongly recommend that you choose a high-quality password. Remember, this single master password can be used to reset any other user account login password.

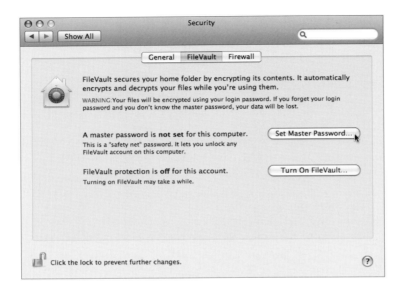

4   Open the Password Assistant by clicking the small key icon to the right of the
    Password field to gauge the quality of your master password choice.

5   Click the OK button to save the master password.

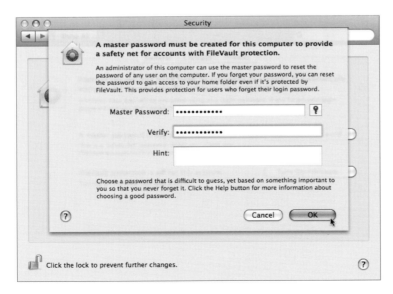

6   Click the Turn On FileVault button, and then enter the user's login password once more.

There are two additional security options you can enable at this point. One is to securely erase the previous unencrypted home folder contents, and the other is to enable secure virtual memory for this particular user account.

7   Select your options and click the Turn On FileVault button once again to start the encryption process.

The user will be logged out, and you will see a slightly modified login window showing the home folder encryption process.

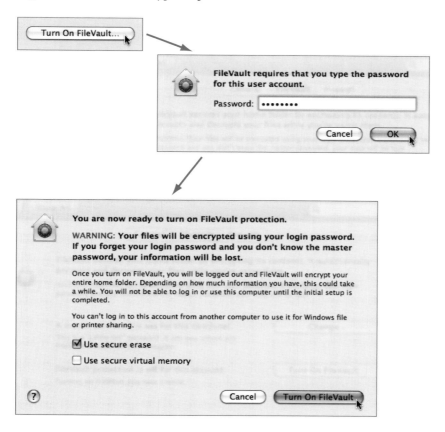

8   Once the encryption process is done, you will return to a normal login window and you can now log in with this user account protected by FileVault.

> **TIP ▶** Once the master password has been set, you can easily enable FileVault as you create new users from the account creation dialog in the Accounts preference.

FileVault Caveats

Enabling advanced security measures nearly always leads to restricted user access. This applies to FileVault as well. There are several caveats you should be aware of when a user account has FileVault enabled:

▶ Only the FileVault user has access to the contents of his home folder. Thus, the normally shared Public and Sites folders will be inaccessible to all other users.

▶ Several sharing services, such as Windows file sharing, Windows printer sharing, and web sharing, do not work with FileVault users.

▶ Even as an administrative user, you must also use the master password to reset a FileVault user account.

▶ The Migration Assistant utility, when started after initial system setup, cannot migrate FileVault users.

▶ The FileVault encryption process may slow disk access to the point that some high-performance applications cannot function properly.

Furthermore, you should be aware that FileVault-protected home folders are more likely to become corrupted than other types of accounts. The home directory is stored in an encrypted bundle, which is like a disk image, but the encrypted data is stored inside the bundle as a collection of separate files. If one of those files gets damaged, it's possible that you could lose the portion of your home directory located in that band.

If all these FileVault caveats have you worried, remember you can always disable FileVault from the Security preference, and protect only your most precious files on a smaller scale. It's relatively easy to manually save your sensitive items into user-created encrypted disk images. Archiving individual files to encrypted disk images will be covered in Lesson 4, "Data Management and Backup."

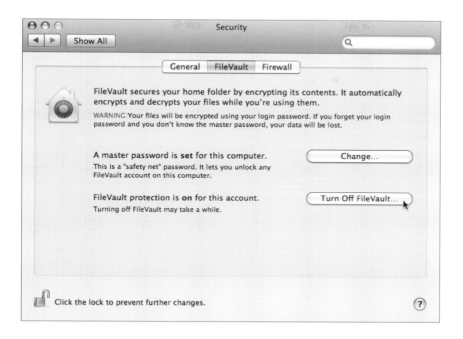

Password Troubleshooting

A user mistyping or forgetting her password is the primary cause of most login and access issues on any platform. The second most common issue, specific to Mac OS X, is when a user's keychain passwords become out of sync with that user's login password. Fortunately, with a few rare exceptions, Mac OS X provides facilities for easily resetting or resolving these types of password issues.

Resetting Login Passwords

By far the most common password issue is when a user simply forgets his login password. Mac OS X provides two methods for easily resetting non-FileVault user login passwords. The first, and most common, method requires administrative authorization. The second method requires configuration and knowledge of the master password and is identical to resetting a FileVault password from the login window.

To reset a non-FileVault login password with administrator authorization:

> **NOTE ▶** Resetting a login password with this method will not reset the user's keychain passwords. Resetting keychain passwords was covered previously in this lesson.

1   If the inaccessible user account is still logged into the computer because of fast user switching, you will need to restart the computer to forcibly log out the user. Alternatively, you can reset the login password from the login window using the master password, as outlined in the "Resetting the Master Password" section.

2   Open the Accounts preference and authenticate as an administrative user to unlock its settings.

3   Select the inaccessible user account from the list, and then click the Reset Password button. When resetting a login password, it's strongly recommend that you choose a high-quality password.

4   Enter the new login password and verification in the appropriate fields.

5   Click the Reset Password button to save the new login password.

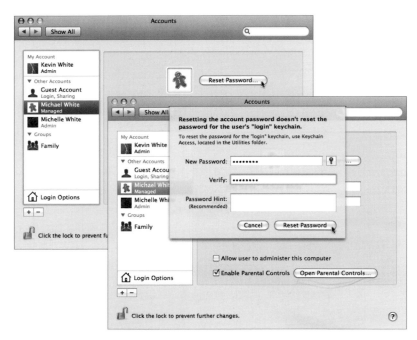

Resetting FileVault Passwords

FileVault accounts are unique because the user's home folder is saved inside an encrypted disk image protected by that user's account login password. Consequently, it is extremely important for an administrator to have the ability to reset a FileVault user's login password if the user ever wants to access her home folder files again.

A normal administrative user account is not enough to reset a lost FileVault password. Frankly, FileVault wouldn't be very secure if just any old administrative user could come along and break in. Therefore, if a FileVault user has forgotten her login password, the master password is required to reset the account. This is why the Mac forces you to create a master password before you enable any FileVault users.

If you have also lost the master password along with the user's FileVault password, then you are completely out of luck. You must have at least one of these two passwords to recover a FileVault account. Otherwise, you are never, ever going to be able to recover the user's data. Not even Apple can help you—they designed FileVault to be as secure as possible and thus only created one way to reset a FileVault account: the master password.

Obviously, if the master password is lost, an administrative user should reset it immediately for the benefit of other FileVault users. Don't get you hopes up, though; just because you can set a new master password for your Mac doesn't mean you can recover a FileVault account that was created with the old master password. Only the master password created when the FileVault user was enabled can unlock an inaccessible account.

If you do know the master password, Mac OS X provides two methods for easily resetting FileVault user passwords. The first method involves the Accounts preference, and the second method uses the login window.

To reset a FileVault password from the Accounts preference:

> **NOTE** ▶ Resetting a login password with this method will not reset the user's keychain passwords. Resetting keychain passwords was covered previously in this lesson.

1 If the inaccessible FileVault user account is still logged into the computer because of fast user switching, you will need to restart the computer to forcibly log out the user. Or, you can reset the FileVault password from the login window, as covered next in this lesson.

2 Open the Accounts preference and authenticate as an administrative user to unlock its settings.

3 Select the inaccessible FileVault account from the list; then click the Reset Password button.

4 Enter the master password in the appropriate field.

When resetting a FileVault password, it's strongly recommended that you choose a high-quality password. Open the Password Assistant by clicking the small key icon to the right of the Password field to gauge the quality of your FileVault password choice.

5 Enter the new FileVault password and verification in the appropriate fields.

6 Finish by clicking the Reset Password button to save the new FileVault password.

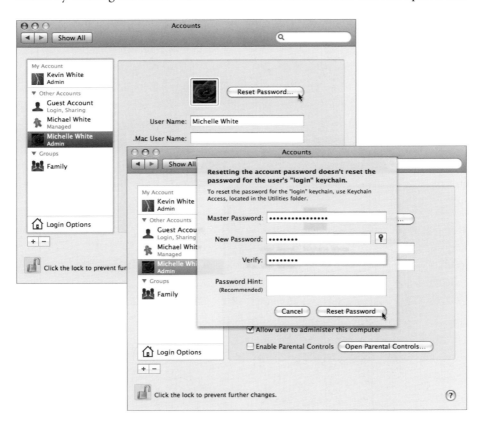

To reset a FileVault or login password from the login window:

NOTE ▸ Resetting a login password with this method will not reset the user's keychain passwords. It will, however, create a new login keychain for the user.

1   Open the login window by logging out, and then select the inaccessible user account. You can also select the inaccessible account from the "fast user switching" menu if it's enabled.

2   Click the Password Reset button.

3   Enter the master password, and then click the Login button.

You will also have to dismiss a keychain password warning dialog by clicking the OK button.

When resetting an account password, it's strongly recommended that you choose a high-quality password.

4   Enter the new account password and verification in the appropriate fields.

5   Finish by clicking the Reset Password button to save the new login or keychain password and log in as the user.

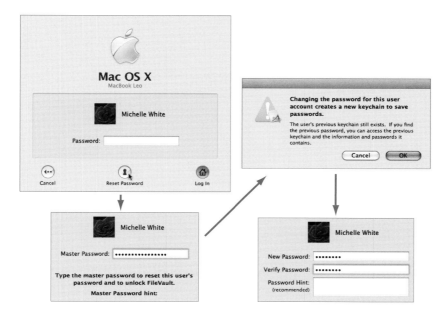

Resetting the Master Password

As mentioned earlier, the master password can be used to reset login passwords and is required to reset FileVault passwords. Thus, it is vital that the master password be properly configured and known by an administrator. There are two distinct situations in which a master password needs to be reset. The first is a situation where the current master password is known, and an administrative user simply wants to reset the password by choice. Changing the master password with this first method is quite easy and will not affect your ability to reset previously enabled FileVault account passwords.

The second situation is when the current master password is lost and a new master password needs to be created. In this case, if you want the new master password to have the ability to reset FileVault account passwords, you will have to reset all FileVault accounts created with the previous master password. Furthermore, because you are dealing with FileVault accounts that were created with a previous unknown master password, you will have to individually log into each account to reset its FileVault encryption. Thus, you must know all the current FileVault account passwords in order to restore the master password reset ability for all accounts. Remember, if both the master password and a user's FileVault password are lost, then that user's home folder contents are lost forever.

To reset a known master password:

1   Open the Security preference and authenticate as an administrative user to unlock its settings; then click the FileVault tab.

2   Click the Change button.

3   Enter the current master password in the appropriate field.

    When resetting the master password, it's strongly recommended that you choose a high-quality password.

4   Enter the new master password and verification in the appropriate fields.

5   Finish by clicking the OK button to save the new master password.

    This new master password can be used to reset all accounts, including FileVault accounts.

To create a new master password because the previous one was lost:

1   Log out all other users on the system, and then log in as an administrative user.

2   From the Finder, locate and delete the /Library/Keychains/FileVaultMaster.cer and /Library/Keychains/FilevaultMaster.keychain files.

3   Open the Security preference and authenticate as an administrative user to unlock its settings; then click the FileVault tab.

4   Click the Set Master Password button, because the computer will think the master password has not been set.

When setting the master password, it's strongly recommended that you choose a high-quality password. Remember, this single master password can be used to reset any other user account login password.

5   Click the OK button to save the new master password.

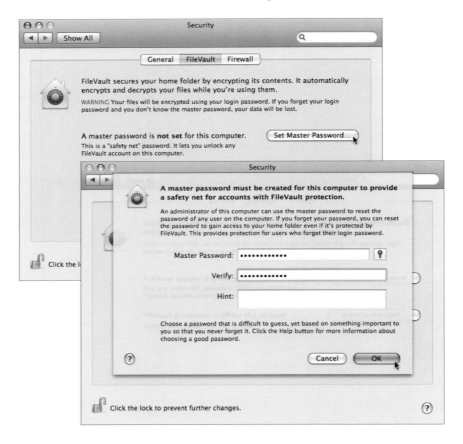

6   Log in using a FileVault account that was created with the previous master password.

7   Open Security preferences and authenticate as an administrative user to unlock its settings; then click the "Turn Off FileVault" button.

8   You will be prompted to enter the current user's password; do so and then click the OK button.

You will be presented with a final warning dialog reminding you that your are decrypting this user's home folder. Click the "Turn Off FileVault" button once more to return this user's home folder to a normal account. The user will be logged out and you will see a slightly modified login window showing the home folder decryption process.

9   Once the user's folder is decrypted, log in to the user's account again and re-enable FileVault. This process is outlined in the FileVault section of this lesson.

10 Repeat steps 6 through 9 for each FileVault user created with the previous master password.

Resetting Keychain Passwords

So that they remain as secure as possible, keychain passwords cannot be changed by any outside password-resetting process. Apple did not design the keychain system with a back door, as doing so would render the system much less secure. Consequently, whenever an administrative user resets a user's login or FileVault password, the keychain password will remain unchanged and will not automatically open as the user logs into her account. This can be easily remedied by resetting the user's keychain password from the Keychain Access utility, assuming the previous keychain password is known. As you'd expect, if you do not know the user's previous keychain password, then the contents of that keychain are lost forever. Using Keychain Access to manage a user's keychain was covered previously in this lesson.

Resetting the Primary Account Password

Many Macs intended for personal use have only the single primary administrator user account that was created when the Mac was initially set up with the Setup Assistant. Even if more than one person uses this Mac, quite often their owner is not very concerned about security. Thus, it's also likely that the primary user account is automatically logged in during startup and the owner has never enabled the master password. All this results in a high likelihood that Mac owners end up forgetting their primary administrator account password and don't have any way to reset this password because they never enabled the master password.

Fortunately, Apple has prepared for these occasions by including a password-resetting utility on the Mac OS X Install DVD. The Reset Password utility will allow you to reset the password of any local user account on the selected system disk.

To reset the primary account password:

1   Boot the Mac from the Mac OS X Install DVD by turning on the Mac while holding down the C key, and as soon as possible, insert the DVD and the computer will boot from it.

2   Once the Installer has started, choose Utilities > Reset Password from the menu bar.

3   Select the system volume containing the inaccessible primary account you wish to reset from the row of system volume icons.

4   Choose the name of the inaccessible primary account from the pop-up menu.

5   Enter and reenter a new password in the appropriate fields.

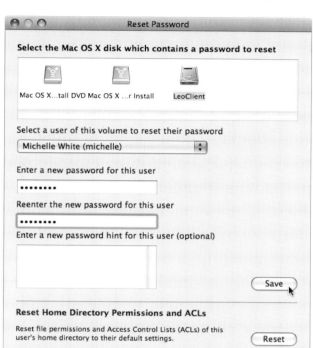

6   Click the Save button to save the new password.

7   Quit the Reset Password utility to return to the Mac OS X Installer.

8   Quit the Mac OS X Installer to restart the Mac.

> **TIP** ▶ You can also use the Reset Password utility to repair home folder permissions and access control lists (ACLs) for the selected account by clicking the Reset button.

Obviously, the Reset Password utility is a dangerous application that can completely eliminate any of the security settings you've configured to protect your Mac. Because of this,
the Reset Password utility will not run if copied off the original media, but this still doesn't

prevent any user with access to the Mac OS X Install DVD from using this utility. Once again, Apple prepared for this situation by providing another utility on the DVD: the Firmware Password utility. Setting a firmware password will prevent any nonauthorized user from booting the machine from a DVD. Using this utility to set a firmware password was covered previously in this lesson.

What You've Learned

▶ There are five types of user accounts, each with its own specific access and capabilities: standard users, administrative users, the guest user, sharing users, and the root user.

▶ Creating, managing, and deleting users is accomplished from within the Accounts preference.

▶ A variety of login and security options are available within the Accounts and Security preferences.

▶ There are five types of passwords, each with its own specific use: login passwords, the firmware password, the master password, resource passwords, and keychain passwords.

▶ Mac OS X provides robust security for users via technologies such as keychains and FileVault.

▶ There a variety of password reset methods you may have to use depending on the type of password you are trying to reset.

References

You can check for new and updated Knowledge Base documents at http://www.apple.com/support.

User Access

106824, "Mac OS X: How to change user short name or home directory name"

107297, "How to get files from a previous home directory after Archive and Install (Mac OS X)"

Fast User Switching

25581, "Mac OS X or Later: About Fast User Switching and home folders on servers"

25619, "Mac OS X 10.3, 10.4: Some applications only work in one account at a time"

Keychain

305146, "Using Keychains with .Mac, troubleshooting keychain issues"

301364, "Mac OS X 10.4: Keychain access asks for keychain 'login' after changing login password"

FileVault

305454, "Mac OS X 10.4: FileVault – 'There isn't enough space on your hard disk...' alert"

301416, "Mac OS X 10.4: If FileVault 'secure erase' is interrupted, data loss may occur"

93460, "iMovie: Using FileVault can affect performance"

93454, "Final Cut Pro and Final Cut Express: About using FileVault"

25695, "Mac OS X 10.3, 10.4: FileVault – How to verify or repair a home directory image"

Firmware Password

106482, "Setting up firmware password protection in Mac OS X 10.1 or later"

Review Quiz

1. What are the five types of user accounts in Mac OS X? How are they different?

2. What are some security risks associated with each type of user account?

3. What default folders make up a user's home folder? What function does each folder serve?

4. What three types of resource contention issues can occur when fast user switching is enabled?

5. What security risk can occur when fast user switching is enabled?

6. How does FileVault secure a user's data?

7. How does resetting the master password affect existing FileVault user accounts?

8. How does resetting a user's password as an administrative user affect that user's keychains?

9. How does the Firmware Password utility help prevent users from making unauthorized password changes?

Answers

1. Standard is the default account type; administrative users can make changes to the system; a guest user does not require a password; sharing users can access only shared files; and the root user has unlimited access.

2. Standard user accounts are very secure, assuming they have good passwords. Administrative users can make changes that may negatively affect the system or other user accounts. A guest user could potentially fill your system drive with unwanted files. Sharing users are generally very secure as long as you don't give them too much access to your items. The potential for mayhem with root user access is nearly unlimited.

3. The default folders in a user's home folder are Desktop, Documents, Downloads, Library, Movies, Music, Pictures, Public, and Sites.

4. Resource contention occurs when fast user switching is enabled and a user tries to access an item that another user already has open in the background. Document contention occurs when a user attempts to open a document that another user has already opened. Peripheral contention occurs when a user attempts to access a peripheral that is already in use by another user's open application. Application contention occurs when the second user attempts to access an application that is designed to run only once on a system.

5. When fast user switching is enabled, all users are allowed to see other users' locally connected volumes.

6. FileVault stores the user's home directory in an encrypted disk image. This disk image is accessible only by the FileVault user.

7. If a known master password is reset using the Security preference, previous FileVault accounts will not be negatively affected. On the other hand, if a master password is reset because it was lost, preexisting FileVault accounts cannot be reset by the new master password until all the old FileVault passwords are reset.

8. If an administrative user resets another user's login or FileVault password, this process will not change any keychain passwords. Therefore, the user's keychains will not automatically open when the user logs in with her new password. The user will have to manually change her keychain passwords using the Keychain Access utility.

9. The Firmware Password utility prevents users from booting off other devices. This in turn prevents them from using the Mac OS X Install DVD to reset local passwords without authorization.

3

Time   This lesson takes approximately 4 hours to complete.

Goals   Recognize the various file systems supported by Mac OS X

Understand and manage file ownership and permissions

Use graphical and command-line file system management utilities

File Systems

Although personal computer processor speed has increased around one-thousandfold since the first Mac was introduced in 1984, storage capacity has easily increased a million times over. Compare 1984's 400 KB floppy to today's average desktop drive at 500 GB, which is roughly equivalent to 524,288,000 KB, or 1.4 million 400 KB floppies. Apple has taken advantage of this tremendous growth in storage by pioneering the Mac as the center of your media hub. Customers have responded by moving thousands of pictures and hundreds of hours of music and video, historically stored in analog form, to the convenience and dynamism of digital storage. They have replaced their shoeboxes and shelves with hard drives and optical discs. Likewise, enterprise customers have replaced filing cabinets and storage rooms with Redundant Array of Independent Disks (RAID) arrays and backup tapes. Even though the Internet recently changed our perception of what a computer is used for, it's clear that the computer's primary task is still that of a tool to organize, access, and store our stuff.

In this lesson, you will examine the storage technology used by Mac OS X. Storage hardware like disk drives and RAID will be covered alongside logical storage concepts like partitions and volumes. Naturally, you will learn how to properly create and manage these storage assets as well. You will also learn to manage storage security through ownership, permissions, and access control lists (ACLs). Finally, this lesson will introduce you to the command-line environment as it relates to file system management.

Storage, Partitions, and Volumes

Before you begin managing storage on Mac OS X, it is important to understand the distinction between storage, partitions, and volumes. Traditionally, computer storage has been defined by disk drive hardware. After all these years, disk drive hardware still maintains the storage lead as it has moved from removable "floppy" disks to enclosed "hard" disks. However, other more convenient removable formats have become extremely popular, as they have increased in size. This includes rewritable optical media like CDs and DVDs, and static-based storage like USB key drives and compact flash cards. All are equally viable storage destinations for Mac OS X.

Without proper formatting, though, any storage technology is nothing more than a big empty bucket of ones and zeros, and consequently not very useful to the Mac. Formatting is the process of applying logic to storage in the form of partitions and volumes. Partitions are used to define boundaries on the storage. You can define multiple partitions if you want the physical storage to appear as multiple separate storage destinations. Even if you want to use the entire space available on a device as a single contiguous storage location, the area must still be defined by a partition.

Once partitions have been established, the system can create usable volumes inside the partition areas. Volumes define how the files and folders are actually stored on the hardware. In fact, it's the volume that is ultimately mounted by the file system and then represented as a usable storage icon in the Finder. Obviously, a storage device with several partitions, each containing a separate volume, will appear as several storage location icons in the Finder.

Using Disk and Flash Drives

The internal disk drive originally included with your Mac is probably the only storage device you will ever come across that is properly formatted for full Mac compatibility.

Most new storage devices are either completely blank or formatted for Windows. For the most part, you will still be able to use Windows-formatted drives on the Mac without reformatting. Conversely, if you want to install the Mac operating system on a drive or you have a new drive that is completely blank, you will have to reformat the drive.

The primary storage management tool included with Mac OS X is /Applications/Utilities/Disk Utility. You may have already used this utility from the Mac OS X Install DVD to reformat the system drive before you installed the operating system. Here you are going to explore all the aspects of this tool for managing disk and flash drives. Though disk and flash drives are very different storage mediums, Mac OS X treats the two similarly because they both provide dynamically writable storage. Optical media, on the other hand, is handled differently by the Mac because it's sequentially written storage. Using optical media will be covered in the "Using Optical Media" section later in this lesson.

Partition Schemes

As mentioned earlier, drives must be partitioned in order to define and possibly segregate the drive's usable space. Every disk requires at least one partition, but Disk Utility in Mac OS X can support up to 16 partitions per disk. You learned the advantages and disadvantages of using single or multiple partitions in Lesson 1, "Installation and Initial Setup."

Mac OS X also supports three different types of partition schemes. This may seem excessive, but it's necessary for Macs to support multiple partition schemes in order to boot computers using both PowerPC and Intel processors and to use standard PC-compatible volumes.

The three partition schemes supported by Mac OS X are:

▶ GUID Partition Table—This is the default partition scheme used by Intel-based Macs. This is also the only partition scheme that allows Intel-based Macs to start up using disk or flash-based storage. However, PowerPC-based Macs running Mac OS X 10.4.6 or later can also access this type of partitioning, but they will not be able to boot from it.

▶ Apple Partition Map—This is the default partition scheme used by PowerPC-based Macs. This is also the only partition scheme that PowerPC-based Macs can start up from. However, all Intel-based Macs can also access this type of partitioning.

▶ Master Boot Record—This is the default partition scheme used by most non-Mac computers, including Windows-compatible PCs. Consequently, this is the default partition scheme you will find on most new preformatted storage drives. This partition scheme is also commonly used by peripherals that store to flash drives such as digital cameras or smart phones. Even though no Mac can boot from this type of partitioning, all Macs can access this type of partitioning.

Obviously, if you have an older drive formatted with the Apple Partition Map you will have to repartition the drive in order for it to be bootable on an Intel-based Mac. But if you don't plan on ever using the older drive as a system disk, there is no advantage to repartitioning. Also, you should keep Master Boot Record drives unmodified if you intend to keep those drives backward-compatible with generic PCs or peripherals.

NOTE ▶ Intel-based Macs can start up from both USB and FireWire external drives; on the other hand, PowerPC Macs can only start up from FireWire external drives.

Volume Formats

The volume format defines how the files and folders are saved to the drive. To maintain compatibility with other operating systems and provide advanced features for newer Mac systems, Mac OS X supports a variety of storage volume formats.

The six primary volume formats supported by Mac OS X are:

▶ Mac OS Extended (Hierarchical File System Plus, HFS Plus)—Mac OS Extended, formerly known as HFS Plus, is the legacy volume format designed and supported by Apple for Macintosh computers. This volume format supports all the advanced features required by Mac OS X, including Unicode filenames, rich metadata, POSIX Permissions, access control lists (ACLs), UNIX-style links, and aliases.

▶ Mac OS Extended, Journaled—The default volume format for Mac OS X, this is a derivation of the Mac OS Extended format that adds advanced file system journaling to help preserve volume structure integrity. In essence, a journaled file system logs when files are changed as they are written to storage. The journal is created in such a way that it is never compromised should the system become inoperative. This way, if a power failure or system crash occurs, after the system restarts it will be able to quickly verify the integrity of the volume based on the journal log.

▶ Mac OS Extended, Journaled, Case-Sensitive—This last derivation of the Mac OS Extended format adds case-sensitivity to the file system. Normally Mac OS Extended is case-preserving but case-insensitive. This means that a normally formatted Mac volume will remember what case you chose for the characters of a file's name, but it cannot differentiate between similar filenames where the only difference is the case. In other words, it would not recognize "MYfile" and "myfile" as different filenames. By adding support for case-sensitivity, Apple resolved this issue. However, this is generally only a problem for volumes with an extremely large number of files, like those shared from Macs or Xserves running Mac OS X Server.

▶ UNIX File System (UFS)—UFS is the legacy native volume format supported by Mac OS X. UFS served as the default UNIX file system for decades. With Mac OS X 10.5, though, UFS volumes are no longer supported as a startup volumes.

▶ File Allocation Table (FAT32)—FAT32 is the legacy volume format used by Windows PCs, and is still used by many peripherals. Apple's Boot Camp supports running Windows XP from a FAT32 volume, but Mac OS X itself cannot start up from such a volume. Boot Camp will be covered in Lesson 5, "Applications and Boot Camp."

▶ New Technology File System (NTFS)—Windows XP, Windows Vista, and Windows Server all use this as their native volume format. Once again Boot Camp supports running Windows XP or Windows Vista from an NTFS volume, but Mac OS X itself cannot start up from such a volume. Further, Disk Utility does not support the creation of NTFS volumes.

NOTE ▶ Even though Disk Utility will not let you create any HFS or FAT16 volumes, Mac OS X still supports these older volume formats.

MORE INFO ▶ A wide variety of file systems are out there. Wikipedia has a great comparison of all file systems: http://en.wikipedia.org/wiki/Comparison_of_file_systems.

Formatting a Drive

Despite all the choices Mac OS X gives you for configuring storage, actually formatting a drive is quite easy. In fact, if you attach an unformatted device, the Mac will automatically prompt you to open Disk Utility. On the other hand, if you have a drive that is already formatted and you want to change the partition scheme or the volume structure, you can just as easily reformat the drive using the same steps.

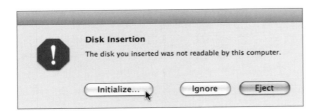

It is important to remember that reformatting a drive will destroy any formatting that is already there; essentially, a reformatted drive is losing its contents. The drive will not technically be erased—all the bits are still stored on the device. Reformatting will simply replace the previously populated volume structure with an empty volume structure. Truly erasing the contents of a drive will be covered in the "Securely Erasing Files" section later in this lesson.

To format a drive:

1   Make sure the drive you wish to format is currently attached to the computer, and then open /Applications/Utilities/Disk Utility.

2   Select the drive you wish to format from the column on the left.

   The size, manufacturer, and model number is usually the name of the drive. If a drive has any volumes, they will appear directly below and indented from the drive entry. If you want to reformat the entire drive, be sure to select the drive, not a volume.

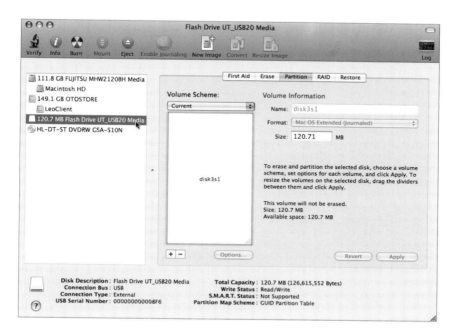

3   Click the Partition tab to the right. This is the only section in Disk Utility that will allow you to change both the partition scheme and the volume format.

4   From the Volume Scheme pop-up menu, choose the number of partitions you want for this drive. You must choose at least one partition.

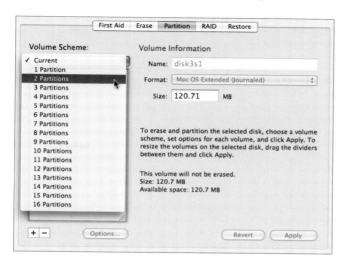

5 Once you have selected the number of partitions you desire, click the Options button at the bottom of the partition diagram to set the partition scheme.

A dialog appears allowing you to select an appropriate partition scheme.

6 Select your partition scheme, and then click the OK button to return.

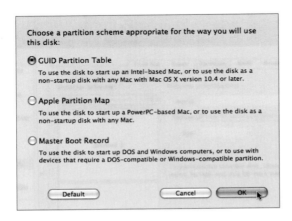

If you have chosen multiple partitions, you can adjust their sizes by clicking and dragging the line between partitions in the partition diagram. You can also specify a precise size by clicking in a partition area and then entering a specific size in the Size entry field to the right.

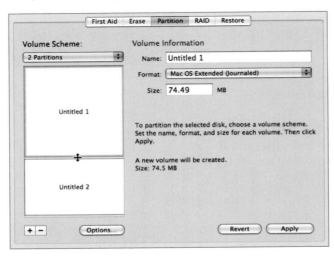

7   Choose a name and volume format for each partition.

If you only have one partition, simply enter an appropriate name and choose the volume format from the Format pop-up menu. If you have chosen multiple partitions, select each partition from the partition dialog first and then set the name and volume structure.

TIP ▶ You can always change the name of a volume in the Finder.

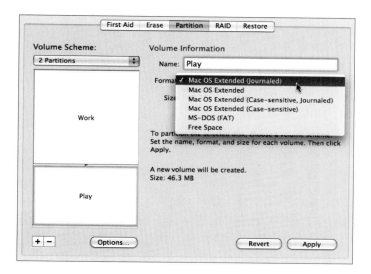

8   Once you have double-checked all your choices, click the Apply button.

You will be presented with a summary dialog, reminding you once again that continuing may destroy any previous volumes. If you are sure this is what you want to do, click the Partition button once more.

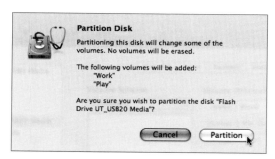

Partitioning and formatting takes only a few moments, and once the process is complete, you should see new volumes in the Disk Utility list and in the Finder.

Repartitioning a Drive

Mac OS X 10.5 has introduced a new feature in Disk Utility that enables you to dynamically repartition a drive without destroying any currently stored data on the drive. This functionality was introduced primarily to facilitate the Boot Camp setup process.

The only downside to dynamic repartitioning is that some drives may not support the partition changes that you want to make. For instance, some drives may be too full for you to repartition. Also, Disk Utility does not support dynamically repartitioning drives formatted with the Master Boot Record partition scheme. If you come across any of these issues, you can resort to using the old method for repartitioning a drive, which does erase any previous formatting, as outlined previously in this lesson.

NOTE ▶ Always back up important data before making changes to a drive's file system.

To dynamically repartition a drive:

1   Quit all open applications, as they may crash while the file system is being changed and consequently cause data corruption or loss.

2   Make sure the drive you wish to change is currently attached to the computer, and then open /Applications/Utilities/Disk Utility.

3   Select the drive you wish to change from the column on the left.

The size, manufacturer, and model number is usually the name of the drive. Do not select any of the drive's volumes.

4   Click the Partition tab to the right.

Any data currently on the drive will appear as a light blue area in the partition diagram. White areas indicate free space.

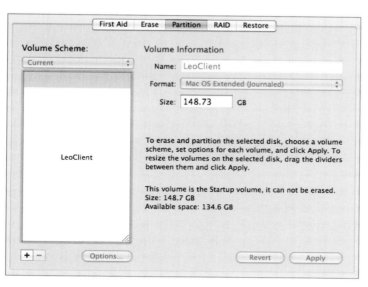

5   Resize any volume, or add new volumes, or delete any volume that isn't the current system drive.

To resize a current volume, click and drag from the bottom-right corner until you reach the desired new size. You will not be allowed to shrink a volume past the light blue that represents data on the drive. You may choose to leave parts of the drive empty if you plan on formatting those parts later using another operating system.

To add a new volume, click the small plus button below the partition diagram. Remember, you can have as many as 16 partitions per drive. Be sure to choose an appropriate name and volume format from the pop-up menu for each new volume.

To delete a volume, select it from the partition diagram and click the minus button below the partition diagram. If you are deleting a preexisting partition, you will be presented with a verification dialog. If you are certain that you want to delete the selected partition, click the Remove button to finish the process. The volume will be deleted immediately, leaving free space where you will be able to resize other volumes or create new volumes.

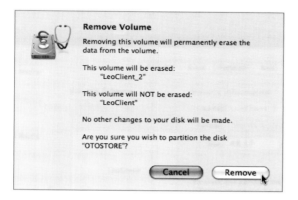

6   Once you have made all your changes and verified your selections, click the Apply button to continue.

7   You will be presented with a summary dialog, reminding you once again that continuing may destroy any previous volumes. If you are sure this is what you want to do, click the Partition button once more.

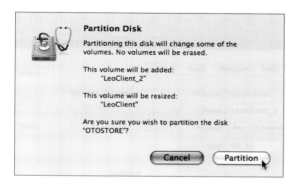

Depending on how much preexisting data must be moved to create your new disk structure, it may take quite a while for the repartitioning process to complete. You should not attempt to interrupt Disk Utility or open any other applications while the system is repartitioning the drive. Doing so may result in catastrophic data loss.

8   Once the process is complete, you should immediately notice the changes in the Disk Utility list and the Finder.

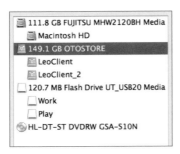

Erasing a Drive or Volume

You have seen earlier in this lesson how Disk Utility can be used to quickly erase an entire drive or volume by reformatting it. Yet, the default reformatting process does not actually erase any files or folders from the drive. This is because Disk Utility simply creates new blank volumes, which only replace the directory data of any volume. The old data still remains on the drive and can be recovered using third-party recovery tools.

In fact, there is no such thing as erasing data from a drive—all you can do is copy new data on top of the old data. Therefore, if you want to truly "erase" a drive or volume, you must somehow copy new nonsensitive data on top of it. Disk Utility includes a variety of options that will let you securely erase old data. You can securely erase an entire drive or volume, or just a volume's remaining free space.

NOTE ▸ Erasing or formatting a disk will not change the drive's partition scheme. To change a drive's partition scheme, you must repartition the drive, as detailed previously in this lesson.

To securely erase an entire drive or volume:

1   Make sure the drive or volume you wish to securely erase is currently available to the computer, and then open /Applications/Utilities/Disk Utility.

2 Select the drive or volume you wish to securely erase from the column on the left.

The size, manufacturer, and model number is usually the name of the drive. If a drive has any volumes, they will appear directly below and indented from the drive entry. If you want to reformat the entire drive, be sure to select the drive, not a volume.

3 Click the Erase tab to the right, and then click the Security Options button.

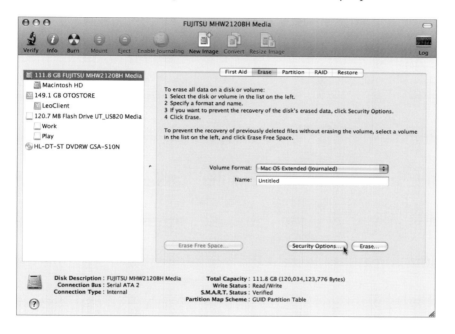

You will be presented with a dialog allowing you to choose one of the four erase options. Select the radio button next to your preferred erase method and click the OK button to continue. The four erase options are:

Don't Erase Data. This is the default action that occurs when you erase or reformat a drive or volume. Obviously, this does not provide any security from drive-recovery utilities. On the other hand, this choice provides a nearly instantaneous erase option.

Zero Out Deleted Files. This option will write zeros over all the data once. This is the quickest of the secure erase options, but it only provides a minimal level of security.

7-Pass Erase. This is a very secure option that writes seven different passes of random information to the drive. This option even meets with U.S. Department of Defense standards for securely erasing data. The downside is that this method will take seven times longer than the standard zero-out method.

35-Pass Erase. This is the most secure option, which certainly borders on paranoia. The Mac will write 35 different passes of random information to the drive. Obviously, this method will take 35 times longer than the standard zero-out method.

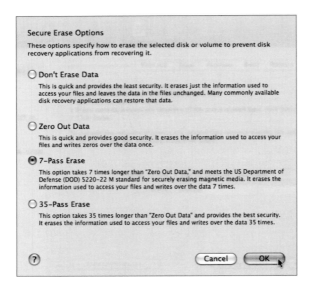

4   At this point you can also change the volume's name or volume format.

5   Double-check all your choices and click the Erase button.

6   You will be presented with a summary dialog, reminding you once again that you will destroy data on any previous volumes. If you are sure this is what you want to do, click the Erase button once more.

Depending on the size of the selected drive or volume and the erase option you chose, this process can take anywhere from seconds to days. If the process is going to take more than a few seconds, Disk Utility will show a progress indicator with the estimated time required to complete the erase task.

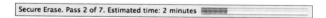

Secure Erase. Pass 2 of 7. Estimated time: 2 minutes

Securely Erasing Files

Because securely erasing an entire drive or volume can take quite a bit of time, you may find it's much quicker to use a more subtle secure erase method. Also, you may not want to erase the entire contents of a volume or disk—you may just want to securely erase a few specific files or only the free space on your drive. Fortunately, Mac OS X provides targeted secure erase options from the Finder and Disk Utility.

To securely erase only select files and folders:

1   In the Finder, move the items you wish to securely erase to the Trash folder.

    There are several ways to accomplish this task: you can drag and drop the items into the trash; you can select the items and then choose File > Move to Trash; or you can select the items and use the Command-Delete keyboard shortcut.

2   Choose Finder > Secure Empty Trash from the menu bar.

    The Finder's Secure Empty Trash feature is a secure erase method, which writes seven different passes of nonsensical information on top of the erased files. This feature even meets with U.S. Department of Defense standards for securely erasing data.

3   You will be presented with a verification dialog. If you are certain you want to securely erase the items in the Trash forever, click the OK button to continue.

Depending on the number and size of the files to be erased, this process can take any-where from seconds to days. The Finder will show you a progress indicator, but it will not show an estimated time.

To securely erase a volume's remaining free space, including any previously deleted files:

1 Make sure the volume with the free space you wish to securely erase is available to the system, and then open /Applications/Utilities/Disk Utility.

2 Select the name of the volume with the free space you wish to securely erase from the column on the left. Do not select the drive.

3 Click the Erase tab to the right, and then click the Erase Free Space button.

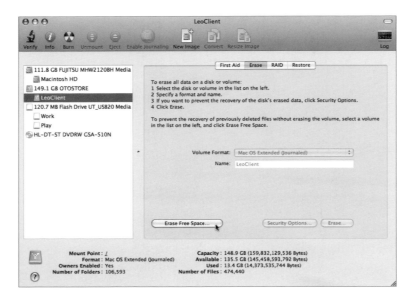

You will be presented with a dialog allowing you to choose one of the three available secure erase options similar to erasing an entire volume or disk: Zero Out Deleted Files, 7-Pass Erase, and 35-Pass Erase.

4   Select the radio button next to your preferred erase method and click the Erase Free Space button to continue.

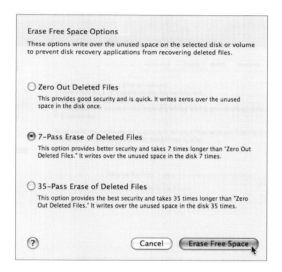

Depending on the amount of free space to erase and the erase option you chose, this process can take anywhere from seconds to days. If the process is going to take more than a few seconds, Disk Utility will show a progress indicator with the estimated time required to complete the erase task.

Secure Erase. Pass 2 of 7. Estimated time: 2 minutes

Using RAID Volumes

The idea behind RAID (Redundant Array of Independent Disks) is that you can combine similar drives together to form large volumes with increased performance and/or reliability. The downside is that you have to have special hardware or software to manage the RAID. Hardware-based RAID solutions are typically external to the computer because they contain many drives and include specialized hardware to manage the RAID. Conversely, software-based RAID solutions don't require any special hardware as they use software running from the computer's processor to manage the RAID.

There are many hardware-based RAID solutions available today, including Apple's own Xserve RAID, which can combine two sets of seven hard drives into multiple large volumes. Because hardware-based solutions manage the RAID internally, the Mac doesn't have to do anything special to take advantage of the storage. When you attach a hardware-based RAID to a Mac, it treats the storage like any other single drive. Simply use Disk Utility to format the storage on the RAID device and make it available to the system.

Mac OS X includes a software-based RAID solution as part of its file system. The advantage of using the built-in software-based RAID is that no special hardware is required. All you have to do is connect two or more similar drives to the Mac via any compatible hardware interface, and then use Disk Utility to create the RAID set. The main disadvantage is that you cannot use advanced RAID types normally available from a hardware-based RAID solution. Specifically, the popular RAID 5 implementation, which provides both increased redundancy and performance, is not available using the built-in software-based RAID solution.

> **TIP** ▶ You can use the built-in software-based RAID to further combine hardware-based RAIDs. This technique is often used to combine the two separate sides of an Xserve RAID into a single huge volume.

Mac OS X built-in software-based RAID supports:

▶ RAID 0—Commonly called *striping*, RAID 0 splits up the data into multiple pieces, and then simultaneously writes each piece to a different drive in the set. This yields a single large volume, with dramatically increased read and write performance, equivalent to the cumulative size of all the drives. On the other hand, RAID 0 offers zero increase in reliability since if just one drive in the set fails, then all the data is lost. In fact, RAID 0 *increases* your chances of data loss because you are introducing more points of failure. In short, RAID 0 is space efficient and fast but provides no redundancy and increased risk.

▶ RAID 1—Commonly called *mirroring*, RAID 1 writes the same data to each drive in the set. This yields a single volume that is only the same size as a single drive. Write performance is no faster than a single drive, whereas read performance is increased. Yet, the primary advantage to a RAID 1 set is that it can survive and recover from hardware failure. RAID 1 decreases your chances of data loss by providing redundancy. In short, RAID 1 is space-inefficient and slower but provides drive redundancy and decreased risk of data loss due to drive failure. Even so, it's very important to remember that mirroring is not a backup solution. Backup solutions create an archive of the data frozen in time and save it to another storage device. If any kind of failure occurs, you can recover from a previous backup version of the data. With a mirrored RAID set, all file system changes are applied immediately to all drives in the set and no archival history is maintained.

► Nested RAID, 1+0 or 0+1—Because RAID 0 and RAID 1 offer opposed feature sets, nesting one type inside of the other can provide the features of both. In other words, you can stripe data between two mirrors, or you can mirror data on two stripes. These nested configurations are certainly more complicated and they require a minimum of four separate drives. However, when you combine their features you get increased performance and redundancy.

► Concatenated disk set—This isn't a true RAID configuration, as not all drives are being used simultaneously. With a concatenated disk set, the system will simply continue on to the next drive once the previous drive is filled. The only advantage here is that the user will see one large volume instead of several separate drives.

MORE INFO ► You can find out more about all the different RAID types by visiting Wikipedia's RAID entry, http://en.wikipedia.org/wiki/RAID.

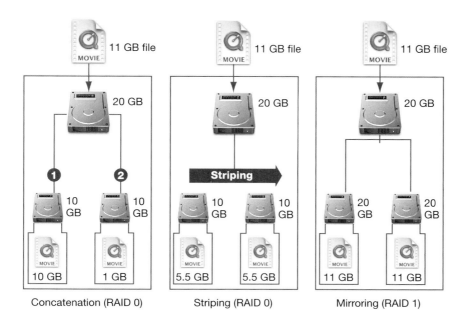

Concatenation (RAID 0)   Striping (RAID 0)   Mirroring (RAID 1)

Creating a RAID Set

Creating a RAID set with Mac OS X is only slightly more complicated than formatting a standard disk or flash drive. Remember, you can use just about any combination of drives to create a RAID set. Nevertheless, you should follow a couple rules to ensure a healthy RAID set.

Here are some software-based RAID guidelines:

▶ Use identical drives if possible—This will ensure consistent size and performance for all drives in the RAID set. RAID sets are susceptible to performance at the lowest common denominator. In other words, all the drives in a RAID set are treated as large or as fast as your smallest and slowest drives. This is not an issue for a concatenated disk set.

▶ Use multiple interfaces to your advantage—This often requires extra hardware, but giving the Mac multiple independent paths to the drives can dramatically increase performance.

▶ Make certain that all drives in a set are simultaneously available to the Mac—This may be a difficult criterion if the drives are using different interfaces, but it's necessary to maintain RAID consistency. If a drive in a RAID set is missing for more than a few seconds, the system will assume the drive has failed and the RAID set is damaged. In other words, make sure all the drives are turned on and plugged into the Mac at the same time.

To create a software-based RAID set:

1   Make sure all the drives for the new, unformatted RAID set are connected to the Mac, and then open /Applications/Utilities/Disk Utility.

2   Select any one of the drives from the column on the left, and then click the RAID tab to the right.

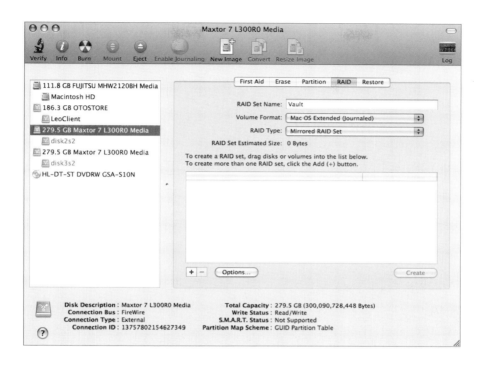

3 Click the small plus button at the bottom of the RAID diagram to create a RAID set. The new RAID set will assume some defaults that you can change at any time before you create the RAID.

4 Configure the newly created RAID set by clicking on its entry in the RAID diagram to select it. For each RAID set, you need to enter a volume name for the RAID set, choose a volume type from the Volume Format pop-up menu, and choose a RAID type from the pop-up menu. Then, click the Options button at the bottom to configure the RAID block size for optimal performance or enable automatic rebuilds if the RAID set is mirrored.

> **NOTE ▶** Disk Utility will only create RAID sets with one volume. Further, it will not let you repartition the RAID set after it was created.

5   If you are creating a nested RAID set, simply click the small plus button to create additional RAID sets.

Be sure to properly configure each new RAID set. Simply drag the nested RAIDs on top of the root RAID set to configure the nesting order.

6   Add the drives by simply dragging the drive icons from the column on the left to the RAID diagram on the right.

To specify a particular RAID set order, continue to drag drive icons around until you set their appropriate locations in the RAID diagram.

If you have added three or more drives to a mirrored RAID set, you can define a spare drive by selecting the drive in the RAID diagram and then choosing Spare from the Drive Type pop-up menu. If one of the other drives becomes unreachable during the life of the RAID set, the system will automatically rebuild the array using the spare drive.

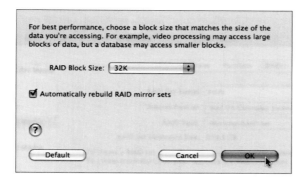

7   Delete items by selecting them from the RAID diagram and then clicking the small minus button below the diagram.

Sometimes if you make too many mistakes it's easier to just start over by quitting and then reopening Disk Utility.

8   Double-check all your choices and click the Create button.

You will be presented with a summary dialog, reminding you once again that continuing may destroy any previous volumes. If you are sure this is what you want to do, click the Create button once more.

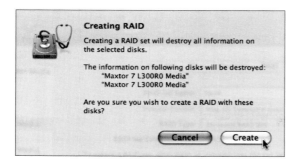

RAID set creation takes only a few moments, and once it's complete, you should see new RAID set volume in the Disk Utility list and in the Finder. Selecting the newly created RAID set from the column on the left, and then clicking the RAID tab, should reveal that the set is "Online."

Rebuilding a RAID Set

As mentioned earlier, using multiple drives in a RAID set actually introduces more points of storage failure. Fortunately, RAID 1 data mirroring configurations are designed specifically to prevent data loss when a drive fails. Mac OS X even includes the ability to automatically repair mirrored RAID sets if you specified that option during RAID creation.

Before the system mounts a RAID volume, it will check the set for consistency. If the system finds a degraded striped RAID 0 set, you'd better have a good backup because all that data is lost. The system will report the degraded RAID set in Disk Utility, but it will not mount the volume. Only a data recovery service, such as DriveSavers, might have a chance at recovering your data.

> **NOTE** ▶ For more about data recovery service providers that can be used without voiding an Apple warranty, see http://docs.info.apple.com/article.html?artnum=31077

On the other hand, if the system finds that a mirrored RAID 1 set is degraded it will either warn you or automatically start rebuilding the RAID set if configured. Either way, the volume will still mount and be accessible to you in the Finder. You should avoid writing new data to a degraded RAID set until you have completed the rebuilding process.

There are two main failure modes for a mirrored RAID 1 set:

One of the drives appears to be responding properly, but the data on the drive is not consistent with the other drives in the set. If configured, the system will automatically start rebuilding the RAID set data by recopying it from a working drive to the apparently corrupted drive. Otherwise, the system will wait for you to manually engage the rebuild process from Disk Utility.

One of the drives in the set is no longer available. If a spare is configured, the system will automatically start rebuilding the RAID set data by copying it from a working drive to the spare drive. Otherwise, the system will wait for you to manually replace the drive and manually engage the rebuild process from Disk Utility.

To manually rebuild a mirrored RAID 1 set:

1 Make sure that all the drives that are part of the RAID set are connected to the Mac, and then open /Applications/Utilities/Disk Utility.

2 Select the degraded RAID set from the column on the left, which should be easy to locate as it will show up onscreen with bright red text for the name.

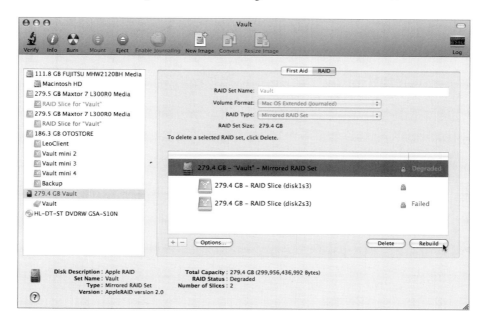

3 Depending on the failure mode of the RAID set, you will need to choose one of two resolutions:

Inconsistent data. The system has discovered that one of the drives does not have the same data as the others. You will see the word "Failed" next to the drive with inconsistent data. Simply click the Rebuild button to repair the RAID set.

Bad or missing drive. The system can no longer access on of the drives. You will see the word "Offline" next to the missing drive. Select the missing drive from the RAID dialog, and then click the small minus button below the RAID dialog to delete the missing drive. Drag the replacement drive from the column on the left to replace the missing drive from RAID diagram. Click the Rebuild button to repair the RAID set.

Depending on the size and bandwidth of the RAID set, the rebuild process can take anywhere from seconds to days. Disk Utility will open a progress dialog with the estimated time required to complete the erase task.

Using Optical Media

Over a decade ago, Apple made headlines by introducing the iMac with only an optical drive, choosing to banish the traditional floppy disk drive from the new computer's revolutionary design. It should come as no surprise, then, that every Mac sold today can at the very least record to CDs, if not DVDs.

> **TIP** ▶ You can easily identify the capabilities of your Mac's optical drive by opening /Applications/Utilities/System Profiler and viewing the Disc Burning information section.

Obviously, Mac OS X provides full support for reading and writing optical media, although the Mac treats optical media differently than disk or flash drives. This is because most optical media formats require that the data be sequentially and permanently written to the disc. This is why the term "burn" is often used to describe the process of writing data to an optical disc. The data is literally burned into the media, and it's common knowledge that you simply can't "un-burn" something once it's been burned.

> **NOTE** ▶ No Mac currently shipping includes the ability to write to DVD-RAM. However, Mac OS X supports this hardware. DVD-RAM media is unique among optical media as it provides a dynamically writable volume. Thus, the Mac will treat a DVD-RAM disc just like it treats any other dynamically writable medium.

Several of the applications included with a new Mac are designed to burn specific types of data to optical discs. For example, iTunes can burn audio and MP3 discs, iDVD is used to create video DVDs, and iPhoto can create cross-platform photo discs. Conversely, if you simply want to burn general-purpose data files onto an optical disc, the Finder is your tool. Finally, Disk Utility rounds out the Mac's optical media functionality by providing the means to burn disk images and prepare rewritable discs for reburning.

Burning a Disc with Finder

The Finder provides no less than three different methods for burning data to an optical disc. The first method enables you to quickly select and burn specific items in the Finder to an optical disc. The other two methods involve creating burn folders that let you organize the contents destined for an optical disc before you burn the data to it. This is a convenient way to burn general-purpose data discs, as you cannot change the contents of most optical discs once they have been burned.

> **TIP** The Finder will automatically burn a cross-platform optical disc that can be accessed by both Macs and PCs.

To quickly burn specifically selected items:

1   Select the items you wish to burn in the Finder.

You can hold down the Shift key to quickly select contiguous lists of items, or hold down the Command key to quickly select noncontiguous items.

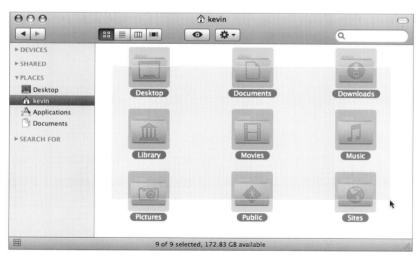

2   Choose File > Burn "Items" to Disc from the menu bar.

The word "Items" in the menu will be replaced by the name of a single item you have selected or the number of items you have selected.

3   The Finder will present you with a dialog asking you to insert a blank disc, and letting you know how much storage space will be required. Insert an appropriately sized blank recordable optical disc.

4   Once the system has verified that the inserted optical disc is adequate, it will present a dialog allowing you to select a name for the disc and the burn speed. Stick with the maximum speed unless you are experiencing problems burning discs.

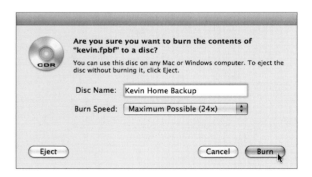

5   Click the Burn button to start the burn and verification process.

Depending on the size of the data and the speed of the drive, the burn and verification process can take anywhere from minutes to hours. The Finder will show a progress dialog that will also allow you to cancel the burn by clicking the small X button on the far right.

6   Once the burn and verification is complete, the Finder will mount the completed disc. Press and hold the Eject key, the furthest top-right key on a Mac keyboard, for a few moments to eject the optical disc.

To use a burn folder:

1   In the Finder, choose File > New Burn Folder from the menu bar.

This will create a special new folder called Burn Folder in the current Finder window or desktop. You can move and rename this folder as you would any other folder.

A burn folder is special because as you drag files and folders inside this folder they will not be moved or copied into the folder. Instead, the system creates aliases to the original items. This allows you to reorganize and rename files and folders inside the burn folder without affecting the originals or wasting drive space. You can even keep burn folders around for future use after you have burned the disc.

2   Once you have perfected the contents of your burn folder, click the Burn button at the top-right corner of the burn folder's Finder window, or select the burn folder and then choose File > Burn "burn folder name" from the menu bar.

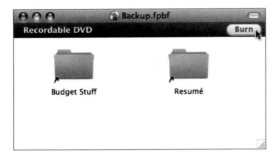

The Finder will present you with a dialog asking you to insert a blank disc, and letting you know how much storage space will be required. Insert an appropriately sized blank recordable optical disc.

3   Once the system has verified that the inserted optical is adequate, it will present a dialog allowing you to select a name for the disc and the burn speed. Stick with the maximum speed unless you are experiencing problems burning discs.

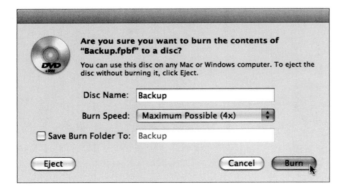

4   Click the Burn button to start the burn and verification process.

Depending on the size of the data and the speed of the drive, the burn and verification process can take anywhere from minutes to hours. The Finder will show a progress dialog that will also allow you to cancel the burn by clicking the small X button on the far right.

5   Once the burn and verification is complete, the Finder will mount the completed disc. Press and hold the Eject key, the furthest top-right key on a Mac keyboard, for a few moments to eject the optical disc.

To use a burn folder for a specific disc size:

1   From within the Finder, insert a blank recordable optical disc.

If this is the first time you have inserted blank optical media in this Mac, you will be presented with a dialog that will let you choose your preferred action when blank media is inserted. Leave the default action to open the media in the Finder, and then click the OK button.

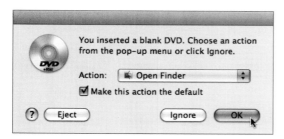

The Finder will create a new burn folder with an optical disc icon named Untitled on your desktop and also create a link to it in the Finder's sidebar. Creating a burn folder this way will cap the size of the burn folder to ensure it will fit once burned to the media you inserted.

2   Continue to reorganize, move, and ultimately burn this burn folder, as you would use a manually created burn folder outlined in the previous steps.

Burning a Disk Image with Disk Utility

One of Disk Utility's many features is its ability to burn the contents of a disk image to optical discs. This is extremely useful for burning backup copies of disk images you have created from original media. In other words, you can use Disk Utility to create a disk image of an original optical disc, and then burn the contents of the newly created disk image to a recordable optical disc. The burned disc will appear identical to the original media. In fact, Apple uses this technology to distribute beta system software installers for testing. After a tester downloads the latest disk image from one of Apple's servers, she will use Disk Utility to burn the contents of that image to an optical disc. Though burning a disk image will be covered here, creating a disk image will be discussed in Lesson 4, "Data Management and Backup."

To burn the contents of a disk image:

1   Open /Applications/Utilities/Disk Utility, and then click the Burn button on the toolbar.

A file browser appears that enables you to browse and select the disk image whose contents you wish to burn to an optical disc.

2   A final burn options dialog appears. Click the small blue arrow button in the upper-right corner to reveal more burn options.

The default burn options are almost always the best choice, but you can make changes here as you see fit.

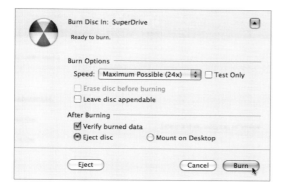

3   Click the Burn button to start the burn and verification process.

Depending on the size of the disk image and the speed of the drive, the burn and verification process can take anywhere from minutes to hours. Disk Utility will open a small progress dialog that will also allow you to cancel the burn by clicking the Cancel button.

4   Once the burn and verification is complete, Disk Utility will either mount or eject the completed disc depending on the options you chose.

Erasing Rewritable Optical Media

One last optical media trick you need to know about Disk Utility is the ability to erase rewritable optical media. Mac OS X requires that you erase rewritable media in order to burn new data to the disc. Most of the time, though, this process takes only a few moments to complete. Only optical media bearing the "RW" initials can be erased and then rewritten again. Also, older optical drive hardware may not support rewritable media. You can easily identify the capabilities of your Mac's optical drive by opening /Applications/Utilities/ System Profiler and viewing the Disc Burning information section.

To erase a rewritable optical disc:

1   Insert the rewritable optical media to be erased, and then open /Applications/Utilities/ Disk Utility.

2   Select the optical drive from the column on the left.

The manufacturer and model number is usually the name of the optical drive. Do not select any disc volumes.

3   Select either the Quickly or the Completely option.

Because erasing completely takes so much longer, you should stick with the Quickly option unless the computer is having problems completing the disc-erase process.

4   Once you have made your choice to quickly or completely erase, click the Erase button to continue.

5   You will be presented with a verification dialog. If you are certain you want to erase the disc, then click the Erase button to start the process.

Depending on the erase option you selected, the erase process will either take a few seconds or up to an hour. If the process is going to take more than a few seconds, Disk Utility will show a progress dialog.

6   Once the erase process is complete, the media will remain in the drive awaiting your next move. Press and hold the Eject key, the furthest top-right key on a Mac keyboard, for a few moments to eject the optical disc.

Mounting, Unmounting, and Ejecting

Mounting volumes is not something users normally concern themselves with on the Mac, because the system will automatically mount any volume connected to the Mac. Simply plug a drive in and the drive's volumes will automatically appear in the Finder and Disk Utility.

At the same time, properly unmounting and ejecting volumes is very important to maintaining data integrity. Unmounting is the process of having the Mac cleanly disconnect from a drive's volumes, whereas ejecting is the process of having the Mac disconnect from the actual hardware drive or media. When you choose eject a drive from the Finder, the computer will actually unmount the volumes first and then eject the drive.

There are three methods to unmount and eject a drive from the Finder:

▶   Pressing and holding the Eject key, the furthest top-right key on a Mac keyboard, for a few moments will only unmount and eject optical media.

▶   Select the volume you wish to unmount and eject from the Finder's sidebar, and then choose File > Eject from the menu bar.

▶   In the Finder's sidebar, click the small eject button next to the volume you wish to unmount and eject.

TIP ▶ If you have more than one optical drive, press Option-Eject to unmount and eject the second optical drive.

When you use the Finder to unmount and eject a single volume that is part of a drive with several mounted volumes, you will be presented with a warning dialog. You will be given the choice to unmount and eject all the volumes on the drive or just the volume you originally selected. You shouldn't experience any problems with a drive by having some volumes mounted while others are unmounted. Just remember to properly unmount the remaining volumes before you disconnect the drive.

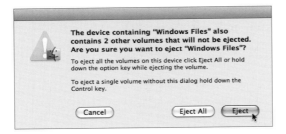

TIP ▶ In the Finder you can eject all the volumes of a drive by holding down the Option key while you click the Eject button.

If you need to remount volumes on a connected drive, from the Finder you will have to unmount and eject the remaining volumes on the drive and then physically disconnect and reconnect the drive. Or, you can choose to manually mount, unmount, and eject items using Disk Utility.

To manually mount, unmount, and eject items:

1 Open /Applications/Utilities/Disk Utility.

2 Select the drive or volume you wish to unmount or eject from the column on the left.

3 If you have selected a volume to unmount, simply click the Unmount button in the toolbar.

The volume will unmount immediately, disappearing from the Finder, although in Disk Utility the volume's name will remain but appear as dimmed text.

4 To mount an unmounted volume on a connected drive, click on the volume's dimmed name and then click the Mount button in the toolbar.

The volume should immediately mount and appear in the Finder, and as normal text in Disk Utility.

5 If you have selected an entire disk to unmount all its volumes and eject, simply click the Eject button in the toolbar.

All the disk's volumes will be unmounted, and then the disk will be disconnected from the system, completely disappearing from the Finder and Disk Utility. You will have to physically disconnect and reconnect the drive for its volumes to be remounted.

Improperly Unmounting or Ejecting

Disconnecting a volume from the Mac that you did not first unmount or eject can lead to data corruption. If you forcibly eject a drive by physically disconnecting it before you eject it, or if the system loses contact with the drive due to power failure, the Mac will warn you with a Device Removal dialog. You should immediately reconnect the device so the Mac can attempt to verify or repair its contents.

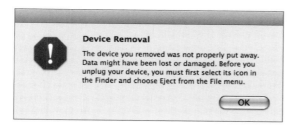

Any time you reconnect a drive that was improperly unmounted, the Mac will automatically run a file system diagnostic on the drive before it remounts any volumes. Depending on the format and size of the drive, it may take anywhere from a few seconds to several hours for the system to verify the contents of the drive. So if you connect a drive and notice there is quite a bit of drive activity but the volumes have not mounted yet, the system is probably running a diagnostic on the drive.

File System Troubleshooting

Because a functional file system is required by the operating system, the software that drives the file system is very reliable. In fact, most file system failures are due to bad hardware or media. It doesn't matter how good the software is, though; if the hardware is no longer reading or writing bits, it's pretty much useless to the file system. If, during troubleshooting, you determine that catastrophic hardware failure is the problem, there really isn't anything you can do to repair the device. Only a data recovery service, such as DriveSavers, might have a chance at recovering your data.

> **NOTE ▶** For more about data recovery service providers that can be used without voiding an Apple warranty, see http://docs.info.apple.com/article.html?artnum=31077

Conversely, if you're experiencing file system issues but the storage hardware still appears to function, you may be experiencing partial hardware failure or file system corruption. In these cases, there are some steps you can try to repair the volumes or at least recover data.

Gathering File System Information

Before attempting any fixes, you should become fully familiar with the file system configuration you're dealing with. Once again, /Applications/Utilities/Disk Utility will be your main tool for gathering file system information. The availability and status of storage hardware in Disk Utility will help determine if you are indeed experiencing hardware failure.

When you open Disk Utility, it will scan the file system for all attached devices and volumes. To gather detailed information about a specific drive or volume in Disk Utility, simply select the item from the column on the left and then click the Info button in the toolbar. Remember, the drive's name is its size and manufacturer information, whereas a drive's volumes appear directly below the drive name in the list.

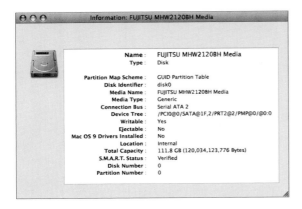

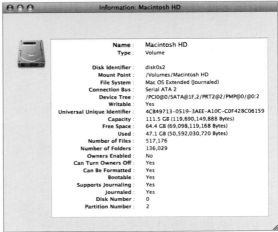

The information gathered from these dialogs will reveal a great deal about the status of a drive or volume. Of most importance for determining hardware failure is a drive's S.M.A.R.T. (Self-Monitoring, Analysis, and Reporting Technology) status. Drives that feature S.M.A.R.T. technology can determine if the drive is suffering from some sort of internal failure.

If a connected drive doesn't even appear in the Disk Utility list, odds are the drive has suffered catastrophic failure. You should double-check the drive's status using /Applications/Utilities/System Profiler to verify that the drive is unreachable. When you open System Profiler, the drive's information should appear when you select the bus that the drive is connected to, such as Serial-ATA or FireWire. If a drive does not appear in System Profiler either, then it is not available to the Mac in its current configuration. At this point you should focus your efforts on troubleshooting the drive hardware.

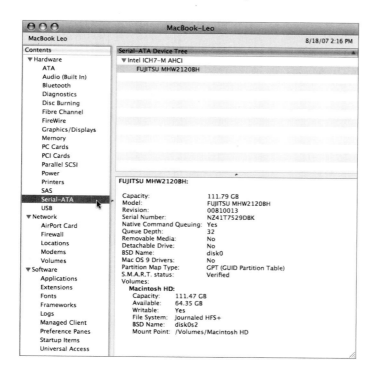

Verify or Repair a Volume

Before any volume is mounted, the Mac will automatically perform a quick consistency check to verify the volume's directory data. The system will also quickly scan the startup volume during the boot process. However, if the system is unable to mount a volume, you are experiencing issues accessing a volume, or you are booting from the startup disk, you can use Disk Utility to thoroughly verify and repair a volume.

Disk Utility can examine and attempt to repair a volume's directory database. The volume's directory database is used by the file system to catalog where files exist on the drive. To access data on the drive, the file system must first check with the directory structure in order to locate the appropriate bits on the drive that make up the requested file. Obviously, any damage to the volume's directory database can lead to serious problems.

To use Disk Utility's verify and repair features:

1   If you're attempting to repair the system drive because the Mac is unable to start up from it, you can boot from the Mac OS X Install DVD and then choose Disk Utility from the Utilities menu.

    If you are on a currently running Mac, make sure the drive you wish to verify or repair is currently attached to the computer, then open /Applications/Utilities/Disk Utility.

2   Select the drive or volume you wish to verify or repair from the column on the left, and then click the First Aid tab to the right.

3   Verify the selected item by clicking the Verify Disk button in the bottom-right corner.

    If the verification process finds any problems, you should repair the volume by clicking the Repair Disk button.

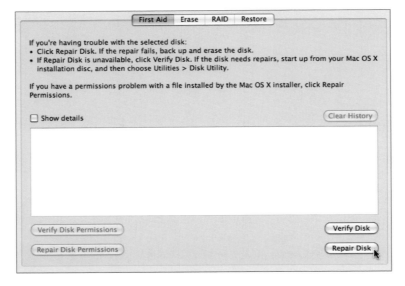

It may take a few minutes to complete the verification or repair process. During this time Disk Utility will show a progress indicator and log entries in the history area. Click the Show details checkbox to view more detail in the history log. You can stop the process at any time by clicking the Stop button.

4   If no problems were found, you should see an entry in the history log with green text. If problems were uncovered, they will appear in bright red text. If you haven't already started the repair process, you should do so now.

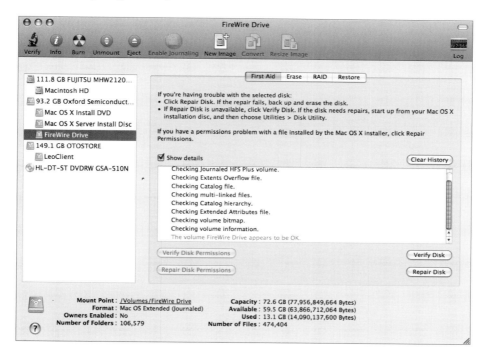

The system will continue to run the repair process until no more problems are found. This may take a while because the system may run through the repair process several times.

FireWire Target Disk Mode

Mac hardware has a unique ability to share its internal drives via a feature called FireWire target disk mode. Basically, when FireWire target disk mode is engaged, instead of booting normally from the system disk the Mac will bridge any internal drives to the FireWire ports. Because target disk mode is a function built into the Mac's hardware, even if the installed operating system is corrupted you can still use this feature.

An administrative user can enable FireWire target disk mode on a currently running Mac by clicking the Target Disk Mode button in the Startup Disk preference. Or, you can engage target disk mode during system startup by holding down the T key while you turn on the Mac. Once target disk mode is engaged, you will see a large FireWire symbol on the screen, and then you can simply plug the targeted Mac into another fully functioning Mac via a normal FireWire cable. The targeted Mac's internal volumes should mount normally on the other Mac as if you had plugged in a normal FireWire-based drive. At this point, you can do anything to the targeted Mac's internal drive that you could do to any local drive, including installations, repairs, and data migration.

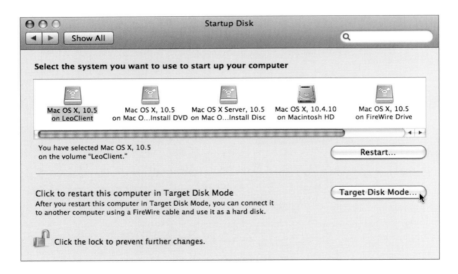

NOTE ► FireWire target disk mode does not support third-party disk drive interfaces and cannot be engaged when using a Bluetooth wireless keyboard.

Recovering Data from an Unbootable System

If you are still stuck with a Mac that refuses to fully boot from its internal system drive, you might still be able to recover important data off the drive as long as it's still functional.

You can use the Mac's built-in FireWire target disk mode to easily access the internal system drive and recover important data.

To recover data using target disk mode:

1   Turn on the troublesome Mac while holding down the T key to engage FireWire target disk mode.

2   Once the FireWire symbol appears on the targeted Mac, connect the machine to another fully functioning Mac using a standard FireWire cable.

3   If the targeted Mac's volume appears in the Finder, you should first attempt to repair the volume using Disk Utility, as detailed previously in this lesson.

4   Once repairs have completed, you have a variety of data recovery options:

    Use the Finder to manually copy data from the targeted Mac to storage attached to the functioning Mac.

    Use Disk Utility on the functioning Mac to create a disk image archive of the targeted Mac's system volume. Creating disk images is covered in Lesson 4, "Data Management and Backup."

    Use the Migration Assistant on a functioning or newly installed Mac to easily migrate user accounts, settings, or applications. The Migration Assistant was covered in Lesson 1, "Installation and Initial Setup."

5   After you have migrated the data, you should use Disk Utility to reformat the targeted Mac's drive and then attempt to reinstall the operating system.

    System installation was also covered in Lesson 1, "Installation and Initial Setup."

Depending on the amount of corruption present on the targeted Mac's system drive, you may not be able to use Disk Utility or the Migration Assistant. The drive may simply be too corrupted to recover all that data. In this case, you will have to resort to manually copying data. In general, the most important items to users are stored in their home folder, so you should start there. You may find this to be a time-consuming process; as the Finder discovers damaged files, you will have to manually restart the copy process and omit the damaged files.

File Ownership and Permissions

The technologies collectively known as ownership and permissions are used to control file and folder authorization for Mac OS X. Ownership and permissions work alongside the user account technologies, which control user identification and authentication, to provide the Mac's secure multiuser environment. Ownership and permissions—again just like user accounts—permeate every level of the operating system, so a thorough investigation of this system is required to fully understand Mac OS X.

Understanding Ownership and Permissions

In short, every single item on every storage device has ownership and permissions rules applied to it by the operating system. Only users and processes with root account access can ignore ownership and permissions rules. Thus, these rules are used to define file and folder access for every normal, administrative, guest, and sharing user. Any user can easily identify the ownership and permissions of a file or folder with the Finder's Get Info window.

To identify ownership and permissions from the Finder:

1   In the Finder, select the file or folder for which you wish to identify the ownership and permissions. You can select multiple items to open multiple Get Info windows.

2   Open the Get Info window.

    There are several methods for doing this. You can choose File > Get Info from the menu bar; use the Command-I keyboard combination; choose Get Info from the Action pop-up menu in a Finder window toolbar; or in the Finder, right-click or Control-click on an item and choose Get Info.

3   Once you have opened a Get Info window, click the Sharing & Permissions disclosure triangle to reveal the item's ownership and permissions.

    Note that the permissions list is broken into two columns. To the left is the name of the user or group, and to the right are the associated permissions. Modifying these settings will be covered in the "Changing Ownership and Permissions" section later in this lesson.

TIP ▶ You can also identify ownership and permissions from the Finder's dynamic Inspector window. This is a single floating window that will automatically refresh as you select different items in the Finder. To open the Inspector window from the Finder, use the Option-Command-I keyboard combination.

Ownership

Every file and folder belongs to at least one owner and one group, and has an ownership setting for everyone else. This three-tiered ownership structure provides the basis for file and folder permissions:

▶ Owner—By default, the owner of an item is the user who created or copied the item to the Mac. For example, the user owns most of the items in his home folder. The system or root user almost always owns system software items, including system resources and applications. Traditionally, only the owner can change the item's ownership or permissions. Despite this, Mac OS X makes management easier by giving every administrative user the ability to change ownership and permissions regardless of who the item's owner is.

▶ Group—By default, the group of an item is based on the user's default group. On Mac OS X, the default group for all users is staff, and root's default group is wheel. Thus, most items belong to the staff, wheel, or admin group. Group ownership is designated to allow users other than the owner to have access to an item. For instance, even though root owns the /Applications folder, the group is set to admin so administrative users can make changes to the contents of this folder.

▶ Everyone—The Everyone setting is used to define access for anyone who isn't the owner and isn't part of the item's group. This includes local, sharing, and guest users.

The simple three-tiered ownership structure presented here has been part of standard UNIX operating systems for decades. However, with only three levels of permissions to choose from, it is quite difficult to define appropriate access settings for a computer with many user accounts and shared files, as is the case with many servers. Fortunately, as you'll see later, access control lists (ACLs) were developed to allow for nearly limitless ownership and permissions configurations.

UNIX Permissions

Mac OS X's basic file and folder permissions structure is also based on decades-old UNIX-style permissions. The system may be old, but for most Mac users it is quite adequate because you can define permissions separately at each ownership tier. In other words, the owner, the group, and everyone else each has an individual permissions setting. Further, because of the inherent hierarchy built into the file system, where folders can reside inside of other folders, you easily create a complex file structure that allows for varying levels of sharing and security.

There is a variety of UNIX permission combinations available from the command line, as will be discussed in the "Ownership and Permissions Commands" section later in this lesson. However, Apple has streamlined the Finder to allow only the most common UNIX permissions configurations.

Permissions that you can assign to a file using the Finder are:

▶ Read and Write—The user can open the file and save changes.

▶ Read Only—The user can open the file but cannot save any changes.

▶ No Access—The user has no access to the file at all.

Permissions that you can assign to a folder using the Finder are:

▶ Read and Write—The user can browse and make changes to the contents of the folder.

▶ Read Only—The user can browse the contents of the folder but cannot make changes to the contents of the folder.

▶ Write Only (Drop Box)—The user cannot browse or make changes to the folder other than copying new items into the folder.

▶ No Access—The user has no access to the contents of the folder.

Access Control Lists (ACLs)

Access control lists (ACLs) were developed to expand the basic UNIX-style ownership and permissions architecture to allow more control of file and folder access. Though there is no common standard for ACLs, Mac OS X has adopted a style of ACL similar to that available on Windows systems. This ACL implementation is extremely flexible but increases complexity by adding more than a dozen unique permission and inheritance attribute types. Further, this implementation supports an unlimited number of ACL attributes for any user or group.

Apple does not expect average users to navigate through all the options available using ACLs, so once again the Finder has been streamlined to allow only the most common ACL permissions configurations. In fact, the Finder only allows you to assign ACL attributes that match the most common UNIX permissions configurations that were previously listed in this lesson. The only feature of ACLs that the Finder actually implements is the ability to have an unlimited number of permissions attributes. In other words, the Finder uses the ACL architecture to let you configure unique privileges for an unlimited number of users or groups. Prior to Mac OS X 10.5, the Finder would only allow you to assign permissions using the standard three-tiered ownership style, with one owner, one group, and one setting for everyone else.

Permissions for Sharing

Once you have an understanding of the ownership and permissions options available to you in Mac OS X, you should explore how the local file system is set up by default to provide a secure environment that still allows for users to share files.

If you don't have fast user switching enabled as outlined in Lesson 2, "User Accounts," you should enable it now to make it easy to test file system permissions as different users. Further, to aide in your exploration of the file system you should use the Finder's Inspector window. This single floating window, which automatically refreshes as you select different items in the Finder, allows you to quickly explore the default ownership and permissions settings without having to open multiple Finder Get Info windows. Open the Inspector from the Finder by using the Option-Command-I keyboard combination, and then click the disclosure triangle to reveal the Sharing & Permissions section.

NOTE ▶ The Inspector window sports a different title bar than the Get Info window. Also, the Inspector window will always float on top of all other windows in the Finder.

Home Folder Sharing

Mac OS X is architected in such a way that the user's files are protected by default and then easily shared when needed. This starts with the user's home folder. Upon inspection, you'll notice that users are allowed read and write access to their home folder, while the staff group is allowed only read access.

Because every local user is in the staff group, this means that every local user can view the first level of every other user's home directory. This may seem insecure until you look at the permissions in context. Most user data is actually stored inside a subfolder in the user's home folder, and if you inspect those subfolders you'll notice that other users are not allowed to access most of them.

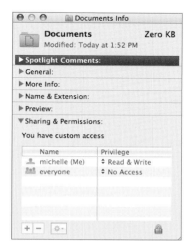

There are a few subfolders in a user's home folder, however, that are specifically designed for sharing. You'll notice the Public and Sites folders remain readable to everyone. A user can easily share files without having to mess with permissions by simply moving the files into those two folders. Others will be able to read those files but they still cannot make any changes to them.

> **NOTE** ▶ User-created files and folders at the root of the home folder will, by default, have permissions like the Public folder's. To secure new items at the root of the home folder, simply change the permissions as outlined in the "Changing Ownership and Permissions" section later in this lesson.

Looking deeper, you'll notice a subfolder of the Public folder is the Drop Box. This folder's permissions allow all other users to copy files into the folder even though they cannot actually see other files in the Drop Box folder. This allows other users to discreetly transfer files without others knowing.

The permissions used to locally protect the Public and Sites folders are also used to protect these folders as they are shared over the network. Sharing files will be covered in Lesson 8, "Providing Network Services."

The Shared Folder

An additional folder set aside for sharing is the /User/Shared folder. You'll notice that this is a general sharing location that allows all users to read and write items to the folder. Normally this permissions setting would also allow any user to delete another user's item in this folder. Yet, the Finder's Inspector window is not showing you the full permissions picture here. There is a unique permissions setting on the Shared folder that prevents other users from being able to delete items that they didn't originally put in the folder. This permission setting, known as the "sticky bit," can only be set using a command-line tool. Inspecting and changing permissions from the command line will be covered in the "Ownership and Permissions Commands" section later in this lesson.

Ownership for External Volumes

Portable external disk and flash drives are very useful tools for transferring files and folders from one computer to another. A downside to this technology, though, is that computers will often improperly interpret file ownership because they don't share the same user account database. In other words, most Macs don't share the same local user accounts, so when a drive is moved from one Mac to another, the system confuses file and folder ownership. In a worst-case scenario, other computers will not be able to access the files on your external storage device.

> **NOTE ▶** The Mac considers any locally mounted volume that is not the system volume to be an external volume. Thus, other partitions on your internal system disk(s) will still be considered external volumes.

Unless you plan to implement a centralized network user database so all your Macs do indeed share the same user account database, ownership on external volumes will have to be ignored to prevent access issues. This is the default behavior on Mac OS X for all external volumes. Keep in mind, however, that this approach introduces the security risk that all local users will have full access to the contents of external volumes. Because some may find this an unacceptable security risk, you can disable the default behavior and force Mac OS X to honor ownership on external volumes.

To honor ownership on external volumes:

1   In the Finder, select the external volume for which you wish the system to honor the ownership, and then open the Get Info window.

2   Once you have opened a Get Info window, click the Sharing & Permissions disclosure triangle to reveal the item's ownership and permissions.

3   Click the small lock icon in the bottom-right corner of the Get Info window and authenticate as an administrative user to unlock the Sharing & Permissions section.

4   Deselect the "Ignore ownership on this volume" checkbox.

    Changes made using the Get Info window are applied immediately.

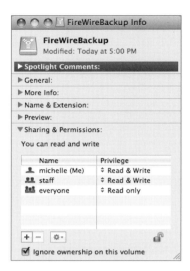

Changing Ownership and Permissions

A significantly redesigned Finder is one of the major new features in Mac OS X 10.5. This includes a new interface for managing ownership and permissions from the Finder's Get Info window. The redesign was necessary to incorporate support for ACLs. As covered previously in this lesson, the Finder uses the ACL architecture so you can configure unique privileges for an unlimited number of users or groups.

To change ownership or permissions in the Finder:

1   In the Finder, select the file or folder for which you wish to change the permissions or ownership, and then open the Get Info window.

2   Once you have opened a Get Info window, click the Sharing & Permissions disclosure triangle to reveal the item's ownership and permissions.

3   Click the small lock icon in the bottom-right corner of the Get Info window and authenticate as an administrative user to unlock the Sharing & Permissions section.

4   To add new users or groups, click the small plus button in the bottom-left corner of the Get Info window.

A dialog will appear allowing you to select a new user or group. To select an existing user or group, choose their name from the list and click the Select button. Alternately, you can create a new Sharing user account by clicking the New Person button or selecting a contact from your Address Book. Creating a new Sharing account in either case requires that you also enter a new password for the account. Details about sharing user accounts, or how to create additional groups, is covered in Lesson 2, "User Accounts."

5 To delete users or groups, select the account from the permission list and click the small minus button in the bottom-left corner of the Get Info window.

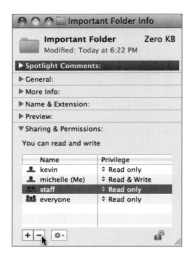

6 To assign new permissions, simply click on any permission and a pop-up menu will appear allowing you to choose another permission option for that user or group. Details about the permission assignments available from the Finder were covered previously in this lesson.

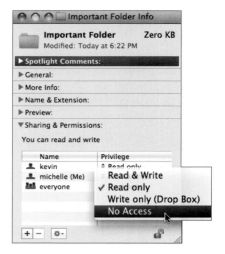

7   If you are changing the permissions of a folder, by default, the Finder will not change the permissions of any items inside the folder. In many cases, you will want to apply the same permissions to the items inside the folder. You can accomplish this quickly by clicking the gear button at the bottom of the Get Info window to reveal a pop-up menu, and then choosing the "Apply to enclosed items" option from this menu.

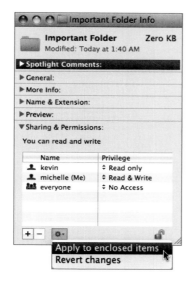

8   Changes made using the Get Info window are applied immediately. When you are done making ownership or permissions changes, close the Get Info window.

As long as you keep the Get Info window open, the Finder will remember the original permissions setting for the item. This is useful for testing different permissions configurations, as you can always revert back to the original permissions setting. To revert to the original permissions setting, click the gear button at the bottom of the Get Info window to reveal a pop-up menu, and then choose the "Revert changes" option from this menu.

Locked Files and Folders

Mac OS X includes a special file and folder extended attribute that trumps all write permissions and even administrative user access. Users can choose to lock a file or folder that they own from the Finder's Get Info window. Locking an item will render it completely unchangeable to all users user except the item's owner. Even administrative users are prevented from making changes to a locked file in the graphical interface. In other words, a standard user could potentially lock an item that the administrative user would have absolutely no ability to change in the graphical interface.

To lock a file or folder in the Finder:

1   In the Finder, select the file or folder you wish to lock, and then open the Get Info window.

2   Once you have opened a Get Info window, click the General disclosure triangle to reveal the Locked checkbox.

3   As long as you are the original owner of the item, you will be allowed to select the Locked checkbox.

Changes made using the Get Info window are applied immediately.

Once an item is locked, no other users can modify, move, delete, or rename it. The owner can modify the content of the item or delete it, but the Finder still prevents the owner from moving, renaming, or changing ownership and permissions of the locked item. The owner can return the file to normal by disabling the locked attribute from the Finder's

Get Info window. An administrative user can disable the locked attribute, but only from the command-line interface using a command such as SetFile. Use of the SetFile command is covered in the "Using Invisible Items" section later in this lesson.

Permissions in Context

It is important to remember that permissions do not exist in isolation; rather, permissions are rules applied in the context of folder hierarchy. In other words, your access to an item is based on the combination of an item's permissions and the permissions of the folder in which it resides. If you're still confused, it's easiest to think of permissions as defining access to an item's content, not the item itself. Remember the word "content" as you consider the following three simplified examples.

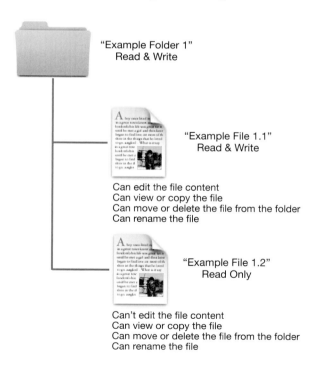

"Example Folder 1"
Read & Write

"Example File 1.1"
Read & Write

Can edit the file content
Can view or copy the file
Can move or delete the file from the folder
Can rename the file

"Example File 1.2"
Read Only

Can't edit the file content
Can view or copy the file
Can move or delete the file from the folder
Can rename the file

Example 1: Your permissions to Example Folder 1 are read and write. It's obvious that you should have full access to Example File 1.1, as your permissions here are read and write as well. You can also view and copy Example File 1.2, but you can't make changes to the file's content because your permissions are read only. Yet you can still move, delete, or rename File 1.2 because you have read and write access to the folder's contents. Thus, File 1.2 isn't secure in this example because you can make a copy of the original file, change the copied file's content, delete the original file, and finally replace it with the modified copy.

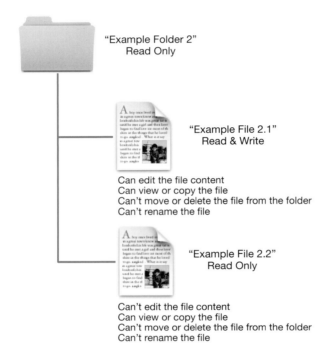

"Example Folder 2"
Read Only

"Example File 2.1"
Read & Write

Can edit the file content
Can view or copy the file
Can't move or delete the file from the folder
Can't rename the file

"Example File 2.2"
Read Only

Can't edit the file content
Can view or copy the file
Can't move or delete the file from the folder
Can't rename the file

Example 2: You have read-only permission to Example Folder 2. You can edit the content of Example File 2.1 because you have read and write access to it, but you can't move, delete, or rename it because you have read-only access to the folder's contents. On the other hand, you can effectively delete the file by erasing its contents. Example File 2.2 is the only truly secure file as you're only allowed to view or copy the file. Granted, you can make changes to the contents of a copied file, but you still can't replace the original.

> **NOTE ▶** Many applications cannot save changes to files inside read-only folders, because these applications attempt to replace the original file during the save process, instead of revising the file's content.

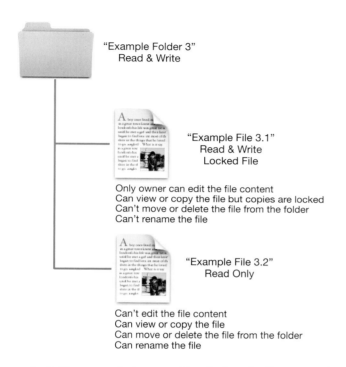

"Example Folder 3"
Read & Write

"Example File 3.1"
Read & Write
Locked File

Only owner can edit the file content
Can view or copy the file but copies are locked
Can't move or delete the file from the folder
Can't rename the file

"Example File 3.2"
Read Only

Can't edit the file content
Can view or copy the file
Can move or delete the file from the folder
Can rename the file

Example 3: Your permissions are identical to the first example, with one significant change. The owner of Example File 3.1 has enabled the locked attribute for it (this attribute was discussed in the previous topic). Even though you have read and write access to Example Folder 3 and File 3.1, the locked attribute prevents all users who aren't the file's owner from modifying, moving, deleting, or renaming the file. Only the owner is allowed to change the file's content or delete it, but the owner can also disable the locked attribute to return the file to normal. You can still make a copy of the locked file, but the copy will be locked as well. However, you will own the copy, so you can disable the locked attribute on the copy, but you still can't delete the original locked file unless you're the owner.

Securing New Items

Once you understand how Mac OS X's file system security architecture works with the folder hierarchy, it's time to consider how this technology is used to enforce specific access needs for new items. You've learned previously in this lesson that Mac OS X is already preconfigured for secure file and folder sharing, but you will find that new items are created with unrestricted read access.

For example, when a user creates a new file or folder at the root of her home directory, by default all other users, including guest users, are allowed to view this item's contents. The same is true for new items created by administrators in local areas such as the root of the system volume and the local Library and Applications folders.

New items are created this way to facilitate sharing, as you do not have to change any permission to share a new item. All that is required of you is to place the new item in a folder that other users can access. It's assumed that if you want to secure a new item, you will place it inside a folder that no one else has access to.

On the other hand, this behavior is inconvenient if you don't want to share your new items. To store items so they are only accessible to the owner requires you to change the item's permissions using the Sharing & Permissions section of the Finder's Get Info window, as outlined previously in this lesson. Specifically, you must remove all nonowner users and all group accounts from the permissions list. You cannot remove the Everyone permission, so you will have to set it to No Access. Once you have made these permissions changes, only the owner will have access to the item.

Permissions Troubleshooting

Permissions issues can be caused from a variety of situations. Many issues are due to user error, but others can be the result of an unintentional failure elsewhere in the system. For instance, some software installers may improperly change permissions during the installation process. You may also experience permissions issues after restarting from a power loss or system freeze.

System and application errors may occur due to incorrect permissions. Example issues include applications that will not open or an inability to empty the Trash. Many of these permissions issues can be resolved by utilities that are part of Mac OS X. If you are having trouble accessing an application, you should attempt to resolve the issue using Disk Utility's Repair Disk Permissions feature. Also, if you are experiencing problems trying to access home folders, you can use the Reset Password utility to reset home folder permissions. The use of these two utilities for resolving permissions issues is covered next in this lesson.

Most general permissions issues are revealed in obvious ways. A user attempting to access a file or folder is immediately stopped and presented with a dialog stating that he doesn't have the appropriate permissions. In this case, a permissions change on the item, or the folder it's inside of, is usually all that's needed to resolve the issue. If you are going to attempt to repair the item's permissions manually, you should be familiar with the methods outlined in this lesson. Changing permissions from the Finder is covered previously in this lesson, while you will learn how to change permissions from the command line in the "Ownership and Permissions Commands" section later in this lesson. For further guidance, you can also refer to Apple Knowledge Base document 106712, "Troubleshooting permissions issues in Mac OS X."

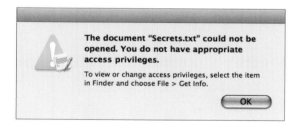

Disk Utility's Repair Permissions

One of the most common troubleshooting techniques for Mac OS X is to use Disk Utility's Repair Disk Permissions feature. Many novice Mac administrators will use this technique every time they encounter any problem. The reality is that this process fixes only file permissions issues specific to certain installed Apple software.

Further, this process will not touch any incorrect permission settings on personal or user data. In other words, this process, though a good starting point for addressing application issues, will not fix every incorrect permissions issue on a problematic Mac. For more information, you can also reference Apple Knowledge Base document 25751, "About Disk Utility's Repair Disk Permissions feature."

To verify or repair disk permissions:

1   Open Disk Utility on a currently running Mac by opening /Applications/Utilities/ Disk Utility, or on a Mac booted from the Mac OS X Install DVD by choosing Disk Utility from the Utilities menu.

2   Select the system volume you wish to repair from the column on the left.

3   Select the First Aid tab to the right.

4   Click the Verify Disk Permissions button to view a log of any potential problems.

5   Click the Repair Disk Permissions button to view and fix any permission problems.

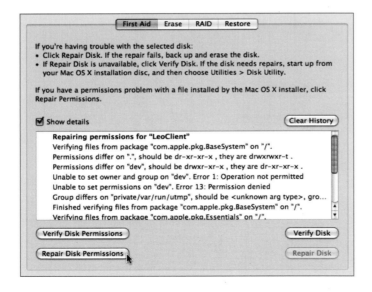

Reset Password's Reset Home Permissions

If a user's home folder becomes inaccessible due to improper permissions, you can attempt to fix the issue by manually adjusting the permissions yourself, or you can try the Reset Password utility found only on the Mac OS X Install DVD. This utility was primarily designed to reset user passwords; nonetheless, this tool also has the ability to reset a user's home folder permissions or ACLs. Keep in mind that this process will reset all home folder permissions, including intentionally changed permissions that may have benefited the user.

To reset home folder permissions and ACLs:

1   Start up the Mac from the Mac OS X Install DVD by turning on the machine while holding down the C key, and as soon as possible, insert the installation disc and the computer will start from it.

2   Once the installer has started, choose Utilities > Reset Password from the menu bar.

3   Select the system volume containing the home folder you wish to reset from the row of system volume icons.

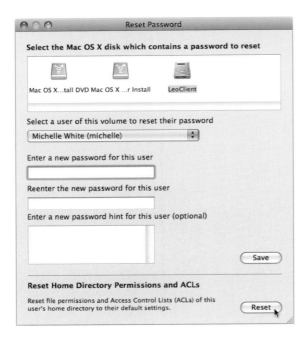

4   Choose the user account whose home folder needs resetting from the user pop-up menu.

5   Click the Reset button at the bottom to reset this user's home folder permissions and ACLs.

6   Quit the Reset Password utility to return to the Mac OS X Installer. Then quit the Mac OS X Installer to restart the Mac.

File Management via the Command Line

Mac administrators can be fairly successful even if they use only the graphical user interface. However, no administrator can be considered fully capable without some knowledge of the Mac's command-line interface (CLI). There are simply too many indispensable management tools that are only available in the CLI. Further, once you become comfortable with the CLI, you'll find many tasks are actually much quicker than their graphical counterpart. In this section, you will discover how powerful the CLI is for advanced file management.

Command-Line Basics

The main application on Mac OS X for accessing the CLI is /Applications/Utilities/ Terminal. The Mac's Terminal application is quite sophisticated, and it has gained a few new features in Mac OS X 10.5, including easier management of interface settings and a new tabbed interface for quickly handling multiple CLIs. You may hear the term "shell" kicked around when CLIs are discussed. A shell is the first command that executes automatically when you open the Terminal, to provide you with the actual CLI. Many types of shells are available, but Mac OS X will start the bash shell by default.

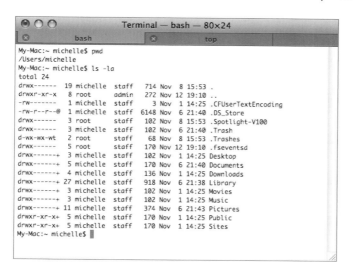

After you open the Terminal for the first time, you may approach the CLI with unnecessary caution. Even though the CLI offers nearly limitless capability, getting started with the basics is not that complicated. In fact, you need only master a few fundamental concepts:

▶ The first thing you'll see in the CLI is the prompt. The prompt is presented to you by the computer to let you know that it's ready for your command. The prompt will always show you where you are in the file system, followed by who you are logged on as, so it will change as you navigate around.

▶ Everything starts with a command. Commands are just like applications, but they are generally more focused; many commands provide very specific functionality.

▶ After the command, you may specify some options that will change the command's default behavior.

▶ After the command and its options, you will typically specify the item that you want the command to modify.

▶ Everything ends with the Return or Enter key. This initiates/executes the command you just entered.

Put these five things in order and you have:

```
prompt$ command options item <return or enter>
```

Here is an example of the user Michelle, who is working on a computer called MyMac. She is deleting an application called Junk inside the /Applications folder. It is assumed that Michelle will press the Return or Enter key once she has entered her command.

```
MyMac:~ michelle$ rm –R /Applications/Junk.app
```

If the command was entered and executed properly, the computer will simply return to a new prompt. The computer will generally let you know if you entered something improperly by returning some sort of error message or help text. Nevertheless, the computer will not prevent you from doing something stupid in the CLI, such as accidentally deleting your home folder. If you remember only one rule about using the CLI, it should be this one: always double-check your typing.

NOTE ▶ The CLI is absolutely case-sensitive and requires that you use filename extensions. In other words, the CLI will not be able to locate the "itunes" application, but it will easily locate the "iTunes.app" application.

Learning About Commands

There are literally thousands of commands, each with dozens of options or requirements for proper usage. In fact, most users are overwhelmed by the CLI simply because they think they have to memorize commands in order to use them. In reality, all you need to know is one command: man.

Most commands have built-in manuals that tell you everything you need to know about a command. Simply enter man followed by the name of the command you are curious about, and you will be shown its manual page. Manual pages include command usage and options and, at the very bottom of the page, often include references to other related commands. Once inside the manual page viewer, you can use a few navigation shortcuts to quickly move through the manual:

- ▶ Use the Up Arrow and Down Arrow keys to scroll through the manual.
- ▶ Use the Space bar to move down one screen at a time.
- ▶ Search through the manual page by entering / and then a keyword.
- ▶ Exit the manual page by simply pressing the Q key.

What if you don't even know the name of the command you're looking for? Simply enter man –k and then a keyword to search the command manual database. For example, entering man –k owner will return a short list of the commands used for changing file and folder ownership, including the proper command, chown. Using the chown command to change file and folder ownership is covered in the "Ownership and Permissions Commands" later in this lesson.

Command-Line Tips

Here are a few CLI tips that will help you customize your experience and save a lot of time typing:

- ▶ Thoroughly explore the Terminal's preferences to customize the look and feel of your CLI.
- ▶ At the command prompt, use the Up Arrow and Down Arrow keys to travel through and reuse your command history.
- ▶ Drag and drop files and folders from the Finder to the Terminal window to automatically enter their locations in the CLI.
- ▶ Enter open . at the prompt to open your current CLI location in the Finder.
- ▶ Press Control-L to quickly clear the Terminal window.
- ▶ To cancel a command gone awry or clear your current command entry, press Command-period.

Navigation via the Command Line

If knowing how to use commands is the first part of conquering the CLI, the second part is learning how to navigate the file system effectively in the CLI. Once again, by the time you master navigation in the CLI you'll find that it can be much faster than navigation using the Finder.

Navigation Concepts

First, a few common navigation terms must be clearly defined. This book has thus far referred to file system containers using the common term "folder." Yet another term, "directory," is often used in the CLI as a synonym for folder. Though the terms can be used interchangeably, this book will continue to favor the word "folder" to describe file system containers, as the word "directory" is often used for other non-folder-like items. For example, network databases used to store user information are often referred to as "directories." Furthermore, the process in Mac OS X for accessing these user databases is called the DirectoryService.

A new term you'll see in this book will is "path." A path represents a file or folder's location in the file system. You have already seen paths in this book used to describe the specific location of an application or utility. For instance, the Disk Utility application's file system path is /Applications/Utilities/Disk Utility. The CLI uses pathnames exclusively for navigating and locating items in the file system.

There are two types of file system pathnames: absolute paths and relative paths. Either type is valid for navigating or locating items in the CLI, but they differ in where they start:

▶ Absolute paths—Absolute paths are full descriptions of an item's location starting from the root, or beginning, of the file system. Thus, an absolute path will always begin with a forward slash to indicate the beginning of the file system. This book uses absolute paths to describe the location of items. An example of the absolute path to the user Michelle's Drop Box folder would be /Users/michelle/Public/Drop Box.

▶ Relative paths—Relative paths are partial descriptions of an item's location based on where you're currently working in the file system from the CLI. When you first open the Terminal application, your CLI session starts out working from the root, or beginning, of your home folder. Therefore, the relative path from the beginning of your home folder to your Drop Box would be Public/Drop Box.

Navigation Commands

You will use three basic commands for navigating the file system in the CLI: pwd, ls, and cd.

pwd. Short for "print working directory," this command will report the absolute path of your current working location in the file system:

```
MyMac:~ michelle$ pwd
/Users/michelle
```

ls. Short for "list," ls will list the folder contents of your current working location. Entering a pathname following the ls command will list the contents of the specified item. The ls command has many additional options for listing file and folder information that will be covered throughout this book.

```
MyMac:~ michelle$ ls
Desktop   Library   Pictures
Documents  Movies   Public
Downloads  Music   Sites
MyMac:~ michelle$ ls Public
Drop Box
```

cd. Short for "change directory," cd is the command you will use to navigate in the CLI. Entering a pathname following the cd command will change your current working location to the specified folder. Entering cd without specifying a path will always return you to your home folder. In the following example, Michelle will use the cd command to navigate to her Drop Box folder, and then she will navigate back to her home folder:

```
MyMac:~ michelle$ cd Public/Drop\ Box/
MyMac:Drop Box michelle$ pwd
/Users/michelle/Public/Drop Box
MyMac:Drop Box michelle$ cd
MyMac:~ michelle$ pwd
/Users/michelle
```

Navigating to Other Volumes

In the CLI, the system volume is also known as the root volume and it's identified by the lone forward slash, /. It may come as some surprise to you, however, that in the CLI other nonroot volumes appear as part of the main file system in a folder called Volumes. In the following example, Michelle will start in her home folder, navigate to and list the items in the /Volumes folder, and then finally navigate into a volume connected to this Mac via a FireWire disk drive:

```
MyMac:~ michelle$ pwd
/Users/michelle
MyMac:~ michelle$ cd /Volumes/
MyMac:Volumes michelle$ pwd
/Volumes
```

```
MyMac:Volumes michelle$ ls
FireWire Drive    Mac OS X Install DVD
LeoClient    Mac OS X Server Install Disc
MyMac:Volumes michelle$ cd FireWire\ Drive/
MyMac:FireWire Drive michelle$ pwd
/Volumes/FireWire Drive
```

Recursive Commands

When you direct a command to execute some task on an item in the CLI, it will only touch the specified item. If the specified item is a folder, the CLI will not automatically navigate inside the folder to execute the command on the enclosed items. If you require that a command be executed on a folder and its contents, you have to tell the command to run recursively. "Recursive" is a fancy way of saying, "Execute the task on every item inside every folder starting from the path I specify." Most commands accept -r or -R as the option to indicate that you want the command to run recursively.

In the following example, Michelle will list the contents of her Public folder normally, and then recursively using the -R option. Notice that when she lists the contents of the Public folder recursively, the system also lists the contents of the Drop Box and Drop Folder:

```
MyMac:~ michelle$ ls Public/
Drop Box  PublicFile1  PublicFile2  PublicFile3
MyMac:~ michelle$ ls -R Public/
Drop Box  PublicFile1  PublicFile2  PublicFile3

Public//Drop Box:
Drop Folder  DroppedFile1 DroppedFile2

Public//Drop Box/Drop Folder:
DropFolderFile1 DropFolderFile2
```

Special Characters

At this point you may have noticed that the CLI is using some special characters in the command prompt and pathnames. Many of these special characters are used as shortcuts to save time. On the other hand, one special character isn't a time-saver; it's an unfortunate necessity. The backslash character, \, is used before a space in a path or filename.

This practice is necessary because the CLI uses the spaces between items to parse the command entry into separate logical pieces. A space in a filename without the backslash will confuse the CLI, and your command will not execute properly.

There are other methods for entering filenames and paths with spaces. One alternative is to surround filenames and paths with quotation marks:

```
MyMac:~ michelle$ cd "Public/Drop Box"
MyMac:Drop Box michelle$ pwd
/Users/michelle/Public/Drop Box
```

Another solution involves dragging and dropping items from the Finder to the Terminal window. The Terminal automatically enters the item's absolute path with the appropriate backslash characters before spaces in names. The most efficient solution, though, is to use the tab-complete feature built into Mac OS X's CLI to automatically complete file and pathnames for you. Saving time by using tab completion is covered next in this lesson.

When navigating the file system, you can also save time by using the double period (..) shortcut to indicate the previous folder. In other words, if you were in working your home folder located at /Users/username, entering cd .. would tell the CLI that you want to navigate to the /Users folder. In the following example, Michelle navigates to her Drop Box folder, backs up to her Public folder, and then finally backs up twice to the /Users folder:

```
MyMac:~ michelle$ cd Public/Drop\ Box/
MyMac:Drop Box michelle$ pwd
/Users/michelle/Public/Drop Box
MyMac:Drop Box michelle$ cd ..
MyMac:Public michelle$ pwd
/Users/michelle/Public
MyMac:Public michelle$ cd ../..
MyMac:Users michelle$ pwd
/Users
```

Finally, there is the ~, or tilde. This little guy is used as shorthand to describe the current user's home folder in a pathname. Once again using the example from earlier, the current user's Drop Box is located at ~/Public/Drop Box. This also helps to explain the tilde you see in the default command prompt. For example, if Michelle opened the Terminal and logged on as herself on a computer called MyMac, the command prompt would show the computer's name, the user's current working location in the CLI, and finally the user's name followed by a dollar sign indicating that the CLI is waiting for the next command:

    MyMac:~ michelle$

If Michelle navigated to her Drop Box, the command prompt would change. Note that the prompt only shows the current working location and not an absolute or even relative path:

    MyMac:Drop Box michelle$

Using Tab Completion

Tab completion is the Mac CLI's absolute top timesaving feature. Not only does using tab completion save time by automatically finishing filenames, pathnames, and command names for you, it also prevents you from making typographical errors and verifies that the item you're entering exists.

Using tab completion couldn't be simpler. Start from your home folder by entering cd, then P, and then press the Tab key. The Terminal window will flash quickly, letting you know there is more than one choice for items that begin with *P* in your home folder. Press the Tab key again, and the computer will display your two choices, Pictures and Public. Now, enter a u after the initial P, then press the Tab key again and the computer will automatically finish Public/ for you. Finally, enter a D and press the Tab key one last time, and the computer will finish the path with Public/Drop\ Box/.

Even in this small example, tab completion turned a command that would take 17 keystrokes (Public/Drop\ Box/) into just 5 (Pu<tab>D<tab>). Further, tab completion helped you avoid mistakes by essentially spell-checking your typing and verifying the item is where you expected it to be. Making tab completion a habit when using the CLI can easily shave hours off the time you have to spend there. Thus, if you remember only two rules about using the CLI, it should be these two: always double-check your typing, and always use tab completion to double-check your typing and save time.

Privilege Escalation Commands

Perhaps the most powerful feature in the CLI is the ability to quickly evoke the access of another user account or even the system root user account.

Using su

The su command, short for "substitute user identity," will allow you to easily switch to another user account in the CLI. Simply enter su followed by the short name of the user you want to switch to, and then enter the account password. The command prompt will change, indicating that you have the access privileges of a different user. You can easily verify your currently logged-on identity by entering who –m in the CLI. You will remain logged on as the substitute user until you quit the Terminal or enter the exit command. In the following example, Michelle will use the su command to change her shell to Kevin's account, and then she will exit back to her account:

```
MyMac:~ michelle$ who -m
michelle ttys001 Aug 20 14:06
MyMac:~ michelle$ su kevin
Password:
bash-3.2$ who -m
kevin ttys001 Aug 20 14:06
bash-3.2$ exit
exit
MyMac:~ michelle$ who -m
michelle ttys001 Aug 20 14:06
```

Using sudo

An even more powerful command is sudo, which is short for "substitute user do," or more appropriately, "super user do." Preceding a command with sudo instructs the computer to execute the command that follows using root account access. The only requirements to use sudo on Mac OS X are that the user be an administrative user and that he authenticate after he enters the command.

In other words, by default on Mac OS X, any administrative user can use sudo to evoke root access in the CLI. Further, sudo works even if the root user account is disabled in the graphical interface. You can, however, adjust the sudo command's configuration file to further restrict its usage. In many environments, granting administrative access to every user is insecure. To find out more about configuring the sudo command, do what you would normally do to learn more about any command; read its manual page entry by entering man followed by the command name in the CLI.

> **TIP** The sudo command can also be used to execute a command as a specific nonroot user. Before a command, simply enter sudo -u *username*, where *username* is the short name of the user you wish to execute the command as.

In the following example, Michelle is not normally allowed to read the text file named Secrets, using the standard CLI text reader command cat. She then uses the sudo command to enable root access for the cat command so she can see the contents of the Secrets text file:

```
MyMac:~ michelle$ cat Secrets.txt
cat: Secrets.txt: Permission denied
MyMac:~ michelle$ sudo cat Secrets.txt
Password:
```

This is the contents of an example text file that the user account Michelle does not normally have access permissions to read. However, because she is an administrative user, she can use the sudo command to envoke root user access and thus read the contents of this file.

If, as an administrative user, you need to execute more than one command with root account access, you can temporarily switch the entire command-line shell to have root level access. Simply enter sudo -s, and then your password to switch the shell to have root access. You can easily verify your currently logged-on identity by entering who –m in the CLI. You will remain logged on as the root user until you quit the Terminal or enter the exit command. In the following example, Michelle will use the sudo command to switch her shell to the root user, and then she will exit back to her own account:

```
MyMac:~ michelle$ who -m
michelle ttys001 Aug 20 14:31
MyMac:~ michelle$ sudo -s
Password:
bash-3.2# who -m
root  ttys001 Aug 20 14:31
bash-3.2# exit
exit
MyMac:~ michelle$ who -m
michelle ttys001 Aug 20 14:31
```

> **TIP** ▶ Once you initially authenticate the sudo command, it will remain "open" for five minutes, so you do not have to reauthenticate subsequent sudo usage during that time.

Remember, with great power comes great responsibility. Using the power of sudo with an improperly typed command can easily wreak havoc on your operating system. The CLI will only warn you the very first time you attempt to use sudo that you could cause serious damage. After that, the CLI assumes you know what you're doing. If you remember only three rules about using the CLI, it should be these: always double-check your typing, always use tab completion to double-check your typing and save time, and, when using sudo, always triple-check your typing.

Ownership and Permissions Commands

Viewing and modifying ownership and permissions in the CLI is a much richer and more complicated experience than in the Finder. The Finder has streamlined ownership, permissions, and ACLs, providing only the most common features that users require. However, the CLI offers every conceivable ownership and permissions option. Further, the CLI often provides more than one method for performing identical tasks.

Viewing Standard Ownership and Permissions

Once again, the ls command is your primary tool for viewing file and folder information in the CLI. The ls command has many options for viewing nearly any file or folder attribute. Naturally, you can learn more about all the options available to ls from its manual entry page. Here, you will be presented with a few fundamental ownership and permissions options.

The most basic ls option for viewing file and folder ownership and permissions is –l:

```
MyMac:~ michelle$ ls -l
total 0
drwx------+ 5 michelle staff 170 Aug 20 15:49 Desktop
drwx------+ 3 michelle staff 102 Aug 20 01:08 Documents
drwx------+ 3 michelle staff 102 Aug 20 01:08 Downloads
drwx------ 19 michelle staff 646 Aug 20 01:08 Library
drwx------+ 3 michelle staff 102 Aug 20 01:08 Movies
drwx------+ 3 michelle staff 102 Aug 20 01:08 Music
drwx------+ 4 michelle staff 136 Aug 20 01:08 Pictures
drwxr-xr-x+ 7 michelle staff 238 Aug 20 15:29 Public
drwxr-xr-x 5 michelle staff 170 Aug 20 01:08 Sites
```

The first string of characters in the listing is shorthand for the item type and permissions. The following information appears from left to right: the number of subitems, the assigned owner, the assigned group, the last modification date, and finally the item's name.

The syntax for the abbreviated information section is:

▶ The first character is item type: - for file, d for folder, and l for symbolic link.

▶ The next three characters indicate the owner's permissions: - for no access, r for read access, w for write access, and x for file execute access or folder browsing access.

▶ The middle set of three rwx characters indicate the group's permissions.

▶ The final set of three rwx characters indicate everyone else's permissions.

▶ Optionally, there may be a + at the end to indicate that the item has ACL rules applied to it.

The execute permission attribute x has not been introduced yet, but it is the third standard UNIX permission attribute after read and write. The execute permission is enabled on files that are commands and folders that are application bundles, to indicate that the item contains executable software code. The execute permission is also required on normal folders to browse the contents of the folder. The Finder doesn't show you when the execute permission is used, but it will properly manage the execute permission when you make permissions changes using the Get Info window.

Viewing Access Control Lists (ACLs)

From the CLI, Mac OS X's ACL implementation provides more than a dozen unique permission attribute types, allows for an unlimited number of user and group permissions per item, and lets you define each permission as a specific allow or deny rule. In other words, you can assign an item an unlimited number of allow or deny rules for any user or group using any of the following permissions attributes:

▶ Administration—Administration attributes, which define a user's or group's ability to make ownership and permissions changes, include change permissions and change ownership.

▶ Read—Read attributes define a user or group's ability to read items and include read attributes, read extended attributes, read file data or list folder contents, execute file or traverse folder, and read permissions.

▶ Write—Write attributes define a user's or group's ability to make changes and include write attributes, write extended attributes, read file data or create files in folder, append file data or create new subfolder inside folder, delete item, and delete subfolders and files.

Furthermore, each permissions entry for a folder can include a static inheritance rule that defines whether the folder's permissions apply to new items placed in the folder. Inheritance attributes include the following: no inheritance, apply to just new items in this folder, apply to any new child folders, apply to any new child files, and apply to all descendants of this folder.

To view the item's ACLs alongside their permissions, simply add the -e option to the -l option:

```
MyMac:~ michelle$ ls -le
total 0
drwx------+ 5 michelle staff 170 Aug 20 15:49 Desktop
 0: group:everyone deny delete
drwx------+ 3 michelle staff 102 Aug 20 01:08 Documents
 0: group:everyone deny delete
drwx------+ 3 michelle staff 102 Aug 20 01:08 Downloads
 0: group:everyone deny delete
drwx------ 19 michelle staff 646 Aug 20 01:08 Library
drwx------+ 3 michelle staff 102 Aug 20 01:08 Movies
 0: group:everyone deny delete
drwx------+ 3 michelle staff 102 Aug 20 01:08 Music
 0: group:everyone deny delete
drwx------+ 4 michelle staff 136 Aug 20 01:08 Pictures
 0: group:everyone deny delete
drwxr-xr-x+ 7 michelle staff 238 Aug 20 15:29 Public
 0: group:everyone deny delete
drwxr-xr-x 5 michelle staff 170 Aug 20 01:08 Sites
```

Modifying Ownership and Permissions

You will use two primary commands for changing file and folder ownership and permissions in the CLI: chown and chmod.

chown. Short for "change ownership," this command will let you change the owner and group associated with a file or folder. Using chown requires root access, so this command is almost always preceded by the sudo command. To use chown, enter the new owner's name, followed optionally by a colon and the new group name, and then finish with the item's path. In the following example, Michelle will use the chown command to change testfile1's ownership to the user account "kevin" and the group account "admin."

```
MyMac:~ michelle$ ls -l Desktop/
total 0
-rw-r--r-- 1 michelle staff 0 Aug 20 15:49 testfile1
drwxr-xr-x 4 michelle staff 136 Aug 20 15:47 testfolder
MyMac:~ michelle$ sudo chown kevin:admin Desktop/testfile1
Password:
MyMac:~ michelle$ ls -l Desktop/
total 0
-rw-r--r-- 1 kevin  admin 0 Aug 20 15:49 testfile1
drwxr-xr-x 4 michelle staff 136 Aug 20 15:47 testfolder
```

chmod. Short for "change file modes," this command will let you change the permissions and ACLs associated with a file or folder. Using chmod on files you don't own requires root access, so the chmod command is often preceded by the sudo command. To use chmod, enter the new permissions or ACLs, and then finish with the item's path.

Adjusting file and folder ACLs goes beyond the scope of this book; however, you can find out how to change ACLs by reading the manual page entry for chmod. As for changing permissions, there are two basic methods when using the chmod command:

▶   Using alphanumeric abbreviations—The basic syntax goes: account type, modifier, and then permission. Account types include u for owner, g for group, and o for everyone else. Modifiers include + for allow, - for deny, and = for exact setting. Permissions are as expected with r for read, w for write, and x for execute. For example, using this method to allow full access for the owner and group but read-only access for everyone else, you'd type ug=rwx,o=r.

▶   Using octal notation—As you can see, the CLI is full of shortcuts and abbreviations. To save even more keystrokes you can use octal notation, which uses numeric abbreviations for defining permissions. The basic syntax for octal notation is to use a single-digit number for the user first, followed by a single number for the group, and then a last single number for everyone else. Octal notation uses: 0, for no access; 1, for execution only; 2, for write-only; and 4, for read-only. To use mixed permissions, simply add the numbers together. For example, using this method to allow for full access for the owner and group but read-only access for everyone else, you'd type 774.

In the following example, Michelle will use the chmod command to change the permissions of testfile1 and testfolder to allow read and write access for the owner and the group but read-only access for everyone else. She will first use alphanumeric abbreviations, and then octal permission equivalents.

> **NOTE ▶** Remember, if you want to change the permissions of a folder and its contents, you must tell the chmod command to run recursively by adding the -R option.

```
MyMac:~ michelle$ ls -l Desktop/
total 0
-rw-r--r-- 1 michelle staff 0 Aug 20 15:49 testfile1
drwxr-xr-x 4 michelle staff 136 Aug 20 15:47 testfolder
MyMac:~ michelle$ chmod ug=rw,o=r Desktop/testfile1
MyMac:~ michelle$ ls -l Desktop/
total 0
-rw-rw-r-- 1 michelle staff 0 Aug 20 15:49 testfile1
drwxr-xr-x 4 michelle staff 136 Aug 20 15:47 testfolder
MyMac:~ michelle$ chmod 664 Desktop/testfolder/
MyMac:~ michelle$ ls -l Desktop/
total 0
-rw-rw-r-- 1 michelle staff 0 Aug 20 15:49 testfile1
drwxrwxr-x 4 michelle staff 136 Aug 20 15:47 testfolder
```

Using the Sticky Bit

As mentioned previously in this lesson, the /Users/Shared folder has a unique permissions setting that allows all local users to read and write items into the folder yet prevents other users from being able to delete files that they didn't originally put in this folder. This special permissions configuration is brought to you courtesy of the "sticky bit." Essentially, enabling the sticky bit on a folder defines it as an append-only destination, or, more accurately, a folder in which only the owner of the item can delete the item.

You can clearly see the sticky bit setting of the /Users/Shared folder when you view its ownership and permissions. Note the t on the end of the permissions information, which indicates that the sticky bit is enabled:

```
MyMac:~ michelle$ ls -l /Users/
total 0
drwxr-xr-x+ 13 Guest  staff 442 Aug 9 18:33 Guest
```

```
drwxrwxrwt 7 root  wheel 238 Aug 10 18:49 Shared
drwxr-xr-x+ 17 kevin  staff 578 Aug 17 00:14 kevin
drwxr-xr-x 16 michael wheel 544 Aug 19 00:06 michael
drwxr-xr-x 15 michelle staff 510 Aug 20 16:43 michelle
```

You can enable sticky bit functionality similar to the /Users/Shared folder on any another folder using a special octal notation with the `chmod` command. In the following example, Michelle has already created a new folder named NewShared. She then uses the `chmod` command with the 1777 octal notation to set sharing for all users with sticky bit functionality:

```
MyMac:~ michelle$ chmod -R 1777 NewShared/
MyMac:~ michelle$ ls -l
total 0
drwx------+ 5 michelle staff 170 Aug 20 15:49 Desktop
drwx------+ 3 michelle staff 102 Aug 20 01:08 Documents
drwx------+ 3 michelle staff 102 Aug 20 01:08 Downloads
drwx------ 19 michelle staff 646 Aug 20 01:08 Library
drwx------+ 3 michelle staff 102 Aug 20 01:08 Movies
drwx------+ 3 michelle staff 102 Aug 20 01:08 Music
drwxrwxrwt 2 michelle staff 68 Aug 20 17:20 NewShared
drwx------+ 4 michelle staff 136 Aug 20 01:08 Pictures
drwxr-xr-x+ 7 michelle staff 238 Aug 20 15:29 Public
drwxr-xr-x 5 michelle staff 170 Aug 20 01:08 Sites
```

File Management Commands

Basic file management is also a much richer experience from the CLI than it is from the Finder. Consequently, basic file management from the CLI can also lead to increased user error. Once again, always make sure to thoroughly check your typing before you execute a command.

Using Invisible Items

To simplify navigation in the file system, both the CLI and the Finder hide many files and folders from your view. Often these files and folders are system support items that are hidden for good reason. While there is no easy way to make the Finder reveal hidden items, it is quite simple to view hidden items in the CLI.

To view hidden items in the CLI, simply add the -a option to the -l option when using the ls command:

```
MyMac:~ michelle$ ls -la
total 32
drwxr-xr-x 15 michelle staff 510 Aug 20 17:33 .
drwxr-xr-x 8 root  admin 272 Aug 20 17:05 ..
-rw------- 1 michelle staff  3 Aug 20 01:08 CFUserTextEncoding
-rw------- 1 michelle staff 2666 Aug 20 16:42 .bash_history
-rw------- 1 michelle staff 48 Aug 20 17:19 .lesshst
-rw------- 1 root  staff 632 Aug 20 14:25 .viminfo
drwx------+ 5 michelle staff 170 Aug 20 15:49 Desktop
drwx------+ 3 michelle staff 102 Aug 20 01:08 Documents
drwx------+ 3 michelle staff 102 Aug 20 01:08 Downloads
drwx------ 19 michelle staff 646 Aug 20 01:08 Library
drwx------+ 3 michelle staff 102 Aug 20 01:08 Movies
drwx------+ 3 michelle staff 102 Aug 20 01:08 Music
drwx------+ 4 michelle staff 136 Aug 20 01:08 Pictures
drwxr-xr-x+ 7 michelle staff 238 Aug 20 15:29 Public
drwxr-xr-x 5 michelle staff 170 Aug 20 01:08 Sites
```

As you can see from Michelle's home folder, any item that has a period at the beginning of its name will be hidden by default in both the CLI and the Finder. These items are created and used by the operating system, so they should be left alone.

There is another way to hide folders from the Finder without having to place a period at the beginning of the folder's name. Items stored on Mac OS X Extended volumes have additional attributes, including an attribute that defines visibility in the Finder. The GetFileInfo and SetFile commands, which are only installed as part of the Xcode Developer Tools package that can be found on the Mac OS X Install DVD, will allow you to view and modify these additional file and folder attributes.

In this first example, Michelle uses the GetFileInfo command to view the additional attributes of a folder she has already created called HiddenFolder. Notice the string of text indicating this folder's attributes. Each character in this string is an abbreviation for a specific attribute. All the characters are lowercase, indicating that the attribute is disabled.

Naturally, you can find out more about each attribute by checking the manual page for the GetFileInfo command.

```
MyMac:~ michelle$ GetFileInfo HiddenFolder/
directory: "/Users/michelle/HiddenFolder"
attributes: avbstclinmedz
created: 08/20/2007 18:00:33
modified: 08/20/2007 18:00:33
```

In the following example, Michelle makes the HiddenFolder folder invisible in the Finder by using the SetFile command to modify the visibility attribute. Notice that when she executes the GetFileInfo command again, the lowercase *v* has changed to a capital *V*, indicating that the folder's visibility attribute is enabled. Ironically, enabling the visibility attribute will make the folder invisible in the Finder.

```
MyMac:~ michelle$ SetFile -a "V" HiddenFolder/
MyMac:~ michelle$ GetFileInfo HiddenFolder/
directory: "/Users/michelle/HiddenFolder"
attributes: aVbstclinmedz
created: 08/20/2007 18:00:33
modified: 08/20/2007 18:00:33
```

TIP ▶ You can use the sudo command in conjunction with the SetFile command to reset any extended attribute, including the notorious locked file or folder attribute.

Modifying Files and Folders

There are a variety of basic commands for modifying files and folders from the CLI, including cp, mv, rm, mkdir, and rmdir.

cp. Short for "copy," this command will copy items from one location to another. The syntax is cp followed by the path to the original item, and ending with the destination path for the copy. In the following example, Michelle uses the cp command to create a copy of testfile located at the root of her home folder and places the copy, testfile2, in her Desktop folder.

NOTE ▶ Remember, if you want to copy a folder and its entire contents you must tell the cp command to run recursively by adding the -R option.

```
MyMac:~ michelle$ ls
Desktop   Library   Pictures   testfile
Documents   Movies   Public
Downloads   Music   Sites
MyMac:~ michelle$ cp testfile Desktop/testfile2
MyMac:~ michelle$ ls Desktop/
testfile2
```

mv. Short for "move," this command will move items from one location to another. The syntax is mv followed by the path to the original item, and ending with the new destination path for the item. In the following example, Michelle uses the mv command to move testfile2 from her Desktop folder to the root of her home folder:

```
MyMac:~ michelle$ ls Desktop/
testfile2
MyMac:~ michelle$ ls
Desktop   Library   Pictures   testfile
Documents   Movies   Public
Downloads   Music   Sites
MyMac:~ michelle$ mv Desktop/testfile2 testfile2
MyMac:~ michelle$ ls
Desktop   Library   Pictures   testfile
Documents   Movies   Public   testfile2
Downloads   Music   Sites
```

The mv command also happens to be the rename command. After all, moving an item into the same folder with a different name is the same as renaming it. In the following example, Michelle, working in her home folder, uses the mv command to rename testfile to testfile1:

```
MyMac:~ michelle$ ls
Desktop   Library   Pictures   testfile
Documents   Movies   Public   testfile2
Downloads   Music   Sites
MyMac:~ michelle$ mv testfile testfile1
MyMac:~ michelle$ ls
Desktop   Library   Pictures   testfile1
Documents   Movies   Public   testfile2
Downloads   Music   Sites
```

rm. Short for "remove," this command will permanently delete items. There is no Trash folder in the CLI. The rm command is forever. The syntax is rm followed by the paths of the items you wish to delete. In the following example, Michelle uses the rm command to delete testifile1 and testfile2.

> **NOTE** ▸ Remember, if you want to delete a folder and its entire contents you must tell the rm command to run recursively by adding the -R option.

```
MyMac:~ michelle$ ls
Desktop   Library   Pictures  testfile1
Documents Movies    Public    testfile2
Downloads Music     Sites
MyMac:~ michelle$ rm testfile1 testfile2
MyMac:~ michelle$ ls
Desktop   Downloads Movies   Pictures  Sites
Documents Library   Music    Public
```

mkdir. Short for "make directory," this command is used to create new folders. The syntax is mkdir followed by the paths of the new folders you want to create. An often-used option is -p, which will tell mkdir to create intermediate folders that don't already exist in the paths you specify. In the following example, Michelle uses the mkdir command with the –p option to create a folder called Private with two folders inside it called Stocks and Bonds:

```
MyMac:~ michelle$ ls
Desktop   Downloads Movies   Pictures  Sites
Documents Library   Music    Public
MyMac:~ michelle$ mkdir -p Private/Stocks Private/Bonds
MyMac:~ michelle$ ls
Desktop   Downloads Movies   Pictures  Public
Documents Library   Music    Private   Sites
MyMac:~ michelle$ cd Private/
MyMac:Private michelle$ ls
Bonds Stocks
```

rmdir. Short for "remove directory," this command will permanently delete folders. Again, there is no Trash folder in the CLI. The rmdir command is forever. The syntax is rmdir followed by the paths of the folders you want to delete. The rmdir command cannot remove folders with any items in them, so in many ways the rmdir command is superfluous, as you can easily remove folders and their contents by using the rm command with the recursive option.

In the following example, Michelle tries to use the rmdir command to delete the Private folder but is unable to because it contains items. She then attempts to use the rm command, but again she is unable to because the folder contains items. Finally, she uses the rm command with the recursive option, -R, to remove the Private folder and all its contents.

```
MyMac:~ michelle$ rmdir Private/
rmdir: Private/: Directory not empty
MyMac:~ michelle$ rm Private/
rm: Private/: is a directory
MyMac:~ michelle$ rm -R Private/
MyMac:~ michelle$ ls
Desktop   Downloads  Movies   Pictures  Sites
Documents  Library   Music   Public
```

What You've Learned

▶ Mac OS X's file system supports a variety of partition schemes and volume types.

▶ Disk Utility is your primary tool for managing the Mac's file system.

▶ Mac OS X includes robust built-in support for software-based RAID sets and burning optical media.

▶ Ownership, permissions, and access control lists (ACLs) are used to manage file and folder access.

▶ There are many useful tools available in the command-line interface (CLI) for managing the Mac's file system that go beyond the capabilities of the graphical user interface.

References

You can check for new and updated Knowledge Base documents at http://www.apple.com/support.

General File System

19516, "Mac OS: Technical overview of disk volume structures"

107249, "Mac OS X: About file system journaling"

25668, "About disk optimization with Mac OS X"

303462, "Mac OS X 10.4: About Disk Utility's secure erase options"

306496, "Mac OS X 10.5: About resizing disk partitions"

File System Troubleshooting

302672, "Using Disk Utility in Mac OS X 10.4.3 or later to verify or repair disks"

106214, "Resolve startup issues and perform disk maintenance with Disk Utility and fsck"

106272, "You can't empty the Trash or move a file to the Trash in Mac OS X"

303118, "Intel-based Macs: 'You have inserted a disk containing no volumes that Mac OS X can read" alert message"

Software RAID

106594, "Mac OS X, Mac OS X Server: How to use Apple-Supplied RAID software"

303692, "Intel-based Macs: Flashing question mark when trying to boot from RAID volume"

Optical Media

302276, "Mac OS X 10.4: About improved disc burning and burn folders"

25402, "Factors that affect writing to or reading from optical media"

301551, "About optical disc drive burning and write speeds"

302191, "About default optical drive burning speeds"

58641, "Using nonstandard discs in optical drives"

Ownership and Permissions

106237, "Unable to move, unlock, modify, or copy an item in Mac OS X"

106712, "Troubleshooting permissions issues in Mac OS X"

25751, "About Disk Utility's Repair Disk Permissions feature"

URLs

Wikipedia entry comparing file systems: http://en.wikipedia.org/wiki/Comparison_of_file_systems

Wikipedia entry comparing RAID types: http://en.wikipedia.org/wiki/RAID

DriveSavers data recovery: http://www.drivesavers.com

Review Quiz

1. What are the difference between disk drives, partitions, and volumes?

2. What are the two primary partition schemes for Mac-formatted drives? What are their differences?

3. What are the six volume formats supported by Mac OS X? How are they different?

4. How does file system journaling work?

5. What differentiates a RAID 0 set from a RAID 1 set?

6. How is Disk Utility's Verify and Repair feature used?

7. What are the four erase options available in Disk Utility? What are the differences between them?

8. How does the Finder's Secure Empty Trash feature work?

9. What is the potential side effect of improperly unmounting or ejecting a drive or volume?

10. What three methods can be used to eject a volume or drive from the Finder?

11. How do you use the Finder's burn folder feature?

12. How do you use Disk Utility to burn an optical disc?

13. What does it mean when you choose the option to "ignore volume ownership" in the Finder? What are the security ramifications of ignoring volume ownership?

14. What is target disk mode and how is it engaged?

15. How do you identify the ownership and permissions of a file or folder in the Finder? In the Terminal?

16. Why is the root, or beginning, level of a user's home folder visible to other users?

17. How are the permissions on the Shared folder set to allow for local user sharing?

18. How does the default organization of the file system allow users to safely share local files and folders?

19. What do the following terms describe: folder, directory, path, absolute path, and relative path?

20. What is the difference between absolute and relative paths?

21. How do permissions in the Finder appear different than permissions in the Terminal?

22. What two methods can you use to hide a file or folder in the Terminal?

23. What is the sticky bit?

Answers

1. Disk drives are the actual storage hardware, partitions are logical divisions of a disk drive used to define the storage space, and volumes, contained inside partitions, are used to define how the individual files and folders are saved to the storage.

2. GUID Partition Table is the default partition scheme on Intel-based Macs, and Apple Partition Map is the default partition scheme on PowerPC-based Macs.

3. The six volume formats supported by Mac OS X are: Mac OS X Extended, the native volume format supported by all Macintosh computers; Mac OS X Extended, Journaled, the default volume format for Mac OS X drives; Mac OS X Extended, Journaled, Case-Sensitive, the default volume format for Mac OS X Server drives; UNIX File System (UFS), a legacy volume format supported by many other UNIX-based systems; File Allocation Table (FAT32), the volume format used by many peripherals and older Windows-based PCs; and New Technology File System (NTFS), the native volume format used by modern Windows-based operating systems.

4. File system journaling maintains a log of changed files as they are actually written to storage. This way, if a power failure or system crash occurs, after the system restarts it will be able to quickly verify the integrity of the volume based on the journal log.

5. RAID 0 uses disk striping to simultaneously write data to all drives providing increased performance but increases your chances of data loss due to drive failure. RAID 1 uses disk mirroring to write the same data to multiple drives, which does not increase performance, but it does greatly decrease your chances of data loss due to drive failure.

6. The Disk Utility's Verify and Repair feature is used to verify or repair the directory structure of a volume. The directory structure contains all the information used to locate files and folders on the volume.

7. The four erase options in Disk Utility are: Don't Erase Data, which simply replaces the volume's directory structure; Zero Out Data, which provides minimal security by writing zeros on top of all the previous drive data; 7-Pass Erase, which provides good security by writing seven separate passes of random information on top of all the previous drive data; and 35-Pass Erase, which provides the best security by writing 35 separate passes of random information on top of all the previous drive data.

8. The Finder's Secure Empty Trash will perform a 7-pass erase on the contents of the Trash folder.

9. Improperly unmounting or ejecting a drive or volume may cause data corruption. The system will automatically verify and repair an improperly unmounted or ejected volume the next time it becomes available to the Mac.

10. The three methods used to eject a volume or drive from the Finder are: press and hold the Eject key for a few moments to unmount and eject optical media; select the volume you wish to unmount and eject from the Finder and choose File > Eject from the menu bar; and finally in the Finder's sidebar click the small eject button next to the volume you wish to unmount and eject.

11. There are two methods for using a burn folder in the Finder. First, you can create a burn folder of any size by choosing File > New Burn Folder from the menu bar. Once you are done adding and arranging items in the burn folder, click the Burn button and then insert a blank recordable optical disc. Or, you can create a burn folder of a specific optical disc size by first inserting a blank recordable optical disc, and then the Finder will automatically create a burn folder that matches the size of the recordable optical disc.

12. Disk Utility can burn the contents of a disk image to an optical disk. Click the Burn button in Disk Utility's toolbar, select a disk image, and then insert a blank recordable optical disc.

13. You can choose to ignore ownership on any nonsystem volume. This will ignore any ownership rules and grant any logged-on user unlimited access to the contents of the volume. This is a potential security risk because it will allow any local user account to have full access to the volume even if that user did not originally mount the volume.

14. Target disk mode is a Mac-specific hardware feature that, when engaged, will share the Mac's internal disk drives through the FireWire ports. Target disk mode can be engaged from the Startup Disk preference or by holding down the T key as you turn on the Mac.

15. An item's ownership and permissions can be identified using the Get Info or Inspector windows in the Finder, or by using the ls -l command in the Terminal.

16. The root level of a user's home folder is visible to other users so they can navigate to the Public and Sites shared folders.

17. The Shared folder is set up to allow all users to read and write files, but only the user who added an item can delete it from the Shared folder. This is accomplished using the sticky bit permissions setting.

18. Every home folder contains a Public folder that other users can read, and a Drop Box folder that other users can write to. All other subfolders in a user's home folder have default permissions that do not allow access to other users. The Shared folder is also set for all users to share items.

19. Folders and directories are both terms used to describe containers in the file system. A path defines directions to a specific item in the file system. Absolute paths are full directions to a specific item, whereas relative paths are partial directions to a specific item based on the user's current working location.

20. Absolute paths always start from the root, or beginning, of the file system, whereas relative paths start from the user's current working location. The default working location of users is at the root of their home folder.

21. The Finder shows only four different permissions options: no access, read and write, read only, and write only. On the other hand, using the options available from the ls command in the Terminal will show you every possible permissions configuration.

22. The two methods for hiding an item in the Terminal are to use a period at the beginning of any item's filename to hide it in the Terminal and the Finder, or to use SetFile –a "V" from the command line.

23. The sticky bit is a special permission used to define a folder as an append-only destination or, more accurately, a folder in which only the owner of the item can delete the item.

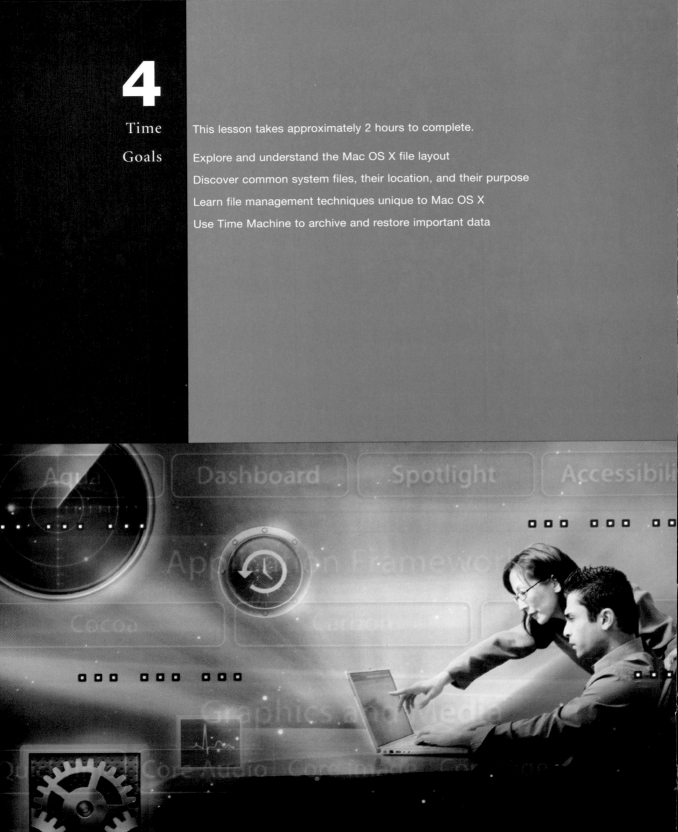

4

Time

Goals

This lesson takes approximately 2 hours to complete.

Explore and understand the Mac OS X file layout

Discover common system files, their location, and their purpose

Learn file management techniques unique to Mac OS X

Use Time Machine to archive and restore important data

Data Management and Backup

It is not unusual for a Mac OS X system drive to contain well over one hundred thousand folders and five hundred thousand files just to support the operating system and its applications. As you can imagine, the number of items in a user's home folder varies widely depending on the user, but even the most frugal of users will have thousands of items in their home folder. It's simply the nature of a modern operating system to compartmentalize each small chunk of data into its own individual file. Avoiding large contiguous files is a conscious design choice that helps to increase reliability and reduce the likelihood of widespread data corruption.

With this many files on hand, attempting to explore and fully comprehend Mac OS X's file layout may seem like a monumental task. On the contrary, like many other technologies Apple has reimagined, Mac OS X's system files have been streamlined and reorganized into an easy-to-understand layout that provides enhanced security and manageability for the Mac administrator.

This lesson builds on the previous lesson, "File Systems," to focus more specifically on the composition and organization of the files and folders that make up Mac OS X. In this lesson you, acting as an administrator, will use the file layout to strategically allocate resources. You will also work with many Mac-specific file technologies, including resource forks, packages, and Spotlight. Finally, you will use the built-in features for archiving data on the Mac, including one of the most significant new features in Mac OS X 10.5, Time Machine.

Mac OS X Volume Hierarchy

Mac OS X's system layout is designed to strike a balance between ease of use and advanced functionality. For the basic user, looking at the root, or beginning, of the file system from the Finder will reveal only four default folders: Applications, Library, Users, and System. The contents of these four folders represent all that most users, and many administrators, will ever need to access. Yet when advanced users look at the system root from the command-line interface, they will see many more items that the Finder would normally hide. Thus, the complexity and flexibility of a UNIX operating system remains for those users who require it.

Exploring Mac OS X's system layout from the command-line interface was covered in Lesson 3 "File Systems," but for now the following describes the default system root folders you'll see from the Finder:

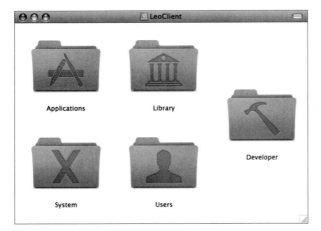

► Applications—Often called the local Applications folder, this is the default location for applications available to all local users. Only administrative users can make changes to the contents of this folder.

▶   Library—Often called the local Library folder, this is the default location for ancillary system and application resources available to all local users. Once again, only administrative users can make changes to the contents of this folder.

▶   System—This folder contains resources required by the operating system for primary functionality. It is very rare that any user should have to make changes to the contents of this folder. Even administrative users are unable to make changes to items in the System folder without reauthenticating.

▶   Users—This is the default location for local user home folders. Specific access to home folder items was discussed earlier in Lesson 2, "User Accounts."

▶   Developer (Optional)—This optional folder contains the Apple Xcode Developer Tools. This is not part of the standard installation, but it's still a fundamental part of the system, and can be found on the Mac OS X Install DVD. Similar to the Applications and Library folders, the Developer folder can only be changed by an administrative user.

System Resources

All Mac OS X–specific system resources can be found in the various Library folders throughout the system volume. System resources can be generally categorized as any resource that is not a general-use application or user document. That's not to say that applications and user data can't be found in the Library folders. However, the concept of the Library folder is to keep system resources organized and separated from the items you use every day. This keeps the Applications folder and user home folders free from system resource clutter.

System Resource Types

Opening any of the Library folders will reveal several dozen categories of items. It is not necessary to explore every single possible Library item, but there are a few system resources you should be familiar with:

▶   Application support—This folder can be found in both the user and local Libraries. Any ancillary data needed by an application may end up in this folder. Once again, application resources are placed here to keep the Applications folders tidy.

▶   Extensions—Also called kernel extensions, these items are only found in the system Library folder. Extensions are low-level drivers that attach themselves to the kernel, or core of the operating system. Extensions provide driver support for hardware, networking, and peripherals. Extensions load and unload automatically, so there is little need to manage extensions as is common in other operating systems. You can view your Mac's currently loaded extensions from the /Applications/Utilities/System Profiler application.

▶ Fonts—Found in every Library folder, fonts are files used to describe typefaces used for both screen display and printing. Font management will be covered in the "Managing Font Resources" section later in this lesson.

▶ Frameworks—Found in every Library folder, frameworks are repositories of shared code used among different parts of the operating system or applications. Frameworks are similar to extensions in that they load and unload automatically, so again there is little need to manage these shared code resources. You can view your Mac's currently loaded frameworks from the /Applications/Utilities/System Profiler application.

▶ Keychains—Found in every Library folder, keychains are used to securely store sensitive information, including passwords, certificates, keys, website forms, and notes. Keychain technology was previously covered in Lesson 2, "User Accounts."

▶ LaunchAgents and LaunchDaemons—These items, found in both the local and system Libraries, are used to define processes that start automatically via the launchd process. Mac OS X uses many background processes, which are all started by launchd. Furthermore, every single process is a child of the launchd process. LaunchAgents are for processes that only need to start up when a user is logged in, whereas LaunchDaemons are used to start processes that will always run in the background even when there are no users logged in. Managing processes is covered next in Lesson 5, "Applications and Boot Camp."

▶ Logs—Many system processes and applications archive progress or error messages to log files. Log files can be found in every Library folder. Log files are viewed using the /Applications/Utilities/Console application.

▶ PreferencePanes—PreferencePanes can be found in any Library folder. These items are used by the System Preferences application to provide interfaces for system configuration. System Preferences usage was covered earlier in Lesson 1, "Installation and Initial Setup."

▶ Preferences—Preferences, found in every Library folder, are used to store system and application configuration settings. In other words, every time you configure a setting for any application or system function, it is saved to a preference file. Because preferences play such a critical role in system functionality, they are often the cause of many software problems. Troubleshooting preference files will be covered in Lesson 5, "Applications and Boot Camp."

▶ StartupItems—StartupItems, found in only the local and system Libraries, are precursors to LaunchAgents and LaunchDaemons. With Mac OS X 10.5, Apple is officially discouraging the use of StartupItems. In fact, you will only have StartupItems if you've installed third-party software that hasn't been updated. In Mac OS X 10.5 the launchd process will still support many StartupItems, but this will probably not be true for future versions.

System Resource Hierarchy

Library folders, and thus system resources, are located in each of the four domain areas: user, local, network, and system. Segregating resources into four domains provides increased administrative flexibility, resource security, and system reliability. Resource domains are more flexible because administrators can choose to allocate certain resources to all users or just specific users. It's more secure because standard users can only add resources to their own home folder and cannot access other users' resources. Finally, it's more reliable because, in most cases, you don't have to make changes to the core system functionality in order to provide more services.

In more detail, the four system resource domains are, in order:

▶ User—Each user has his own Library folder in his home folder for resources. When resources are placed here, only the user has access to them. Also, a user can have his own Applications folder in his home folder.

▶ Local—Both the root Applications and root Library folders are part of the local resource domain. This is why they are known as the local Applications and local Library folders. Any resources placed in these two folders are available to all local user accounts. By default, only administrative users can make changes to local resources.

▶ Network—Mac OS X can access system resources and applications from a network file share. Administrators must configure an automounted share in order to enable the Network resource domain. Configuring automounted shares goes beyond the scope of this guide. However, it is covered in Lesson 5, "Using File Services," of *Apple Training Series: Mac OS X Server Essentials Second Edition*.

▶ System—Finally, the system domain encompasses all the items necessary to provide core system functionality. There are many hidden items at the root of the system volume that make up the system resource domain, but the only one you will see in the Finder is the root System folder. In many cases, you do not need to add any resources here.

With four different domains containing resources, there is a strong likelihood for overlap in resources. In other words, there may be multiple copies of similar resources available to the system and user at any given time. The system is designed to handle this by searching for resources from the most specific resources, those in the user domain, to the least specific, those in the system domain. If multiple similar resources are discovered, the system will use the resource most specific to the user. For example, if multiple versions of the font Times New Roman are found, one in the local Library and one in the user's Library, the copy of the font in the user's Library will be the one used.

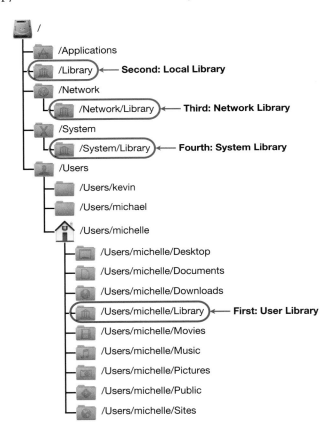

Managing Font Resources

An excellent way to experience the system resource domain hierarchy is by managing fonts. Mac OS X has advanced font-management technology that enables an unlimited number of fonts using nearly any font type, including bitmap, TrueType, OpenType, and all PostScript Type fonts. As mentioned earlier, fonts are installed in the various Font folders located in the Library folders throughout the system. A user can manually install fonts by simply dragging them into a Fonts folder.

On the other hand, Mac OS X includes a very nice font-management tool, /Applications/Font Book, which will automatically install fonts for you. Font Book can also be used to organize fonts into more manageable collections, enable or disable fonts to simplify font lists, and resolve duplicate fonts.

> **NOTE ►** Third-party font-management tools, such as Extensis's Suitcase Fusion, will interrupt Font Book and take over font management for the system.

To manage fonts with Font Book:

1 Open /Applications/Font Book.

The main Font Book window appears, allowing you to preview any currently installed font by clicking on it in the Font list.

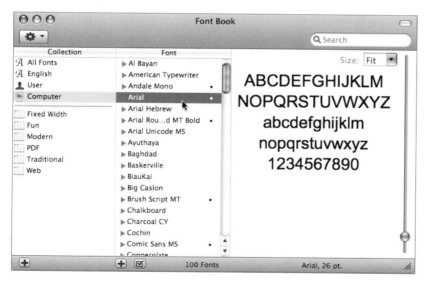

2 Choose Font Book > Preferences to adjust where Font Book will install new fonts.

By default, Font Book will install fonts to the user's Library. If you are an administrative user, you can choose to install fonts to the local Library by choosing Computer from the pop-up menu. Close the Font Book Preference dialog once you have made your selections.

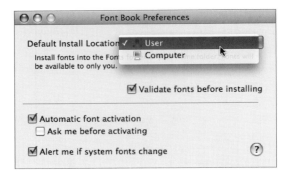

3 From the Finder, simply double-click on the font you wish to install. Font Book will automatically open the font and show you a preview.

4 Click the Install Font button to install the font to your selected default Library folder.

5 If you feel overwhelmed by the number of installed fonts, you can temporarily disable fonts within Font Book by selecting the font and then clicking the small checkbox button at the bottom of the font list.

Disabled fonts will appear dimmed in the font list with the word *Off* next to their name. To enable the font, simply select it again and click the same button at the bottom of the font list.

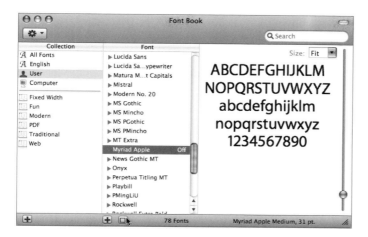

6 Fonts that appear more than once in your font list will have a small dot next to their name. You can automatically disable fonts that are duplicated in your system with FontBook, by choosing Edit > Resolve Duplicates from the menu bar.

7 To remove a font, select it from the font list and press the Delete key. You will be presented with a summary dialog, reminding you that continuing will move the selected fonts to the Trash folder. If you are sure this is what you want to do, then click the Remove button.

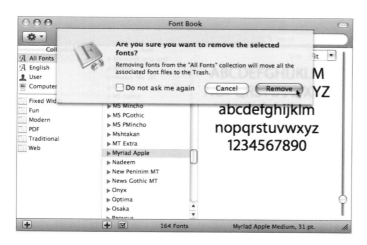

TIP ▶ Some applications may need to be restarted to take advantage of recently added fonts.

System Resource Troubleshooting

System resource issues are usually rare, and they are generally easy to identify. You will occasionally see an error message calling out an issue with a specific item, but you may also experience a situation where the item appears to be missing. In some cases, the system resource in question may be missing, but many times the system will simply ignore a system resource if it determines that the resource is in some way corrupted. The solution for both of these situations is to simply replace the missing or suspect item with a known working copy.

When troubleshooting system resources, you must also remember to heed the resource domain hierarchy. Once again using fonts an example, you may have loaded a specific version of a font in the local Library that is required by your workflow to operate properly. In spite of this, a user may have loaded another version of the same font in her home folder. In this case, the system will load the user's font and ignore the font you installed. Therefore, this user may experience workflow problems even though it appears that she is using the correct font.

> **TIP** If fonts are missing from within applications but they appear to be properly installed, remember to check Font Book as the font may be temporarily disabled.

Logging in with another account on the Mac is always a quick way to determine if the problem is in the user's home folder. You can also use /Applications/Utilities/System Profiler to list active system resources. System Profiler will always show the file path of the loaded system resources, so it's easy to spot resources that are loading from the user's Library.

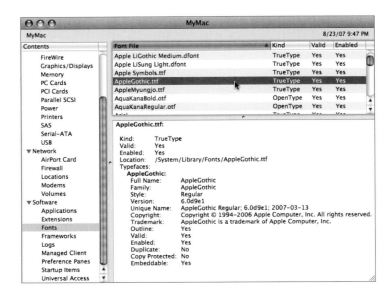

Finder vs. Command-Line Interface

Mac OS X 10.5 is a fully compliant UNIX operating system, and as such requires a number of files that will never be used by the average user. The root level of the Mac's system volume is littered with resources that are required by UNIX processes and expected by UNIX administrators. Apple made the wise choice of configuring the Finder to hide these items from the average user. On a daily basis, the average user—and even most administrative users—do not need to access any of these items from the graphical interface. Realistically, the only people who even care about these normally hidden resources are going to be using the command-line interface (CLI) to do their work anyway. In other words, keeping these system items hidden in the Finder not only provides a tidier work environment but also prevents average users from poking around in places they don't need to go.

Files and folders are hidden in the Finder using two methods. The first is by simply using a period at the beginning of the item's name, and the second method is by using the visibility attribute. File and folder visibility was covered in great detail in Lesson 3, "File Systems."

In the following CLI example, Michelle will use the ls command with the option to list all items at the root of the system drive:

```
MyMac:~ michelle$ ls -a /
.               Desktop DF      etc
..              Developer       home
.DS_Store       Library         mach_kernel
.Spotlight-V100 Network         mach_kernel.ctfsys
.Trashes        System          net
.fseventsd      Users           private
.hotfiles.btree Volumes         sbin
.vol            bin             tmp
Applications    cores           usr
Desktop DB      dev             var
```

Of the 30 items at the root of the system volume shown in this example, only 5 of them are shown in the Finder: Applications, Developer, Library, System, and Users.

> **NOTE ▶** If you are unfamiliar with using the CLI, you should thoroughly examine the CLI introduction in Lesson 3, "File Systems."

Revealing Hidden Folders in the Finder

Should you want or need to reveal normally hidden items in the Finder, there are two methods. The first involves use of the Finder only; the second involves using the open command from the CLI.

To reveal hidden folders in the Finder:

1   From the Finder, choose Go > Go to Folder from the menu bar, or you can use the Command-Shift-G keyboard combination.

This will reveal a dialog allowing you to enter an absolute path to any folder on the Mac. A good starting place is the /private folder, as many UNIX system configuration files are found in this folder.

2   Click the Go button once you have entered the path.

The Finder will reveal the hidden folder in a window. Note the dimmed folder icon representing the normally hidden folder. To save time when you return to the Go dialog, the previous path you entered will be there.

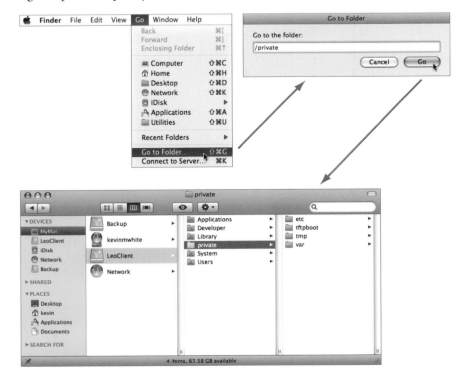

Using the open Command

The open command is a rather unique command that spans the chasm between the CLI and the graphical interface. The open command can be used to open files, folders, and URLs from the CLI to an application in the graphical interface. Folders are opened in a Finder window, the default web browser opens URLs, and files are opened by the default application for the specified file type. The only caveat when using the open command is that the user who executes the open command must also be logged into the graphical interface. In other words, the same user account must be logged into the graphical interface and the CLI to use the open command.

The following example will open the user's current working folder from the CLI to a Finder window:

```
MyMac:~ michelle$ open .
```

The next example will open the /private folder, which is normally hidden, in a Finder window:

```
MyMac:~ michelle$ open /private/
```

This next example will open a document on Michelle's Desktop called Proof.pdf with the default PDF reader, most likely the Preview application:

```
MyMac:~ michelle$ open Desktop/Proof.pdf
```

This final example will open Apple's main website page in the default web browser, most likely the Safari application:

```
MyMac:~ michelle$ open http://www.apple.com/
```

> **TIP** Remember, you can automatically enter paths from the Finder to the CLI by dragging a file or folder on top of the Terminal window.

Mac OS X Metadata

Metadata is data about data. More specifically, metadata is information used to describe content. The most basic forms of file and folder metadata employed by nearly every operating system are names, paths, modification dates, ownership, and permissions. These metadata objects are not part of the item's content, yet they are necessary to describe the item in the file system. Mac OS X utilizes advanced metadata technology to simplify the file system layout and provide lightning-fast rich content searches via Spotlight.

File System Metadata

Aside from the normal file and folder metadata information (names, paths, modification dates, ownership, and permissions), Mac OS X uses additional metadata information stored as either resource forks or additional attributes.

Resource Forks

Resource forks have a long history in the Macintosh operating system, dating back to the original Mac OS. To simplify the user experience, Apple created a forked file system to make complex items, such as applications, appear as a single icon. Forked file systems allow multiple pieces of data to appear as a single item in the file system. In this case, a file will appear as a single item, but it would actually be composed of two separate pieces, a data fork and a resource fork. For many years the Mac OS relied on forked files for storing both applications and documents.

This may have made the user experience simpler in most cases, but because most other operating systems don't normally use a forked file system, compatibility was an issue. Only volumes formatted with the Mac OS or Mac OS Extended file system could properly use forked files. Third-party software has been developed for Windows-based operating systems to allow them to access Mac OS Extended volumes and cope with forked files. More often users would use the compatibility software built into Mac OS to help other file systems cope with a forked file.

Versions of Mac OS X previous to Mac OS X 10.5 will store the resource fork information in a hidden file on non-Mac OS volumes. For example, if you were to copy a forked file called Report.doc on a FAT32 volume, the Mac's file system would automatically split the forked file and write it as two discrete pieces on the FAT32 volume. The data fork would have the same name as the original, but the resource fork would end up in a file called ._Report.doc, which would remain hidden from the Finder. This worked out pretty well for most files because Windows applications only care about the contents of the data fork. Consequently, some files do not take well to being split up and all the extra dot-underscore files created a bit of a mess on other file systems.

Mac OS X version 10.5 introduced an improved method for handling forked files on NTFS volumes and SMB network shares from NTFS volumes. The native file system for modern Windows-based computers, NTFS, supports something similar to file forking known as alternative data streams. The Mac's file system will now write the resource fork to the alternative data stream so the file will appear as a single item on both Windows and Mac systems.

> **NOTE ▶** Mac OS X 10.5 will revert to the previous method of splitting forked files when writing to FAT32 and UFS volumes or NFS shares.

Resource Forks via Command Line

Most UNIX operating systems do not use forked files. As a result, most UNIX commands do not properly support forked files. These commands can manipulate the data fork just fine, but they often ignore the resource fork, leaving files damaged and possibly unusable. Fortunately, Apple has made some modifications to a few of the most common file management commands, thus allowing them to properly work with forked files. Resource fork–aware commands on Mac OS X include cp, mv, and rm.

In the following example, Michelle will use the fork-aware cp command to copy a forked file on from her Desktop called ForkedDocument.tiff to a FAT32 volume. Note that the file is a single item on her Desktop, but on the FAT32 volume it is two items. The resource fork part is named with a preceding period-underscore. Finally, Michelle will remove the file using the fork-aware rm command to remove the document. Note that both the document and the resource part are removed from the FAT32 volume.

```
MyMac:~ michelle$ ls -a Desktop/
.        .localized
..       ForkedDocument.tiff
MyMac:~ michelle$ cp Desktop/ForkedDocument.tiff /Volumes/FAT32VOLUME/
MyMac:~ michelle$ ls -a /Volumes/FAT32VOLUME/
.        ._.Trashes
..       ._ForkedDocument.tiff
.DS_Store    .fseventsd
.Spotlight-V100    ForkedDocument.tiff
.Trashes
MyMac:~ michelle$ rm /Volumes/FAT32VOLUME/ForkedDocument.tiff
MyMac:~ michelle$ ls -a /Volumes/FAT32VOLUME/
.        .Spotlight-V100 .fseventsd
..       .Trashes
.DS_Store ._.Trashes
```

Additional File and Folder Attributes

Mac OS X also supports additional file and folder attributes for items stored on Mac OS Extended volumes. The GetFileInfo and SetFile commands, which are only installed as part of the Xcode Developer Tools package, will allow you to view and modify these additional file and folder attributes. Usage of these two commands to enable the invisibility attribute is covered in Lesson 3, "File Systems."

> **NOTE ▶** The GetFileInfo and SetFile commands are installed as part of the optional Xcode Developer Tools package that can be found on the Mac OS X Install DVD.

Examples of additional file and folder attributes include:

▶ Alias file—Setting this attribute indicates to the file system that the specified item is an alias, or file system shortcut. Aliases can be created in the Finder.

▶ Bundle folder—Setting this attribute indicates to the file system the folder is a package or bundle. Packages and bundles are covered in the next section of this lesson.

▶ Hide extension—Setting this attribute indicates to the file system that the item's filename extension should be hidden in the Finder. This attribute can be enabled or disabled from the Get Info or the Inspector window in the Finder.

▶ Locked—Setting this attribute indicates to the file system that the item is locked from editing. Locking an item prevents any edits of the item's content or attributes. The owner of an item can lock or unlock it from the Get Info or the Inspector window in the Finder.

▶ Invisible—Setting this attribute indicates to the file system that the item should be invisible in the Finder. Setting the visibility attribute is covered in Lesson 3, "File Systems."

▶ Busy—Setting this attribute indicates to the file system that the item is being used by another process and cannot be edited. An application that is actively modifying an item may temporarily enable the busy attribute to avoid corruption, thus preventing another process from modifying the item at the same time.

Packages and Bundles

When Apple moved to Mac OS X, it wanted to avoid the use of resource forks while still retaining the ability to make complex items appear as single icons. Instead of creating a new container technology, Apple simply modified an existing file system container, the common folder. Packages and bundles are nothing more than common folders with the bundle attribute enabled so they appear as single opaque items in the Finder. This allows software developers to easily organize all the resources needed for a complicated product into a single package or bundle, while making it harder for normal users to interfere with the resources. In other words, where a user sees only a single icon in the Finder representing an application, in reality it is a folder potentially filled with thousands of resources.

Packages and bundles both use the same technique of hiding resources inside special folders. The only difference between a package and a bundle is semantics. The word *package* typically refers to archived files used by the installer application to install software—that is, installer packages—whereas the word *bundle* is typically used when describing applications, software resources, or complex documents—that is, software bundles.

The anatomy of an installer package is quite simple; it usually contains only a compressed archive of the software to be installed and a few configuration files used by the installer application. Software bundles, on the other hand, are often much more complex as they contain all the resources necessary for the application or software.

Software bundles often include:

- ▶ Executable code for multiple platforms
- ▶ Document description files
- ▶ Media resources such as images and sounds
- ▶ User interface description files
- ▶ Text resources
- ▶ Resource forks
- ▶ Resources localized for specific languages
- ▶ Private software libraries and frameworks
- ▶ Plug-ins or other software to expand capability

You can easily view the contents of a package or bundle from the Finder. Nevertheless, you should be very careful when exploring this content. Modifying the content of a package or bundle can easily leave the item unstable or unusable. If you can't resist the desire to tinker with a package or bundle, you should always do so from a copy and leave the original safely intact.

To access the content of a package or bundle in the Finder, simply right-click or Control-click on the package or bundle you wish to explore, and then choose View Package Contents from the shortcut menu.

> **TIP** ▶ Tools for creating and modifying packages and bundles are included with the optional Xcode Developer Tools package that can be found on the Mac OS X Install DVD.

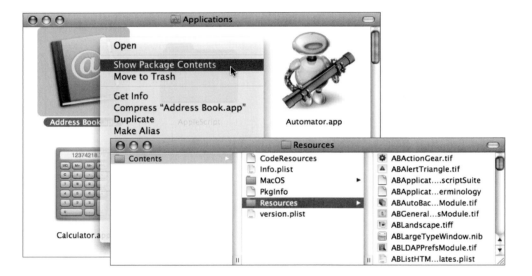

Spotlight Search

Spotlight was a significant new feature in Mac OS X 10.4 that revolutionized the way users searched for files on their Macs. Spotlight enables you to perform nearly instantaneous searches that go wider and deeper than previous desktop search technology. Spotlight has the ability to go beyond simple file system searches and actually search for relevant metadata inside application documents and databases. For example, an application like Address Book stores contact information in a database that appears opaque to the file system. Nevertheless, Spotlight can return search results from inside the Address Book database along with results from dozens of other databases and the entire file system hierarchy nearly instantly.

Though Spotlight was pretty amazing when it debuted in Mac OS X 10.4, Apple has added a few new tricks to Spotlight in Mac OS X 10.5. Spotlight is now able to search through the contents of other Mac clients and servers shared over the network. The new QuickLook feature has improved your ability to quickly view the content of Spotlight's search results. Finally, you are now able to use advance search operations while performing Spotlight searches from the Finder or menu bar.

Mac OS X 10.5's advanced Spotlight search operations include:

▶ The use of Boolean logic by using AND, OR, or NOT

▶ The use of exact phrases and dates by using quotation marks

▶ The use of search ranges by using greater-than and less-than symbols

Spotlight Indexes

Spotlight is able to perform wide and deep searches quickly because it works in the background to maintain highly optimized databases of indexed metadata for each volume. When you first set up Mac OS X, it will create these databases by indexing all the available volumes. Mac OS X will also index new volumes when they are first attached. A background process called the Metadata Server will update the index databases on the fly as changes are made throughout the file system. Because these indexes are kept current, the Spotlight process need only search through the databases to return thorough results. Essentially, Spotlight preemptively searches everything for you in the background so you don't have to wait for the results when you need them.

> **NOTE** ▶ Spotlight does not create index database on read-only volumes or write-once media such as optical discs.

You can find the Spotlight general index databases at the root level of every volume in a folder named .Spotlight-V100. A few applications maintain their own databases separate from these general index databases. One example is the built-in email application Mail. It maintains its own optimized email database in each user's folder at ~/Library/Mail/Envelope.index. Also, the Spotlight index database for a FileVault user is stored at the root level inside his encrypted home folder for greater security. If you are experiencing problems with Spotlight, you can force it to rebuild the index databases by deleting them and restarting your Mac.

> **NOTE** ▶ You must restart the Mac to have Spotlight rebuild missing index databases.

Spotlight Plug-ins

Spotlight is able to create indexes, and thus search, from an ever-growing variety of metadata using a plug-in technology. Each Spotlight plug-in is designed to examine a specific type of file or database. Many Spotlight plug-ins are included by default, but Apple and third-party developers can create additional plug-ins to expand Spotlight's search capabilities.

Included Spotlight plug-ins enable you to:

▶ Search via basic file metadata, including name, file size, creation date, and modification date

▶ Search via media specific metadata from picture, music, and video files, including time code, creator information, and hardware capture information

▶ Search through the contents of a variety of document types, including text documents, PDF documents, iWork documents, and Microsoft Office documents

▶ Search through personal information like the Address Book contacts and iCal calendar events

▶ Search for correspondence information like the contents of Mail emails and iChat chat transcripts

▶ Search for highly relevant information like your favorites or web browser bookmarks and history

Spotlight plug-ins, like any other system resource, are stored inside the various Library folders. Apple's built-in Spotlight plug-ins are always found in the /System/Library/Spotlight folder. Third-party plug-ins can be installed in either the /Library/Spotlight or the ~/Library/Spotlight folder, depending on who needs access to it.

> **TIP** You can create custom metadata for Spotlight by entering Spotlight comments in the Get Info and Inspector windows from the Finder.

Using Spotlight

You can initiate a Spotlight search any time by clicking the Spotlight icon on the far right of the menu bar or using the Command-Space bar keyboard combination. The Spotlight search is so fast that the results will actually change in real time as you type in your search query. Selecting an item from the results will open it immediately.

Selecting Show All from the Spotlight search results menu will open a new Finder window with the results. You could have also arrived at this same window by opening a new Finder window and entering your search in the Spotlight field from the Finder's toolbar. Selecting an item from the search results will show you the path to the selected item at the bottom of the Finder window. Selecting an item and then tapping the Space bar will open a QuickView of the selected item.

You can refine your Spotlight search from the Finder window by clicking the small plus buttons on the right below the search field. This will allow you to choose as many specific search criteria settings as you need. Clicking the Save button on the right will save these search criteria as a Smart Folder. Smart Folders are like normal folders in that they can be given a unique name and placed anywhere you like, but they are special because their contents will always match your search criteria no matter how the file system changes. In fact, the Search For items in the Finder's sidebar are simply predefined Smart Folders for Today, Yesterday, Past Week, All Images, All Movies, and All Documents.

MORE INFO ► You can create highly specialized Smart Folders using detailed search criteria by choosing "Other" from the search criteria pop-up menu. Search options include specifying audio file tags, digital camera metadata, authorship information, contact information, or any other metadata that is recognized by Spotlight plug-ins.

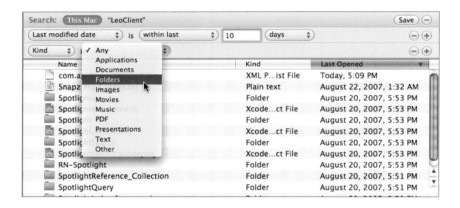

NOTE ► Smart Folders do not work from the command-line interface.

Spotlight Security and Privacy

In order to provide security on par with the rest of the file system, Spotlight also indexes every item's ownership and permissions. Even though Spotlight indexes every single item on a volume, it will automatically filter search results to only show items that the current user has permissions to access. There is still a security concern, though, when users search through locally attached nonsystem volumes because they can choose to ignore ownership on these volumes. In other words, all users can search through locally attached nonsystem volumes even if another user attached the drive.

From the Spotlight preference, any user can choose to disable specific categories from appearing in Spotlight searches. A user can also prevent volumes from being indexed by specifying those volumes in the privacy list. However, by default all new volumes are automatically indexed, so a user must manually configure Spotlight to ignore a volume. The Spotlight privacy list is a computer-level setting that remains the same across all user accounts, but it's not protected by administrative access, which means any user can change the privacy list. In this case, the Spotlight privacy list isn't any less secure than the rest of the file system, as any user can still have full access to locally connected nonsystem volumes by choosing to ignore ownership on those volumes.

To change Spotlight settings:

1   Open the Spotlight preferences by choosing Apple menu > System Preferences, and then click the Spotlight icon.

    The Spotlight preferences will open to the Search Results tab, allowing you to disable specific categories from the search results.

2   Simply deselect the checkboxes next to the categories you wish to ignore.

    You can also drag categories to change their order in the search results. Each user has her own separate Search Results settings.

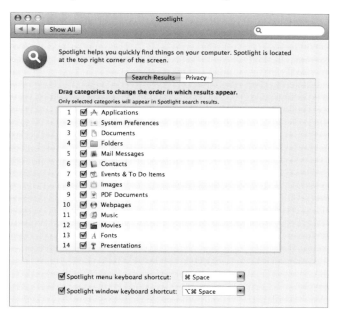

3   To prevent Spotlight from indexing specific items, click the Privacy tab, and then click the small plus icon at the bottom of the privacy list.

A file browser dialog will appear, allowing you to select any folder or volume.

4   Once you have located the item you want Spotlight to ignore, click the Choose button.

You can delete an item from the privacy list by selecting it and then clicking the minus icon at the bottom of the privacy list.

All Spotlight settings are applied immediately.

Document Binding

Document binding is the technical term for how the computer almost always knows the correct application to open when you double-click on a document. Mac OS X handles document binding with a background processes named Launch Services. When you double-click on a document from the Finder, it asks Launch Services to open the document with the appropriate application. Launch Services identifies the document based on its type and then references an application registration database to determine which application should open the document.

Document Identification

Apple pioneered document binding when it first introduced the Macintosh operating system. Apple designed the document identification system to use four-character file type and creator signature file attributes, which were normally hidden from the user. This was a brilliant design that separated the file's type and default application binding from the file's name.

Unfortunately, the popularity of other operating systems forced the awkward practice of adding a file type identifier to the end of a file's name, thus complicating the practice of naming files by requiring the user to identify and maintain the appropriate filename extension. You probably recognize many of these filename extensions, like .mp3 for compressed audio files, .jpg for compressed picture files, or .doc for Microsoft Word documents. Using filename extensions has become standard practice, so modern operating systems have been designed to work around this poor design choice by simply hiding the filename extension from the user.

For the sake of compatibility, Apple adopted this later method of file type identification as the default for Mac OS X. Nevertheless, Mac OS X still supports the legacy file type and creator signature file attributes. Both styles of file type identifiers are recognized by Launch Services when a user attempts to open a document.

Again, to keep things simple for users and to prevent them from messing things up, the Finder hides all file type extensions by default. You can toggle file type extension visibility from the Finder's preferences by choosing Finder > Preferences from the menu bar. Then click the Advanced button and select or deselect the checkbox next to "Show all file extensions."

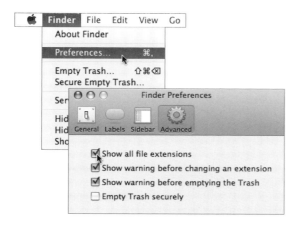

NOTE ▶ Choosing to show all file extensions in the Finder will override the individual file attribute for hiding the extension as configured from the Get Info and Inspector windows in the Finder.

Application Registration

When a user attempts to open a document, Launch Services reads from a database of applications and the types of files each can open to determine a match. After every reboot or login, a background process automatically scans for new applications and updates this database. Further, both the Finder and Installer keep track of new applications as they arrive on your system and add their supported file types to the database. If you attempt to open a document type that is not stored in the Launch Services database, the computer will prompt you to find an application that supports the document. The application registration system is pretty good at finding matches, so odds are if you're prompted to find a match, you don't have the correct application for the document.

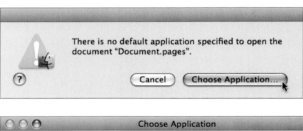

The Launch Services databases are stored in the /Library/Caches folder. There is a separate database for every user who has logged on to the computer that holds an attribute for each trusted application. When a user opens a new application for the first time, the computer asks him if he trusts this new application; if the user clicks the OK button, the trusted attribute is set for that application. Finally, each user can define his own document bindings that will override the default Launch Services bindings. These custom bindings are saved to a LaunchServices.plist preference file in each user's ~/Library/Preferences folder.

To change document binding in the Finder:

1   In the Finder, select the document or documents you wish to change the bindings for, and then open the Get Info or Inspector window.

2   To open the Get Info window, do one of the following (performing the same tasks while holding the Option key will open an Inspector window):

   ▶   Choose File > Get Info from the menu bar.

   ▶   Use the Command-I keyboard combination.

   ▶   Choose Get Info from the Action pop-up menu in a Finder window toolbar.

   ▶   Choose Get Info from the Finder's shortcut menu by right-clicking or Control-clicking on an item.

3   Once you have opened a Get Info window, click the "Open with" disclosure triangle to reveal the default document bindings.

4   To change just the selected documents' bindings, select another application from the pop-up menu.

5   To change the document binding for all documents of this type, click the Change All button.

   NOTE ▶ If you do not click the Change All button, the binding settings will only be saved to the selected documents. These settings will, however, stay with the selected document until changed again.

6   All document binding changes take place immediately.

 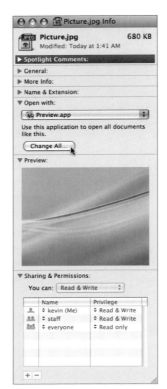

TIP ▶ You can also modify document bindings in the Finder by right-clicking or Control-clicking the selected documents and then choosing Open With from the shortcut menu. Holding down the Option key will change the menu command to Always Open With.

File Examination Commands

There are a variety of basic commands for locating and examining files and folders from the CLI, including cat, less, which, file, and find. As always, you can find out more detailed information about each one of these commands by reading their manual entry.

cat. Short for "concatenate," this command will read a file sequentially to the standard output, often the Terminal window. The syntax is cat followed by the path to the item you wish to view. The cat command can also be used to append text files using the >> operand. In the following example, Michelle uses the cat command to view the content of two text files in her Desktop folder, TextDocOne.txt and TextDocTwo.txt. Then she uses the cat command with the >> operand to append the second text file to the end of the first text file.

```
MyMac:~ michelle$ cat Desktop/TextDocOne.txt
This is the contents of the first plain text document.
MyMac:~ michelle$ cat Desktop/TextDocTwo.txt
This is the contents of the second plain text document.
MyMac:~ michelle$ cat Desktop/TextDocTwo.txt >> Desktop/TextDocOne.txt
MyMac:~ michelle$ cat Desktop/TextDocOne.txt
This is the contents of the first plain text document.
This is the contents of the second plain text document.
```

less. A play on words from the previously popular text-viewing command more, the less command is much better for viewing long text files, as it will let you interactively browse and search through the text. The syntax is less followed by the path to the item you wish to view. The less viewer command is actually the same interface used to view manual pages, so the navigation shortcuts are identical to what you find when you use the man command:

▶ Use the Up and Down Arrow keys to scroll through the text.

▶ Use the Space bar to move down one screen at a time.

▶ Search though the text by entering /, then a keyword.

▶ Exit the less viewer command by simply pressing the Q key.

> **NOTE ▶** In Mac OS X 10.5 attempting to run the more command will actually run the less command instead.

which. This command will locate the file path of a specified command. In other words, it will show you which file you're actually using when you enter a specific command. The syntax is which followed by the commands you wish to locate. In the following example, Michelle uses the which command to locate the file path of the man, ls, pwd, and cd commands:

```
MyMac:~ michelle$ which man ls pwd cd
/usr/bin/man
/bin/ls
/bin/pwd
/usr/bin/cd
```

file. This command will attempt to determine a file's type based on its content. This is a useful command for identifying files that do not have a filename extension. The syntax is file followed by the path to the file you're attempting to identify. In the following example, Michelle uses the file command to locate the file type of two documents in her Desktop folder, PictureDocument and TextDocument:

```
MyMac:~ michelle$ ls Desktop/
PictureDocument TextDocument
MyMac:~ michelle$ file Desktop/PictureDocument
Desktop/PictureDocument: TIFF image data, big-endian
MyMac:~ michelle$ file Desktop/TextDocument
Desktop/TextDocument: ASCII English text
```

find. This command is used to locate items in the file system based on search criteria. The find command does not use the Spotlight search service, but it does allow you to set very specific search criteria and use filename wildcards. (Filename wildcards are covered in the next section.) The syntax is find followed by the beginning path of the search, then an option defining your search criteria, and then the search criteria within quotation marks. In the following example, Michelle uses the find command to locate any picture files in her home folder by only searching for files with names ending in *.tiff*:

```
MyMac:~ michelle$ find /Users/michelle/ -name "*.tiff"
/Users/michelle//Desktop/PictureDocument.tiff
/Users/michelle//Pictures/FamilyPict.tiff
/Users/michelle//Pictures/MyPhoto.tiff
```

> **TIP** ▶ To use the Spotlight search service from the CLI, use the mdfind command. The syntax is simply mdfind followed by your search criteria.

Using Filename Wildcards

One of the most powerful features in the CLI is the ability to use filename wildcards to define path name and search criteria. Here are three of the most commonly used filename wildcards:

▶ Asterisk (*)—The asterisk wildcard is used to match any string of characters. For instance, entering * matches all files, while entering *.tiff matches all files ending in *.tiff*.

▶ Question mark (?)—The question mark wildcard is used to match any single character. For example, entering b?ok matches *book* but not *brook*.

▶ Square brackets ([ ])—Square brackets are used to define a range of characters to match in that specific space. For example, [Dd]ocument would locate any item named "Document" or "document," and doc[1-9] matches any file named "doc#" where # is any number between 1 and 9.

Combining filename wildcards can be used to great effect. Consider a collection of five files with the names ReadMe.rtf, ReadMe.txt, read.rtf, read.txt, and It's All About Me.rtf. Using wildcards among these files:

▶ *.rtf* matches ReadMe.rtf, read.rtf, and It's All About Me.rtf

▶ *????.** matches read.rtf and read.txt

▶ *[Rr]*.rtf* matches ReadMe.rtf and read.rtf

▶ *[A-Z]** matches ReadMe.rtf, ReadMe.txt, and It's All About Me.rtf

Archiving and Backup

Archiving and backup are both synonymous with copying data to another location for safekeeping, yet in the context of this lesson and Mac OS X, they are different processes serving different purposes. In Mac OS X, archiving is typically a manual process that involves creating compressed copies of selected data. Archive formats are efficient from a storage and data transfer perspective, but they add a layer of complexity that requires user interaction. On the other hand, the backup service introduced with Mac OS X 10.5, Time Machine, is an automated process that allows users to easily browse the backup history of their entire file system. As you can imagine, maintaining a history of your file system is not space efficient, but it is extremely useful.

Archiving Data

At its essence, archiving is the practice of saving copies of important information to another location or format better suited for long-term storage or network transfer. Large amounts of hard disk drive storage has become much less expensive in the last few years, but it's still not as reliable as tape or optical media in terms of longevity. This type of archival media has not kept up with the tremendous growth of hard drives, so storing archival data in a more efficient form by compressing it is still relevant. Also, no matter how robust your

Internet connection is, there never seems to be enough bandwidth, so compressing items in preparation for data transfer is almost always a time-saver. Mac OS X includes two archival technologies that allow you to combine multiple files and compress the data into a more efficient file suited for long-term storage or network data transfer.

First, the Mac's Finder will allow you to create zip archives from a selection of files or folders. This is an efficient method for archiving relatively small amounts of data quickly. The zip archive format is also widely compatible, as many operating systems include software to decompress zip archives back to their original items. However, zip archives on Mac OS X do not offer the flexibility provided by disk images.

Disk images, created using Disk Utility, are more widely used in Mac OS X for archival purposes because they offer many features not available from zip archives. Primarily, disk images allow you to archive the contents of an entire file system into a single file that can be compressed or encrypted. The only downside to disk images created using Disk Utility is that, by default, only Macs can access the content—other systems require third-party software to access Mac disk image content.

Using Zip Archives

Expanding a zip archive in the Finder is as simple as double-clicking on the zip archive file. The Finder will decompress the archive file and place the resulting files and folders in the same folder as the original zip archive. The Finder will not delete the original zip archive. Mac OS X's Finder also allows you to quickly create a compressed zip archive from any number of selected items. Likewise, creating a zip archive in the Finder will not delete the original documents you've selected to compress.

To create a zip archive in the Finder:

1   Select the items you wish to archive and compress in the Finder.

    You can hold down the Shift key to quickly select contiguous lists of items, or hold down the Command key to quickly select noncontiguous items. It's best to put all of the items in one folder and then compress that, as opposed to selecting multiple items.

2   Choose File > Compress "Items" from the menu bar.

The word "Items" in the menu will be replaced by the name of a single item you have selected or the number of items you have selected.

If the archival process is going to take more than a few seconds, the Finder will show a progress dialog with the estimated time required to complete the erase task. You can also choose to cancel the archive by clicking the small X button on the far right.

3   When the archival process has completed, you will be left with a zip archive named either Archive.zip or *Item*.zip, where *Item* is the name of the single item you chose to archive and compress.

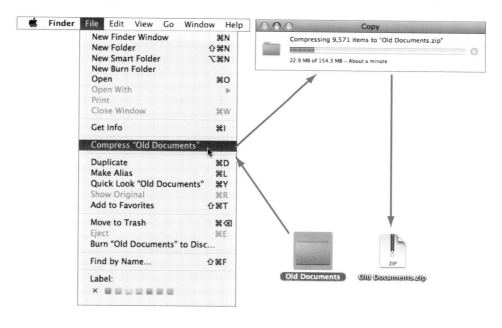

TIP You can also archive and compress items in the Finder by right-clicking or Control-clicking the selected documents and then choosing Compress "Items" from the shortcut menu.

Once the archive process is complete, it's always interesting to compare the original items' size with the archive's size using the Get Info or Inspector windows in the Finder. In many cases you can expect a 50 percent decrease in file size. On the other hand, many media formats are already quite compressed in their original form, so you may not experience very good results when compressing these types of files.

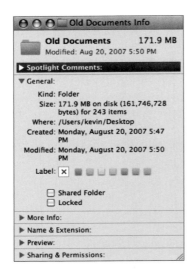 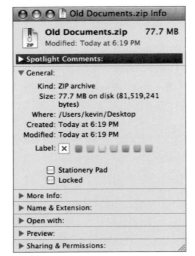

Using Disk Images

Disk images are files that contain entire virtual drives and volumes. Mac OS X relies on disk images for several core technologies, including software distribution, system imaging, NetBoot, and FileVault. Disk images are also useful as a personal archive tool. Though Mac-created disk images only work on Mac computers by default, they are much more flexible to use than zip archives. Disk images provide advanced compression and encryption, but their greatest benefit is that they can be treated like a removable volume.

To access the contents of a disk image, you simply double-click on the disk image file in the Finder. This will mount the volume inside the disk image file as if you had just connected a normal storage device. Even if the disk image file is located on a remote file server, you can still mount it as if it was a local drive. You can treat the mounted disk image volume as you would any other storage device by navigating through its hierarchy and selecting files and folders as you need them. Further, if the disk image is read/write you can add to the contents of the disk image by simply dragging items to the volume.

NOTE ▶ When you are done with a disk image volume, be sure to properly unmount and eject it as you would any other removable volume.

Using /Applications/Utilities/Disk Utility to make disk images allows you to create blank images or images containing copies of selected folders or even entire file systems. Mac OS X supports disk images up to at least 2 terabytes. Disk images also feature a number of configuration options, including:

▶ Image format—Disk images can be read-only or read/write. They can also be a set size or expandable as a sparse disk image. Sparse disk images will only take up as much space as necessary and automatically grow as you add items to them.

▶ Compression—Read-only disk images can be compressed to save space. With a compressed disk image, any free space becomes negligible in size, and most other files average a 50 percent reduction in size.

▶ Encryption—Any disk image can be protected with a password and encrypted with strong 128-bit or 256-bit AES encryption. Choosing a higher bit rate is more secure but degrades performance. This feature is useful for securing data stored on otherwise unsecure volumes like removable drives and network shares. The encryption always happens on the local computer, so even if the disk image file is physically stored externally, as on a network file share, the data is always encrypted as it travels across the connection.

▶ File system—Disk images can contain any partition scheme or volume format that Mac OS X supports, including support for optical media formats. You learned about differences between file system options in Lesson 3, "File Systems."

Creating New Disk Images

To create an automatically resizing blank disk image:

1 Open /Applications/Utilities/Disk Utility, and then choose File > New > Blank Disk Image from the menu bar.

2   Enter a name for the disk image file, and then select a destination for the disk image file from the Where pop-up menu. Also, enter a name for the volume inside the disk image.

The disk image file and volume names do not have to match, but should be similar so that you can recognize their relationship.

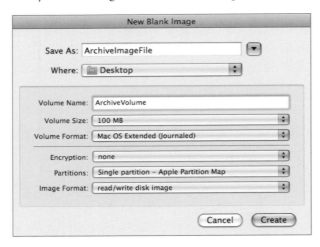

3   Select a volume size from the pop-up menu.

Remember this disk image will only occupy as much space as the files you copy inside it. Obviously if this disk image is going to be saved on an external volume of limited size, that should define your maximum size.

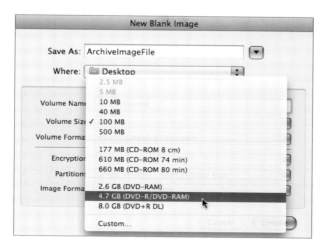

4 You can select a different volume format or partition scheme from the pop-up menus, but in most cases you will want to stick with the default Mac OS Extended (Journaled) and Apple Partition Map selections.

5 You can also select an encryption at this point from the pop-up menu. For most uses, 128-bit AES is secure enough and still provides good performance.

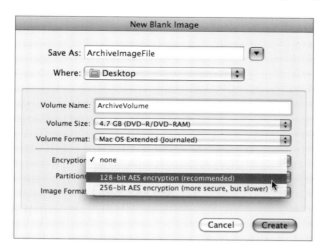

6   Choose "sparse disk image" from the Image Format pop-up menu to create an automatically resizable disk image.

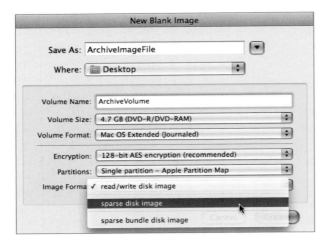

7   Click the Create button to create the disk image.

8   If you have selected an encrypted disk image you will be prompted to enter a password for the disk image. After you have selected a secure password, click the OK button to finish the disk image creation process.

After the system has created the new blank disk image, it will automatically mount it. From the Finder, you can open Get Info windows on both the disk image file and the disk image volume to verify that the volume size is much larger than the image size. As you copy files to the volume, the disk image file will grow accordingly.

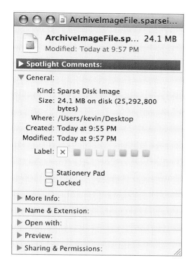 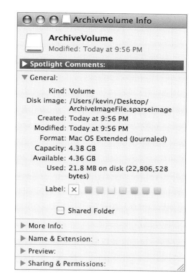

TIP You can change the format of a disk image at any time in Disk Utility by choosing Images > Convert from the menu bar. This will open a dialog allowing you to select the image you want to change and save a copy of the image with new options.

To create a disk image from selected items:

1   Open /Applications/Utilities/Disk Utility.

2   At this point you can choose to create a new disk image from the contents of a folder or the contents of a volume:

   To create a disk image from the contents of a folder, choose File > New > Disk Image From Folder from the menu bar, and then select the folder you wish to copy into a new disk image from the file browser window. Once you have made your selection, click the Image button to continue.

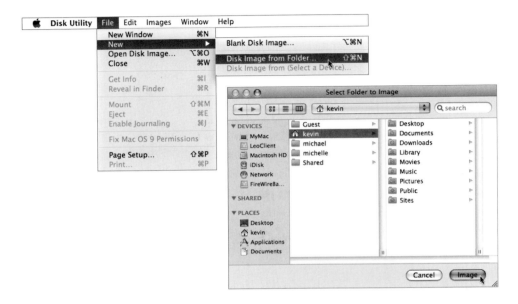

To create a disk image from the contents of a volume, select the volume you wish to copy into a new disk image from the Disk image column on the left, and then choose File > New > Disk Image from disk (volumename) where volumename is the name of the selected volume.

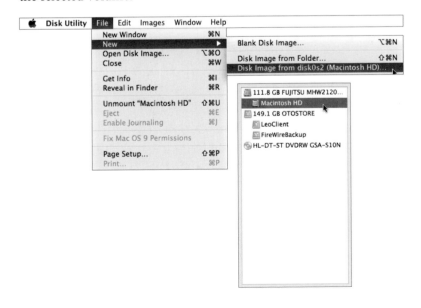

3   Enter a name for the disk image file, and then choose a destination for the disk image file from the Where pop-up menu.

Again, the disk image file and volume names do not have to match, but should be similar so that you can recognize their relationship.

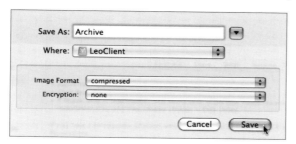

4   Choose an image format from the pop-up menu. Remember, compressed images are also read-only.

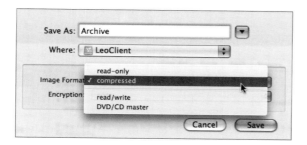

5   You can also choose an encryption at this point from the pop-up menu.

For most uses, 128-bit AES is secure enough and still provides good performance.

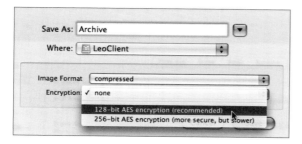

6   Click the Save button to create the disk image.

If you have selected an encrypted disk image, you will be prompted to enter a password for the disk image. After you have selected a secure password, click the OK button to start the disk image creation process.

Depending on the amount of data that has to be copied and the image format you chose, it can take anywhere from minutes to hours for the disk image copy process to complete. Disk Utility will open a small progress dialog that will also allow you to cancel the disk image copy by clicking the Cancel button.

NOTE ▶ It takes nearly twice as much free space to create a compressed disk image—the system must create a noncompressed image first and then convert the first image to a compressed image.

Time Machine Backup

There are several mature and relatively easy-to-use backup solutions for the Mac, so you may be wondering why Apple chose to invent a new backup architecture for Mac OS X 10.5.

The folks at Apple did a little research and discovered that only 4 percent of Mac users back up their data on a regular basis. That is an unacceptable number, so Apple decided that the only way to convince users to do so on a regular basis was to create a new backup process that's as easy as possible and also surprisingly fun to use. Apple's solution is Time Machine.

Aside from being built into the operating system, Time Machine has two features that make it fundamentally different than any other solution currently out there. First, configuring Time Machine is so easy it's nearly automatic. The system practically begs you to set up Time Machine if you haven't already, and with as little as one click the system is configured. The second, more significant feature is that Time Machine is so tightly integrated with the operating system that users don't even have to exit the application they are currently using to recover data. Applications, both built-in and third party, can tie directly into the Time Machine backup system. From applications supporting Time Machine, a user can activate the visually striking Time Machine interface and travel back through time to see the application's data as it was in the past. If an application doesn't yet support Time Machine, you can use the Finder while in Time Machine's interface to browse the entire file system through time.

Time Machine Backup Archives

Time Machine can save backup archives to any locally connected Mac OS X Extended volume that is not the startup volume. You are allowed to select a backup destination volume that resides as another partition on the system disk drive, but this is an incredibly bad idea—if the system drive dies, so does your backup. If you don't have a local volume suited for backup, you can also select a shared network volume as your backup destination. Time Machine supports network shares by creating a disk image on the share to store the backups. Time Machine currently only supports backing up to Apple Filing Protocol (AFP) network shares hosted from Mac OS X or Mac OS X Server.

Logistically, Time Machine uses a sophisticated background process to automatically create new backups of the entire file system every hour. Obviously, Time Machine employs some tricks to keep these backups as small as possible so that you can maintain a deep history. The initial Time Machine backup will copy almost the entire contents of your file system to the specified backup volume. Between backups, a background process, similar to the one used by the Spotlight search service, will automatically track any changes to the file system. When the next scheduled backup occurs, only the items that have changed will be copied to the backup volume. Time Machine will then combine this new content with hard link file system pointers (which occupy nearly zero disk space) to the previous backup content, and create a simulated view of the entire file system at that point in time.

> **NOTE ▶** Do not confuse Time Machine with snapshot technology common on other operating systems. While snapshots do create multiple instances of a file system through time, they do not provide you with a backup, as they don't actually copy data to another storage device. In other words, if a drive containing file system snapshots dies, those snapshots are just as lost as the current data on the dead drive.

Time Machine also saves space by ignoring files that do not need to be backed up, as they can be re-created after a restoration. Specifically, Time Machine ignores the /tmp, ~/Library/Caches, and /Library/Caches folders. Software developers can also tell Time Machine to ignore specific application data that does not need to be backed up.

Eventually, so as not to waste space on your backup volume with historical data that has outlived its usefulness, Time Machine will start "aging out" backups. Time Machine will only keep hourly backups for a day, daily backups for a week, and weekly backups until your backup volume is full. After your backup volume is full, Time Machine will start deleting the oldest items first. However, Time Machine will always keep at least one copy of every item that is still also on your current file system.

NOTE ▶ If the backup volume isn't available when a backup is scheduled to execute, Time Machine will continue to keep track of all the changes to the file system and save them to the backup volume once it becomes available again.

Configuring Time Machine

Despite the rather complex process going on behind the scenes to make Time Machine possible, configuration couldn't be easier. In fact, Time Machine is enabled by default and simply waiting for you to pick a backup destination. If you haven't configured a Time Machine backup destination, the system will automatically scan the network for a Time Machine network share or wait for you to attach an external drive. If the system locates either, you will be prompted to select it as your backup destination. If you select your backup destination with this method, after you click the Use as Backup Disk button Time Machine is fully configured. It's just that easy.

On the other hand, you can choose to manually configure Time Machine:

1   Open the Time Machine preferences by choosing Apple menu > System Preferences, and then click the Time Machine icon.

2   Enable Time Machine by sliding the switch to the On position, and then click the Choose Backup Disk button.

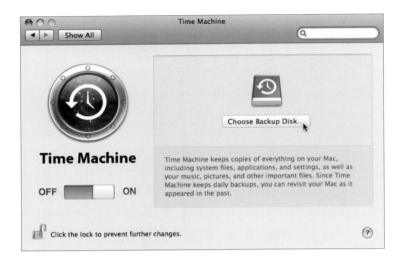

This will reveal a dialog allowing you to select a backup destination. Once you have selected an appropriate volume, click the Use for Backup button.

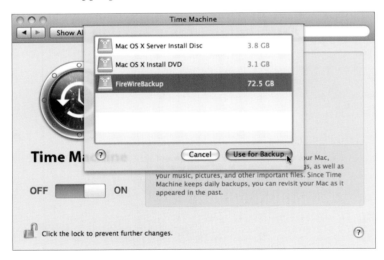

At this point Time Machine will wait two minutes, allowing you to make further configuration changes, before it starts the first backup.

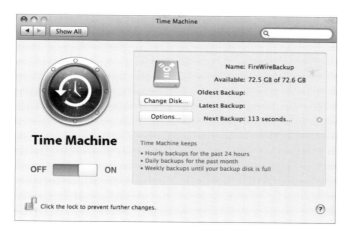

3   Click the Options button to reveal a dialog allowing you to create a list of folders or volumes to exclude from the backup.

You can drag and drop items into the list field, or you can click the small plus button at the bottom of the list to reveal a file browser, allowing you to select specific folders or volumes to exclude.

4   Click the Save button when you are done making changes.

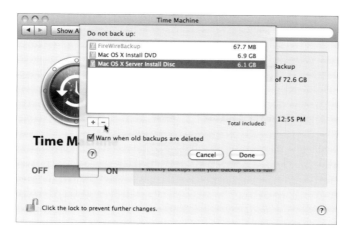

The two-minute timer will reset every time you make a Time Machine configuration change. Once you are done, simply wait two minutes and the initial Time Machine backup will commence.

Depending on the amount of data that has to be backed up, it can take from minutes to hours for the initial backup to complete. Time Machine will open a small progress dialog that will also allow you to cancel the backup by clicking the small "X" button to the right of the progress bar. The Time Machine preferences pane has a similar progress bar.

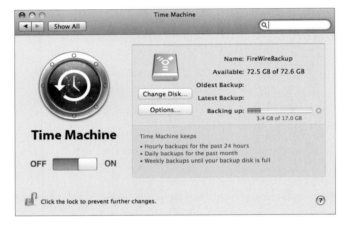

Subsequent backups will occur automatically in the background. Revisiting the Time Machine preferences will show you the time and date of the oldest, last, and next backup.

Restore from Time Machine

Using Time Machine to restore data is what many will consider the best part because of the dynamic interface Apple has created to look through time. Clicking the Time Machine icon in the Dock will bring up the Time Machine history browser. Few applications currently support the Time Machine interface, so in most cases you will be presented with a historical view in the Finder. The Finder windows will let you browse as normal with one significant addition. You can use the navigation arrows on the bottom right, or the navigation timeline on the right side, to view Finder contents as they change through time. To aide in your search through time, the Spotlight search field remains active, and you can quickly preview any item using the Finder's new QuickLook feature. Once you have found the item you were looking for, simply click the Restore button at the bottom-right corner and the Finder will return to normal with your recovered file intact where it once was.

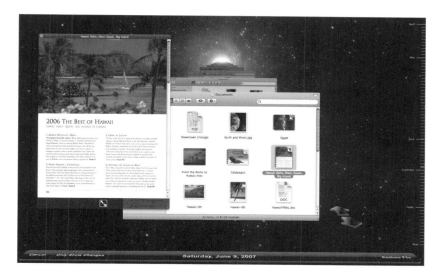

TIP ▶ Right-click or Control-click the Time Machine icon in the Dock to reveal a shortcut menu allowing you to adjust Time Machine preferences, start a backup immediately, or browse another Time Machine backup.

You can also restore a complete user home folder or other nonsystem data from a Time Machine archive using the Migration Assistant. First, make sure the Time Machine backup volume is available to the destination Mac. The Migration Assistant will automatically open as part of the initial setup on new Mac systems, but you can also open it on a currently running Mac system by opening /Applications/Utilities/Migration Assistant. When the Migration Assistant opens, simply choose to restore from a Time Machine backup. The rest of the Migration Assistant process is identical to the standard migration process covered earlier in Lesson 1, "Installation and Initial Setup."

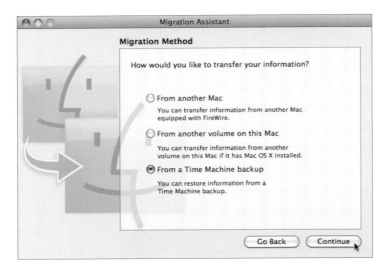

Finally, you can restore an entire system volume when booted from the Mac OS X Install DVD. Once the installer has started the Mac, choose Utilities > Restore System From Backup from the menu bar. This will open the Time Machine system restore assistant. The assistant will first scan for local and network Time Machine backup volumes. Once you have selected the Time Machine volume, you can restore the entire system from any backup instance on that volume to your new system drive. Accessing utilities from the Mac OS X Install DVD is covered in Lesson 1, "Installation and Initial Setup."

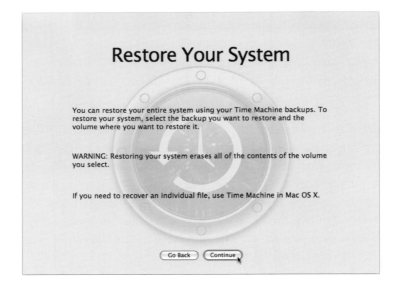

Troubleshooting Time Machine

Though Time Machine is revolutionary, it is not without flaws. Time Machine's backup architecture does not lend itself well to large files that change often. For example, many database documents appear as large, single files to the file system. While the database application may be able to change just a few bytes of the large file as a user edits the database, Time Machine will not recognize this and it will have to create another copy of the entire database file during the next backup. This will obviously fill your backup volume much quicker than if the database had been stored as many smaller files.

This leads to the next Time Machine issue: running out of backup space. Once Time Machine fills up the backup volume, it will begin deleting older items to make room for newer ones. Therefore, the depth of your backup history will vary based not only on the size of your backup volume, but also on how often you change your files and how Time Machine recognizes those changes. Because you cannot change how Time Machine chooses to delete older items, you may discover that items you thought would still be on the backup volume have already been deleted.

If you are experiencing problems using one of the Time Machine restoration interfaces, you can always browse the backup archive from the Finder. Time Machine's archive technology uses file system features that are part of standard Mac OS X Extended volumes, so no special software is needed to browse through archive contents. Time Machine archives are located on the root of your backup volume in a folder named Backups.backupdb. Once inside the backup database folder, you will see folders with the names of each computer that is backed up to that volume. Inside each computer folder you will see folders named with a date and time indicating each backup. Finally, inside each dated folder you will see folders representing each volume that was backed up.

NOTE ▶ You should not directly modify the contents of a Time Machine backup archive, as doing so could damage the archive hierarchy. The default file system permissions will not give you write access to these items.

What You've Learned

▶   Mac OS X's file system is laid out to enhance ease of use and administration.

▶   System resources are stored in various Library folders throughout the system, and these folders provide different levels of access.

▶   Font Book is the primary tool for managing font resources.

▶   Mac OS X uses extensive metadata to provide robust file system searches with Spotlight.

▶   Time Machine backup, along with other archival tools like disk images, provides ample means to secure your data from human or hardware failure.

References

You can check for new and updated Knowledge Base documents at http://www.apple.com/support.

Font Management

106417, "Mac OS X: Font locations and their purposes"

25251, "Mac OS X: Font file formats"

Spotlight

301533, "Mac OS X 10.4: Where does Spotlight search?"

301562, "Spotlight: How to re-index folders or volumes"

Review Quiz

1.   What are the four default top-level folders visible in the Finder?

2.   What are the four system resource domains? What purpose does each domain serve?

3.   What are six common system resources? What purpose does each resource serve? Where are they located in the file hierarchy?

4.   Why does the Finder hide certain folders at the root of the system volume?

5.   What are resource forks and why have they fallen out of favor?

6. What are some of the common additional file attributes used by Mac OS X?

7. What does Mac OS X use packages or bundles for?

8. How does the Spotlight search service use metadata?

9. What are some privacy and security concerns with the Spotlight service?

10. Where does Spotlight store its metadata index databases? How about the Spotlight plug-ins?

11. How does the system identify which application to open when a user double-clicks on a document?

12. What are five common UNIX commands for locating and examining files? What function does each command perform?

13. What three common UNIX commands support resource forks?

14. What are the differences between zip archives and disk images?

15. How does Time Machine maintain a backup history of the file system?

16. What types of files are omitted from Time Machine backups?

17. Why is Time Machine inefficient at backing up large databases?

18. What backup destinations does Time Machine support?

19. Why might a previously backed-up item be no longer available in Time Machine?

Answers

1. The four default top-level folders visible in the Finder are: Applications, containing applications all local users have access to; Library, containing system resources all local users have access to; System, containing necessary system resources; and finally, Users, containing all the local user home folders.

2. The four system resource domains are: User, containing applications and system resources specific to each user account; Local, containing applications and system resources available to all users on the local Mac; Network (optional), containing applications and system resources available to any Mac that has an automated network share; and finally, System, containing applications and system resources required to provide basic system functionality.

3. Six common system resources are: extensions, which attach themselves to the system kernel to provide hardware and peripheral driver support; frameworks, which are shared code libraries that provide additional software resources for both applications

and system processes; fonts; preferences files, which contain application and system configuration information; LaunchAgents and LaunchDaemons, used by launchd to provide services that automatically start when they are needed or at system startup; and finally, logs, which are text files that contain error and progress entries from nearly any application or system service.

4. The Finder hides traditional UNIX resources from average users because they don't need to have access to those items. If users do need access to these UNIX items, they can access them from the Terminal.

5. Resource forks are used to make the file system appear less complex. Data forks and resource forks are combined to appear as one single item in the file system. They have fallen out of favor because they are not directly compatible with non-Mac OS volumes.

6. Common additional file attributes are: the alias bit, which defines a file as a Mac-specific file system pointer; the bundle bit, which defines a folder that will appear as a single icon in the Finder; the hide extension bit, which hides the item's filename extension in the Finder; the locked item bit, which ensures that only the owner can edit the item; the invisible bit, which prevents the item from appearing in the Finder at all; and finally, the busy bit defines the item as busy.

7. Packages and bundles are used to combine complex items into what appear as a single item in the Finder. This allows software developers to combine resources into a single item and prevents users from messing with those resources.

8. The Spotlight search service creates index databases of file system metadata so that it can perform normally time-intensive searches nearly instantly.

9. Though Spotlight indexes file and folder permissions, it will allow other users to search the contents of locally attached nonsystem volumes when ownership is ignored on those volumes.

10. Spotlight metadata index databases are stored at the root of every volume in a /.Spotlight-V100 folder. However, a FileVault user's database is stored in his encrypted home folder. Also, the Mail application maintains its own database in each user's home folder at ~/Library/Mail/Enveloper.index. Spotlight plug-ins can be located in any Library in a folder named Spotlight.

11. Documents are identified either by their file type attributes or their filename extension. Launch Services maintains a database of known applications and which file types they can open. When you double-click on a document in the Finder, Launch

Services tries to find an appropriate match. You can override the default application selection in the Finder.

12. Five common UNIX commands for locating and examining files are: the cat command, which reads a text file to the standard output; the less command, a more sophisticated text reader for searching and navigating and search through text files; the which command, which reveals the path used when a command is called; the file command, which attempts to determine a document's type by examining its contents; and finally, the find command, which can be used to locate an item in the file system based on search wildcards.

13. Three common UNIX commands that have been updated to support resource forks are cp, mv, and rm.

14. Zip archives are created with the Finder from a specific selection of items. Zip archives are compatible with many operating systems. On the other hand, disk images are created using Disk Utility and allow you to create highly flexible archive volumes that can contain nearly anything.

15. Time Machine starts with a full copy of the file system; then it records any changes to the file system and only copies the changes. It creates a simulation of the full file system using hard links for files that have not changed.

16. Time Machine always ignores the /tmp, ~/Library/Caches, and /Library/Caches folders. Time Machine will also ignore any files an application has defined as exempt, or any files you have defined as exempt in the Time Machine preference.

17. Time Machine is inefficient at backing up large databases because it must back up the entire database file every time any change, no matter how small, is made to the database.

18. Time Machine can back up to any Mac OS X Extended volume, including volumes from disk images stored on an AFP share from a Mac OS X or Mac OS X Server.

19. A previously backed-up item will not be available if your backup volume has become full and Time Machine has had to start deleting older items to make room for newer items.

5

Time   This lesson takes approximately 4 hours to complete.

Goals   Understand and support the various application types

Monitor and control processes and applications

Locate and manage application preferences

Configure and administer Boot Camp for Windows compatibility

Lesson 5
Applications and Boot Camp

People acquire computers because they want to run certain applications, not operating systems. Most users don't care about the technologies underneath as long as the applications they want run smoothly. This is why, despite Mac OS X's superiority in many ways to other operating systems, non-Mac users are apprehensive about switching. It cannot be ignored that there are many applications that run only on Windows-based computers.

Yet, there are many Mac-only applications that tempt non-Mac users because they represent the best solutions available. For several years now, Apple has held a strong lead on advanced media creation applications with the iLife and Pro production suites. Third-party developers have stepped up their game in the last few years as well, as Mac OS X provides a robust development platform with many unique features. For hundreds of examples, you need look no further than the Apple Products Guide, http://guide.apple.com/.

Ultimately, with Apple's move to Intel processors for Mac hardware, users can finally have one computer that runs Mac OS X, UNIX, and Windows applications. This means that modern Intel-based Macs have the unique ability to run nearly every application available today.

In this lesson you will explore the application environments available to Mac OS X, and you will learn how to monitor and control applications and processes. You will also learn proper application configuration and troubleshooting techniques. Finally, this lesson will walk you through the configuration of Apple's Boot Camp technology, which facilitates running Windows on Mac hardware.

Applications and Processes

A process is any instance of executable code that is currently activated and addressed in system memory. Mac OS X handles processes very efficiently, so although an idle process will likely consume zero processor resources, it's still considered an active process because it has dedicated address space in system memory. The three general process types are applications, commands, and daemons.

Applications are a specific category of process that is generally identified as something the user opened in the graphical interface. Commands are also normally opened by the user, but they exist only in the command-line interface (CLI). Both applications and commands can be opened automatically, but they are still considered part of the user's space because they are executed with the same access privileges as the user.

Processes that run on behalf of the system fall into the final category, daemons, which are also called background processes because they rarely have any user interface. Daemons usually launch during system startup and stay on the entire time the Mac is up and running. These background daemons are responsible for most of the automatic Mac OS X system features like the software update checker and the Spotlight search metadata indexer.

Mac OS X is a desirable platform for running applications and other processes because it combines a rock-solid UNIX foundation with an advanced graphical user interface (GUI). Users will most likely recognize the GUI elements right away, but it's the underlying foundation that keeps things running so smoothly. Specifically, a few fundamental features of Mac OS X are responsible for providing a high level of performance and reliability:

▶   Preemptive multitasking—This gives Mac OS X the ability to balance computing resources without letting any single process take over. This allows the system to maintain dozens of background processes without significantly slowing down user applications.

▶ Symmetric multiprocessing—Whenever possible the system will use all available computing resources to provide the best performance. This is a key feature since every currently shipping Mac includes at least two processor cores.

▶ Simultaneous 32-bit and 64-bit support—Mac OS X is one of the few operating systems that supports both 32-bit and 64-bit modes simultaneously. Mac OS X 10.5 improves 64-bit support by allowing both command-line and graphical interface applications to access 64-bit resources. A 64 bit–capable process has the ability to access more than 4 GB of system memory, and can perform higher-precision computational functions much faster. Only Macs featuring 64 bit–capable processors can take advantage of 64-bit system features. Currently, Macs with PowerPC G5, Intel Core2Duo, or Intel Xenon processors can take advantage of 64-bit support.

▶ Protected memory—Similar to how the file system prevents users from meddling with items they shouldn't, processes are also kept separate and secure in system memory. The system manages all memory allocation so processes are not allowed to interfere with each other's system memory space. In other words, an ill-behaved or crashed application will not affect any other process on the system.

▶ Dynamic memory allocation—The operating system will automatically manage system memory for processes at their request. Though real system memory is clearly limited by hardware, the system will dynamically allocate virtual memory when needed. Thus, the only memory limitation in Mac OS X is the amount of free space you have available on your system volume.

▶ Security architecture—At both the command line and graphical interface level, processes are not allowed to access resources unless they are authorized. Again, access restrictions at the file system are responsible for much of the security here. However, privilege escalation is allowed when needed. The most obvious example of this is the Installer application, which requires administrative authorization to install software that affects more than one user. The security architecture built into Mac OS X is one of the primary reasons Macs remain relatively free of malware.

▶ Signed applications—Mac OS X 10.5 introduces support for secure signed applications. Signed applications include a digital signature in the application's bundle, which is used by the system to verify the authenticity and integrity of the software code and resources. Applications are verified not only on disk but also as they are running. Therefore, even if some part of the application is inappropriately changed while it's active, the system can automatically kill the application. Application signing is also used by the Keychain, Parental Controls, and Managed Client settings to verify applications after they have been updated.

Application Environments

Mac OS X supports a wide range of application environments. Several of these environments are required solely to provide backward compatibility for legacy Mac applications, while others add support for popular UNIX-based tools. Most important, though, average users do not need to concern themselves as to which application environment their application is using—the system will provide the appropriate resources automatically. The five application environments in Mac OS X are Cocoa, Carbon, BSD, X11, and Java.

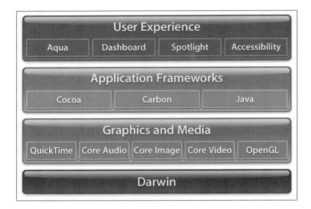

MORE INFO ► To learn more about Mac OS X system architecture and application environments, see Apple's development resources, http://developer.apple.com/macosx/architecture/index.html.

NOTE ► The Classic compatibility environment, which enables users to run software created for Mac OS 9, is no longer supported as of Mac OS X 10.5.

Cocoa

Cocoa is the application environment most specific to Mac OS X, as Cocoa-based applications run only on Mac OS X. Cocoa is based on the Objective-C object-oriented programming language. Often, developers must use the Cocoa environment if they want to take advantage of the latest Mac features. For this reason, most of the built-in system software and new third-party software is developed for the Cocoa environment.

MORE INFO ► To learn more about the Cocoa application environment, refer to Apple's own development resources, http://developer.apple.com/cocoa/.

Carbon

The Carbon application environment is a streamlined and updated version of the previous Mac OS 9 environment. Developers can update their legacy Mac applications, often with little work, to run natively in Mac OS X. In many cases, developers create Carbon applications that run natively in both Mac OS 9 and Mac OS X.

Carbon is based on the industry-standard C and C++ programming languages. On the surface, it's nearly impossible to identify any differences between Carbon and Cocoa applications. With every new version of Mac OS X, Apple has further blurred the lines between Cocoa and Carbon. In fact, many modern applications contain code that takes advantage of both environments.

> **MORE INFO** ▶ To learn more about Carbon, see Apple's development resources, http://developer.apple.com/carbon/.

BSD

Mac OS X's system foundation, named Darwin, is based on the open source Free Berkeley Software Distribution (FreeBSD) UNIX command-line interface (CLI). The CLI is most often accessed via the /Applications/Utilities/Terminal application. Various CLI utilities are covered throughout this guide, but a CLI introduction is part of Lesson 3, "File Systems."

> **MORE INFO** ▶ To learn more, visit Apple's UNIX resource website, http://www.apple.com/macosx/technology/unix.html

X11

X11 is a common GUI platform for UNIX workstations. Apple's implementation of X11 is based on the popular open source XFree86 project. The X11 environment is an optional system install, as outlined in Lesson 1, "Installation and Initial Setup." You can access X11 applications by simply double-clicking on their executable binary, or by opening the X11 interface located at /Applications/Utilities/X11.

> **MORE INFO** ▶ To learn more, visit Apple's X11 resource website, http://developer.apple.com/opensource/tools/X11.html

Java

Java is an application environment developed by Sun Microsystems with the goal to create non-platform-specific applications. This means a developer can create software code once and it can run on many different environments. Mac OS X includes the full Java 2, Standard Edition (J2SE) software. This implementation supports Java in three distinct methods: JavaScript, Java applets, and full Java applications.

Safari, the built-in Mac OS X web browser, is your primary interface for executing JavaScripts and Java applets. Many users won't even notice that they are using Java code, as Safari will automatically execute Java code as it would any other web resource.

Most full Java applications are also delivered via a web download from a small Java Web Start (.jnlp) file. Double-clicking on a .jnlp file opens /Applications/Utilities/Java/Java Web Start, which downloads the remainder of the Java application to ~/Library/Caches. Once the download is complete, the Java application runs in its own environment alongside your other Mac applications. When you open a Java application the second time, the Java Web Start application automatically converts the small .jnlp file to a stand-alone Java application.

> **MORE INFO** ▶ To learn more, visit Apple's Java resource website, http://www.apple.com/macosx/features/java/.

Universal vs. Rosetta

With the introduction of Intel-based Macs, Apple had to introduce an entirely new code base to Mac OS X. At the hardware level, PowerPC and Intel processors are so different that they require their own separate versions of software. Apple had been secretly maintaining an Intel-compatible version of Mac OS X since its inception, so when Apple announced that the entire Mac lineup was moving to Intel processors, Mac OS X and all its included applications were already Intel native.

However, every other Mac application was not Intel native. Apple did preannounce the arrival of Intel-based Macs six months early to allow software developers to create Universal applications. Universal applications contain software code that runs on both PowerPC and Intel-based Macs. Yet for some third-party developers, updating software to Universal proved more difficult than others. In fact, some popular Mac applications still have not made the move to Universal.

So as not to leave both users and developers stranded with new hardware that couldn't run their old software, Apple includes the Rosetta compatibility environment on all Intel-based Macs. Rosetta is software that efficiently translates PowerPC code to Intel code on the fly. In typical Apple style, most users will never even know that their application is running through the Rosetta translation process. When a user double-clicks on a non-Universal application from an Intel-based Mac, Rosetta automatically starts providing translation for the application, and the application should open and run as normal.

Rosetta, like many compatibility solutions, is not without flaws. In some cases, there simply isn't an Intel equivalent for certain PowerPC software code. In other cases, such as support for Classic, it was simply prudent for Apple to stop supporting such old technology.

Rosetta does not support the following software:

▶ Applications created for any version of the Mac OS earlier than Mac OS X

▶ The Classic compatibility environment

▶ Screen savers written for the PowerPC architecture

▶ Software that inserts PowerPC preference panes in System Preferences

▶ Applications that specifically require a PowerPC G5 processor

▶ Applications that depend on one or more PowerPC-only kernel extensions

▶ Kernel extensions or hardware drivers written for the PowerPC architecture

▶ Java applications with JNI libraries

▶ Java in applications that Rosetta can translate (this means a web browser that Rosetta can run translated will not be able to load Java applets)

▶ Plug-ins written for the PowerPC architecture if the software they tie into runs as Intel native

Application Monitoring

Mac OS X provides several methods for identifying and managing processes and applications. You can use the Finder or System Profiler to identify application and command information, including what processor architecture—PowerPC, Intel, or both—the application supports. Activity Monitor is used for viewing and managing all processes as they are running on your Mac.

To quickly locate basic application information from the Finder:

1   In the Finder select the application or command you wish to identify, and then open the Get Info or Inspector window.

There are several ways to open the Get Info window: choose File > Get Info from the menu bar; press Command-I; choose Get Info from the Action pop-up menu in a Finder window toolbar; or right-click/Control-click an item and choose Get Info from the shortcut menu.

2   Once you have opened a Get Info window, click the General disclosure triangle to reveal general application information.

This will reveal that the selected application is one of four types:

Application (Universal). Designed for Mac OS X on both PowerPC and Intel-based Macs. It has both types of code embedded in it, so it will run natively on whichever platform it is opened from.

Application (Intel). Designed for Mac OS X only on Intel-based Macs.

Application or Application (PowerPC). Designed for Mac OS X on PowerPC-based Macs, and will open on Intel-based Macs using the Rosetta translation service.

Application (Classic). Designed only for older PowerPC-based Macs running Mac OS 9 or Mac OS X prior to version 10.5 from the Classic compatibility environment.

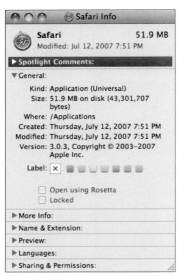

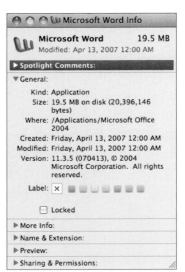

System Profiler

If the Finder doesn't provide enough application information for your needs, try the /Applications/Utilities/System Profiler application. Upon opening, System Profiler scans the contents of all available Application folders, including the /System/Library/CoreServices folder. Select Applications from the Contents list to see which applications System Profiler found. Selecting an application from the list reveals its name, version number, modification date, and application type.

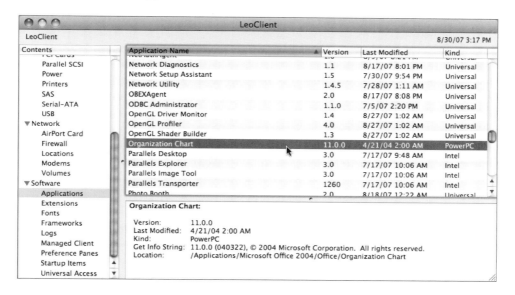

Activity Monitor

The primary Mac OS X application for monitoring processes as they are running is Activity Monitor. This extremely useful tool shows you the vital signs of any currently running process and the system as a whole. If an application has stopped responding or has become noticeably slow, check Activity Monitor. Also check here if the overall system is running noticeably slower. Activity Monitor will help you identify an application or background process that is using a significant percentage of system memory or processor resources.

To view your Mac's currently running processes with Activity Monitor:

1   Open /Applications/Utilities/Activity Monitor.

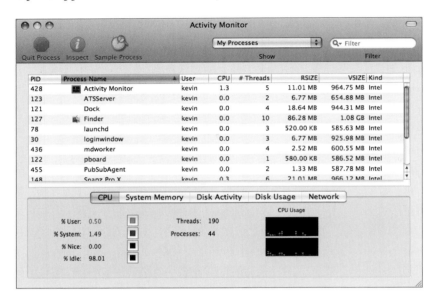

The main Activity Monitor list shows you, by default, detailed process information updated every other second and broken into the following individual columns:

Process Identification (PID). Each process has a unique identifier that is chosen based on the order in which it was opened since system startup.

Process Name. This is the human name chosen for the process by its creator.

User. Each process is opened on behalf of a particular user. Thus, each application has file system access based on the assigned user account.

CPU. This number is the percentage of total CPU usage the process is consuming. Note that the maximum percentage possible is 100% times the number of processor cores.

Threads. Each process is further broken down into the number of thread operations. Multithreading a process helps increase responsiveness by enabling the process to perform multiple simultaneous tasks. Multithreading also increases performance as each thread of a single process can run on a separate processor core.

Resident Memory Size (RSIZE). This represents the amount of active system memory that the process is currently occupying.

Virtual Memory Size (VSIZE). This represents the amount of total system memory, including both virtual and real memory, that the process is currently occupying.

Kind. This shows what processor architecture the application is currently using: PowerPC or Intel.

2   Click a column title to sort the process list by that column.

Click the column title again to toggle between ascending and descending sorts. You can also adjust the number of columns and the update frequency from the View menu.

PID	Process Name	User	▼CPU	# Threads	RSIZE	VSIZE	Kind
467	Safari	kevin	20.0	8	43.23 MB	980.13 MB	Intel
428	Activity Monitor	kevin	1.6	5	11.50 MB	981.36 MB	Intel
127	Finder	kevin	0.4	9	86.24 MB	1.08 GB	Intel
148	Snapz Pro X	kevin	0.2	6	21.01 MB	966.13 MB	Intel
436	mdworker	kevin	0.1	4	2.62 MB	600.58 MB	Intel
78	launchd	kevin	0.0	3	520.00 KB	585.63 MB	Intel
444	SyncServer	kevin	0.0	2	3.81 MB	600.15 MB	Intel
122	pboard	kevin	0.0	1	580.00 KB	586.52 MB	Intel
455	PubSubAgent	kevin	0.0	2	1.33 MB	587.78 MB	Intel
30	loginwindow	kevin	0.0	3	6.79 MB	925.98 MB	Intel

3   By default, Activity Monitor will only show processes running for the currently logged-in user. To view all active processes, choose All Processes from the Show pop-up menu.

Use the Spotlight search field in the upper-right corner of the Activity Monitor window to quickly pare down the list of running processes.

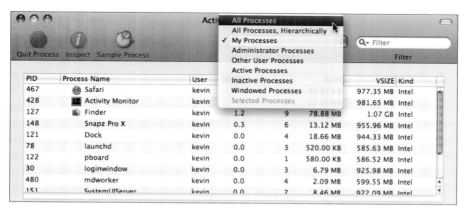

By viewing all processes and then re-sorting the list by either CPU or RSIZE, you can determine whether any process is using excessive resources.

4   To further inspect a process, double-click on its name in the Activity Monitor list. This reveals a window showing detailed process information.

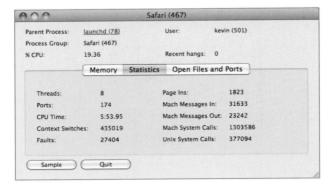

5   Finally, to inspect overall system information click through the tabs at the bottom of the Activity Monitor window.

These monitoring features are invaluable for troubleshooting as they show you real-time system statistics.

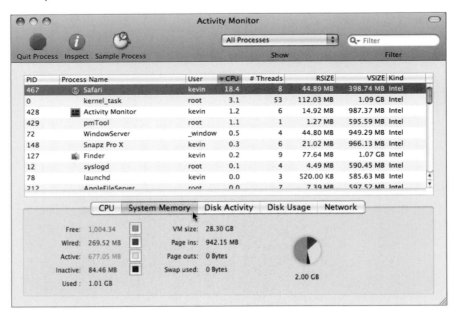

TIP ▶ Take time to explore all the features available from the Activity Monitor menu options. For an even more detailed process inspector, check out the Xray application installed as part of the optional Xcode Developer Tools package that can be found on the Mac OS X Install DVD.

Application Preferences

Applications primarily access two types of files during their use: the documents that the application is responsible for viewing or editing and the preference files that contain all the application's settings. From an administration perspective, preference files are often more important, as they may contain important settings that are required for an application to work properly. For instance, an application's serial number or registration information is often stored in a preference file.

Preference files can be found in any Library folder, but most application preferences end up in the user's Library, specifically in the ~/Library/Preferences folder. This is because the local and system Libraries should only be used for system preferences. More important, it enables each user to have his or her own application settings that do not interfere with other users' application settings.

Most application and system preference files are saved as a property list file. The naming scheme for a property list file is usually in the form of a reverse uniform resource locator (URL) followed by the file extension .plist. For example, the Finder's preference file is named com.apple.finder.plist. This naming scheme may seem strange at first, but it helps avoid confusion by identifying the software's maker along with the application.

The content of a property list file is formatted either as plain-text Extensible Markup Language (XML) or binary XML. The XML format is relatively human-readable with normal text interspersed alongside special text tags that define the data structure for the information. Thus, you can view and attempt to decipher the XML code of plain-text-formatted property list files using any text-reading application. Binary-encoded XML files are only readable using special tools designed to convert the binary code into human-readable format. One such tool, Property List Editor, not only decodes binary property list files but also enables you to view and edit any property list in an easy-to-read format. The

Property List Editor application is installed as part of the optional Xcode Developer Tools package on the Mac OS X Install DVD.

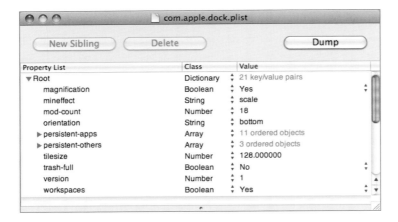

NOTE ▶ A few third-party applications do not store their preference files as property lists. Thus, they will likely sport a different naming convention, and you will probably not be able to view or edit the file's contents.

Application Accessibility

Apple has worked hard to ensure that Mac OS X remains approachable for all users, including users who have difficulty using the standard Mac interface via keyboard, mouse, and video display. Apple has built an extensive accessibility architecture into Mac OS X called Universal Access. Universal Access enables assistive interaction features for Apple and many third-party applications.

You can enable these features from the Universal Access system preference by choosing Apple menu > System Preferences, then click the Universal Access icon. General preferences include showing the Universal Access menu item and enabling access for assistive devices like electronic Braille interfaces. The remaining Universal Access preferences are presented in four separate tabs representing different assistance features:

▶   Seeing—The accessibility features in this section are designed to assist those who have difficulty viewing the screen or who are unable to view the screen at all. Options include enabling dynamic screen zooming and adjusting display settings to enhance clarity. The VoiceOver spoken-word interface, covered next in this lesson, is also enabled here.

▶ Hearing—The accessibility features in this section are designed to assist those who have difficulty hearing or who cannot hear sound. The primary option here is to enable screen flashing as an alternative to the alert sound.

▶ Keyboard—The accessibility features in this section are designed to assist those who have difficulty using a keyboard. Options include enabling sticky keys to assist with using keyboard combinations and slow keys to help with initial or repeated keystrokes.

▶ Mouse & Trackpad—The accessibility features in this section are designed to assist those who have difficulty using or who cannot use a mouse or trackpad. Options include increasing the cursor size so it's easier to see and enabling mouse keys that allow you to use the keyboard arrow keys in place of a mouse or trackpad.

MORE INFO ▶ To learn more, visit Apple's Accessibility resource website, http://www.apple.com/accessibility/.

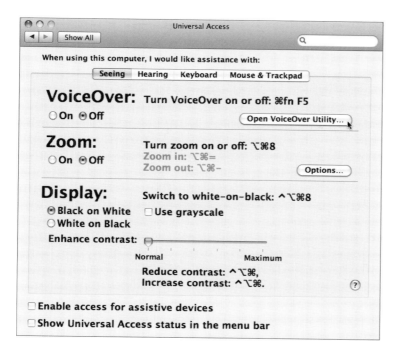

VoiceOver

VoiceOver is an interface mode that enables you to navigate the Mac OS X user interface using only keyboard control and spoken English descriptions of what's happening onscreen. You enable VoiceOver from the Seeing section of the Universal Access system preference, but you access all of the VoiceOver configuration options from the /Applications/Utilities/VoiceOver Utility application.

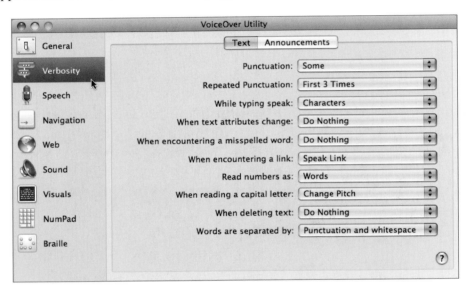

MORE INFO ▸ To learn more about VoiceOver, including an interactive Quick Start tour, visit the VoiceOver resource site, http://www.apple.com/accessibility/voiceover/.

Accessibility Preferences

It is important to note that almost all Universal Access preferences are saved on a per-user basis. Thus, each user will have a unique com.apple.universalaccess.plist located in his or her ~/Library/Preferences folder. In other words, each user has unique accessibility preferences that are only active when that user's account is logged in to the Mac. The one exception is that an administrative user can enable the VoiceOver feature for use by all accounts at the login window. This preference is available in the Accounts system preference by clicking the Login Options button.

Dashboard Widgets

Mac OS X 10.4 introduced the Dashboard as a new interface concept that provides instant access to narrowly focused, but usually very attractive, mini-applications called widgets. When the Dashboard is activated, your chosen mini-applications will instantly spring to life and appear "on top" of the Mac's normal interface. A simple click on the Mac's normal interface will dismiss the Dashboard just as quickly. The convenience of using these mini-applications from the Dashboard caught on quickly, and within a few months after its introduction hundreds of new third-party widgets were available.

Apple has added a few new tricks for Dashboard with Mac OS X 10.5, including the ability for any user to quickly make new widgets from any website using the Safari Web Clip button. Apple has also completely reworked the widget runtime architecture to run more efficiently and securely than before. Finally, Apple formalized the widget creation process by introducing a full widget development environment called Dashcode. Dashcode is installed as part of the optional Xcode Developer Tools package on the Mac OS X Install DVD.

Widget Management

By default, the Dashboard is activated by pressing the F12 key or the scroll wheel button on a compatible mouse. You can adjust the Dashboard keyboard key and activate an Active Screen Corner for Dashboard from the Exposé & Spaces system preference. Further, you can adjust the Dashboard mouse button from the Keyboard & Mouse system preference.

Built-in Apple widgets are located in /Library/Widgets, while third-party widgets are typically installed in ~/Library/Widgets in the user's home folder. Most users will use the automatic Widget Installer to add new widgets to their Dashboard.

To automatically test and install a widget:

1   From the Finder, double-click on a widget to start the Widget Installer. Alternatively, downloading a widget using a web browser will, by default, automatically start the Widget Installer.

2   When the Widget Installer dialog appears, click the Install button to open the widget in the Dashboard for installation.

The Dashboard will open the new widget in a test environment.

3   Thoroughly explore the widget and, if you like it, click the Keep button to complete the installation process.

The widget will be installed in the currently logged-in user's home folder, in the ~/Library/Widgets folder, and will always be available to the Dashboard from the widget bar.

You can also manually install widgets by simply dragging them into one of the Widgets folders. As with all system resources, widgets installed in the user's home folder will only be available to that user, and widgets installed in the local Library folder will be available to all local users. If you manually install a widget, users will have to manually add that widget to their Dashboard from the widget bar.

To remove a widget, locate it in either the local or user Library Widgets folder and drag it to the trash. If the widget is still active in the Dashboard after you have removed it from the Widgets folder, log the user out and then back in again to restart the Dashboard process.

Widget Architecture

The widget runtime architecture was reworked for Mac OS X 10.5 to provide a more efficient and secure Dashboard environment. When a user logs in, the launchd process starts the Dock process. The first time a user attempts to access the Dashboard, the Dock process starts the DashboardClient process. The DashboardClient process is responsible for running the Dashboard environment, including all widgets. This means that even if you have dozens of widgets open, you will still have only one active process handling all those widgets.

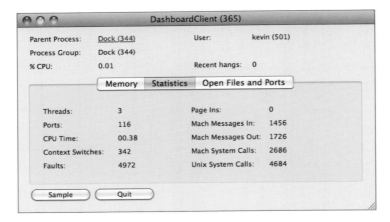

The DashboardClient process maintains three general Dashboard preference files in the ~/Library/Preferences folder: com.apple.dashboard.client.plist, com.apple.dashboard .installer.plist, and com.apple.dashboard.plist. Each open widget also maintains its own preference file in the user Preferences folder named widget-com.*widgetmaker*.widget .*widgetname*.plist, where *widgetmaker* is the name of the software developer who created the widget, and *widgetname* is the name of the widget.

The DashboardClient process has the same access privileges as the user. So generally, widgets are as secure as any other normal application. Nevertheless, it is possible for someone to create and distribute widgets that have a negative effect. Widgets are basically miniature specialized web browsers, so just about any data transfer or software that can run from a web browser can also be run by a widget. The Dashboard is only as safe as the widgets a user chooses to run. If you are at all suspicious of a third-party widget, simply avoid using it.

> **TIP** ► Although an administrator can't prevent a user from downloading third-party widgets, she can limit a user's ability to use third-party widgets with the Parental Controls preference, as covered in Lesson 2, "User Accounts."

Widget Troubleshooting

If a widget appears to stop working or becomes unresponsive, your first step should be to attempt to reset the widget. From the Dashboard, click once on the widget, then press Command-R to reset the widget. Widgets use a swirling animation to indicate that they have reset.

If the widget is still having problems, or you're having trouble using all the widgets, restart the DashboardClient process. You can forcibly quit the DashboardClient process by using /Applications/Utilities/Activity Monitor. More information about forcibly quitting processes is available in the "Forcibly Quit" section later in this lesson. After you quit the DashboardClient process, reactivate the Dashboard and the DashboardClient, and all open widgets will reopen. Another method is to restart all user processes by logging the user out and then in again.

If restarting the widget and the DashboardClient process doesn't work, you may have a corrupted widget or widget preference file. Widgets are similar to other applications in that they are susceptible to errors from corrupted files. Start by removing the specific widget preference file, and then restart the DashboardClient process. If you're having trouble with a third-party widget, download a new copy and replace the widget itself. Finally, you can reset the entire Dashboard system by removing all Dashboard and widget preference files and then logging the user out and back in again.

Application Troubleshooting

The application issues are as diverse as the applications themselves. Just as each application is designed to provide unique features, problems often manifest in unique ways as well. Fortunately, there several general troubleshooting steps you can take when diagnosing and resolving an application issue. The actions in the following list are presented from the least invasive and time-consuming to the most invasive and time-consuming. The actions are also generally presented by the likelihood of their success in resolving the issue, from most to least likely.

General application troubleshooting methods include:

▶ Restart the application—Often restarting an application will resolve the issue, or at least resolve application responsiveness. In some cases, the application may become unresponsive and you have to forcibly quit the application to restart it.

▶ Try another known working document—This is an excellent method to determine if a document has become corrupted and is the cause of the problem. If you discover that the problem's source is a corrupted document file, usually the only solution is to restore the document from an earlier backup. Mac OS X includes a sophisticated and yet easy-to-use backup system called Time Machine. Time Machine was covered earlier in Lesson 4, "Data Management and Backup."

▶ Try another user account—Use this method to determine if a user-specific resource file is the cause of the problem. If the application problem doesn't appear when using another account, you should search for corrupted application caches, preferences, and resource files in the suspect user's Library folder.

▶ Check log files—This is the last information-gathering step you take before you start replacing items. Few applications keep detailed log files; however, every time an application crashes, the CrashReporter process saves a log of the crash information. Open the /Applications/Utilities/Console application to view these log files. The CrashReporter creates logs with the name of the application followed by ".crash.log" saved in the user's ~/Library/Logs folder.

▶ Delete cache files—To increase performance, many applications create cache folders in the /Library/Caches and ~/Library/Caches folders. A specific application's cache folder almost always matches the application's name. While not the most likely application resource to cause problems, cache folders can be easily deleted without affecting the user's information. Once you delete an application's cache folder, the application will create a new one during the next time you open it.

▶ Replace preference files—Corrupted preference files are the most likely of all application resources to cause problems, as they change often and are required for the application to function properly. Application preference troubleshooting is covered later in this lesson.

▶   Replace application resources—Although corrupted application resources can certainly cause problems, they are the least likely source of problems, since application resources are rarely changed. Application resource troubleshooting is covered in the "Preference Troubleshooting" section later in this lesson.

Forcibly Quit

It's pretty easy to tell when an application becomes unresponsive—it stops reacting to your mouse clicks and the cursor changes to a spinning beach ball. Hence, the term "beach-balling" has become slang for a frozen Mac application. Because the forward-most application controls the menu bar, it may seem as if the application has locked you out of the Mac entirely. But this simply isn't so, because moving the cursor from the frozen application windows to another application window or the desktop usually returns the cursor to normal—and you can then click on the desktop to regain control of your Mac.

Mac OS X provides no less than three methods for forcibly quitting applications from the graphical interface:

▶   From the Force Quit Applications dialog—Choose Apple menu > Force Quit or use the Option-Command-Escape keyboard combination to open the Force Quit Applications dialog. A frozen application will appear in red text with "(not responding)" next to it. To forcibly quit, select any application and click the Force Quit button. Note that you can only restart the Finder from this dialog.

▶   From the Dock—Control-click or right-click on the application's icon in the Dock to display the Dock's application shortcut menu. If the Dock has recognized that the application is frozen, simply choose Force Quit from this menu. Otherwise, hold down the Option key to change the Quit menu command to Force Quit.

▶   From Activity Monitor—Open /Applications/Utilities/Activity Monitor and select the application you wish to quit from the process list. Next, click the Quit Process button in Activity Monitor's toolbar, and then click the Force Quit button. Activity Monitor is the only built-in application that will allow administrative users to quit or forcibly quit any user or system process.

Safe Relaunch

If an application unexpectedly quits, the system will present a dialog enabling you to restart the application. Click the Report button to send a crash report to Apple via the Internet, or just click the Relaunch button to try using the application again.

If the application crashes upon restart, the system open the safe relaunch dialog, which enables you to restart the application using a new preference file based on the application's defaults. Corrupted application preference files are one of the most common causes of application crashes. The safe relaunch system automates the common troubleshooting task of removing the old preference file and restarting the application. Click the "Reset and relaunch" button to try a new preference file for this application.

Hopefully, the application will restart given the new preference file. You may have to spend some time reconfiguring the application, as those settings are often saved to the application preference file. If the application appears to be working properly, quit the application to complete the safe relaunch feature. A final dialog appears allowing you to permanently save the new preference file. The system saves the previous application preference file and appends ".saved" to the file's name in case you want to try to use the preference file again.

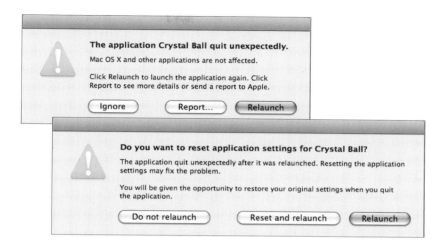

Preference Troubleshooting

Application preference files are the most common application resources to cause problems. These files contain both internal application configuration information and user-configured preferences. Even if you haven't changed any preferences, odds are the application is constantly storing new information in this file. It is the only file required by the application that is constantly being rewritten, so it's ripe for corruption. Corrupted preferences typically result in an application that crashes frequently or during startup.

Not all applications are compatible with the safe launch feature, so you may have to resolve corrupted preferences issues manually. As covered earlier in this lesson, application preferences are located in the ~/Library/Permissions folder and are named by the application and its maker. The most convenient method of isolating a corrupted preference in this case is to rename the suspect preference file in the Finder by adding an identifier to the end of the file name—something like ".bad." Restarting the application creates a new preference file based on the application's defaults. If this resolves the issue, go ahead and trash the old preference file; if not, you should move on to application resource troubleshooting. If you eventually resolve the problem elsewhere, you can restore the user's previous settings by deleting the newer preference file and then removing the filename identifier you added to the original preference file.

Resource Troubleshooting

Although rare, corrupted application software and associated nonpreference resources can be a source of application problems. These types of files rarely, if ever, change after the initial application installation, so the likelihood that such a resource is the cause of a problem is low. However, keep in mind that many applications use *other* resources from the local and user Library folders, such as fonts, plug-ins, and keychains, as well as items in the Application Support folder. The hard part is locating the suspect resource; once you have, the fix is to simply remove or replace the corrupted resource and restart the application.

If you've followed along, at this point you've attempted to replicate the application issue with another user account, and you've checked the /Applications/Utilities/Console application for application and CrashReporter logs. Corrupted resources in the user's home folder Library affect only that user, while corrupted resources in the local Library affect all users. Further, application and CrashReporter logs may tell you what resource the application was attempting to access when it crashed. Obviously, those resources should be your primary suspects.

If the application exhibits problems with only one user, attempt to locate the specific resource at the root of the problem in the user's Library folder. Start with the usual suspects; if you find a resource that you think could be causing the problem, move that resource out of the user's Library and restart the application.

If you've determined that the application issue is persistent across all user accounts, start by reinstalling or upgrading to the latest version of the application. You will probably find that there is almost always a newer version of the application available that likely includes bug fixes. At the very least, by reinstalling you will replace any potentially corrupted files that are part of the standard application. If you continue to experience problems after reinstalling the application, search through the local Library resources to find and remove or replace the corrupted resource.

Application Management via the Command Line

Three primary commands exist for viewing and forcibly quitting processes from the command-line interface (CLI): top, ps, and kill. Find out more detailed information about each one of these commands by checking the manual.

NOTE ▶ If you are unfamiliar with the CLI, review the CLI introduction in Lesson 3, "File Systems."

top. So named because it's typically used to show the "top" processes that are using the most processor resources. However, by default on Mac OS X, top lists commands in reverse order based on their process ID number. To have top sort by processor usage, include the -u option. The top command takes over the Terminal window when you open it. To return to the command prompt, press the Q key. The following code shows the default output of the top command. Notice the similarities to Activity Monitor.

```
Processes: 46 total, 2 running, 44 sleeping... 188 threads 3:18
Load Avg: 0.16, 0.05, 0.02 CPU usage: 0.48% user, 1.92%
SharedLibs: num = 8, resident = 63M code, 652K data, 4132K
MemRegions: num = 5327, resident = 110M + 11M private, 67M
PhysMem: 221M wired, 251M active, 65M inactive, 538M used,
VM: 4306M + 364M 35721(0) pageins, 0(0) pageouts

PID COMMAND  %CPU TIME #TH #PRTS #MREGS RPRVT RSHRD
953 top   3.6% 0:05.52 1 19  33 496K 188K
952 PubSubAgen 0.0% 0:00.02 2 54  26 352K 2532K
925 bash   0.0% 0:00.01 1 14  18 148K 184K
922 launchd  0.0% 0:00.00 3 29  24 116K 284K
921 sshd   0.0% 0:00.02 1 12  57 140K 816K
917 sshd   0.0% 0:00.07 1 17  53 128K 816K
831 Finder  0.0% 0:04.46 7 173 297 6420K 18M
```

ps. Short for "process status," this command lists active processes, but it does not take over the Terminal window as the top command does. Sometimes you have so many active processes that the top command simply can't show them all on your monitor, and this is where the ps command comes in handy. The syntax is ps, followed by any listing options you specify. The most useful options are -A (to show all processes), -c (to only show the process name instead of the absolute path to the process), and -u followed by a user's short name (to only list processes belonging to that user). In the following example, Michelle first uses the ps command with the -c and -u options to shorten the process name and list active processes belonging to her user account. She then uses the ps command with only the -A option to view all active processes with full pathnames. The results were too long to print so they have been cut off at process 10 in this example.

```
LeoClient:~ michelle$ ps -cu michelle
UID PID TTY   TIME CMD
502 922 ??   0:00.05 launchd
502 1113 ??   0:00.65 sshd
502 1205 ??   0:00.35 Spotlight
502 1206 ??   0:00.17 UserEventAgent
502 1208 ??   0:00.13 Dock
502 1210 ??   0:00.76 SystemUIServer
502 1211 ??   0:00.00 pboard
502 1212 ??   0:01.18 Finder
502 1214 ??   0:00.12 ATSServer
502 1367 ??   0:00.58 ScreenSaverEngine
502 1369 ??   0:00.14 mdworker
502 1115 ttys001 0:00.12 -bash
0 1371 ttys001 0:00.00 ps
LeoClient:~ michelle$ ps -A
PID TTY   TIME CMD
1 ??   0:03.65 /sbin/launchd
9 ??   0:00.86 /usr/libexec/kextd
10 ??   0:05.01 /usr/sbin/DirectoryService
...
```

kill. The intent of this command is clear by its name. This command is used to forcibly quit processes. The syntax is kill, followed by the process identification number of the process you wish to forcibly quit. In the following example, Michelle attempts to use the kill command to kill process 1129, which happens to be the Finder process of another user account. Initially she isn't allowed because the process belongs to another user, so being an administrative user, she uses the sudo command to execute the kill command as the root user.

```
LeoClient:~ michelle$ kill 1129
-bash: kill: (1129) - Operation not permitted
LeoClient:~ michelle$ sudo kill 1129
Password:
LeoClient:~ michelle$
```

Boot Camp

Mac hardware, aside from generally having superior industrial design, higher build quality, and the unique ability to run Mac OS X, isn't that much different than other Intel-based PCs. In fact, Apple hardware is a great platform for running Windows or any other operating system that supports the Intel chipset.

When Apple introduced the first Intel-based Macs, users were scrambling for solutions to run Windows on Mac hardware. For several months, dedicated hackers attempted to get Windows working on Mac hardware; Apple, however, had already been working on the problem and eventually introduced the Boot Camp Public Beta. With the introduction of Mac OS X 10.5, the testing is done and Boot Camp is a complete product that provides users with full support for running Windows natively on their Mac.

> **NOTE** ▶ Although it is possible to run any Intel-compatible operating system on Intel-based Macs, Boot Camp provides only setup and hardware driver support for Windows XP SP2 and Windows Vista.

Your Mac's Intel-based hardware is what primarily enables Windows to run natively. Boot Camp simply provides the means for you to easily prepare the Mac hardware for Windows installation. The Boot Camp Assistant will quickly partition and prepare your Mac OS X system drive to accept a Windows installation. You then install Windows from optical media as you would on any other PC hardware. Finally, the Mac OS X Install DVD includes Windows drivers for your Mac's hardware, including support for Mac-specific features such as integrated iSight cameras and Apple keyboards, mice, and trackpads.

Boot Camp Requirements

The following is required to install and set up Windows on your Mac:

▶ An Intel-based Mac computer—If you're not sure what processor type your Mac uses, you can identify it by choosing Apple menu > About This Mac to open the About This Mac dialog.

▶ Directly attached input devices—The Windows installation process does not support Bluetooth wireless input devices, which means you must use either a USB keyboard and mouse, or a built-in keyboard and trackpad.

▶ Mac OS X 10.5 or later—The latest version of Mac OS X is strongly recommended. You can check for Apple software updates if your Mac is connected to the Internet by choosing Apple menu > Software Update to launch the Software Update application. You can also check Apple's Support Download website at http://www.apple.com/support/downloads/.

▶ All firmware updates for your Mac—The latest version of firmware is strongly recommended. Again, you can check for Apple firmware updates by using the Software Update application. Another source is the Apple Knowledge Base document 303880, "Mac OS X: Firmware updates for Intel-based Macs."

▶ A Mac OS X 10.5 installation disc—You can use either a store-purchased "box copy" Mac OS X Install DVD or, if your Mac came with OS X 10.5 preinstalled, you can use the Mac OS X Install Disc 1 that came with your Mac.

▶ At least 10 GB of free disk space dedicated to Windows—Remember that Windows cannot natively access other Mac-formatted volumes, so you should probably carve out more than the minimum amount of disk space. If you have a Mac Pro with multiple drives, you can dedicate an entire drive to Windows.

▶ 2 GB or more of RAM when running Windows Vista on a Mac Pro—Windows Vista is a notorious resource hog. Mac Pros require more memory when used by Windows Vista because they use Intel Xeon processors.

▶ Boot Camp Assistant—Included with Mac OS X 10.5 or later, Boot Camp Assistant is located at /Applications/Utilities/Boot Camp Assistant.

▶ A single full-install Windows install disc—Specifically, Boot Camp supports full installations of Windows XP Home Edition or Professional with Service Pack 2 or later, or Windows Vista Home Basic, Home Premium, Business, or Ultimate.

Boot Camp Caveats

Before installing Windows using Boot Camp, be aware of its known limitations:

▶ Boot Camp supports only 32-bit versions of Windows.

▶ The Boot Camp Assistant cannot be used on drives containing more than one partition.

NOTE ▶ You can dynamically repartition your Mac's internal hard drive and restore it to a single partition using Disk Utility, as covered in Lesson 3, "File Systems."

► Boot Camp does not work with external hard drives.

► If you are installing Windows on a portable computer, always connect the power adapter to ensure that the laptop remains on during the entire Windows installation process.

► Do not use Windows-based tools to create or modify partitions on drives containing Mac volumes. Doing so may delete Mac-formatted volumes or render your system drive unbootable. However, you can use Windows-based tools to modify individual volume formatting.

► Mac OS X includes support for mounting NTFS volumes as read only. So, while using Mac OS X you'll be able to view and copy the contents of Windows volumes, but you won't be able to write changes.

    NOTE ► You can add NTFS volume write support to Mac OS X by installing two open source software packages. MacFUSE adds support for third-party file system drivers: http://code.google.com/p/macfuse/. The NTFS-3G package adds support for the NTFS file system through MacFUSE: http://www.ntfs-3g.org/.

► Windows can't mount Mac OS Extended formatted volumes. So, while using Windows you won't be able to view any Mac volumes.

    NOTE ► You can add Mac OS Extended volume support to Windows by installing the MacDrive software package by Mediafour: http://www.mediafour.com/products/macdrive/.

► Finally, just because you're using Mac hardware doesn't mean Windows is any less susceptible to viruses, spyware, and malware. Keep Windows updated at all times with the latest security updates and be sure to install Windows protection software.

Set Up Boot Camp

Setting up Boot Camp is a significant process that can take up to several hours. Apple has worked hard to make the setup process as easy as possible, but there isn't much Apple can do to make the Windows system installation and setup process any less complex or time consuming. In fact, the majority of setup time is spent with Windows setup.

Here are a few things to do before setting up Boot Camp:

▶ Always back up important items before making any significant changes to the Mac. Needless to say, setting up Boot Camp is a very significant change.

▶ Print out the Boot Camp Installation & Setup Guide accessible from the Boot Camp Assistant introduction screen.

▶ Update to the latest version of Mac OS X 10.5 and to the latest firmware for your Mac. You can use the built-in Software Update or visit the Apple Support Downloads website at http://www.apple.com/support/downloads/.

The three primary steps for setting up Boot Camp are:

▶ Use Boot Camp Assistant—This assistant will create a new partition on your internal startup disk for the Windows system. If you have multiple internal disks, you can use this assistant to prepare a specific disk for Windows. This assistant will automatically restart the Mac from the Windows installation disc.

▶ Install and set up Windows—In addition to correctly choosing and possibly reformatting the Windows partition, you will have to complete the standard Windows installation and setup process.

▶ Install Boot Camp drivers for Windows—These drivers add support for Mac-specific hardware like the built-in iSight camera and Apple input devices.

Boot Camp Assistant

The Boot Camp Assistant process is used to start the Boot Camp setup process. It's easy to follow and takes only a few minutes to complete.

To start the Boot Camp setup process with Boot Camp Assistant:

1 Quit all currently running applications, as they may stop responding and lose data during the repartitioning process.

2 As an administrative user, open /Applications/Utilities/Boot Camp Assistant and click the Continue button after you heed the Introduction warning.

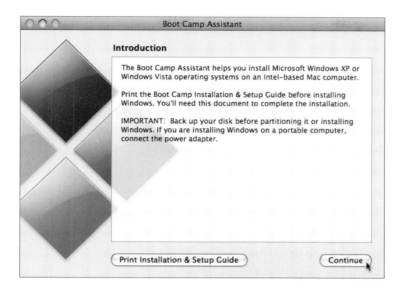

3   Depending on your hardware situation, you'll see one of two options. If you have only a single internal drive, click and drag the divider to specify the size of the Windows partition. You can also use the two buttons below the partition diagram to make a quick choice.

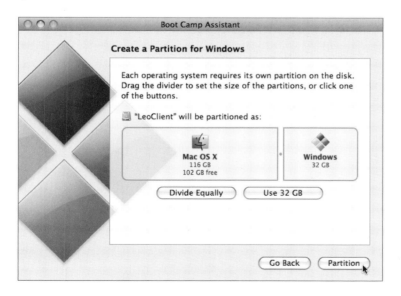

If you have multiple internal drives, you'll be able to select any drive for the Windows partition. You can dedicate an entire drive to Windows, or you can choose to create a second partition.

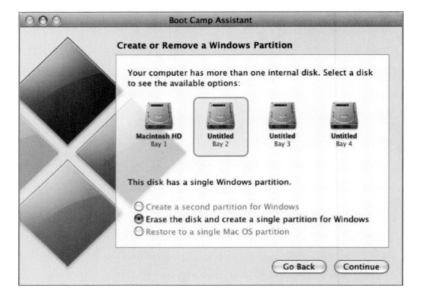

The Boot Camp Assistant won't let you choose a partition size larger than the amount of free space your drive has available. If you're installing Windows Vista, it's strongly advised that you choose a minimum partition size of 32 GB.

4   Click the Partition or Continue button to repartition the drive and create the Windows volume.

It may take several minutes for this process to complete; the system will have to verify the integrity of the volume and possibly move any data that would interfere with the new partition space. It's important that you do not open any other applications while the repartition process is under way.

When the repartition process is complete, the Boot Camp Assistant will format the new Windows partition as a FAT32 volume named BOOTCAMP. In most cases, you will have to reformat this volume later using the Windows installer.

Once the Windows partition has been created, you will be prompted to start the Windows installation process.

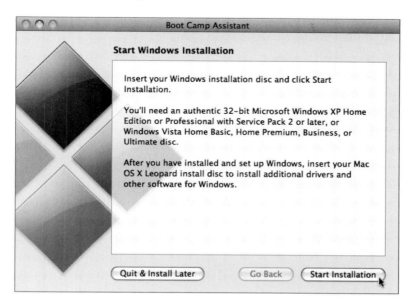

5   Insert a compatible Windows installation disc and click the Start Installation button.

The Mac will restart from the inserted disc and start the Windows installation process.

If you want to install Windows later, simply click the Quit & Install Later button. The next time you open the Boot Camp Assistant, it will automatically detect the Windows partition and again prompt you to start the Windows installation process.

NOTE ▶ If the Boot Camp Assistant cannot complete the repartition process, you have a few solutions to try. First, you should repair the disk as outlined in Lesson 3, "File Systems." You can also restart the Mac and try the Boot Camp Assistant again.

Install and Set Up Windows

The installation and setup process for Windows on a Mac using Boot Camp is nearly identical to the process used on a standard Windows-compatible PC. The Windows installation and setup process isn't difficult, but it does require quite a bit of time, an Internet connection, and several restarts.

> **NOTE** ▸ The following installation and setup overview assumes you're installing Windows Vista, but the main points still apply to installing Windows XP.

To install and set up Windows using Boot Camp:

1   The Mac will take a few minutes to boot from the Windows installation disc. Once the installer begins, advance through the language, Windows activation, and license terms screens.

2   Because no previous version of Windows exists on your Mac, the installer forces you to choose a Custom (Advanced) installation process. Click anywhere in the Custom (Advanced) area to continue.

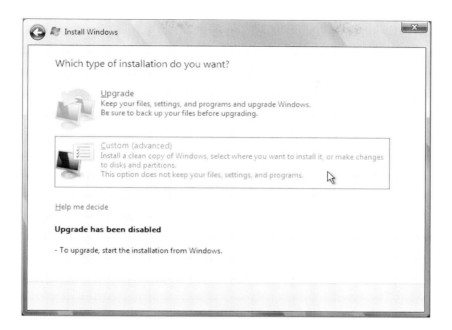

3   The Windows installation process will scan the Mac's local drives for any available volumes.

Because Windows doesn't fully comprehend the GUID partitioning scheme, you may see several "Unallocated Space" or unnamed partitions listed. It's critical that you choose the correct Windows partition that you created earlier for Boot Camp. The partition created by the Boot Camp Assistant should appear as "BOOTCAMP," but Windows can also identify the Boot Camp partition by its size.

4   Once you have selected the correct partition, you have to reformat it with the NTFS file system. Click "Drive options (advanced)" below the partition list. Then click Format to reformat the selected partition.

You will have to dismiss a final dialog by clicking OK to format the partition. By default, Windows will not name formatted volumes, so they will show up in Mac OS X as "Untitled."

Do not attempt to format other partitions or extend any partition. Doing so may corrupt the drive's partition structure or erase the Mac's system volume. Either will result in catastrophic data loss.

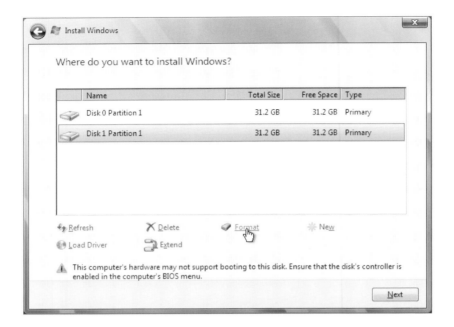

5   Once you have selected and reformatted the Windows partition, click the Next button to start the installation process. This process may take several hours, and the Mac will restart several times.

6   Finally, work through the Windows first-run setup, complete any Windows activation, and always make sure to check for any Windows updates.

The Windows Update system is managed from the Windows Update Control Panel.

NOTE ▶ You may not be able to initially check for Windows updates until you install the appropriate network drivers via the Boot Camp drivers for Windows.

Install Boot Camp Drivers for Windows
You could theoretically continue to use Windows without installing the Boot Camp drivers, but the generic drivers included with Windows do not fully support all of your Mac's advanced hardware. Most important, though, installing the Boot Camp drivers allows you to restart into Mac OS X from Windows.

NOTE ▶ Again, the following instructions assume you're installing Windows Vista, but the main points still apply to installing Windows XP.

To install the Boot Camp drivers for Windows:

1   Once you have Windows installed and set up, you need to eject the Windows installation disc, but because you haven't installed the proper drivers yet, the Mac's keyboard Eject key will be useless.

    To eject the Windows installation disc, choose Computer from the Windows Start menu, select the Windows install disc icon, and click the Eject button.

TIP ▶ From the Computer view you can also rename the Local Disk (C:) volume to something more recognizable for when you're using Mac OS X, as demonstrated in the previous screen shot.

2   Insert the Mac OS X Install DVD, and the Windows AutoPlay service automatically opens the Boot Camp Installer.

Windows Vista requires that you click "Run setup.exe" to validate that you want to run the Boot Camp Installer.

3   Proceed through the Boot Camp Installer welcome, license agreement, and install screens.

When the installer is done, you will be prompted to restart Windows. Click the Yes button to restart immediately.

4   After Windows restarts, you should have full access to all the Mac's hardware features. You will also have access to the Boot Camp system tray item in the Windows Taskbar, the Boot Camp Control Panel, and the Boot Camp Help system.

Switching Between Systems

Although switching between Mac OS X and Windows requires a full restart of the Mac, there are three convenient methods for choosing which operating system you want to engage:

▶ The Startup Manager allows you to temporarily select the operating system before the computer fully starts up.

▶ The Mac OS X Startup Disk preference allows you to set the Mac's startup disk.

▶ The Windows Boot Camp Control Panel allows you to set the Mac's startup disk.

Startup Manager

The Startup Manager is a feature built into the Mac's firmware that allows you to temporarily select the startup disk. This selection is considered temporary because as soon as you restart the Mac, it reverts to the startup disk that was selected by one of the other two methods.

Holding down the Option key during the very first moments when the Mac is starting up activates the Startup Manager. It scans all locally attached volumes and the network for valid operating systems, and displays those choices to you using a Mac-like graphical interface. You can use the arrow and Return keys or the mouse to select a startup disk from multiple choices.

> **NOTE** ▶ Access to the Startup Manager can be password protected with the Firmware Password Utility, as covered in Lesson 2, "User Accounts."

Switching from Mac OS X to Windows

The Mac OS X Startup Disk system preference allows an administrative user to set the Mac's startup disk. When you select a startup disk using this method, the Mac will adhere to the selection until you change it again using this tool or the Windows Boot Camp Control Panel. This selection can also be temporarily overridden by the Startup Manager.

To use the Startup Disk preference, choose Apple menu > System Preferences and then select the Startup Disk preference icon. The Startup Disk preference scans all locally attached volumes and the network for valid operating systems. Keep in mind that volumes formatted by Windows will, by default, be named "Untitled." Select the operating system you wish to set as the startup disk from the list, and then click the Restart button to restart the Mac.

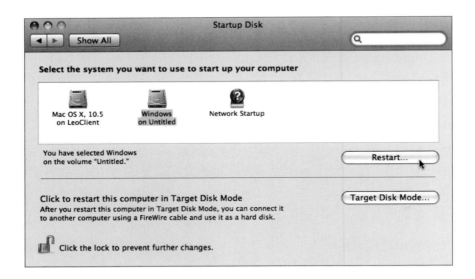

Switching from Windows to Mac OS X

The Windows Boot Camp Control Panel also allows an administrative user to set the Mac's startup disk. Additionally, when you select a startup disk using this method the Mac will adhere to the selection until you change it again using this tool or the Mac OS X Startup Disk preference. Once more, this selection can also be temporarily overridden by the Startup Manager.

The quickest route to the Boot Camp Control Panel is clicking on the Boot Camp system tray item, which looks like a gray diamond, in the Windows Taskbar. This reveals a pop-up menu allowing you to open the Boot Camp Control Panel. Notice this pop-up menu also allows you to access the Boot Camp Help system and, with one click, restart back into Mac OS X.

The Boot Camp Control Panel will open to the Startup Disk section, which scans all locally attached volumes and the network for valid operating systems. Mac OS X volumes appear with their given name, but the Windows volume always appear as simply "Windows." Select the operating system you wish to set as the startup disk from the list, and then click the Restart button to restart the Mac. Finally, take a few minutes to explore the other sections of the Boot Camp Control Panel that allow you to control Mac-specific hardware functions.

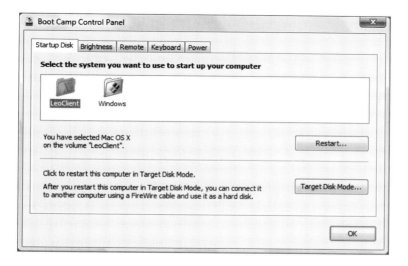

Removing Windows

If for some reason you decide to remove Windows from your Mac, the Boot Camp Assistant makes quick work of the process.

To remove Windows:

1   While in Mac OS X, as an administrative user open /Applications/Utilities/Boot Camp Assistant, and then click the Continue button to advance past the Introduction screen.

2   The Boot Camp Assistant will automatically recognize that Windows is already installed and present you with the choice to "Create or remove a Windows partition." Click Continue once more.

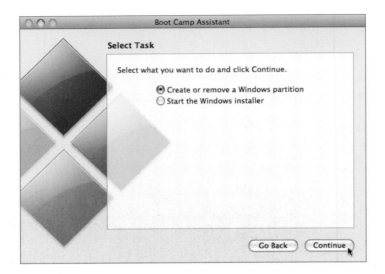

The next screen shows the final size of the Mac volume once the Windows partition has been removed.

3 Click the Restore button to remove the Windows partition and reclaim the storage space into a single Mac volume.

What You've Learned

▶ Mac OS X supports a variety of applications on both PowerPC and Intel-based Mac systems.

▶ You can use Activity Monitor in the graphical interface, or top and ps in the command-line interface to monitor applications and processes.

▶ Mac OS X includes application accessibility interfaces via Universal Access and VoiceOver.

▶ The Dashboard provides instantaneous access to useful mini-applications called widgets.

▶ Application troubleshooting involves locating the problem source by taking steps from the least invasive and time-consuming action to the most invasive and time-consuming action.

▶ Boot Camp allows Intel-based Macs to natively run Windows XP SP2 or Windows Vista.

References

You can check for new and updated Knowledge Base documents at http://www.apple.com/support.

Rosetta

304302, "Intel-based Mac: Some migrated applications may need to be updated"

303059, "Safari, Intel-based Macs: Internet plug-in not installed alert or blank page when loading plug-in content"

303814, "Some QuickTime components may display white instead of video on Intel-based Macintosh computers"

Application Monitoring

107918, "Mac OS X: Reading system memory usage in Activity Monitor"

24721, "Mac OS X Server: ps Command (Process Status)"

106415, "Mac OS X: How to View Memory Usage With the 'top' Utility"

Application Accessibility

75459, "Mac OS X keyboard shortcuts"

303070, "Mac OS X: Computer Speaks unexpectedly, or a black box unexpectedly appears around a file, folder, or other item"

Dashboard

302240, "Mac OS X: Installing and removing Dashboard widgets"

301572, "Mac OS X: Downloaded Dashboard widgets don't automatically install"

Application Troubleshooting

25398, "Mac OS X: How to troubleshoot a software issue"

107199, "Mac OS X: If your computer stops responding, 'hangs,' or 'freezes'"

301084, "Mac OS X: Reopening an application after it unexpectedly quits"

303572, "Mac OS X: How to troubleshoot a software issue."

Boot Camp

303880, "Mac OS X: Firmware updates for Intel-based Macs."

306538, "Mac OS X 10.5: System requirements for Boot Camp and Microsoft Windows"

306703, "Mac 101: Using Windows via Boot Camp with Mac OS X 10.5 Leopard"

306823, "Boot Camp 2.0, Mac OS X 10.5: Frequently asked questions"

306580, "Intel-based Mac: Startup issues after using unsupported version of Windows installer via Boot Camp"

306759, "Mac OS X 10.5, Boot Camp: Understanding how Apple localized keyboard character combinations are mapped in Window"

306891, "Boot Camp 2.0: Video issues with Windows Vista or XP"

306882, "Mac OS X 10.5, Boot Camp: Windows Vista 'Problem Reports and Solutions' indicates compatibility issues before Boot Camp drivers installation"

URLs

Apple's product guide: http://guide.apple.com

Mac OS X architectural overview: http://developer.apple.com/macosx/architecture/index.html

Cocoa application environment: http://developer.apple.com/cocoa/

Carbon application environment: http://developer.apple.com/carbon/

Apple's UNIX implementation: http://www.apple.com/macosx/technology/unix.html

Apple's X11 implementation: http://developer.apple.com/opensource/tools/X11.html

Apple's Java implementation: http://www.apple.com/macosx/features/java/

Apple's Accessibility resource: http://www.apple.com/accessibility/

VoiceOver resource: http://www.apple.com/accessibility/voiceover/

MacFUSE file system provides full support for NTFS: http://code.google.com/p/macfuse/ and http://www.ntfs-3g.org/

Mediafour's MacDrive, which provides Mac OS Extended file system support for Windows: http://www.mediafour.com/products/macdrive/

Apple's Support Downloads: http://www.apple.com/support/downloads/

Review Quiz

1. What is protected memory? What is 64-bit memory addressing?
2. What are the five application environments supported by Mac OS X? What is each one used for?
3. What is Rosetta? What types of items are not supported by Rosetta?
4. What three ways can you forcibly quit an application from the graphical interface?
5. Where are application preferences stored? What format is often used for preference files?
6. What does the safe relaunch feature do?
7. What system preference enables the accessibility features in Mac OS X? What accessibility features are available in Mac OS X? Finally, where is the preference file for these features located?
8. What are the advantages of signed applications?
9. What steps should you use when troubleshooting application issues?
10. How do Dashboard widgets work?
11. How does Boot Camp work?
12. What are the minimum system requirements for Boot Camp?
13. What are the three primary steps for setting up Boot Camp with Windows?
14. What three methods can be used for selecting the startup disk on a Mac with Windows installed?

Answers

1. The system keeps applications from interfering with one another by segregating their memory usage using protected memory. Macs with 64-bit capable processors can address more than 4 GB of system memory.

2. The five application environments supported by Mac OS X are: Cocoa, the native application environment for Mac OS X; Carbon, which is based on Mac OS 9 but still provides native Mac OS X performance; BSD, which is Mac OS X's command-line interface (CLI) and is based on Berkeley Software Distribution (BSD) UNIX; X11, which is a popular UNIX windowing environment; and Java, which was originally created by Sun Microsystems.

3. Rosetta is translation software built into Mac OS X that allows Intel-based Macs to use software originally designed for PowerPC-based Macs. Rosetta does not support applications created for any version of the Mac OS earlier than Mac OS X, the Classic compatibility environment, screen savers written for the PowerPC architecture, software that inserts PowerPC preference panes in System Preferences, applications that specifically require a PowerPC G5 processor, applications that depend on one or more PowerPC-only kernel extensions, kernel extensions or hardware drivers written for the PowerPC architecture, Java applications with JNI libraries, Java in applications that Rosetta can translate, or plug-ins written for the PowerPC architecture if the software they tie into runs as Intel native.

4. The three ways to forcibly quit an application from the graphical interface are from the Force Quit Application dialog accessed from the Apple menu, from the Dock's application shortcut menu accessed by Control-clicking or right-clicking on the application's icon, or from the /Applications/Utilities/Activity Monitor application.

5. Application preferences are almost always stored in the user's Library folder in the ~/Library/Preferences folder. Most application preferences are property lists, which are XML-formatted files that use the ".plist" filename extension.

6. The safe relaunch feature restarts a recently crashed application using fresh application preferences. If this prevents the application from crashing again, the system automatically saves the new working preference file as the permanent preference file.

7. Mac OS X's accessibility features are accessed from the Universal Access system preference. Universal Access includes options to assist users who have difficulty seeing, hearing, using the keyboard, or using the mouse and trackpad. The Universal Access preference file is com.apple.universalaccess.plist, located in ~/Library/Preferences.

8. Signed applications include a digital signature that the system can use to verify the authenticity and integrity of the application and its resources.

9. General application troubleshooting steps include restarting the application, trying another known working document, trying another user account, checking log files, deleting cache files, replacing preference files, and replacing application resources.

10. The Dock process starts the DashboardClient process on behalf of the currently logged-in user. All open widgets run inside the DashboardClient process.

11. Boot Camp allows Windows XP SP2 or Windows Vista to run natively on Mac hardware. The Boot Camp Setup Assistant automatically repartitions the system volume in preparation for the Windows installation. Users install Windows as they would on any other PC, and then load Mac hardware drivers for Windows from the Mac OS X Install DVD.

12. The minimum system requirements for Boot Camp are:

   ▶ An Intel-based Mac computer

   ▶ Directly attached input devices

   ▶ Mac OS X 10.5 or later

   ▶ All firmware updates for your Mac

   ▶ A Mac OS X 10.5 installation disc

   ▶ At least 10 GB of free disk space you'll be installing Windows on

   ▶ 2 GB or more of RAM when running Windows Vista on a Mac Pro

   ▶ Boot Camp Assistant

   ▶ A single full-install Windows Installation disc

13. To set up Boot Camp, you must start with the Boot Camp Assistant, then install and set up Windows from the Windows installation disc, and then finally install the Boot Camp drivers for Windows from the Mac OS X Install DVD.

14. If you have both Mac OS X and Windows installed, you can select the startup disk from the Startup Manager as soon as you turn on the Mac, from the Mac OS X Startup Disk preference, or from the Windows Boot Camp Control Panel.

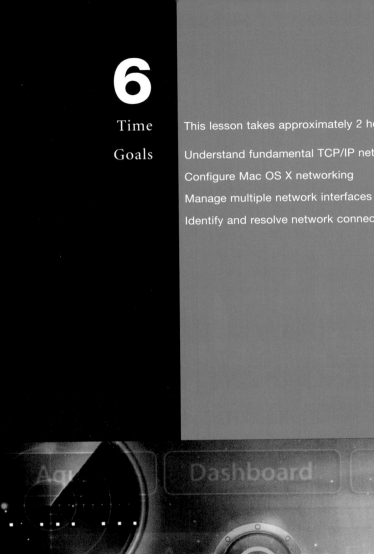

6

Time   This lesson takes approximately 2 hours to complete.

Goals   Understand fundamental TCP/IP network concepts

Configure Mac OS X networking

Manage multiple network interfaces

Identify and resolve network connectivity issues

Network Configuration

The capability to share information between computers across a network has always been paramount. During the early years of personal computer development, vendors designed their own proprietary local network systems. Apple was no exception with its implementation of AppleTalk and LocalTalk network standards for file sharing and network printing. Yet, although these vendor-specific technologies were suitable for smaller networks, they didn't scale very well once customers wanted to create more complicated networks with large numbers of computers over long distances. Further, special hardware or software had to be put in place to translate from one vendor's network to another.

Around the same time, researchers were working at the behest of the United States Department of Defense to create a wide area network standard for military and governmental use. From this research was born the Internet protocol suite known as TCP/IP. The marriage of the Transmission Control Protocol (TCP) and the Internet Protocol (IP) became the universal language that allows computers to communicate on the Internet. This standard became so pervasive that nearly every network today, including small local networks all the way up to the largest long-distance network on Earth, the Internet, is based on the TCP/IP suite.

It should come as no surprise then that Mac OS X includes a robust TCP/IP implementation. In fact, the first computer systems to popularize the use of TCP/IP were UNIX systems. Thus, much of the TCP/IP software built into Mac OS X is based on open source UNIX software that was established long before Mac OS X ever existed as a product from Apple.

In this lesson, you will configure network settings and troubleshoot network connectivity issues using Mac OS X. Before that, though, you must have a fundamental understanding of core network concepts. Accordingly, the first part of this lesson presents these fundamental concepts for your edification.

Fundamental Network Concepts

Properly configuring and troubleshooting networking on any operating system requires a basic understanding of fundamental network concepts. Due to the widespread adoption of standardized network technology, the following network overview applies to nearly any operating system, Mac OS X included. Basic network terminology is covered first, followed by an overview of the processes involved in actual data delivery across a network.

Fundamental Network Terminology

It's best to explore networking from a layered perspective. In fact, there is an established seven-layer model used to describe network technologies, the Open Systems Interconnection Reference Model (known as the OSI model). Exploring networking using the OSI model goes well beyond the scope of this text. Consequently, networking concepts will be presented in a more simplistic abstraction of three basic elements:

▶ Network interface—The network interface is the actual medium through which the network data flows. Network interfaces can be physical or virtual. The most common physical network interfaces for computers are Ethernet and wireless, which is known in the Apple world as AirPort. Virtual network interfaces are also available that can be used to secure otherwise insecure network connections by creating a virtual private network (VPN) riding on top of a standard network interface.

▶ Network protocol—A protocol defines a set of standard rules used for data representation, signaling, authentication, or error detection across network interfaces. Primarily, protocols are designed to ensure that all data is communicated properly and completely. Specific protocols have a narrow focus, so often multiple protocols are combined or layered to provide a complete network solution. For example, the combined TCP/IP protocol suite provides only for the addressing and end-to-end transport of data across the Internet; dozens of other protocols are required for something as simple as checking your email or browsing a website.

▶ Network service—In the context of the Network preference, the term *network service* describes a network interface's settings, which are necessary to define a network connection. A fundamental feature of Mac OS X is the ability to support multiple network services, or connections, per each individual network interface. As you will learn in Lesson 7, "Accessing Network Services," a network service is also more generally defined as information provided on the network by a server for use by clients. Common examples include network configuration services, file-sharing services, messaging services, and collaboration services. Often a specific set of protocols is used to define how the particular service works.

TIP ▶ For more information regarding the OSI model for describing computer networks, refer to this Wikipedia entry: http://en.wikipedia.org/wiki/OSI_model.

Simplifying computer network technology to only three distinct elements does not provide a detailed abstraction, but it still shows clearly how each is related. When a network interface, service, or protocol is created, it is often put through a review process before it's deemed a network standard. Standards committees are formed with members from multiple network organizations and vendors to ensure that new network standards remain interoperable with existing network standards. Most networking technologies in use today have been ratified by some standards body, so you may often come across an interface, protocol, or service labeled as a "standard."

Media Access Control (MAC) Address

The Media Access Control (MAC) address is used to uniquely identify a physical network interface on a local network. Each physical network interface has at least one MAC address associated with it.

NOTE ▶ The Intel-based Xserve has two MAC addresses per Ethernet interface to provide functionality for lights-out management.

Because the most common network interface is Ethernet, people often refer to MAC addresses as "Ethernet addresses." Still, nearly every other network interface type also uses some type of MAC address for unique identification. This includes, but isn't limited to, wireless, Bluetooth, FireWire, and Fibre Channel.

A MAC address is usually a 48-bit number represented by six groups of two-digit hexadecimal numbers, known as octets, each separated by colons. For example, a typical MAC address would look something like this: 00:1C:B3:D7:2F:99.

The first three octets are the Organizationally Unique Identifier (OUI), and the last three octets identify the network device itself. In other words, you can use the first three octets of a MAC address to identify who made the network device. The Institute of Electrical and Electronics Engineers (IEEE) maintains a searchable database of publicly listed OUIs at their website: http://standards.ieee.org/regauth/oui/index.shtml.

Internet Protocol (IP) Address

Communicating with computers on both local and remote networks requires an Internet Protocol (IP) address. IP addresses, unlike MAC addresses, are not permanently tied to a network interface. Instead, IP addresses are assigned to the network interface based on the local network it's connected to. This means, if you have a portable computer every new network you connect to will probably require a new IP address. If necessary, you can assign multiple IP addresses to each network interface, but this approach is often only used for computers that are providing network services.

There are currently two standards for IP addresses: IPv4 and IPv6. IPv4 was the first widely used IP addressing scheme and is by far the most common today. An IPv4 address is a 32-bit number that is represented by four groups of three-digit numbers, also known as octets, separated by periods. Each octet has a value between 0 and 255. For example, a typical IPv4 address would look something like this: 10.1.45.186.

With IPv4 there are a little over 4 billion unique addresses. This may seem like a lot, but considering every new network-ready gadget that comes out and the number of people who want to own multiple network-ready gadgets, this number isn't really big enough. For the time being, the available IPv4 addresses are extended by using network routers that can share a single real IPv4 address to a range of reusable private network addresses. This is how most home networks are configured, but it is only a temporary solution for what's to come next.

The successor to IPv4 is IPv6, but because IPv4 is so entrenched in the backbone of the Internet, the transition to IPv6 has been slow. The main advantage to IPv6 is a much larger address space—so large in fact, every person on Earth could have roughly 1.2×10^{19} copies of the entire IPv4 address range. This may appear to be a ridiculous amount of IP addresses, but the design goal of IPv6 was to eliminate the need for private addressing and allow for easier address reassignment and changing to a new network. An IPv6 address is a 128-bit number that is presented in eight groups of four-digit hexadecimal numbers separated by colons. Hexadecimal numbers use a base-16 digit system, so after the number 9 you use the letters A through F. For example, a typical IPv6 address would look something like this: 2C01:0EF9:0000:0000:0000:0000:142D:57AB. Large strings of zeros in an IPv6 address can be abbreviated using a double colon, resulting in an address more like this: 2C01:0EF9::142D:57AB.

Subnet Mask

The computer uses the subnet mask to determine the IPv4 address range of the local network. Networks based on the IPv6 protocol do not require subnet masks. A subnet mask is similar to an IPv4 address in that it's a 32-bit number arranged in four groups of octets. The computer applies the subnet mask to its own IP address to determine the local network's address range. The non-zero bits in a subnet mask are used to specify which bits of the IP address define the local network address range. For example, assuming your computer has an IP address of 10.1.5.3 and a commonly used subnet mask of 255.255.255.0, the local network IP address range would be 10.1.5.0 to 10.1.5.255.

Whenever the computer attempts to communicate with another network device, it applies the subnet mask to the destination IP address of the other device to determine if it's on the local network as well. If so, the computer will attempt to directly access the other network device. If not, the other device is clearly on another network and the computer will send all communications bound for that other device to the router address.

Router Address

Routers are network devices that manage connections between separate networks. Routers, as their given name implies, route network traffic between the networks they bridge. Routing tables are programmed into the routers to determine where network traffic goes. Even if a router is presented with traffic destined for a network that the router is unaware of, it will still route the traffic to another router that it thinks is closer to the final destination. Thus, routers literally are the brains of the Internet.

Your computer's router address is the IP address of the router that connects the local network with another network, or more commonly in residential situations, an Internet service provider. Typically the router's address is at the beginning of the local address range, and it's always in the same subnet. Using the previous example, assuming your computer has an IP address of 10.1.5.3 and a commonly used subnet mask of 255.255.255.0, the local network IP address range would be 10.1.5.0 to 10.1.5.255 and the router address would most likely be 10.1.5.1.

Transmission Control Protocol (TCP)

The Transmission Control Protocol (TCP) is the primary protocol used to facilitate end-to-end data connectivity between two IP devices. TCP is the preferred transport mechanism for many Internet services because it guarantees reliable and in-order delivery of data. In other words, IP provides network addressing and data routing, and TCP ensures that the data arrives at its destination complete. The combination of these two protocols encompasses the TCP/IP suite, commonly known as the Internet protocol suite.

The TCP/IP protocol suite chops contiguous data streams into many individual packets of information before they are sent across the network. This is because IP networks use packet-switching technology to route and transmit data. Almost all digital networking technologies are packet-based because this provides efficient transport for network connections that aren't always reliable. Remember, the TCP/IP protocol was originally designed with the military in mind, so packet-based network technology is ideal because it's designed to work around communications link failure. This is why sophisticated routing hardware was originally developed for TCP/IP networks, so data could be literally rerouted and re-sent should a network link go down.

A lesser-used protocol known as Universal Datagram Protocol (UDP) is also attached to the TCP/IP suite. UDP is a simpler protocol that does not guarantee the reliability or ordering of data sent across networks. This may seem like a poor choice for networking, but in some cases UDP is preferred because it provides better performance than TCP. Examples of network services that use UDP include the Domain Name System (DNS), media streaming, voice over IP (VoIP), and online gaming. These services have been designed to tolerate lost or out-of-order data so they can benefit from UDP's increased performance.

TIP ▶ For more information regarding the Internet protocol suite, refer to this Wikipedia entry: http://en.wikipedia.org/wiki/internet_protocol_suite.

Networks in Action

Manually assigning an IP address, a subnet mask, and a router address is technically all that is needed to configure a computer to use TCP/IP-based networking on both local area networks (LANs) and wide area networks (WANs). Yet, there are two other network services that are almost always involved in basic network functionality: Dynamic Host Configuration Protocol (DHCP) and the Domain Name System (DNS). These two services, combined with TCP/IP, characterize core network functionality that provides the foundation for nearly any network service.

Dynamic Host Configuration Protocol (DHCP)

Although not required to provide network functionality, the Dynamic Host Configuration Protocol (DHCP) is used by nearly all network clients to automatically acquire preliminary TCP/IP configuration. In some situations, an administrative user may still choose to manually enter TCP/IP networking configuration information. This is often the case with network devices that are providing network services. However, manually configuring multitudes of network clients is tedious work that is prone to human error. Thus, even on rigorously managed networks, DHCP is still widely used to configure network clients.

> **NOTE ▶** A precursor to DHCP is the Bootstrap Protocol (BOOTP). DHCP is backward compatible with BOOTP but provides greater functionality and reliability.

A DHCP server is required to provide the service. On many networks, the network routers provide the DHCP service, but in some cases a dedicated server can be used for this purpose. When a network device becomes active on the network, it first negotiates a link with the hardware interface, and then it sends out a broadcast to the local network requesting DHCP information. Because the new network client doesn't yet have an IP address, it uses the network interface's MAC address for identification. If a DHCP server that is listening has available addresses, it will send back a reply to the client with TCP/IP configuration information. At a minimum, this information includes IP address, subnet mask, router, and a DHCP lease time that defines how long the client can retain the address before it's given away. Ancillary DHCP information can include DNS information, directory service information, and NetBoot information.

If the DHCP server has run out of available network addresses, or there is no DHCP service available, as is the case with small ad hoc networks, the client will automatically generate a self-assigned link-local address. Link-local addresses are always in the IP address range of 169.254.xxx.xxx. The network client will automatically generate a random link-local address and then check the local network to make sure no other network devices are using that address. Once a unique link-local address is established, the network client will only be able to establish connections with other network devices on the local network.

> **TIP** ▶ For more information regarding DHCP, refer to this Wikipedia entry: http://en.wikipedia.org/wiki/Dhcp.

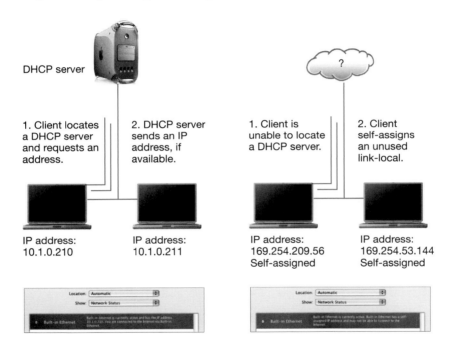

DHCP server

1. Client locates a DHCP server and requests an address.

2. DHCP server sends an IP address, if available.

1. Client is unable to locate a DHCP server.

2. Client self-assigns an unused link-local.

IP address: 10.1.0.210

IP address: 10.1.0.211

IP address: 169.254.209.56 Self-assigned

IP address: 169.254.53.144 Self-assigned

Local Area Network (LAN) Traffic

Most local area networks (LANs) use some form of wired or wireless connection. When an Ethernet network connection is established, the network device will typically send out an Address Resolution Protocol (ARP) broadcast request to discover what other devices are on the local network. Other active network devices will respond with their known MAC and IP addresses. Each network device will maintain and continuously update a routing table of all known local addresses. Once the network interface has been established, TCP/IP networking must be configured, either manually or via DHCP. Once both these steps are complete, network communication can begin.

TCP/IP packets are encased inside Ethernet frames to travel across the local network. The TCP/IP packet includes the originating IP and destination IP addresses along with the data to be sent. The network device applies the subnet mask setting to determine if the destination IP address is on the local network. If so, it will consult the routing table of known addresses to find the MAC address associated with the destination IP address. If no record is found, it will re-query the local network with another ARP request to locate the MAC address associated with the destination IP address. The outgoing Ethernet packet, encasing the TCP/IP packet, will be sent using the destination MAC address.

The other network device will likely return some information as well using the same technique of transferring TCP/IP packets inside of MAC addressed Ethernet packets. This goes on and on for thousands of packets every second to complete a data stream. The standard Ethernet packet size is only 1,500 bytes (that's roughly 1.5 kilobytes or 0.0015 megabytes) so you can imagine how many packets are necessary to transmit even a small file.

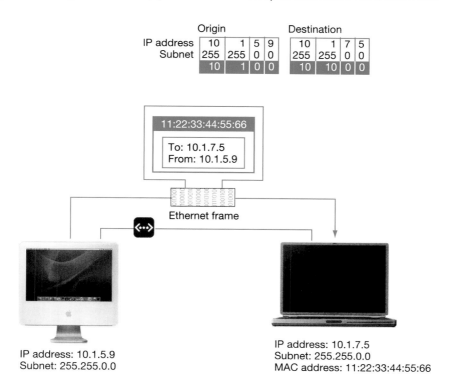

Wide Area Network (WAN) Traffic

Sending data over a wide area network (WAN) differs only in that data is sent through one or more network routers to reach its intended destination. WANs exist in all shapes and sizes, from a small WAN perhaps used to connect separate LANs in a large building, all the way up to the biggest and most popular WAN, the Internet.

Initially transferring data across a WAN is similar to transferring data on a LAN. After all, the first stop for the data destined for the WAN is to the network router on the local network. The network device will prepare the packets as before by encasing the TCP/IP packets inside Ethernet frames. Once again, the subnet mask will be applied to the destination IP address to determine if the address is on the local network. In this case, the network device determines that the destination is not on the local network, so it sends the data to the router. Because the router is on the local network, the transmission between the local network client and the router is identical to standard LAN traffic.

Once the router receives the Ethernet-encased TCP/IP packets, it will examine the destination IP address and use a preconfigured routing table to determine the next closest destination for this packet. This almost always involves sending the packet to another router closer to the destination. In fact, only the very last router in the path will send the data to the destination network device.

Network routers also often perform some sort repackaging and readdressing of the data because WAN network links are rarely standard Ethernet connections. The router will strip the Ethernet container away from the original TCP/IP packet and then rewrap it in another container that is appropriate for the WAN connection. Obviously, the final router will have to prepare the TCP/IP packet for the last leg of the journey on the destination device's local network by rewrapping it in an Ethernet frame addressed to the destination's MAC address.

In most cases, network data will be transferred back and forth several times to establish a complete connection. Remember, these packet sizes are very small. The default packet size for Internet traffic is also 1,500 bytes with a maximum packet size of 65,535 bytes for most TCP/IP connections. Network routers are highly optimized devices that can easily handle thousands of data packets every second, so for small amounts of data many WAN connections "feel" as fast as LAN connections. Conversely, a lot of latency is introduced from all the different routers and network connections involved in transferring data across a WAN, so often sending large amounts of data across a WAN is much slower than across a LAN. Thus, many a user's favorite time-wasting computer practice was born: waiting for an Internet download or upload.

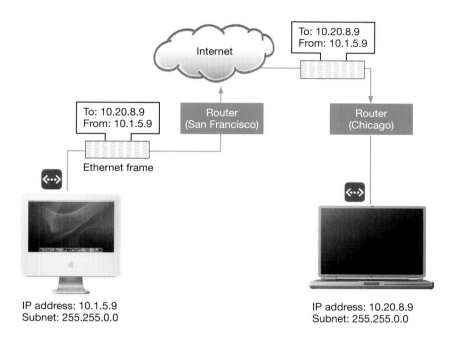

IP address: 10.1.5.9
Subnet: 255.255.0.0

IP address: 10.20.8.9
Subnet: 255.255.0.0

NOTE ▶ The previous network diagram uses nonroutable IP addresses for the purposes of this example. These addresses would not normally be used on any true WAN.

Domain Name System (DNS)

Most people are notoriously bad at remembering strings of seemingly arbitrary numbers used to define addresses, so additional technology is often implemented to help users find addresses. Even the most humble of cell phones features a contact list so users don't have to remember phone numbers. For TCP/IP networks, the Domain Name System (DNS) makes network addressing much more approachable to normal humans.

In essence, the DNS is a worldwide network of domain servers with the single task of maintaining human-friendly host names used to easily locate specific network IP addresses.

If you've spent any time at all on the Internet, you're already familiar with the DNS naming convention. For example, Apple's main website is located at http://www.apple.com. All network devices have a host name, but only those network devices providing a service that needs to be easily located on the Internet will have host name entries on a DNS server. Websites and mail servers are the most common devices to have DNS entries.

The hierarchical DNS naming convention relates directly to the hierarchical structure of the DNS domain architecture. As you know, DNS names are broken into labels separated by periods. Each label represents a different level, or domain, of the DNS hierarchy. The domains at the top of the DNS hierarchy are the familiar abbreviations at the end of nearly every Internet resource. Common examples are .com, .edu, .gov, and others, including various country codes. These top-level domains (TLDs) are hosted by a consortium of commercial and governmental organizations.

Below the TLDs, individual organizations or users host or rent their own DNS domain. For example, Apple hosts several DNS servers that are known by the TLD servers in order to maintain the apple.com domain. Apple can host an unlimited number of host names inside the apple.com domain. Apple can create unlimited domain names by preceding any text before apple.com. Examples include http://www.apple.com, http://training.apple.com, and http://developer.apple.com.

When a local network device needs to resolve a DNS name, it sends the name query to the IP address of a DNS server. The IP address for a DNS server is usually configured along with the other TCP/IP address information for the network device. The DNS server will search its local and cached name records first. If the requested name isn't found locally, the server will query other domain servers in the DNS hierarchy. This process may take a while, so DNS servers will temporarily cache any names they have recently resolved to provide a quicker response for future requests. Querying a DNS server to resolve an IP address given a known host name is called a forward lookup, whereas querying a DNS server to resolve a host name from a known IP address is called a reverse lookup. When initially configured, network clients will query the DNS server with a reverse lookup of its own IP address to determine if the network client has its own DNS name.

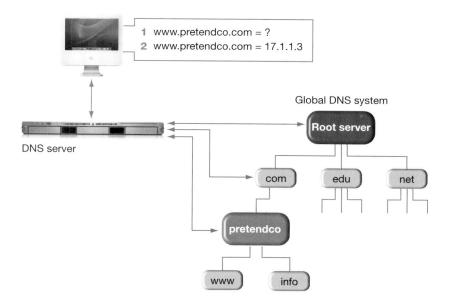

Configuring Mac OS X Networking

Initial networking configuration is handled by the Setup Assistant, which runs the first time you start up a new Mac or a fresh Mac OS X system installation. The Setup Assistant makes it easy for even a novice user to configure Mac OS X's network settings. Yet, even if you choose to not set up networking during the initial system setup process, the Mac will automatically enable any active network interface, including connecting to unrestricted wireless networks, and attempt to configure TCP/IP via DHCP. Consequently, for many users Mac OS X does not require any initial network configuration at all.

If network changes are required after initial setup, you can still use the Network Setup Assistant to help guide you through the network configuration process. You can access the Network Setup Assistant by clicking the Assist me button at the bottom of the Network system preference. Although this assistant is helpful for novice users, you should be familiar with all network configuration options so you're prepared for any potential network situation or troubleshooting issue.

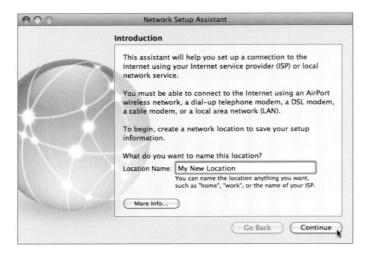

Apple didn't introduce many changes to the underlying network technology in Mac OS X 10.5, but it completely redesigned the network configuration user interface to further simplify network configuration. The fundamental change is a consolidation of previously separate network configuration windows into a new, unified Network system preference. With Mac OS X 10.5, all network settings can be found in the new Network system preference.

Despite this change, Mac OS X maintains a three-tiered system for network configuration. This three-tiered system enables you to easily maintain multiple separate but easily accessible network configurations, each supporting multiple interfaces and protocols. The top tier is network locations, which are used to define a specific set of network configurations. Next, within each network location you can configure a variety of network interfaces. Finally, each network interface can support multiple network services and protocols.

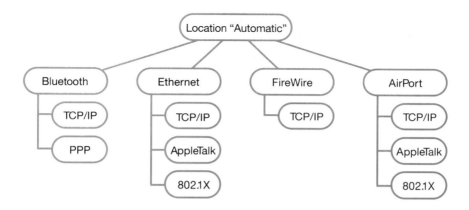

Using Network Locations

Similar to how applications are designed to save information to any number of individual documents, Mac OS X allows you to save network settings to any number of individual network configurations known as network locations. A network location contains all network interface, service and protocol settings, allowing you to configure as many unique network locations as you need for different situations. For example, you could create one network location for home and a different network location for work. Each location would contain all the appropriate settings for that location's network situation.

It is not necessary to add new network locations to change network settings, but it is more convenient as you can easily switch back to the pervious network location should you make a mistake. Creating additional network locations is also an essential network troubleshooting technique. Also, Mac OS X always requires one active network location, so if you ever want to temporarily turn off networking, you will have to create a new location with all the interfaces and services disabled.

Configuring Network Locations

The default network location on Mac OS X is called Automatic. In spite of this, this first location is no more automatic than any other network location you create. The initial location is simply called Automatic to indicate that it will attempt to automatically initialize any network interface to establish a TCP/IP connection via DHCP, but all network locations regardless of their name attempt this as well.

To configure network locations:

1   Open the Network preference by choosing Apple menu > System Preferences, then clicking the Network icon.

    You may have to click the lock icon in the bottom-left corner and authenticate as an administrative user to unlock the Network preference.

2   Choose Edit Locations from the Location pop-up menu.

    This will reveal the network locations editing user interface.

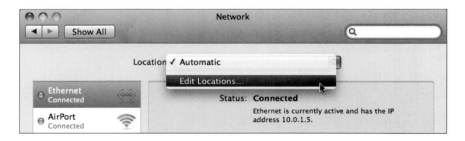

3   To add a new location based on the default "Automatic" location, click the small plus button at the bottom of the locations list, and then enter a new name for the location.

    Or, you can duplicate an existing location by selecting its name from the locations list and clicking the gear icon at the bottom of the list and then choosing Duplicate Location from the pop-up menu.

    Finally, double-clicking on a location name will allow you to rename any location.

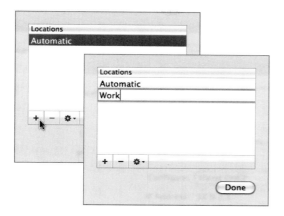

4 When you are finished making locations changes, click the Done button to return to the Network preference.

The Network preference will automatically load the newly created location, but it will not apply the location settings to the system.

If you want to work with another location, simply choose it from the Locations pop-up menu, and the Network preference will load it but won't apply it to the system.

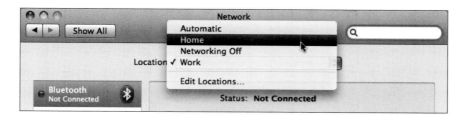

5 Once you have completed all the necessary network locations changes, click the Apply button at the bottom-right corner of the Network preference to activate the currently selected network location.

> **TIP** If you make a mistake at any time using the Network preference, click the Revert button in the bottom-right corner to return to the current active network configuration.

You may have noticed that the Network preference is different from all the other system preferences in that you must click the Apply button to activate the new settings. This allows you to easily prepare new network locations and settings without disrupting the current network configuration.

Changing Network Locations

Though you can certainly choose and apply a different network location from the Network preference, only administrative users have this ability as normal users do not have access to the Network preference. Conversely, all users who can log in to the Mac OS X graphical user interface can quickly and easily change the network location by choosing Apple menu > Locations > *location name* from the menu bar. This will apply the selected network location. Keep in mind that changing locations may interrupt network connections. Once a network location is selected, it will remain active until another location is selected. Even as other users log in to the Mac, or the Mac is restarted, the selected network location will remain active.

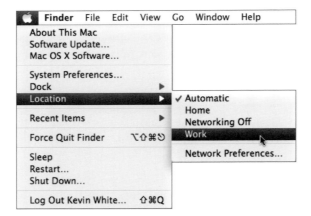

Using Hardware Network Interfaces

Mac hardware has a long history of providing built-in network connectivity. Apple started including Ethernet on Macs as early as 1991, and was the first manufacturer to have wireless as a built-in option when it introduced the iBook in 1999. Mac models have varied over the years as network technologies have grown increasingly faster and more affordable.

You can identify the hardware network interfaces and services available to your Mac from the /Applications/Utilities/System Profiler application. Detecting network information and troubleshooting with the Network Utility will be covered later in this lesson. Virtual network interfaces, like those used for virtual private networks (VPNs) or link aggregation, will also be covered later in this lesson.

Mac OS X includes built-in support for the following hardware network interfaces:

▶ Ethernet—Ethernet is the family of IEEE 802.3 standards that define most modern wired LANs. Every Mac since 1997 has included standard built-in Ethernet connectivity, with some models even featuring multiple Ethernet ports.

▶ FireWire—FireWire is Apple's marketing name for the IEEE 1394 connection standard. Though not a common network standard, Mac OS X includes software that allows you to create small ad hoc networks using daisy-chained FireWire cables. FireWire 400 is standard on every currently shipping Mac, with some models featuring FireWire 800.

▶ Analog modem—Although no currently shipping Mac includes an analog modem, it's available via an optional USB adapter and still supported by Mac OS X. For many years the analog modem was the standard method for home users to connect to the Internet. With the proliferation of high-speed and wireless Internet connections, analog modems are usually only necessary from the most remote of locations.

▶ AirPort—AirPort is Apple's marketing name for the family of IEEE 802.11 wireless standards, which has become the default implementation for most for wireless LANs. Every nonserver Mac since 2006 has included standard built-in AirPort connectivity.

▶ Bluetooth—This relatively low-speed wireless interface has become popular as a short-range connectivity standard. Mac OS X supports Bluetooth as a network bridge to modern cell phones that can provide Internet connectivity via a cell phone network.

Using Multiple Simultaneous Interfaces

Mac OS X supports these network interfaces via a multilink networking architecture. This means that Mac OS X supports multiple simultaneous network interfaces. For example, you can have both an active wired Ethernet connection and an active AirPort, or wireless

Ethernet, connection at the same time. Typically, having multiple active network interfaces means you will also have multiple active IP addresses. To handle multiple IP addresses, Mac OS X also features IP network multihoming. In fact, Mac OS X supports multiple IP addresses for each network interface.

In other words, you can configure as many separate network interfaces with as many unique IP addresses as you need. This may seem like overkill for most Mac clients, but remember Mac OS X and Mac OS X Server share the same underlying architecture. For some servers, multilink multihoming networking is a requirement, but Mac clients can also benefit from this technology. You may have a work environment where you have one insecure network for general Internet traffic and another network for secure internal transactions. With Mac OS X you can be on both of these networks at the same time.

When multiple IP addresses are available, the system can communicate via any of those interfaces but will attempt to pick the most appropriate route for every network connection. As described earlier, a network client will use the subnet mask to determine if an outgoing transmission is on the LAN. Mac OS X takes this a step further by examining all active LANs when determining a destination for outgoing transmission. Because a LAN connection is always faster than a WAN connection, Mac OS X will always route outgoing transmissions to the most appropriate LAN.

Any network connections that are not destined for a LAN that your Mac is connected to will be sent to the router address of the primary active network interface. Therefore, all Internet traffic will also connect via the primary active network interface. Any active network interface with a valid TCP/IP setting will be considered, but the primary active network interface is automatically selected based on the network service order. You can manually configure the network service order, as outlined later in this lesson.

Using the previous example where you have a Mac active on both wired and wireless Ethernet, the default network service order prioritizes wired over wireless Ethernet because wired is almost always faster. Thus, in this example, even though you have two active valid network interfaces, the primary active interface will be the wired Ethernet connection.

Configuring Hardware Network Interfaces

Every time you open the Network system preference, the system identifies all available network interfaces. Even if an interface is not connected or properly configured, it will create a service for that interface, which will show up in the network services list. In the Network preference, each network interface is tied to one or more network services.

A quick glance at the network services list clearly shows the status of all network interfaces and their configured services. Network services with a red indicator are not connected, a yellow indicator shows services that are connected but not properly configured, and a green indicator shows connected and configured network services. The active service at the top of this list is the primary network service as defined by the network service order. This list updates dynamically as new interfaces become active or as active interfaces become disconnected, so it's always the first place you should check when attempting to troubleshoot a network issue.

To manage network interfaces and their configured services:

1   Open and unlock the Network preference.

Choose the network location you wish to edit from the Locations pop-up menu, or configure a new network location, as detailed previously in this lesson.

2   To configure a particular network service, simply select it from the network services list.

Remember, each network service has its own settings separate from the other services. The configuration area to the right of the list will change to reflect primary options available to the selected service. Clicking the Advanced button in the bottom-right corner of the Network preference will reveal all the network protocol options available to the selected network service. Network protocol configuration will be covered later in this lesson.

3   To make a service inactive, select it from the services list, click the gear icon at the bottom of the list, and then choose Make Service Inactive from the pop-up menu.

An inactive service will never activate even if connected and properly configured. You can also delete an existing network service by selecting its name from the services list and then clicking the minus button at the bottom of the list.

Inactivating or deleting a network service from this list is the only way to disable a hardware network interface in Mac OS X.

4   To create another configurable instance of a network interface, click the small plus button at the bottom of the network services list.

This reveals a dialog that allows you to choose a new interface instance from the Interface pop-up menu and then assign it a unique service name to identify it in the services list. Click the Create button to continue. Or, you can duplicate an existing network service by selecting its name from the services list, clicking the gear icon at the bottom of the list, then choosing Duplicate Service from the pop-up menu. Using this menu you can also rename an existing network service.

Creating additional instances of a network service allows you to assign multiple IP addresses to a single network interface.

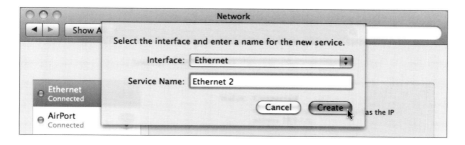

5   To change the network service order, click the gear icon at the bottom of the network services list, and then choose Set Service Order from the pop-up menu.

This reveals a dialog that allows you to click and drag network services into your preferred order for selection as the primary network interface. Click the OK button when you have finished reordering.

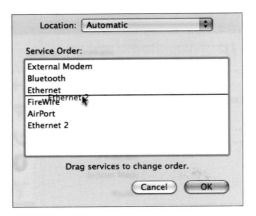

6   Once you have completed all the necessary network interface and service changes, click the Apply button at the bottom-right corner of the Network preference to activate the currently selected network location.

> **TIP** ▶ If you make a mistake at any time using the Network preference, click the Revert button in the bottom-right corner to return to the current active network configuration.

Using Virtual Network Interfaces

Virtual network interfaces are logical networks within a hardware network interface. Think of a virtual network interface as providing another unique network interface by carving out a section of an established network connection.

Some virtual network services are used to increase security by encrypting data before it travels across an IP network, and others are used to segregate or aggregate network traffic across LAN connections. Mac OS X includes the necessary client software that will allow you to connect to many common virtual network services and establish a virtual network interface.

If necessary, you can define multiple separate virtual network interfaces for each network location. Virtual network interfaces are not always tied to a specific hardware network interface, as the system will attempt to seek out the most appropriate route when there are multiple active connections. Likewise, any virtual network interface that is not destined for a LAN connection will always be routed to the primary active network interface.

NOTE ▶ Third-party virtualization tools, like Parallels, also use virtual network interfaces to provide networking for multiple simultaneous operating systems. In fact, when you install Parallels you will notice multiple virtual Ethernet services in the Network preference.

Mac OS X includes built-in support for the following virtual network interfaces:

▶ Virtual private network (VPN)—By far the most commonly used virtual network service, VPNs are primarily used to create secure virtual LAN connections over the Internet.

▶ Point-to-Point Protocol over Ethernet (PPPoE)—Primarily used for directly connecting your Mac to a modem providing a high-speed Digital Subscriber Line (DSL) Internet connection.

▶ 6 to 4—Creates a VPN of sorts to transfer IPv6 packets across an IPv4 network. There is no enhanced security when using a 6 to 4 connection, but your Mac will appear to be directly connected to a remote IPv6 LAN. The differences between IPv4 and IPv6 were covered earlier in this lesson.

▶ Virtual local area network (VLAN)—Mac OS X's VLAN implementation allows you to define separate independent LANs on a single network hardware interface.

▶ Link aggregation—Allows you to define a single virtual LAN interface using multiple network hardware interfaces.

Configuring PPPoE

The PPPoE is a connection protocol that encapsulates PPP packets inside standard Ethernet packets. This protocol is primarily used by high-speed Digital Subscriber Line (DSL) providers. You may or may not need to use PPPoE for your DSL connection.

To manage PPPoE connections:

1 Open and unlock the Network preference.

   Choose the network location you wish to edit from the Locations pop-up menu, or configure a new network location, as detailed previously in this lesson.

2 Click the small plus button at the bottom of the services list to add a PPPoE virtual network interface.

   This will reveal a dialog allowing you add a new network interface and service.

3   Choose PPPoE from the Interface pop-up menu.

PPPoE is tied to a specific Ethernet interface, so you must choose the specific interface that will be used for the PPPoE connection from the Ethernet pop-up menu. Finally, enter a descriptive name and click the Create button to make a new PPPoE virtual network interface and service.

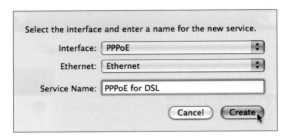

4   Select the PPPoE service from the network services list to configure PPPoE settings.

Basic PPPoE configuration settings will appear to the right of the services list. At a minimum you will need to enter the account name and password given by the service provider. You should also probably check the "Remember this password" checkbox to save the PPPoE authentication information to the system keychain so other users don't have to remember it.

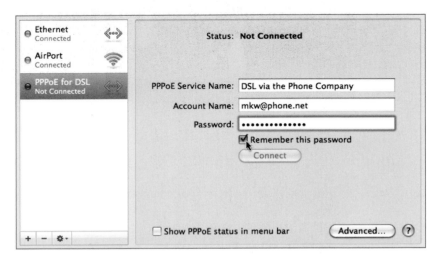

5 To configure advanced PPPoE settings, click the Advanced button in the bottom-right corner of the Network preference.

This reveals the advanced settings dialog. Click the PPP tab to view PPP-specific settings.

Because PPPoE is based on PPP, they share the same advanced configuration options. Probably the most significant settings are to optionally connect automatically when needed and to not disconnect when switching to another user account. Click the OK button when you have made all your selections.

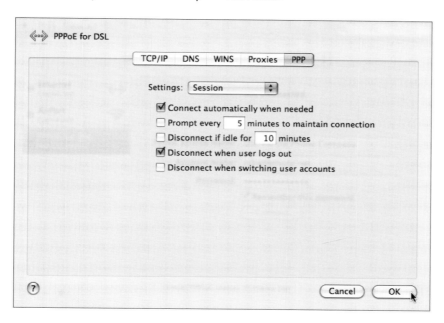

6 Once you have completed all PPPoE settings, click the Apply button at the bottom-right corner of the Network preference to save and activate the changes.

7   You can make accessing PPPoE connectivity options much easier by clicking the "Show PPPoE status in menu bar" checkbox. The PPPoE menu bar item allows you to easily connect, disconnect, and monitor PPPoE connections.

As you can see, PPPoE connections are not always on like other high-speed services. Mac OS X supports automatically connecting PPPoE when needed, but you can also manually connect and disconnect the PPPoE link from the PPPoE menu bar item or by clicking the Connect button in the Network preference. Once the connection is established, the PPP process automatically configures TCP/IP and DNS settings. You can also manually configure these settings, as outlined later in this lesson. PPPoE services are also automatically placed above all other services in the network service order, so as soon as the PPPoE service is connected and completely configured it will be the primary network interface for all Internet traffic. Reordering the network service order was covered previously in this lesson.

Configuring VPN

A VPN is an encrypted tunnel from your client to the network routing device providing the VPN service. Once established, your Mac will appear to have a direct connection to the LAN that the VPN device is sharing. So, even if you're on a wireless Internet connection thousands of miles away from your LAN, a VPN connection provides a virtual network interface as if your computer is directly attached to that LAN. Mac OS X supports two common VPN protocols: Point-to-Point Tunneling Protocol (PPTP) and the Layer 2 Tunneling Protocol (L2TP) over Internet Protocol security (IPsec).

> **NOTE** ▶ Some VPN services require a third-party VPN client. Third-party VPN clients usually include a custom interface for managing the connection. Although you may see the virtual network interface provided by the third-party VPN client appear in the Network preference, it's usually not configurable from there.

To manage VPN connections:

1 Open and unlock the Network preference.

Choose the network location you wish to edit from the Locations pop-up menu, or configure a new network location, as detailed previously in this lesson.

2 To add a VPN virtual network interface, click the small plus button at the bottom of the services list.

This reveals a dialog that allows you to add a new network interface and service.

3 Choose VPN from the Interface pop-up menu.

You must choose the appropriate VPN protocol from the VPN Type pop-up menu. Again, Mac OS X supports the PPTP or L2TP over IPsec VPN protocols. Both have similar configuration options, but for the purposes of this lesson L2TP will be used because it has a few more authentication options.

Finally, if you're only going to have one VPN service, you should enter a descriptive name for the service. Otherwise, you can leave the service name as is because you can define multiple VPN configurations per VPN service. Click the Create button to make the new VPN virtual network interface and service.

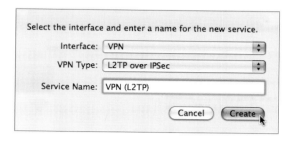

4 To begin configuring VPN settings, select the VPN service from the network services list, and basic VPN configuration settings will appear to the right of the services list.

5 If you plan to have only one VPN configuration, leave the Configuration pop-up menu as is and continue to the next step.

Conversely, if you want to set multiple VPN configurations, choose Add Configuration from the Configuration pop-up menu. This reveals a dialog where you can name and create a new VPN configuration. You can also delete and rename your configuration from this pop-up menu.

Continue editing VPN configurations, and when finished you will have to enter the settings for each VPN configuration, as outlined in the following steps.

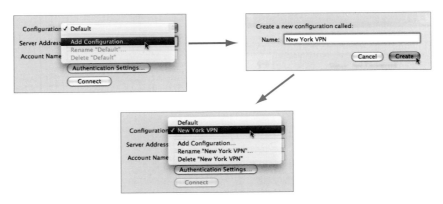

6   To configure VPN settings, first enter the VPN server address and then your VPN account name.

You must also define authentication methods by clicking the Authentication Settings button.

This will reveal a dialog allowing you to specify user and machine authentication settings. The VPN administrator should provide you with the appropriate authentication settings. When you have made your selections, click the OK button to save the authentication settings.

7 To configure advanced VPN settings, click the Advanced button in the bottom-right corner of the Network preference. In the advanced settings dialog that opens, click the Options tab to view general VPN options.

The most important optional setting is to send all traffic over the VPN connection. By default, active VPN connections will not act as the primary network interface, so the system will only route traffic to the VPN if the destination IP address is part of the LAN that the VPN service is providing. Selecting the "Send all traffic over VPN connection" checkbox will force the VPN connection to act as the primary network interface.

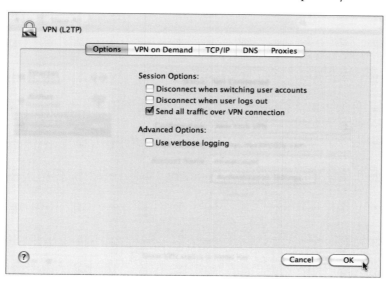

8 To enable automatic VPN connections, click the VPN on Demand tab. The options on this tab allow you to assign domains that, when accessed, will automatically activate specific VPN configurations.

Click the small plus button at the bottom of the list to add a domain and an associated VPN configuration. Double-click on a domain name to change it, and click once on the VPN configuration name to choose an alternate configuration from the pop-up menu. When you have finished, click the OK button to save the VPN on Demand settings.

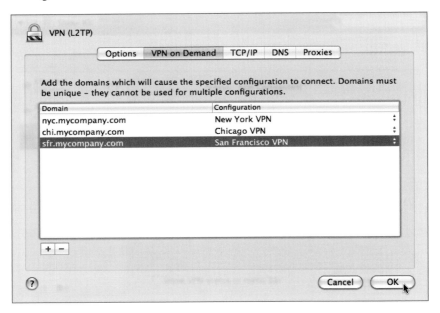

9 Once you have completed all VPN settings, click the Apply button at the bottom-right corner of the Network preference to save and activate the changes.

10 You can make accessing VPN connectivity options much easier by clicking the "Show VPN status in menu bar" checkbox. The VPN menu bar item allows you to easily select VPN configurations, and connect, disconnect, and monitor VPN connections.

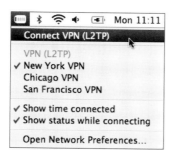

TIP ▶ VPN connections can be complicated and take a while to configure properly, so you can save time and prevent mistakes by using VPN configuration files. Click the gear icon at the bottom of the services list and use the Import and Export configuration menu options to use VPN configuration files.

VPN connections are not typically always-on connections. As you saw in the instructions, Mac OS X supports automatic VPN connections with the VPN on Demand feature, but most users will manually enable VPN connections when necessary. You can manually connect and disconnect the VPN link from the VPN menu bar item or by clicking the Connect button in the Network preference. VPNs are usually implemented in situations where security is required, so for many, initiating a VPN connection will prompt an authentication dialog.

Once the connection is authenticated and established, the VPN process will automatically configure TCP/IP and DNS settings using the PPP protocol. You can also manually configure these settings, as outlined later in this lesson. VPN interfaces are, by default, set at the bottom of the network service order, so they will not automatically become the primary network interface when activated. This behavior is overridden when the optional "Send all traffic over VPN connection" checkbox is enabled, as covered in the instructions. You can also manually reorder the network service order, as explained earlier in this lesson.

Configuring VLANs

VLANs are used to define separate independent logical LANs on a single network interface. In other words, your Mac could have a single Ethernet connection that allows it to simultaneously connect to multiple separate LANs. VLANs are configured in software, which gives network administrators much greater control over how network traffic is allocated and routed. VLAN services require special network infrastructure, but Mac OS X includes the appropriate network client software to support VLANs. Mac OS X supports the standard protocol used for VLAN configuration: the IEEE 802.1Q specification.

To manage VLANs:

1   Open and unlock the Network preference.

Choose the network location you wish to edit from the Locations pop-up menu, or configure a new network location, as detailed previously in this lesson.

2   To add a VLAN interface, click the gear icon at the bottom of the services list and choose Manage Virtual Interfaces from the pop-up menu.

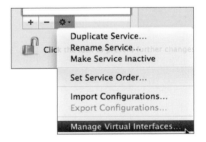

This will reveal a dialog allowing you add a new virtual network interface and services. Click the small plus button at the bottom of the virtual interface list and then choose New VLAN from the pop-up menu.

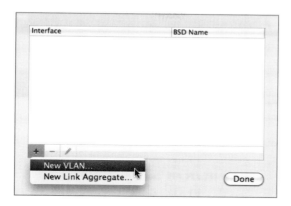

3   The dialog will transition to the VLAN creation dialog.

Enter a recognizable name for the new VLAN, and select a VLAN Tag as indicated by the network administrator. VLANs are tied to a specific wired Ethernet interface, so if you have multiple interfaces you must specify one from the Interface pop-up menu. When you have finished configuring the VLAN, click the Create button to continue.

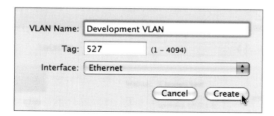

4   The dialog will transition back to the virtual interface dialog.

Here you can edit any virtual interface by double-clicking on its name. You can also delete a virtual interface by selecting it from the list and clicking the minus button at the bottom of the list.

When you have finished managing virtual interfaces, click the Done button.

5   Once you have completed all VLAN settings, click the Apply button at the bottom-right corner of the Network preference to save and activate the changes.

If properly configured, the VLAN interface should activate a few moments after you click the Apply button. The VLAN interface will act like any other Ethernet interface and automatically attempt to configure using DHCP-supplied TCP/IP and DNS settings, but you can also manually configure these settings, as outlined later in this lesson. New virtual network interfaces are, by default, set at the bottom of the network service order, so they will not automatically become the primary network interface when activated. You can manually reorder the network service order as covered previously in this lesson.

Configuring Link Aggregation

Link aggregation, also known as interface bonding, allows you to define a single LAN interface using multiple separate hardware network interfaces. The advantage here is that you greatly increase network performance by using multiple physical connections. Link aggregation also increases network reliability by introducing connection redundancy, so if a network interface goes down there is at least one other interface to fall back on. Link aggregation services also require special network infrastructure, but again, Mac OS X includes the appropriate network client software to support link aggregation. Mac OS X supports the standard protocol used for link aggregation: the IEEE 802.3ad specification.

To manage link aggregation:

1   Open and unlock the Network preference.

    Choose the network location you wish to edit from the Locations pop-up menu, or configure a new network location, as detailed previously in this lesson.

2   To add a new aggregate virtual interface, click the gear icon at the bottom of the services list and choose Manage Virtual Interfaces from the pop-up menu.

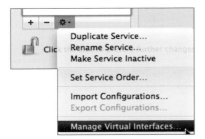

This will reveal a dialog allowing you add a new virtual network interface and service. Click the small plus button at the bottom of the virtual interface list and then choose New Link Aggregate from the pop-up menu.

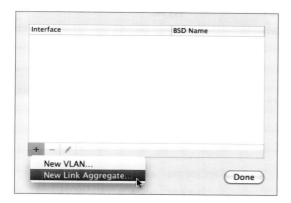

3   The dialog will transition to the link aggregate creation dialog.

Enter a recognizable name for the new aggregate interface, and select the checkboxes next to the Ethernet interfaces you want to bond together. Once bonded, these Ethernet interfaces cannot be used for another service. When you have finished configuring the aggregate interface, click the Create button to continue.

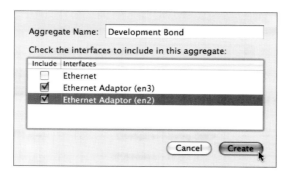

4   The dialog will transition back to the virtual interface dialog.

Here you can edit any virtual interface by double-clicking its name. You can also delete a virtual interface by selecting it from the list and clicking the minus button at the bottom of the list.

When you have finished managing virtual interfaces, click the Done button.

5   Once you have completed all link aggregation settings, click the Apply button at the bottom-right corner of the Network preference to save and activate the changes.

If properly configured, the link aggregate interface should activate a few moments after you click the Apply button. You can check the status of the link aggregate interface by clicking the Advanced button in the bottom-right corner of the Network preference, and then clicking the Bond Status tab. The Development Bond in the following example is obviously not properly configured.

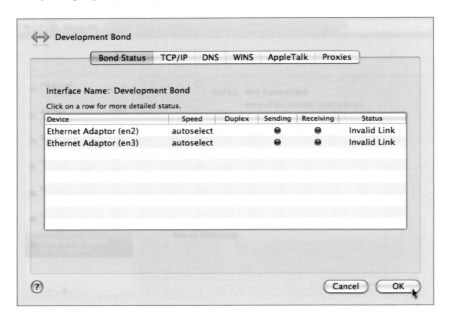

The link aggregate interface will act like any other Ethernet interface and automatically attempt to configure using DHCP-supplied TCP/IP and DNS settings, but you can also manually configure these settings, as outlined later in this lesson. New virtual network interfaces are, by default, set at the bottom of the network service order, so they will not automatically become the primary network interface when activated. You can manually reorder the network service order, as explained earlier in this lesson.

Using Network Protocols

Each hardware or virtual network interface provides connectivity for a number of standard networking protocols. The Network system preference shows primary protocol settings whenever you select a service from the services list, but many protocol configuration options are only available by clicking the Advanced button. The remainder of this section covers how to configure each built-in networking protocol supported by Mac OS X.

Mac OS X includes built-in support for the following network protocols:

▶ TCP/IP configured via DHCP—As explained previously in this lesson, TCP/IP is the primary network protocol for LANs and WANs, and DHCP is a popular network service that will automatically configure TCP/IP clients.

▶ TCP/IP configured manually—If you do not have DHCP service on your local network or if you want to ensure that the TCP/IP settings never change, you can manually configure TCP/IP settings.

▶ DNS—As covered previously, DNS provides host names for IP network devices. DNS settings are often configured alongside TCP/IP settings either by DHCP or manual configuration. Mac OS X supports multiple DNS servers and search domains.

▶ Network Basic Input/Output System (NetBIOS) and Windows Internet Naming Service (WINS)—NetBIOS and WINS are protocols most often used by Windows-based computers to provide network identification and service discovery.

▶ AppleTalk—AppleTalk is a suite of legacy network protocols designed by Apple to facilitate network identification, service discovery, and data transfer.

▶ Authenticated Ethernet via 802.1X—The 802.1X protocol is used to secure Ethernet networks by allowing only properly authenticated network clients to join the LAN.

▶ IP proxies—Proxy servers act as intermediaries between a network client and a requested service, and are used to enhance performance or provide an additional layer of security.

▶ Wired Ethernet Protocol options—Mac OS X supports both automatic and manual Ethernet configuration.

▶ Wireless Ethernet (AirPort) Protocol options—The wireless nature of AirPort requires additional configuration to facilitate network selection and authentication.

▶ Analog modem with PPP—Likewise, the very nature of analog modems requires manual configuration to activate a connection.

▶ Bluetooth with PPP—Again, the wireless nature of Bluetooth requires additional configuration to facilitate peripheral selection and authentication.

▶ Point-to-Point Protocol (PPP)—As PPP is used for both analog modem and Bluetooth connectivity, additional configuration is required.

Configuring TCP/IP and DNS

Many network situations do not require any manual intervention to configure TCP/IP and DNS, as the DHCP or PPP service will automatically configure these settings. The default configuration for all Ethernet services is to automatically engage the DHCP process as soon as the interface port becomes active. To verify TCP/IP and DNS settings for hardware or virtual Ethernet services when using the DHCP service, simply select the service from the Network system preference.

NOTE ▶ IPv6 addressing information is automatically detected as well if available. However, automatic IPv6 configuration is not provided by standard DHCP or PPP services.

Interfaces that may require a manual connection process, like AirPort, analog modems, VPN, and PPPoE interfaces, will automatically engage the DHCP or PPP process to automatically configure TCP/IP and DNS settings. To verify TCP/IP and DNS settings when using these interfaces, select the service from the services list, and then click the Advanced button in the bottom-right corner of the Network preference. This will open the advanced settings dialog, where you can click the TCP/IP or DNS tabs to view their respective settings. You can also verify network settings of any other interface this way.

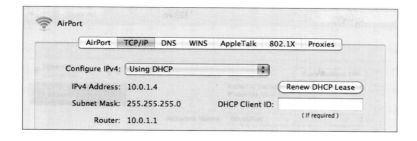

TIP ▶ Automatically configured DNS settings will show as gray text. This indicates that you can override these settings by manually entering DNS information.

Despite the convenience of automatic TCP/IP and DNS configuration, there may be times where manual configuration is required. For example, the network server providing the DHCP service will require a manual configuration. In fact, most network devices that provide services use manually entered network configuration information so they don't run the risk of changing to a different TCP/IP address if DHCP resets.

To manually configure TCP/IP and DNS settings:

1   Open and unlock the Network preference.

Choose the network location you want to edit from the Locations pop-up menu, or configure a new network location, as detailed previously in this lesson.

2   Select the network service you wish to configure from the network services list.

At this point, you could configure TCP/IP settings from the general information area to the right of the services list, but for the purposes of this lesson you need to click the Advanced button in the bottom-right corner of the Network preference to open the advanced settings dialog.

3   Click the TCP/IP tab at the top to view the TCP/IP settings.

4   If you want to keep using DHCP but only assign a manual IP address, choose "Using DHCP with manual address" from the Configure IPv4 pop-up menu.

You will have to manually enter an IPv4 address only for this Mac. When you have entered the appropriate IP address, click the OK button to dismiss the advanced network options dialog, and then click the Apply button in the bottom-right corner of the Network preference to save and activate the changes.

You can disregard the rest of these steps because the DHCP service will continue to manage the rest of the TCP/IP and DNS settings.

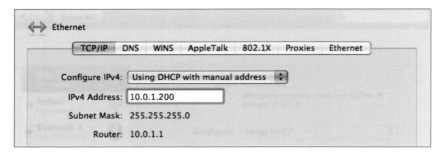

5   If you want to manually enter all TCP/IP settings, choose Manually from the Configure IPv4 pop-up menu.

At a minimum you will have to manually enter the IP address, the subnet mask, and the router address. The user interface will cache the TCP/IP settings from the DHCP service so you may only have to enter a new IPv4 address.

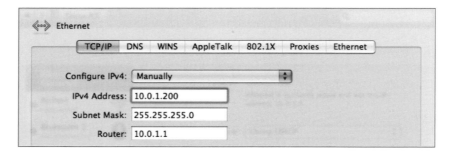

6   If you have to manually set up IPv6 settings as well, choose Manually from the Configure IPv6 pop-up menu.

At a minimum you will have to manually enter the IPv6 address, router address, and the prefix length. The user interface will cache any automatic IPv6 settings so you may only have to enter a new IPv6 address.

7   To configure DNS, click the DNS tab at the top to view the DNS settings.

Again, the user interface will cache the DNS settings from the DHCP service so you may not have to enter any DNS settings at all.

You should configure at least one DNS server. Click the plus button at the bottom of the DNS server list to add a new server, and then enter the server's IP address. Entering a search domain is optional. Click the plus button at the button at the bottom of the Search Domains list, and then enter the domain name.

If you configure multiple DNS servers or search domains, the system will attempt to access those resources in the order they appear in the list. To edit an address, double-click on its entry in the list, or you can delete an entry by selecting it and clicking the minus button at the bottom of the list.

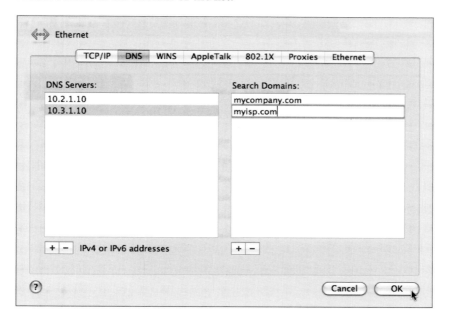

8   When you have entered all the appropriate IP and DNS settings, click the OK button to dismiss the advanced network options dialog, and then click the Apply button in the bottom-right corner of the Network preference to save and activate the changes.

Whenever you manually configure TCP/IP or DNS settings, you should always test network connectivity to verify that you properly entered all information. Using standard applications to access network and Internet resources is one basic test, but you could also test more thoroughly using the included network diagnostic utilities. Using network diagnostic tools built into Mac OS X is covered later in this lesson.

Configuring NetBIOS and WINS

Network Basic Input/Output System (NetBIOS) and Windows Internet Naming Service (WINS) runs on top of TCP/IP to provide network identification and service discovery. NetBIOS and WINS are used primarily by Windows-based systems to provide identification and service discovery on LANs, while WINS is used to identify and locate NetBIOS network devices on WANs. You can think of WINS as a form of DNS for NetBIOS network clients.

NOTE ▶ Mac OS X supports NetBIOS and WINS on any active network interface except for VPN connections.

Mac OS X automatically configures your computer's NetBIOS name, and for small networks this should be sufficient. If your Mac is on a larger network and you want to share resources from your Mac with other network clients, you may want to manually select the NetBIOS workgroup. NetBIOS workgroups are used make navigation easier on large networks by grouping devices into smaller collections. You may have to manually configure the WINS service to provide faster NetBIOS resolution.

To manually configure NetBIOS and WINS settings:

1   Open and unlock the Network preference.

    Choose the network location you wish to edit from the Locations pop-up menu, or configure a new network location, as detailed previously in this lesson.

2   Select the network service you wish to configure from the network services list, and then click the Advanced button in the bottom-right corner of the Network preference.

3   In the advanced settings dialog that opens, click the WINS tab at the top to view the NetBIOS and WINS settings.

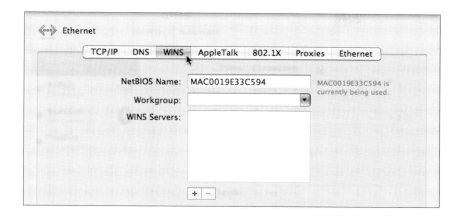

4   To manually configure NetBIOS, enter a unique name, and then choose a workgroup from the pop-up menu.

It may take a while for the NetBIOS workgroup list to refresh, so if you already know the name of the workgroup you want the Mac to be in you can manually enter the workgroup name.

NOTE ▶ NetBIOS workgroup names are in all capital letters and cannot contain any special characters or spaces.

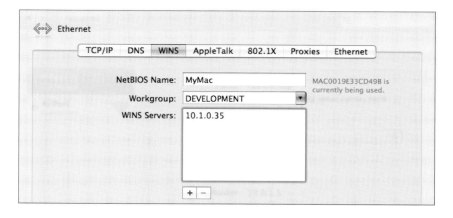

5   To enable WINS, enter at least one WINS server IP address. Click the plus button at the bottom of the WINS server list to add a new server, and then enter the server's IP address.

If you configure multiple WINS servers, the system will attempt to access those resources in the order they appear in the list. To edit a server address, double-click its entry in the list, or you can delete a server by selecting it and clicking the minus button at the bottom of the list.

6   When you have entered all the appropriate NetBIOS and WINS settings, click the OK button to dismiss the advanced network options dialog, and then click the Apply button in the bottom-right corner of the Network preference to save and activate the changes.

Once NetBIOS and WINS are fully configured, you should be able to browse and share resources with other Windows-compatible network clients as if you were running Windows natively. Accessing shared network services using these two protocols is covered in Lesson 7, "Accessing Network Services." Sharing resources from your Mac over the network using these two protocols is covered in Lesson 8, "Providing Network Services."

Configuring AppleTalk

AppleTalk is a suite of network protocols that was originally designed by Apple before the proliferation of TCP/IP networks. AppleTalk runs on Ethernet networks alongside TCP/IP but uses a separate set of protocols. With the introduction of Mac OS X, and more important, with the dominance of the TCP/IP standard, AppleTalk support has been reduced to the minimum required for network identification, service discovery, and printing.

AppleTalk is disabled by default on Mac OS X. If you don't have a reason to use it, leave it disabled. The most common reason to continue using AppleTalk is to support older printers. In Mac OS X Leopard, the system will automatically enable and disable AppleTalk as required to support those printers. You do not need to enable AppleTalk in the Network preference. Managing printers is covered in Lesson 9, "Peripherals and Printing."

> **NOTE ▶** AppleTalk is only supported on wired and wireless (AirPort) Ethernet connections. Further, it's only supported on a single network interface at a time.

To manually enable AppleTalk for resource discovery:

1   Open and unlock the Network preference.

Choose the network location you wish to edit from the Locations pop-up menu, or configure a new network location, as detailed previously in this lesson.

2 Select the network service you wish to configure from the network services list, and then click the Advanced button in the bottom-right corner of the Network preference.

This will reveal the advanced settings dialog.

3 Click the AppleTalk tab at the top to view the AppleTalk settings, and then click the Make AppleTalk Active checkbox to enable the AppleTalk protocol.

4 If you're on a large AppleTalk network, you will be able to access AppleTalk zones and define the zone to which your Mac belongs.

It may take a while for the AppleTalk zone list to refresh, but you can click the Refresh Zones button to force a list refresh. Once you have a zone list, choose the zone you want your Mac to appear in from the AppleTalk Zone pop-up menu.

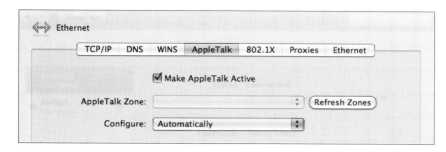

NOTE ▸ Only in the rarest of circumstances will you need to manually configure any of the AppleTalk node ID or network ID settings, so it's best to leave AppleTalk in automatic configuration mode.

5 Once you have enabled AppleTalk, click the OK button to dismiss the advanced settings dialog, and then click the Apply button in the bottom-right corner of the Network preference to save and activate the changes.

Once AppleTalk is activated and fully configured, you should be able to browse and provide AFP sharing resources using AppleTalk for identity and service discovery. Accessing shared network services using these two protocols is covered in Lesson 7, "Accessing Network Services." Sharing resources from your Mac over the network using these two protocols is covered in Lesson 8, "Providing Network Services."

Configuring 802.1X

The 802.1X protocol is used to secure wired and wireless (AirPort) Ethernet networks by only allowing properly authenticated network clients to join the LAN—802.1X-protected networks will not allow any traffic until the network client properly authenticates to the network.

To facilitate 802.1X authentication, Mac OS X provides three configuration choices:

▶ User authentication—With this configuration the user must manually choose to authenticate to the 802.1X network using account information you've configured. This method requires that users be logged in to the machine before they can join the 802.1X network.

▶ System authentication—If you want the Mac to always have access to the 802.1X network, you can set a single 802.1X account for the machine as a whole. The account information is saved to the system keychain, and the system will automatically join the network on boot.

▶ Login window authentication—Many larger networks use the same usernames and passwords for access to the computers and to their networks. Setting 802.1X for the login window allows the system to pass to the network the same credentials that are used to log in to Mac OS X.

To configure 802.1X on Ethernet:

1   Open and unlock the Network preference.

    Choose the network location you wish to edit from the Locations pop-up menu, or configure a new network location, as detailed previously in this lesson.

2   Select the Ethernet or AirPort network service you wish to configure from the network services list, and then click the Advanced button in the bottom-right corner of the Network preference.

    This will reveal the advanced settings dialog.

    Click the 802.1X tab at the top to view the 802.1X settings.

3   You must first choose one of the three 802.1X configurations from the Domain pop-up menu: User, System, or Login Window.

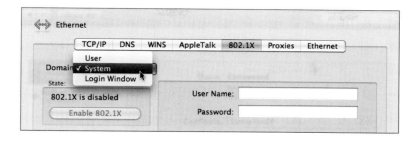

4   At this point you will you will perform one of three routines based on your 802.1X configuration domain choice.

If you picked the User configuration domain, click the plus button at the bottom of the configurations list to create a new 802.1X configuration, and then enter the account information and select authentication settings provided by your network administrator. You can configure multiple 802.1X user configurations. To rename a configuration, simply double-click on its entry in the list, or you can delete a configuration by selecting it and clicking the minus button at the bottom of the list.

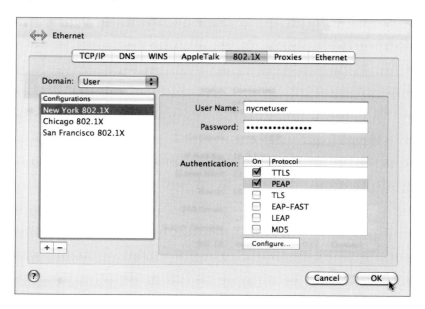

If you picked the System configuration domain, enter the 802.1X account information and select authentication settings provided by your network administrator. Then click the Enable 802.1X button to immediately enable 802.1X authentication.

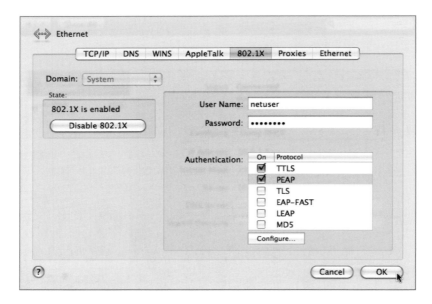

If you picked the Login Window configuration domain, configure the certificate and authentication settings as provided by your network administrator. Then click the Enable 802.1X Login button to allow the Login Window to authenticate 802.1X connections based on user-entered authentication information.

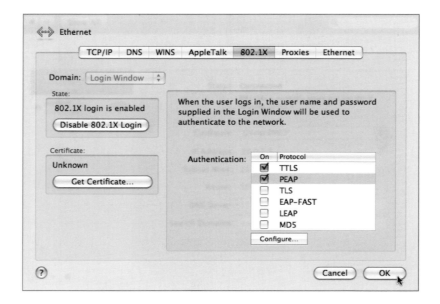

5 When you have entered all the appropriate 802.1X settings, click the OK button to dismiss the advanced settings dialog, and then click the Apply button in the bottom-right corner of the Network preference to save and activate the changes.

Once 802.1X is properly configured, you should be able to authenticate to the protected Ethernet network. System 802.1X configurations will automatically connect as soon as you click the Apply button. Login Window 802.1X configurations will start to authenticate the next time you log in to the Mac. Finally, to connect User 802.1X configurations you will have to manually click the Connect button in the Network preference.

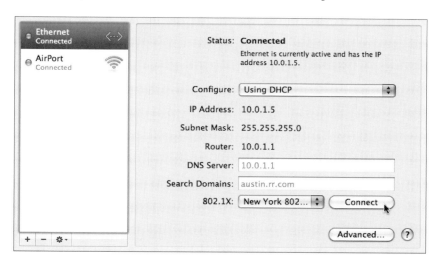

Configuring IP Proxies

Proxy servers act as intermediaries between a network client and a requested service. Proxy servers are often used to enhance the performance of slow WAN or Internet connections by caching recently requested data so future connections appear faster to local network clients. Primarily, though, proxy servers are implemented so network administrators can limit network connections to unauthorized servers or resources. Administrators can manage lists of approved resources, having the proxy servers allow access only to those resources.

Mac OS X supports proxy services for File Transfer Protocol (FTP), web protocols (HTTP and HTTPS), streaming (RTSP), SOCKS, and Gopher. Mac OS X also supports manual proxy configuration or automatic proxy configuration using a local or network hosted .pac proxy configuration file.

To configure proxy settings:

1   Open and unlock the Network preference.

Choose the network location you wish to edit from the Locations pop-up menu, or configure a new network location, as detailed previously in this lesson.

2   Select the network service you wish to configure from the network services list, and then click the Advanced button in the bottom-right corner of the Network preference.

This will reveal the advanced settings dialog.

3   Click the Proxies tab at the top to view the proxy settings.

4   To use an automatic proxy configuration file, select the Automatic Proxy Configuration checkbox at the bottom of the proxy protocols list.

You must then specify a .pac proxy configuration file. To specify a local file, click the Choose File button and then select the file using the file browser dialog. To specify a network-hosted file, enter the full network path to the file in the URL entry field.

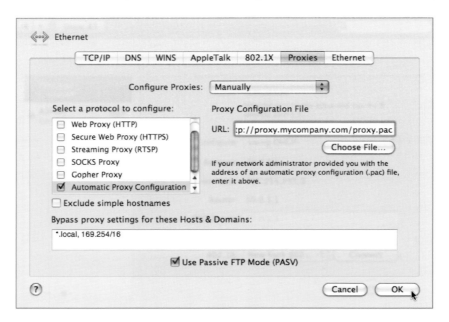

5 To manually configure proxy settings, select the checkboxes next to each protocol you wish to send through the proxy servers.

Select each protocol individually to enter the proxy connection information provided by the network administrator.

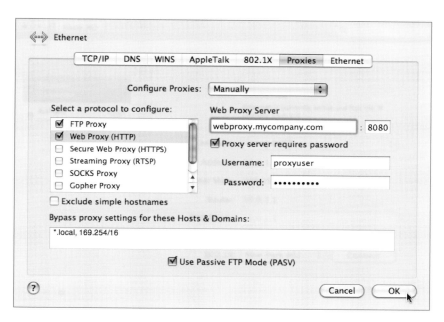

6 When you have entered all the appropriate proxy information, click the OK button to dismiss the advanced settings dialog, and then click the Apply button in the bottom-right corner of the Network preference to save and activate the changes.

Configuring Ethernet Protocol Options

Wired Ethernet connections are designed to establish connection settings automatically. Yet Mac OS X allows you to manually configure wired Ethernet options from the Network preference.

To manually configure wired Ethernet settings:

1 Open and unlock the Network preference.

Choose the network location you wish to edit from the Locations pop-up menu, or configure a new network location, as detailed previously in this lesson.

2   Select the wired Ethernet service you wish to configure from the network services list, and then click the Advanced button in the bottom-right corner of the Network preference.

This will reveal the advanced settings dialog.

3   Click the Ethernet tab at the top to view the current automatically configured Ethernet settings.

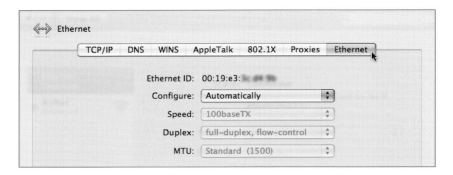

4   To manually configure Ethernet options, choose Manually from the Configure pop-up menu. The system will cache the current automatically configured Ethernet settings so you will not have to change all the settings.

The system will prepopulate the Speed, Duplex, and MTU Ethernet options based on your Mac's network hardwire. Make your custom selections from these pop-up menus.

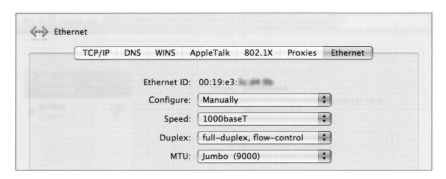

5   When you have selected all the appropriate Ethernet settings, click the OK button to dismiss the advanced settings dialog, and then click the Apply button in the bottom-right corner of the Network preference to save and activate the changes.

Configuring AirPort Protocol Options

Apple made basic wireless Ethernet (AirPort) network management a breeze with the AirPort menu item. The AirPort menu item will automatically appear in the menu bar if your Mac has an AirPort card installed. From this menu you can easily join established open and secure wireless networks. The AirPort background process will automatically scan for any advertised networks that are within range for you to choose from. If you select an open wireless network, the Mac will immediately connect, but if you select a secure wireless network, as indicated by the small lock icon, you will have to enter the network password. By default, the system will automatically remember secure networks by saving the passwords to the system keychain so all users can access the wireless network.

To increase security, some wireless networks do not advertise their availability. You can connect to these hidden wireless networks (also called closed networks) as long as you know their network name by choosing Join Other Network from the AirPort menu item. This will reveal a dialog where you can enter all the appropriate information to join the hidden wireless network. Again, the system will save this information to the system keychain by default.

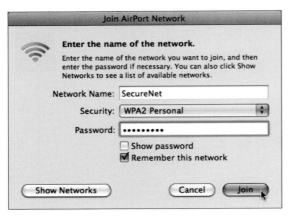

Lastly, if you are unable to connect to a standard wireless network, you can create an ad hoc wireless network using your Mac's AirPort card to share files wirelessly with other computers. Choose Create Network from the AirPort menu item and then enter the wireless network information that will be used to connect to your ad hoc network.

> **NOTE** ▶ It is a security risk to leave an ad hoc network enabled on your Mac. To disable the ad hoc network, turn off AirPort or choose another wireless network from the AirPort menu.

Some administrators may find the need to restrict some of the wireless features. You may want to require that the Mac connect only to specific secure wireless networks, or that the Mac always connect to one particular network. In these situations you will access the advanced AirPort configuration options in the Network system preference.

To manage AirPort options and connections:

1   Open and unlock the Network preference.

Choose the network location you wish to edit from the Locations pop-up menu, or configure a new network location, as detailed previously in this lesson.

2   Select the AirPort service from the services list.

At this point you can configure basic AirPort settings, including the ability to join or create another wireless network, from the Network Name pop-up menu. You can also disable the AirPort menu item by deselecting the "Show AirPort status in menu bar" checkbox, or you can turn off the AirPort card completely by clicking the Turn AirPort Off button.

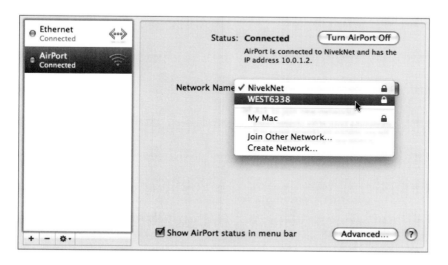

3   Click the Advanced button in the bottom-right corner of the Network preference to reveal the advanced settings dialog. Click the AirPort tab at the top to view the advanced AirPort settings.

You can create a list of preferred wireless networks by clicking the plus button at the bottom of the preferred network list, and then by either joining the wireless networks in range or manually entering all the network information. To edit a network, simply double-click on its entry in the list, or you can delete a network by selecting it and clicking the minus button at the bottom of the list.

Perhaps the most important optional setting here is to require administrative authentication to manage AirPort connections. By selecting this option and creating a list of preferred networks, you can lock down the Mac's AirPort configuration but still allow specific wireless network access.

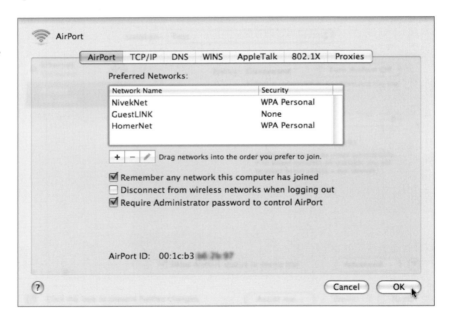

4   When you have entered the appropriate AirPort settings, click the OK button to dismiss the advanced settings dialog, and then click the Apply button in the bottom-right corner of the Network preference to save and activate the changes.

Configuring Analog Modem Connections

The Point-to-Point Protocol (PPP) was developed to act as a control and transport mechanism for TCP/IP connections transferred via analog modems over phone lines. Though slow, the combination of using an analog modem to establish a PPP-based TCP/IP connection over the phone system, commonly known as a dial-up connection, provided the basis for many users' first Internet connection. With the abundance of high-speed Internet options, though, dial-up connections have been slowly dwindling. For some unlucky souls, however, this is still their only option.

To manage analog modem (PPP) connections:

1 Open and unlock the Network preference.

Choose the network location you wish to edit from the Locations pop-up menu, or configure a new network location, as detailed previously in this lesson.

2 To begin configuring modem settings, select the analog modem service from the network services list, and basic modem configuration settings will appear to the right of the services list.

3 If you plan to have only one modem configuration, leave the Configuration pop-up menu as is and continue to the next step.

Conversely, if you want to set multiple modem configurations, choose Add Configuration from the Configuration pop-up menu. This will reveal a dialog where you can name and create a new modem configuration. You can also delete and rename configurations using this pop-up menu.

Continue adding modem configurations, and then you will have to enter the settings for each modem configuration, as outlined in the following steps.

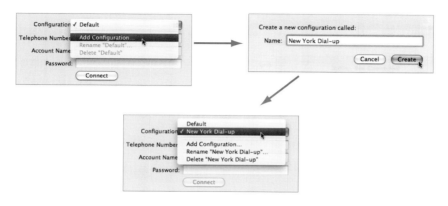

4   To configure basic modem settings, enter the dial-up phone number and account
information as provided by your Internet service provider.

5   To configure advanced modem settings, click the Advanced button in the bottom-
right corner of the Network preference. This will reveal the advanced settings dialog.
Click the Modem tab to view advanced modem options.

There are a lot of settings here, but for most situations the default settings are adequate.
The most important configuration to double-check is the analog modem vendor and
model selection.

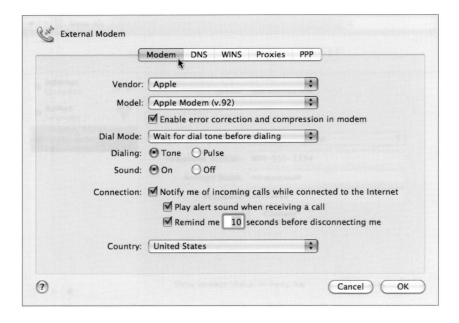

6   To configure advanced PPP settings, click the PPP tab.

Again, there are a lot of settings here, but the defaults are usually adequate. Probably the most significant settings are to optionally connect automatically when needed and to disconnect when logging out or switching to another user account. Click the OK button when you have made all your selections.

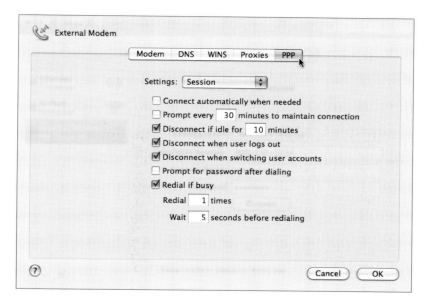

7   Once you have completed all modem settings, click the Apply button at the bottom-right corner of the Network preference to save and activate the changes.

8   You can make accessing modem connectivity options much easier by clicking the "Show modem status in menu bar" checkbox. The modem menu bar item allows you to easily select modem configurations, and connect, disconnect, and monitor modem connections.

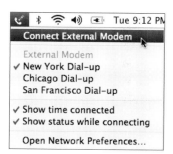

> **TIP** ▶ Modem connections can be complicated and take a while to configure properly, so you can save time and prevent mistakes by using modem configuration files. Click the gear icon at the bottom of the services list and use the Import and Export configuration menu options to use modem configuration files.

Modem connections are not typically always-on connections. Mac OS X supports automatically connecting the modem when needed, but you can also manually connect and disconnect the modem link from the modem menu bar item or by clicking the Connect button in the Network preference. Once the connection is established, the PPP process will automatically configure TCP/IP and DNS settings. You can also manually configure these settings, as outlined earlier in this lesson. Modem interfaces are also automatically placed above all other interfaces in the network service order, so as soon as the modem interface is connected and completely configured it will be the primary network interface for all Internet traffic. Reordering the network service order was covered previously in this lesson.

Configuring Bluetooth Connections

On Mac OS X, accessing the Internet via a Bluetooth connection is similar to accessing it via an analog modem connection. The only difference is that instead of using an analog modem directly connected to your Mac, you're using a cell phone connected via a Bluetooth wireless connection, which requires a cell phone capable of re-sharing an Internet connection via Bluetooth, and a Bluetooth-enabled Mac.

Configuring a Bluetooth connection is nearly identical to an analog modem because Bluetooth connections also use PPP as a control and transport mechanism for the TCP/IP connection. Only one extra step is required: pairing your Mac to the mobile phone providing the Internet access via Bluetooth. If you have already paired your Bluetooth-enabled mobile phone to your Mac, then all you have to do is enter the rest of the connection information as if you were configuring an analog modem. Otherwise, follow the instructions presented later in Lesson 9, "Peripherals and Printing," to pair your Mac to a Bluetooth-enabled mobile phone.

Network Troubleshooting

The most important thing to remember about troubleshooting network issues is that it is often not the computer's fault. There are many other points of failure to consider when dealing with WAN and Internet connection issues. So, the second most important thing to remember about troubleshooting network issues is to isolate the cause of the problem before attempting generic resolutions.

To help you isolate network issues, you can categorize them into three general areas:

▶ Local issues—These issues are usually either related to improperly configured network settings or disconnected network connections.

▶ Network issues—Network issues are by far the hardest to nail down, as there could be literally hundreds of points of failure involved. In this case it always helps to be familiar with the physical topology of your network. Start by checking the devices that provide network access closest to your Mac. Something as simple as a bad Ethernet port on a network switch can cause problems. As you move on to investigating devices farther away from your Mac, you will find that it's often easiest to start your investigation using the network diagnostic utilities included with Mac OS X.

▶ Service issues—Service issues are related to the actual network device or service you are trying to access. For example, the devices providing DHCP or DNS services could be temporarily down or improperly configured. It's often easy to determine if the problem is with the service alone by testing other network services. If the other network services work, you're probably not dealing with network or local issues. Again, Mac OS X provides some useful diagnostic tools for testing service availability. Troubleshooting network services is also covered in Lesson 7, "Accessing Network Services."

You will be using three main tools for diagnosing network issues on Mac OS X: the Network system preference, the Network Diagnostics assistant, and the Network Utility.

Network System Preference

The first diagnostic tool you should always check is the Network system preference. The Network preference features a dynamically updating list that will show you the current status of any network interface. If a network connection is not working, you will find it here first.

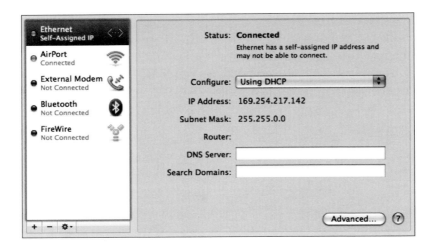

Network status indicators include:

▶ Green status—The connection is active and configured with TCP/IP settings. This, however, does not guarantee that the service is using the proper TCP/IP settings. For instance, in the previous screenshot of the Network preference you'll note that the Ethernet service appears with a green status indicating proper TCP/IP settings. Nevertheless, if you look closer you'll see that the service is using a link-local TCP/IP configuration, indicating this interface is not receiving proper configuration from the DHCP service. If you are still experiencing problems with this service, double-check the network settings. If the settings appear sound, move on to the other diagnostic utilities.

▶ Yellow status—The connection is active but the TCP/IP settings are not properly configured. Double-check all the network settings until you get things right and the service goes green.

▶ Red status—These issues are usually either related to improperly configured network settings or disconnected network interfaces. If this is an always-on interface, check for proper physical connectivity. If this is a virtual or PPP connection, double-check the settings and attempt to reconnect.

> **TIP** Remember that the interface order plays a huge part in how the Mac routes network traffic. Become familiar with how the Mac uses multiple network connections, as covered earlier in this lesson.

Network Diagnostics Assistant

Mac OS X includes the Network Diagnostics assistant to help you troubleshoot common network issues. Some networking applications will automatically open this assistant when they encounter a network issue. You can also open it manually by clicking the Assist Me button at the bottom of the Network system preference, and then clicking the Diagnostics button.

The Network Diagnostics assistant will ask you a few simple questions about your network setup and then, based on your answers, run a battery of tests to determine where the problem might be occurring. Test results are displayed using colored indicators on the left side of the window. If there are problems, the assistant makes suggestions for resolution. In the following example, the modem connection has failed and the Network Diagnostics assistant is suggesting that you double-check your modem settings.

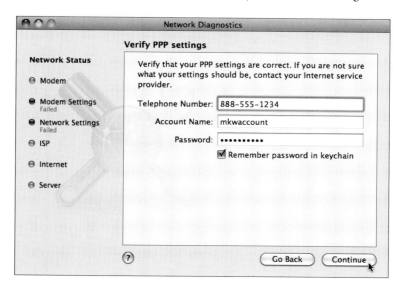

Network Utility

The Network system preference and Network Diagnostics assistant are good places to start troubleshooting network issues, but the most powerful application in Mac OS X for diagnosing network issues is /Applications/Utilities/Network Utility. The Network Utility provides an array of popular network identification and diagnostic tools. In fact, most of the tools in the Network Utility are based on UNIX command-line network utilities that have been used by network administrators for years.

The Network Utility is broken up into the following sections:

- ► Info—Allows you to inspect details regarding hardware network interfaces.

- ► Netstat—Shows routing information and network statistics.

- ► AppleTalk—Provides detailed AppleTalk protocol information.

- ► Ping—This fundamental network troubleshooting tool lets you test network latency.

- ► Lookup—This very important tool lets you test DNS resolution.

- ► Traceroute—This powerful tool lets you analyze how your network connections are routed to their destination.

- ► Whois—Lets you query whois database servers and find the owner of a DNS domain name or IP address.

- ► Finger—Enables you to gather information based on a user account name from a network service.

- ► Port Scan—The most important tool for determining if a network device has services available.

The Network Utility can also be opened when your Mac is booted from the Mac OS X Install DVD. Any time you are booted from this DVD, you can open the Network Utility by choosing it from the Utilities menu. However, when booted from the Mac OS X Install DVD you do not have access to any network configuration user interfaces, so the Mac will only activate built-in wired Ethernet connections on networks providing DHCP services. If your Mac is connected in this manner, you will be able to use the Info, Netstat, Ping, and Traceroute sections to isolate local network configuration issues.

Network Interface Information

When you open the Network Utility, you will first see the Info section. This section lets you view the detailed status of any hardware network interface. Even if you've opened the Network Utility to use another section, always take a few moments to verify that the network interface is properly activated.

Start by selecting the specific interface you're having issue with from the pop-up menu. You'll notice the selections here do not match the service names given in the Network preference. Instead, this menu shows the interfaces using their UNIX-given names. When working properly, the en0 interface should be the first internal Ethernet port, and in most cases the en1 interface is the AirPort interface. If you have a Mac or an Xserve with two internal Ethernet ports, the second internal port will be en1 and the AirPort interface will be bumped to en2. The FireWire interface will be labeled as fw0.

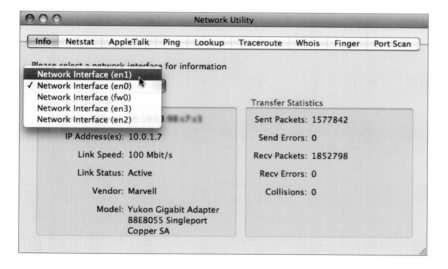

Once you have selected an interface, you can view general interface information to the left and transfer statistics to the right. The primary pieces of information you're looking for here are the Link Status, Link Speed, and IP Address(es). Only active hardware network interfaces will show as such, and the link speed will indicate if the interface is establishing a proper connection. Obviously, a proper IP address is required to establish a TCP/IP connection. You can also identify the selected interface's MAC address, which is used to identify this particular interface on the LAN.

As a final validation of the selected network interface, you can view recent transfer statistics. If you open other network applications to stir up some network traffic, you will be able to verify that packets are being sent and received from this interface. If you are seeing activity here but still experiencing problems, the issue is most likely due to a network or service problem and not the actual network interface. Or, if this interface is experiencing transfer errors, a local network hardware connectivity issue may be the root of your problem.

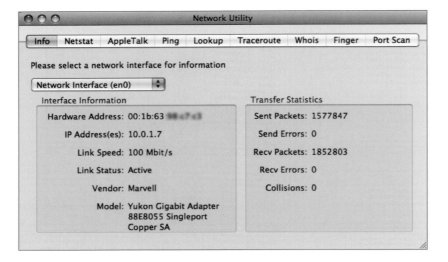

To resolve hardware network interface issues, always start by checking the physical connection. With wired networks, try different network ports or cabling to rule out physical connection issues. With wireless networks, double-check the AirPort settings and the configuration of any wireless base stations. In only the rarest of occasions, you may find that the Mac's network hardware is somehow no longer working properly, in which case you should take your Mac to an Apple Authorized repair center.

Using Ping

If you have determined that your network settings are properly configured and that the hardware network interface appears to be working correctly but you are still experiencing network issues, your next step is to test network connectivity using the ping tool. The ping tool is the most fundamental network test to determine if your Mac can successfully send and receive data to another network device. Your Mac will send a ping data packet to the destination IP address, and the other device should return the ping packet to indicate connectivity.

To use ping:

1   Open /Applications/Utilities/Network Utility, and then click the Ping tab at the top.

2   Enter the IP address or host name of a network device to test connectivity to that device.

    Start by entering an IP address to a device on the LAN that should always be accessible, like the network router.

    Remember, using a domain name assumes that your Mac is properly communicating with a DNS server, which might not be the case if you're troubleshooting connectivity issues.

3   Click the Ping button to initiate the ping process.

    If the ping is successful, it should return with the amount of time it took for the ping to travel to the network device and then return. This is typically within milliseconds, so experiencing ping times any longer than a full second is unusual.

4   Once you have established successful pings to local devices, you can branch out to WAN or Internet addresses.

    Using the ping tool, you may find that everything works except for the one service you were looking for that prompted you to start troubleshooting the network.

    NOTE ▶ Some network administrators view excessive pinging as a threat, so many configure their network devices to not respond to any network pings.

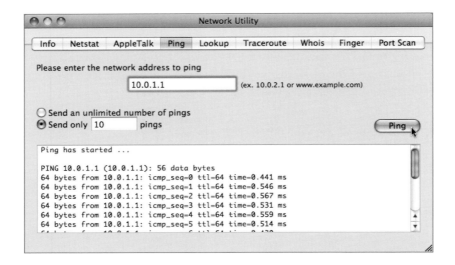

Using Lookup

If you are able to successfully ping other network devices by their IP address but attempting to connect to another device by its host name doesn't work, then you are experiencing issues related to DNS. The network lookup process will allow you test name resolution against your DNS server.

To use lookup:

1   Open /Applications/Utilities/Network Utility, and then click the Lookup tab at the top.

2   Enter the IP address or host name of a network device to test DNS resolution.

Start by entering the host name of a device or service in your local domain. If you can resolve local host names but not Internet host names, this indicates that your local DNS server is resolving local names but it's not properly connecting to the worldwide DNS network.

If you don't have a local domain, you can use any Internet host name as well.

3   Click the Lookup button to initiate the network lookup process.

A successful forward lookup will return the IP address of the host name you entered. A successful reverse lookup will return the host name of the IP address you entered.

4   If you are unable to successfully return any lookups, this means that your Mac is not connecting to the DNS server. You can verify this by pinging the DNS server IP address to test for basic connectivity.

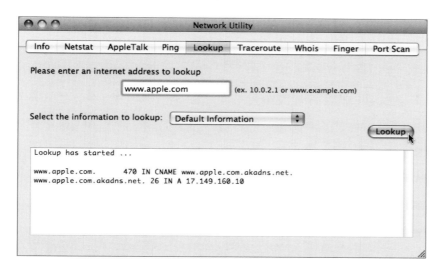

Using Traceroute

If you are able to connect to some network resources but not others, you should use the network traceroute utility to determine where the connection is breaking down. Remember that WAN and Internet connections require the data to travel through many network routers to find their destination. The traceroute tool will examine every network hop between routers using the ping tool to determine where connections fail or slow down.

To use traceroute:

1   Open /Applications/Utilities/Network Utility, and then click the Traceroute tab at the top.

2   Enter the IP address or host name of a network device to trace the connectivity to that device.

     Start by entering an IP address to a device on the LAN that should always be accessible, like the network router.

Remember, using a domain name assumes that your Mac is properly communicating with a DNS server, which might not be the case if you're troubleshooting connectivity issues.

3   Click the Trace button to initiate the ping process.

If the traceroute is successful, it should return with the list of routers required to complete the connection and the amount of time it took for the ping to travel to each network router. Again, the ping is typically measured within milliseconds, so experiencing ping times any longer than a full second is unusual.

4   Once you have established successful routes to local devices, you can branch out to WAN or Internet addresses.

Using the traceroute tool, you may find that a specific network router is the cause of the problem.

NOTE ▶ Some network administrators view traceroute as a threat, so many configure their network devices to not respond to any network traceroute queries.

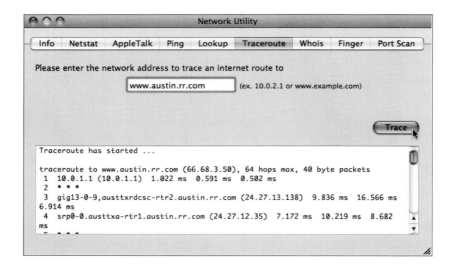

What You've Learned

▶ The Internet protocol suite, TCP/IP, provides the basis for nearly all local and wide area networks. DHCP provides automatic configuration for TCP/IP networks, and DNS provides local and worldwide TCP/IP host naming.

▶ Mac OS X supports a wide array of hardware network interfaces, virtual network interfaces, and network protocols, all managed via the Network system preference.

▶ Mac OS X includes a variety of network troubleshooting tools, among them the Network system preference, the Network Diagnostics assistant, and the Network Utility.

References

You can check for new and updated Knowledge Base documents at http://www.apple.com/support.

General Network

30821, "TCP/IP: IP Addresses for private networks"

106439, " 'Well-known' TCP and UDP ports used by Apple software products"

303262, "Apple USB modem: Frequently asked questions"

106433, "Mac OS X: Frequently asked questions for PPP modem connections"

106432, "Mac OS X: DSL/PPPoE frequently asked questions"

Network Troubleshooting

106796, "Mac OS X: Connect to the Internet, troubleshoot your Internet connection, and set up a small network"

106797, "Mac OS X: Slow startup, pauses at 'Initializing network' or 'Configuring network time' "

106260, "Your computer's name does not appear on the network"

106748, "Mac OS X: Troubleshooting a dial-up (PPP) Internet connection"

106747, "Mac OS X: Troubleshooting a PPPoE Internet connection"

URLs

Wikipedia entry about the OSI reference model: http://en.wikipedia.org/wiki/OSI_model

IEEE's searchable database of OUIs used for MAC addresses: http://standards.ieee.org/regauth/oui/index.shtml

Wikipedia entry about the Internet protocol suite: http://en.wikipedia.org/wiki/internet_protocol_suite

Wikipedia entry about DHCP: http://en.wikipedia.org/wiki/Dhcp

Review Quiz

1. What is the purpose of the Internet Protocol (IP) addresses and subnet masks? What is their format?

2. How does the IP use the MAC address to send messages between computers on a local area network (LAN)?

3. How does the IP transfer messages between computers over a wide area network (WAN)?

4. How is the Domain Name Service (DNS) used to facilitate network naming?

5. What do the terms *interface*, *protocol*, and *service* mean in relation to computer networks?

6. What interfaces and protocols are supported by default in Mac OS X?

7. How do Mac OS X computers acquire and use link-local TCP/IP addresses?

8. What functionality does Mac OS X support with the AppleTalk protocol?

9. What are four common issues that can interrupt network services on a Mac OS X computer?

10. How does network service order affect network connectivity?

Answers

1. The Internet Protocol (IP) address identifies the location of a specific network device. IP addresses are the primary identification used by the Internet protocol suite TCP/IP for both local and wide area networks. Subnet masks are used by network devices to

identify their local network range, and to determine if outgoing data is destined for a network device on the LAN. Most common IP addresses and subnet masks share the same IPv4 formatting. IPv4 addresses are a 32-bit number represented in four groups of four-digit numbers, known as octets, separated by periods. Each octet has a value between 0 and 255.

2. If a network device needs to send data to another network device on the same LAN, it will address the outgoing packets based on the destination device's MAC address.

3. A network client uses the subnet mask to determine if the destination IP address is on the LAN. If the destination IP address is not on the LAN, then it's assumed the destination address is on another network and it will send the data to the IP address of the local network router. The network router will then send the data, via a WAN connection, on to another router that it thinks is closer to the destination. This will continue across WAN connections from router to router until the data reaches its destination.

4. The DNS service is used to translate host names to IP addresses via forward lookups, and translate IP addresses to host names via reverse lookups. DNS is architected as a hierarchy of worldwide domain servers. Local DNS servers provide name resolution and possibly host names for local clients. These local DNS servers connect to DNS servers higher in the DNS hierarchy to resolve both unknown host names and host local domain names.

5. An *interface* is any channel through which network data can flow. Hardware network interfaces are defined by physical network connections, while virtual network interfaces are logical network connections that ride on top of hardware network connections. A *protocol* is a set of rules used to describe a specific type of network communication. Protocols are necessary for separate network devices to communicate properly. Finally, a network *service* is the collection of settings that define a network connection.

6. Mac OS X supports the following network interfaces and protocols:

   ▶ Wired Ethernet IEEE 802.3 family of hardware network interface standards

   ▶ Wireless (AirPort) IEEE 802.11 family of hardware network interface standards

   ▶ FireWire IEEE 1394 hardware network interface

   ▶ Analog modem hardware network interface

   ▶ Bluetooth wireless hardware network interface

> ▶ Virtual private network (VPN) virtual network interface via the Point-to-Point Tunneling Protocol (PPTP)

> ▶ VPN virtual network interface via the Layer 2 Tunneling Protocol (L2TP) over Internet Protocol security (IPsec)

> ▶ Point-to-Point Protocol over Ethernet (PPPoE) virtual network interface

> ▶ 6 to 4 virtual network interface

> ▶ Virtual local area network (VLAN) virtual network interface via the IEEE 802.1Q standard

> ▶ Link Aggregation virtual network interface via the IEEE 802.3ad standard

> ▶ Transmission Control Protocol/Internet Protocol (TCP/IP), also known as the Internet protocol suite

> ▶ Dynamic Host Configuration Protocol (DHCP)

> ▶ Domain Name Service (DNS) protocol

> ▶ Network Basic Input/Output System (NetBIOS) and Windows Internet Naming Service (WINS) protocols

> ▶ AppleTalk protocol suite

> ▶ Authenticated Ethernet via the 802.1X protocol

> ▶ Point-to-Point Protocol (PPP)

7. If DHCP is specified as the configuration for a TCP/IP connection and no DHCP service is available, the computer will automatically select a random IP address in the 169.254.xxx.xxx range. It will check the local network to ensure that no other network device is using the randomly generated IP address before it applies the IP address.

8. While Mac OS X supports full AppleTalk addressing, identification, and service discovery, the only AppleTalk service still supported is the Printer Access Protocol (PAP).

9. Four common issues that interrupt network services on Mac OS X are:

> ▶ A disconnected network cable will cause the hardware network interface to become inactive.

> ▶ A nonfunctioning network interface port will cause the hardware network interface to become inactive.

▶   A DHCP service issue will prevent proper TCP/IP configuration.

▶   A DNS service issue will prevent host name resolution.

10. The network service order list is used to determine the primary network interface if there is more than one active interface. All network traffic that isn't better handled via local connection to an active network interface is sent to the primary network interface. Thus, all Internet traffic is sent through the primary network interface.

7

Time This lesson takes approximately 3 hours to complete.

Goals Connect to common network services using built-in Mac OS X network applications

Browse and access network file services using the Finder

Use remote control tools to access other network clients

Access network directory service information

Accessing Network Services

Modern operating systems provide a wide range of network and Internet service options, but all of them share the similar basic network architecture of client software, which accesses services, and server software, which provides services. Mac OS X includes support for many popular network protocols, allowing you to access a wide variety of network services.

In this lesson, you will focus on using Mac OS X as a network client to access a variety of network and Internet services. First, you will learn how to access popular Internet and file services using Mac OS X. You will also discover how to control network clients remotely and troubleshoot general network service access issues. Then we introduce you to the client side of Mac OS X's directory services architecture, where you will learn how to manage identification and authorization technologies.

Lesson 8, "Providing Network Services," expands on the content of this lesson by focusing on how to use Mac OS X to provide network services.

Network Services

At a minimum, accessing a network service requires you to have the service's network location and some way to prove your identity to the service provider. For some network services, you will have to manually identify the service's location with an Internet Protocol (IP) address or Domain Name Service (DNS) host name. Others feature automatic service discovery that allows you to easily locate a network service by simply browsing from a list of available services. Once you have selected a network service to connect to, you must prove your identity to that service provider. This process is called authentication, and authenticating a network successfully will establish a connection to that service.

Network Services Architecture

From an architectural standpoint, network services are defined by client software (designed to access the service) and server software (designed to provide the service). The network service communication between the client and server software is facilitated by commonly known network protocols or standards. By adhering to such standards, software developers can create unique yet compatible network client and server software. This allows you to choose the software tool that best fits your needs. For instance, you can use the built-in Mac OS X Mail client created by Apple to access mail services provided by software created by Sun Microsystems or Microsoft.

Network Services Software

Some client software takes the form of dedicated applications, as is the case with many Internet services like email and web browsing. Other client software is integrated into the operating system—file and print services, for example. In either case, when you establish a network service connection, settings for that service are saved on the local computer to preference files. These client preferences often include resource locations and authentication information.

On the other side of this relationship is the server software. Properly setting up server software is usually a much more complicated affair. Server administrators may spend months designing, configuring, and administering the software that provides network services. Server-side settings include configuration options, protocol settings, and account information. Lesson 8, "Providing Network Services," offers detailed information about configuring the network server software built into Mac OS X.

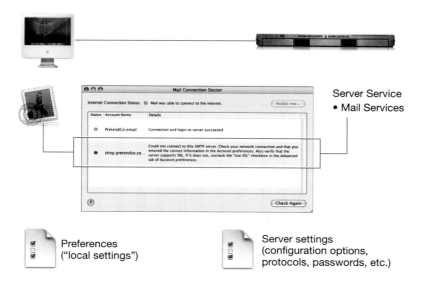

Server Service
• Mail Services

Preferences
("local settings")

Server settings
(configuration options,
protocols, passwords, etc.)

Network Services Communication

Network clients and servers, sometimes of different makes, communicate using commonly known network protocols or network standards. The distinction is that a protocol becomes a standard once it is widely adopted and ratified by a standards committee. Part of what defines a specific network protocol is which TCP or UDP ports are used for communications.

A primary feature of both the TCP and UCP transport mechanisms is the ability to handle multiple simultaneous connections and service protocols. This is accomplished by assigning each communication service to a specific port number or port range. Both TCP and UDP connection ports are defined between 0 to 65,535. For instance, the standard TCP port for web browser traffic is port 80. When troubleshooting a network service, you must know the port numbers or ranges for that service. Apple maintains a list of commonly used network services and their associated TCP or UDP ports at Knowledge Base document 106439, "'Well Known' TCP and UDP ports used by Apple software products."

NOTE ▶ This book assumes the default port numbers and port ranges for each network service. Network administrators may choose to use a different port number than the default for testing or to "hide" a service.

Accessing Internet Services

Because of the widespread adoption of the Internet protocol suite TCP/IP for nearly all LAN, WAN, and Internet communications, there really isn't any difference between how you access a "standard network service" and an "Internet service." With few exceptions, nearly all network services work the same way across a LAN as they do across the Internet. The primary difference between the two is scope of service. Services like email and instant messaging can certainly work on a local level, but these services are also designed to communicate across separate networks and between servers.

Mac OS X includes a range of client applications designed to access different network services. Although this book focuses only on the network client software built into Mac OS X, many excellent third-party network clients are available for the Mac. In fact, when troubleshooting a network access problem using an alternative network client is an excellent way to determine if the issue is specific to your primary client software.

> **MORE INFO** ▶ You can find third-party network client software at Apple's Macintosh Products Guide, http://guide.apple.com/.

Safari 3 for Web Browsing

By far the most popular and ubiquitous network service, web communication is handled via the Hypertext Transfer Protocol (HTTP) using TCP port 80. Secure web communications, known by the acronym HTTPS, encrypts the HTTP protocol over a Secure Sockets Layer (SSL) connection and by default uses TCP port 443. Generally, little additional network configuration is required to use web services, as you only need to provide the web browser with the Uniform Resource Locator (URL) or web address of the resource you desire to connect to. The only exception is if you have to configure web proxies, as described in Lesson 6, "Network Configuration."

Mac OS X 10.5 includes Apple's Safari 3 web browser. Safari is an efficient and robust web browser that supports most websites. However, you may find that some websites do not render properly or flat out don't work with Safari. If you are unable to access certain websites with Safari, try a third-party web browser. Several third-party web browsers are available for the Mac, including popular alternatives like Camino, Firefox, OmniWeb, and Opera.

Mail 3 for Email

A close second for popularity, email communications is handled by several protocols. The protocol used between mail clients and mail servers for receiving mail is either Post Office Protocol (POP) on TCP port 110 or Internet Message Access Protocol (IMAP) on TCP port 143. Both protocols can also be encrypted with an SSL connection. By default, encrypted POP uses TCP port 995 and encrypted IMAP uses TCP port 993. The protocol used for sending mail from clients to servers and from server to server is Simple Mail Transfer Protocol (SMTP) on TCP port 25. Again, SMTP can be encrypted with an SSL connection on ports 25, 465, or 587. The ports used for secure SMTP vary based on mail server function and administrator preference.

Mac OS X 10.5 includes the Mail 3 application for handling electronic mail communications along with mail-based notes and task lists. Mail supports all three common email protocols and their encrypted counterparts along with a variety of authentication standards. With this many service options, properly configuring mail service settings can be quite daunting. Fortunately, Mail includes an account setup assistant that will walk you through the process of configuring mail account settings. The assistant will even attempt to automatically determine mail protocol security and authentication mail protocol settings. Finally, email settings for users with .Mac accounts will be configured automatically based on the .Mac system preference settings.

NOTE ▶ Microsoft Exchange servers often use the Message Application Program Interface (MAPI) protocol for email communications. The Mac OS X Mail application does not support MAPI, but it does support IMAP and SMTP connections to Exchange Servers.

iChat 4 for Instant Messaging

Instant messaging has grown well beyond text chatting with iChat 4 included with Mac OS X 10.5. The latest iChat supports ten-way audio conferencing, four-way video conferencing, peer-to-peer file sharing, and remote screen sharing. iChat also features an account setup assistant that walks you through the configuration process.

iChat 4 supports three categories of chat services:

▶ Messaging services that are open to the public—iChat 4 supports .Mac, AOL Instant Messenger, and Google Talk accounts. Assuming you have already registered for an account through one of these service providers, configuring iChat simply involves entering your account name and password. Once again, .Mac accounts will be configured automatically based on the .Mac system preference settings.

▶ Privately hosted messaging services—iChat 4 supports open source Jabber servers, including Mac OS X Server's iChat service. If your Mac is connected to a directory server that is hosting Jabber account information, iChat will be automatically configured based on those settings. Otherwise, you will have to manually enter Jabber server and account information.

▶ Ad hoc messaging—iChat 4 will use the Bonjour network discovery protocol to automatically find other iChat users. No configuration is necessary to access Bonjour messaging. Bonjour details will be covered in the "Dynamic Network Service Discovery" section later in this lesson.

iChat supports a wide variety of messaging features and instant messaging protocols—which means it uses far too many TCP and UDP ports to list here. However, Knowledge Base document 93208, "Using iChat with a firewall or NAT router" lists all the possible ports iChat may attempt to use.

NOTE ▶ iChat's advanced features, such as videoconferencing and screen sharing, are not supported by many third-party chat clients. When you select a chat participant, iChat will automatically determine the client software's messaging capabilities and allow you to use only supported features.

iCal 3 for Shared Calendaring

Mac OS X 10.5 includes iCal 3, which supports shared calendaring in two ways. The first method is through Web-based Distributed Authoring and Versioning (WebDAV) calendar publishing and subscriptions. WebDAV is an extension to the HTTP protocol, so it runs over TCP port 80 or TCP port 443 if encrypted. iCal allows you to share your calendar information by publishing iCalendar files to WebDAV-enabled web servers. You can also subscribe to iCalendar files hosted on WebDAV servers. Configuration is fairly easy, as accessing a shared calendar is identical to accessing a webpage. Simply provide iCal with the URL of the iCalendar file. You can subscribe to hundreds of shared calendars at http://www.icalshare.com.

Although calendar publishing allows you to easily share calendars one way over the web, it doesn't provide a true collaborative calendaring and scheduling environment. Other users can see your calendar but they cannot invite you to new calendar events. Thus, iCal 3 also supports an emerging calendar collaboration standard known as CalDAV. As the name implies, CalDAV also uses WebDAV as a transport mechanism, but CalDAV adds the administrative processes required to facilitate calendar and scheduling collaboration. Mac OS X Server's iCal service is based on CalDAV. Furthermore, CalDAV is being developed as an open standard so any vendor can create software that provides or connects to CalDAV services. Configuring iCal to use a CalDAV account is also straightforward, requiring you to enter only a URL for the server address and an account name and password.

> **MORE INFO** ▶ You can find out more about the CalDAV protocol by visiting the main CalDAV resource page at http://ietf.osafoundation.org/caldav.

Accessing Network File Services

There are many protocols for transferring files across networks and the Internet, but the most efficient are those designed specifically to share file systems. Network file servers can make entire file systems available to your client computer across the network. The key distinction is that client software built into Mac OS X's Finder can mount a network file service similar to mounting a locally connected storage volume. Once a network file service is mounted to the Mac, you will be able to read, write, and manipulate files and folders as if you were accessing a local file system. Additionally, access privileges to network file services are defined by the same ownership and permissions architecture used by local file systems. Details regarding file systems, ownership, and permissions were covered in Lesson 3, "File Systems."

Mac OS X provides built-in support for these network file service protocols:

▶ Apple File Protocol (AFP) on TCP port 548 or encrypted on TCP port 22—This is Apple's native network file service. AFP supports all the features of Apple's native file system HFS+.

▶ Server Message Block (SMB) on TCP port 139—This network file service is mainly used by Windows systems, but many other platforms have adopted support for this protocol. SMB also supports many of the advanced file system features used by Mac OS X.

▶ Network File System (NFS), which may use a variety of TCP or UDP ports—Used primarily by UNIX systems and supports many advanced file system features used by Mac OS X.

▶ Web-based Distributed Authoring and Versioning (WebDAV) on TCP port 80 or encrypted on TCP port 443—This protocol is an extension to the common HTTP service and provides basic file services.

> **TIP** ▶ Apple uses the WebDAV protocol to facilitate .Mac iDisk services.

▶ File Transfer Protocol (FTP) on TCP ports 20 and 21—This protocol is in many ways the lowest common denominator of file systems. FTP is supported by nearly every computing platform, but it provides only the most basic of file system functionality. Further, the Finder supports only read capability for FTP volumes.

> **MORE INFO** ▶ The command-line interface (CLI) includes a full FTP client with the ftp command. Additionally, you will find several third-party FTP clients on Apple's Macintosh Products Guide.

The Finder provides two methods for connecting to a network file system: manually connecting by entering the address of the server providing the file service and automatically discovering shared resources by browsing to them in the Finder's Network folder.

Manually Connecting Network File Services

To manually connect to a file service, you at least have to specify the network address of the file server providing the service. You may also have to enter authentication information and choose or enter the name of a specific shared resource path. When connecting to an AFP or SMB service, you will normally have to authenticate first and then choose a shared resource. Conversely, when connecting to an NFS, WebDAV, or FTP service you specify the shared resource as part of the server address and then you authenticate if needed.

To manually connect an AFP or SMB file service:

1 From the Finder, choose Go > Connect to Server from the menu bar or use the Command-K keyboard shortcut.

This will open the Finder's Connect to Server dialog.

2 In the Server Address field, enter afp:// or smb:// followed by the server's IP address, DNS host name, or local host name.

Or after the server address you can enter another slash and then the name of a specific shared volume.

Click the Connect button to continue.

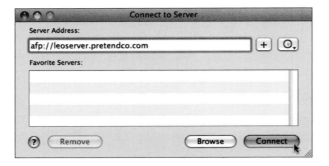

TIP ▶ If you don't specify a protocol, the Connect to Server dialog will default to the AFP protocol.

3 A dialog will appear requiring you to enter authentication information.

Selecting the Connect as Guest radio button indicates that you wish to connect anonymously to the file service. Remember that guest access is an option on file servers that many administrators will disable.

If you do have proper authentication information, enter it here. Or you can select the checkbox that saves this information to your login keychain.

Click the Connect button to continue.

NOTE ▶ If you are using Kerberos or you have previously saved your authentication information to a keychain, the computer will automatically authenticate for you and will not present the authentication dialog.

4   You will be presented with the list of shared volumes that your account is allowed to access.

Select the volume or volumes you wish to mount. Hold down the Command key to select multiple volumes from the list.

Click the OK button to mount the selected shared volumes.

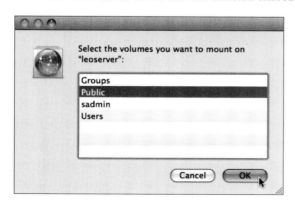

To manually connect an NFS, WebDAV, or FTP file service:

1   From the Finder choose Go > Connect to Server from the menu bar or use the
    Command-K keyboard shortcut.

    The Finder's Connect to Server dialog opens.

2   In the Server Address field, enter one of the following:

    ▶   nfs:// followed by the server address, another slash, and then the absolute file path
    of the shared volume.

    ▶   http:// for WebDAV (or https:// for encrypted WebDAV), followed by the server address.
    If there are multiple WebDAV volumes on the server, enter another slash and the
    name of the specific shared volume you wish to mount.

    ▶   ftp:// followed by the server address. FTP servers have only one mountable root
    volume, but you can optionally enter another slash and then specify a folder inside
    the FTP volume. When connecting to an FTP server that allows both anonymous and
    authenticated access, if you want to authenticate enter the user name in the Server
    address field. In this case, enter ftp:// followed by the account name, then the @ symbol,
    and then the server address.

    Click the Connect button to continue.

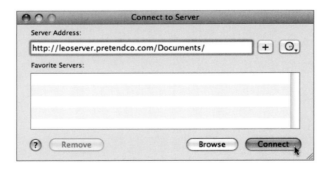

3   Depending on the protocol settings, you may be presented with an authentication
    dialog: NFS connections will never display an authentication dialog.

    The NFS protocol uses the local user that you're already logged in as for authorization
    purposes. In addition, WebDAV and FTP both allow anonymous guest connections
    and will not show an authentication dialog if guest authentication is allowed.

If you are presented with an authentication dialog, enter the appropriate authentication information here. Optionally you can select the checkbox that will save this authentication information to your login keychain.

Click the OK button to mount the shared volume.

NOTE ▶ If you are using Kerberos or you have previously saved your authentication information to a keychain, the computer will automatically authenticate for you and will not display the authentication dialog.

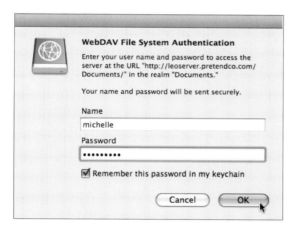

Once the Mac has mounted the network file system, it can appear in several locations from the Finder depending on your preference settings. Mounted network volumes will always appear at the Computer location in the Finder accessible by choosing Go > Computer from the menu bar or by pressing Shift-Command-C. You can also set Finder preferences to show mounted network volumes on the desktop and in the Sidebar's Shared list. Finally, from the CLI, mounted network volumes will appear where all other nonsystem volumes appear: in the /Volumes folder.

Manually entering server information every time you connect to a server is a hassle. Two features in the Connect to Server dialog make this process efficient for your users. The Connect to Server dialog maintains a history of your past server connections. You can access this history by clicking the small clock icon to the right of the Server Address field. Also, you can create a list of favorite servers in the Connect to Server dialog by clicking the plus button to the right of the Server Address field.

> **TIP** ▶ Clicking the Browse button in the Connect to Server dialog will bring you to the Finder's Network folder. The Network folder is covered in the "Browsing Network File Services" section later in this lesson.

Dynamic Network Service Discovery

Requiring users to manually enter server addresses isn't very user-friendly. What if you were to join a new network where you don't know the exact names of all the available resources? Or what if the shared resource you need is hosted from another client computer that doesn't have a DNS host name or the same IP address every time? To address these issues, Mac OS X supports several dynamic network service discovery protocols.

Dynamic network service discovery protocols allow you to browse local and wide area network resources without having to know specific service addresses. In a nutshell, network devices that are providing a service advertise their availability on the network, and clients that are looking for services request and receive this information to provide the user with a list of available network service choices. As available network resources change, or as you move your client to different networks, the service discovery protocols will dynamically update to reflect the current state network resources.

On small LANs the list of available resources is usually short enough that it's not hard to locate and select your desired resource. But on larger networks and WANs, there may be hundreds or thousands of available resources to choose from. Network administrators organize the service discovery systems on these large networks into smaller, more manageable groups of network devices known as zones or workgroups. Both server and client computers can be placed inside a specific zone or workgroup when their network settings are configured. Often the logical or physical layout of the network will also determine what zone or workgroup a network device resides in.

Mac OS X makes ample use of dynamic network service discovery throughout. For example, dynamic network service discovery allows you to browse for available network file systems from the Finder and locate new network printers from the Print & Fax system preference. Other network applications built into Mac OS X use it to locate a variety of shared resources, including iChat, Image Capture, iPhoto, iTunes, Safari, and the Mac OS X Server Admin Tools. Countless third-party network applications also take advantage of dynamic network service discovery.

Mac OS X provides built-in support the following dynamic network service discovery protocols:

▶   Bonjour on TCP ports 5297 and 5298 and UDP ports 5298 and 5353—Bonjour is Apple's implementation of Zero Configuration Networking, or Zeroconf, an emerging standard that provides automatic local network configuration, naming, and service discovery. Bonjour is the primary dynamic network service discovery protocol used by Mac OS X native services and applications. Bonjour is preferred because it integrates well with other TCP/IP-based network services. Mac OS X 10.5 adds support for Wide-Area Bonjour, allowing you to browse WAN resources as well as LAN resources. To access Wide-Area Bonjour, your Mac must be configured to use a DNS server and search domain that supports the protocol. Configuring DNS is covered in Lesson 6, "Network Configuration."

    MORE INFO ▶ You can find out more about Zeroconf at http://www.zeroconf.org.

▶   Network Basic Input/Output System (NetBIOS) on UDP port 138 and Windows Internet Naming Service (WINS) on UDP port 137—NetBIOS and WINS are used primarily by Windows-based systems, but other operating systems have also adopted these protocols for discovering SMB-based file and print sharing services. Details regarding NetBIOS and WINS are covered in Lesson 6.

► AppleTalk—AppleTalk is a suite of network protocols that was originally designed by Apple before the proliferation of TCP/IP networks. In many ways the dynamic network service discovery abilities in AppleTalk are a precursor to Bonjour. AppleTalk is disabled by default; enabling it allows you to browse for AppleTalk-compatible AFP servers, print servers, and network printers. Details regarding AppleTalk are covered in Lesson 6.

NOTE ► With Mac OS X 10.5 you can no longer disable Bonjour or NetBIOS/WINS from the graphical interface.

It is important to remember the discovery protocol is only used to help you and the system locate the name and IP address of an available service. Once the discovery protocol provides your computer with a list of available services, their names, and their IP addresses, its job is done. When you connect to a discovered service, the Mac will establish a connection to the service using the service's native communications protocol. For example, the Bonjour protocol will provide the Mac with a list of available file services, but when you select a file server from this list the Mac will establish a connection to the server using the AFP protocol.

Browsing Network File Services

You can browse for dynamically discovered file services from two locations in the Finder. The first location is the Shared list located in the Finder's Sidebar. If enabled in the Finder preferences, the Shared list is ideal for quickly discovering computers providing file services on a small network. The Shared list will show only the first eight discovered computers providing services and will also show only services that can be discovered using the Bonjour protocol. If additional servers are discovered, the last item in the Shared list, All Items, is a link to the Finder's Network folder.

TIP ► The Finder's Shared list can also show servers that you are currently connected to even if they didn't originally appear in the Shared list.

The Finder's Network folder is a special place on Mac OS X. The Network folder is not a standard folder at all; it's an amalgamation of all dynamically discovered network file services and all currently mounted file systems, including manually mounted file systems. Obviously the Network folder is constantly changing based on information gathered from the three dynamic network service discovery protocols supported by Mac OS X—Bonjour, NetBIOS/WINS, and optionally AppleTalk—so you can only browse AFP or SMB file services from the Network folder.

On smaller networks there may only be one level of network services. Conversely, if you have a larger network that features service discovery network zones or workgroups, they will appear as subfolders inside the Network folder. Each subfolder will be named by the zone or workgroup it represents. Items inside the zone or workgroup subfolders represent shared resources configured for that specific network area.

> **NOTE** ▶ From the CLI environment, the Network folder will only show file systems that were mounted by Mac OS X's automatic network file mounting system. Automatic mounts are covered in Lesson 5, "Using File Services," of *Apple Training Series: Mac OS X 10.5 Server Essentials.*

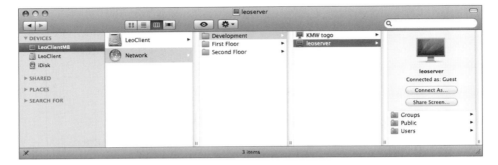

To browse and connect to an AFP or SMB file service:

1   From the Finder's Sidebar, select the computer you wish to connect to from the Shared list, or select a computer from the Finder's Network folder. The quickest routes to the Network folder are to either choose Go > Network from the menu bar, or use the Shift-Command-K keyboard shortcut.

Selecting a computer from either the Shared list or the Network folder will yield similar results.

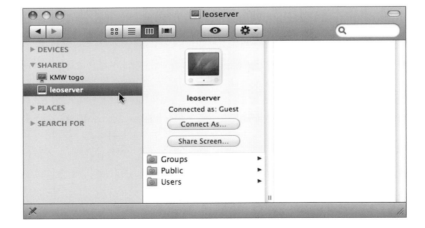

2   The moment you select a computer providing services, the Mac will attempt to automatically authenticate using one of three methods:

▶   If you are using Kerberos authentication, the Mac will attempt to authenticate to the selected computer using your Kerberos credentials.

▶ If you are using non-Kerberos authentication but you have connected to the selected computer previously and chose to save the authentication information to your keychain, the Mac will attempt to use the saved authentication information.

▶ The Mac will attempt to authenticate as a guest user. Keep in mind guest access is an option on file servers that many administrators will disable.

If the Mac succeeds in authenticating to the selected computer, the Finder will show you the account name it connected with and also list the shared volumes available to this account.

3   If the Mac was unable to automatically connect to the selected computer, or you need to authenticate with a different account, click the Connect As button to open an authentication dialog.

Choosing the Connect as Guest radio button will indicate that you wish to connect anonymously to the file service. Otherwise, if you have proper authentication information, enter it here. Or you can select the checkbox that will save this authentication information to your login keychain.

Click the Connect button and the Mac will re-authenticate with the new account and show you a new list of shared volumes available to the account.

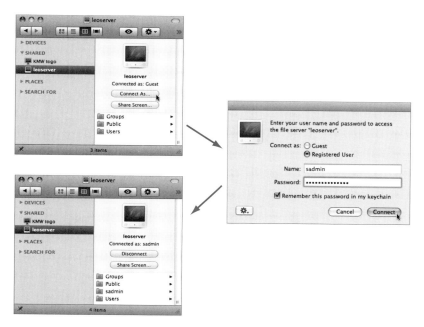

4 Each available shared volume will appear as a folder. Click once on a shared volume to connect and mount its file system.

Again, once the Mac has mounted the network file system it can appear in several locations from the Finder, including the Computer location, the desktop, and the Sidebar's Shared list. Also, again from the CLI, mounted network volumes will appear where all other nonsystem volumes appear, in the Volumes folder.

Managing Network Volume Mounts

It is important to recognize that the Mac treats mounted network volumes similarly to locally attached volumes, so you must remember to always properly unmount and eject network volumes when you are done with them. Mounted network volumes are unmounted and ejected from the Finder using the exact same techniques you would use on a locally connected volume. Unmounting and ejecting mounted volumes was covered previously in Lesson 3, "File Systems."

In practice, though, it's difficult for users to remember they have network volumes mounted, as there is no locally attached hardware device to remind them. Further, laptop users will often roam out of wireless network range without even thinking about what network volumes they may have mounted. If a network change or problem disconnects the Mac from a mounted network volume, the Mac will spend several minutes attempting to reconnect to the server hosting the volume. If after several minutes the Mac cannot reconnect to the server, you will see an error dialog allowing you to fully disconnect from the server.

On a positive note, because the Finder treats mounted network volumes similar to other file system items, you can save time and make life easier for you and your users by creating shortcuts to often-used network volumes. One method involves creating aliases on the user's desktop that link to often-used network volumes or even specific items inside a network volume. You can also create Dock shortcuts by dragging network volumes or their enclosed items to the right side of the Dock. Or you can configure network volumes to automatically mount when a user logs in by adding network volumes to the user's login items. Managing login items was covered in Lesson 2, "User Accounts."

TIP ▶ Remember that by using Kerberos authentication or by saving authentication information to the keychain you can bypass authentication dialogs as well.

Controlling Shared Network Clients

Providing remote phone support can be arduous. Inexperienced users don't know how to properly communicate the issues they are experiencing or even what they are seeing on the screen. Attempting to describe the steps involved in performing troubleshooting or administrative tasks to an inexperienced user over the phone is at best time consuming and at worst a painful experience for both parties.

When it comes to troubleshooting or administration, nothing beats actually seeing the computer's screen and controlling its mouse and keyboard. Mac OS X includes built-in software that allows you to access shared network clients using two methods. The first method lets you control another computer's graphical interface, and the second allows you to control another computer's CLI.

Using Screen Sharing

Previous versions of Mac OS X included the client-side software of Apple Remote Desktop (ARD) built in, which allows network-based remote control of a Mac's graphical interface from another administrative computer. The administrative side of ARD used to control other computers was not included with previous versions of Mac OS X. However, Mac OS X 10.5 introduces full screen-sharing capabilities that support both sharing the Mac's graphical interface and controlling other computers' graphical interfaces natively from the Finder.

MORE INFO ▶ The Apple Remote Desktop (ARD) administration software provides advanced functionality that goes well beyond simple screen sharing. You can find out more about ARD at http://www.apple.com/remotedesktop.

NOTE ▶ Although client-side support for ARD is still included in Mac OS X 10.5, the full ARD administration software is not included.

Mac OS X 10.5's built-in screen sharing is based on Apple's implementation of the Virtual Network Computing (VNC) protocol running on TCP and UDP ports 5900. With it, you can remotely view another computer's graphical interface and control its keyboard and mouse input. VNC is a cross-platform standard for remote control, so Mac OS X's screen-sharing technology integrates well with other third-party VNC-based systems. So your Mac can control (or be controlled by) any other VNC-based software regardless of operating system.

NOTE ▶ Previous versions of Mac OS X that have Apple Remote Desktop 3 remote control enabled are also compatible with Mac OS X 10.5 screen-sharing and other VNC software.

The process to connect to another computer for screen sharing is similar to how you connect to a shared file system. From the Finder you can connect to another computer for screen sharing by either manually entering its network address in the Connect to Server dialog or by browsing to the computer from the Shared list or Network folder.

NOTE ▶ Browsing for screen-sharing computers works only for Bonjour-compatible clients.

To control the graphical interface of another computer with screen sharing, Apple Remote Desktop 3, or VNC enabled:

1   From the Finder initiate a connection to the computer you wish to control using one of two methods:

▶   In the Finder's Connect to Server dialog, enter vnc:// followed by the computer's IP address, DNS host name, or local host name. Then click the Connect button to continue.

▶   Browse to and select the computer from the Finder Sidebar's Shared list, or select the computer from the Finder's Network folder. Then click the Share Screen button to continue.

The Mac automatically opens the /System/Library/CoreServices/Screen Sharing application.

2   You are presented with a dialog where you must enter the authentication information. Optionally you can select the checkbox that will save this information to your login keychain.

Click the Connect button to continue. The Screen Sharing application will establish a VNC connection to the other computer.

NOTE ▶   If you are using Kerberos or you have previously saved your authentication information to a keychain, the computer will automatically authenticate for you and will not present the authentication dialog.

A new window opens, titled with the controlled computer's name, showing a live view of the controlled computer's screen(s). Anytime this window is active, all keyboard entries and mouse movements will be sent to the controlled computer.

For example, using the Command-Q keyboard shortcut will quit the active application on the computer being controlled. Thus, in order to quit the Screen Sharing application you have to click the close (X) button at the top-left corner of the window.

While using the Screen Sharing application, be sure to check out the preference options by choosing Screen Sharing > Preference from the menu bar. Use these preferences to adjust screen size, encryption, and quality settings. If you are experiencing slow performance, adjust these settings for fastest performance. Keep in mind that some network connections, such as crowded wireless or dial-up connections, are so slow that these preferences won't matter much and you will simply have to wait for the screen to redraw.

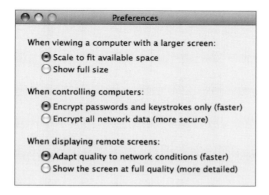

Using iChat 4 Screen Sharing

The included iChat 4 instant messaging application can now be used to initiate screen sharing, and as an added bonus will simultaneously provide voice chat services between the administrator Mac and the controlled Mac. iChat screen sharing also makes it much easier to locate other Macs to control, as iChat will automatically resolve the location of remote computers based on your active chats or available buddies. Further, iChat also supports reverse screen sharing—the administrator Mac can push its screen to display on another Mac for demonstration purposes.

> **NOTE** ▶ iChat 4's screen-sharing feature is only compatible with other computers running iChat 4. When you select chat participants, iChat will automatically determine if their computer is using iChat 4.

iChat does not require either Mac to have screen sharing enabled in the Sharing preferences because iChat includes a quick and easy authorization process to initiate each screen-sharing session.

To initiate an iChat screen-sharing session:

1 From iChat, select an available chat user from a buddy list and then click the screen sharing button at the bottom of the buddy list.

This opens the screen sharing pop-up menu, where you can choose "Share My Screen with <*chatuser*>" or "Ask to Share <*chatuser*>'s Screen," where <*chatuser*> is the name of the user whose machine you are asking to control.

The user on the other computer will see an authorization dialog where he or she can choose to accept or decline your request to share screens.

2 If the other user clicks the Allow button, the screen-sharing session will begin.

The following screen capture shows the screen-sharing "controller's" point of view. The other user will see the same screen without the small My Computer window in the bottom-left corner.

3 Both users will have simultaneous control of the Mac being shared, including the ability to end the screen-sharing session at any time from the screen-sharing menu item on the right side of the menu bar.

NOTE ▸ Even as an administrative user, you cannot force other users to share screens using iChat 4; they have the sole power to allow or deny your request. However, with Finder-initiated screen sharing, administrative users can force a screen-sharing connection.

Using Command-Line Remote Login

Mac OS X 10.5 includes support for (CLI) remote login via the Secure Shell (SSH) protocol, which by default runs on TCP port 22. Apple's implementation of remote login is based on the popular OpenSSH project. OpenSSH provides a robust and secure environment for remotely accessing the CLI of another network device.

With graphical user interface (GUI) screen sharing so readily accessible in Mac OS X 10.5, you may wonder why the ability to remotely log in to the CLI is still relevant. After all, if you need to remotely access another Mac's CLI you can always use screen sharing to open and control the Terminal application on the remote Mac. Well, aside from screen sharing being a bandwidth hog, there are many uses for CLI remote login and SSH that remote screen sharing does not provide.

For starters, using remote login is much more efficient than screen sharing because only text is transmitted. Often, remote login is so fast that it's indistinguishable from using the CLI on a local computer. From an administration standpoint, remote login is a much more subtle approach for remote management, as users logged in to the GUI can't tell that someone has remotely logged in to their Mac's CLI. So as an administrative user, you can remotely log in to a Mac and resolve an issue from the CLI without the user even knowing you were there. Even if the Mac is sitting idle at the login window, you can still remotely log in to the CLI and take care of business.

Aside from providing a secure network connection for remote login, the SSH protocol can also provide secure connections for any other network protocol. You can use SSH to create an encrypted tunnel between two SSH-enabled network devices and then pipe any other TCP- or UDP-based network protocol through the SSH connection. In fact, this method is used by Mac OS X to encrypt AFP and VNC traffic. As with any CLI tool, you can learn more about SSH by reading the ssh man page. Lesson 3, "File Systems," contains an overview of the CLI.

The primary interface for SSH is the ssh command. The syntax for initiating a remote login connection using SSH is ssh followed by the name of the user you will be logging in as, then the @ symbol, and then the address or host name of the computer you wish to log in to. If you're logging in to a computer for the first time using SSH with standard password authentication, you'll be prompted to trust the authenticity of the remote host. If a network administrator has given you a public key for authentication, you won't have to enter a user password.

In the following example, Michelle starts off in the CLI on a Mac named "leoclient." She issues the ssh command to connect to the "leoserver.pretendco.com" Mac using the user name "sadmin." She has never established an SSH connection between these two computers, so she is asked if she wants to trust the authenticity of the leoserver computer. In most cases, the answer to this question is "yes." Michelle then enters the sadmin user's password, but note that it is never shown onscreen. Notice how the command prompt changes to show that Michelle is using the leoserver Mac. The using CLI environment remotely with SSH is nearly indistinguishable from using it locally. Michelle issues the who command on leoserver to see who is currently using that Mac. You can see that a user has logged in to the GUI, "console," using the sadmin account, and you can also see Michelle's SSH connection, "ttys000." Finally in this example, Michelle logs out and closes the SSH connection by issuing the exit command.

```
leoclient:~ michelle$ ssh sadmin@leoserver.pretendco.com
The authenticity of host 'leoserver.pretendco.com (10.0.1.200)' can't be established.
RSA key fingerprint is bd:34:8c:1e:c6:bf:9a:46:e9:2a:b1:cc:81:7c:a3:02.
Are you sure you want to continue connecting (yes/no)? yes
Warning: Permanently added 'leoserver.pretendco.com,10.0.1.200' (RSA) to the list of known hosts.
Password:
Last login: Sat Oct 6 18:19:09 2007
leoserver:~ sadmin$ who
sadmin console Oct 2 11:57
sadmin ttys000 Oct 6 22:13 (leoclient.pretendco.com)
leoserver:~ sadmin$ exit
logout
Connection to leoserver.pretendco.com closed.
leoclient:~ michelle$
```

TIP▶ The OpenSSH software includes a secure copy command, scp, and sftp. These commands can be used to securely transfer files to and from a Mac with remote login enabled.

Troubleshooting Network Services

To effectively troubleshoot a network issue you must isolate the issue into one of three categories: local, network, or service. Most issues involving failure to access network services will probably fall under the service category. This means that you should probably focus most of your efforts toward troubleshooting the specific service that you're having issues with.

However, before digging too deep into troubleshooting the service, check for general network issues. First, check to see if other network services are working. Opening a web browser and navigating to a few different local and Internet websites is always a good general network connectivity test. To be thorough, also test other network services, or test from other computers on the same network. If you're experiencing problems connecting to a file server but you can connect to web servers, chances are your TCP/IP configuration is fine, and you should concentrate on the specifics of the file server. If you're only experiencing problems with one particular service, you probably don't have local or network issues and you should focus your efforts on troubleshooting just that service.

If other network services aren't working, your issue is likely related to local or network issues. Double-check local network settings to ensure proper configuration from both the Network preference and Network Utility. If you find that other computers aren't working, you might have a widespread network issue that goes beyond troubleshooting the client computers. Again, general network troubleshooting was covered in Lesson 6, "Network Configuration and Troubleshooting."

Using Network Port Scan

Once you decide to focus on troubleshooting a problematic network service, one of your most important diagnostic tools will be the network port scan utility. Part of the Network Utility application, port scan will scan for any open network service ports on the specified network address. As covered earlier in this lesson, network protocols are tied to specific TCP and UDP network ports. Network devices providing a service must leave the appropriate network ports open in order to accept incoming connections from other network clients. A port scan will reveal if the required ports are indeed open. If the ports aren't open, that device is either not providing the expected service or is configured to provide the service in a nonstandard method. Either way, this indicates that the issue lies with the device providing the service, not your Mac.

To use network port scan:

1   Open /Applications/Utilities/Network Utility and click the Ping tab at the top.

    Before performing a port scan, check for basic network connectivity by attempting to ping the device that is supposed to be providing the service. Enter the device's network address or host name and click the Ping button.

If the ping is successful, it should return with the amount of time it took for the ping to travel to the network device and then return. Assuming you have network connectivity to the other device, continue to the next step.

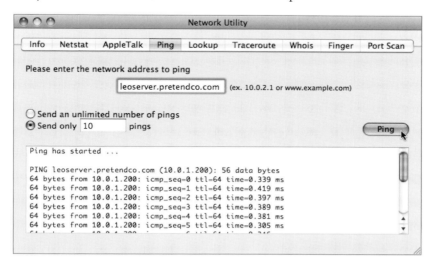

2   Click the Port Scan tab at the top of the Network Utility window.

Again, enter the network address or host name of the device that is supposed to be providing the service.

There are 65,535 available TCP and UDP network ports, so a full port scan can take quite some time. To save time, you can optionally configure the port scan utility to test only a specified range. Most common ports are between 0 and 1024, but if you're only troubleshooting a specific service, limit the port scan to just that service's default ports.

3   Click the Scan button to initiate the port scan process.

Depending on the scan range you chose, it may take several minutes to complete the scan. Any open ports that were discovered will be listed along with the associated network protocol if known.

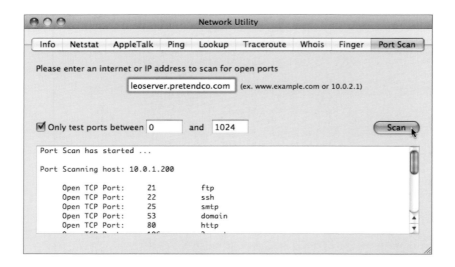

NOTE ► Because some network administrators view network pings or port scans as a threat, some network devices are configured to not respond even when working properly.

Troubleshooting Network Applications

Aside from general network service troubleshooting, there are a few application-specific troubleshooting techniques you can try. First, double-check any application-specific configuration and preference settings. It takes only a few moments, and you may find that users have inadvertently caused the problem by changing a setting they shouldn't have.

Be aware of these issues when troubleshooting network applications:

► Safari—Safari is a good web browser, but it's not perfect. There are certain webpages that Safari just can't get right. The only resolution is to try a different web browser. Several third-party web browsers are available for the Mac, including popular alternatives like Camino, Firefox, OmniWeb, and Opera.

► Mail—Improper mail account configuration settings are the most common cause of Mail application issues. Fortunately, the Mail application includes a built-in account diagnostic tool called the Mail Connection Doctor that will attempt to establish a connection with all configured incoming (POP and IMAP) and outgoing (SMTP) mail servers. To open the Mail Connection Doctor, choose Window > Connection Doctor within the Mail application. If a problem is found a suggested resolution will be offered, but for a more detailed diagnostic view click the Show Detail button to reveal the progress log and then click the Check Again button to rerun the tests.

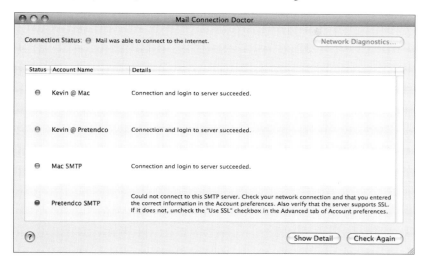

▶   iChat—iChat also suffers from occasional improper account configuration, but it's a less frequent occurrence than with the Mail application. More often iChat suffers from connectivity issues when attempting advanced messaging features like voice and videoconferencing. As such, iChat also features a Connection Doctor that will let you view conference statistics, chat capabilities, and the iChat error log. To open the iChat Connection Doctor, within the iChat application choose Video > Connection Doctor. If you have experienced recent errors the Connection Doctor will open to the error log, but you can view other information from the Show pop-up menu.

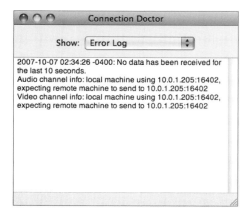

Network File Services Issues

There are a few known Mac OS X file service issues that you should be aware of. They aren't software bugs in the sense that something is broken and requires a fix. These issues represent compatibility and design choices that are intentional but may still cause you problems.

Some Mac files use separate data and resource forks. The NFS and WebDAV file sharing protocols do not support forked files of this type. Thus, when forked files are written to a mounted NFS or WebDAV volume, Mac OS X will automatically split these files into two separate files. The data fork will retain the original name, but the resource fork will be saved with a period and underscore before the original name. The Finder will recognize these split files and show only a single file to the user. However, users on other operating systems will see two separate files and may have trouble accessing the appropriate file.

You may encounter another issue when trying to access an AFP network volume from a Windows file server. Windows servers include Services for Macintosh (SFM), which provides only the legacy AFP 2 file service. Mac OS X is still compatible with AFP 2 but is optimized for AFP 3.1. There are many known performance issues with AFP 2, so you should avoid it at all costs. Ideally, you should use a Mac OS X Server to provide AFP services for your network. However, if you must keep the Windows file server, you can add AFP 3.1 support by installing Group Logic's ExtremeZ-IP (http://www.grouplogic.com). Mac OS X 10.5 clients include a robust SMB client that will natively connect to your Windows server without compatibility problems.

Directory Services

Directory service is a generic term used to describe the that are used to locate network and resource information. Apple's implementation of directory services is branded as Open Directory. Open Directory (OD) is integrated into the foundations of Mac OS X's core system software known as Darwin. It's responsible for providing Mac OS X with fundamental network and resource information. The OD process, appropriately named DirectoryService, is started during system startup and is always running as a background system process.

The first of two main OD functions is to act as the primary authority for network identification information. When a system process or application needs information about a network host name or needs to discover a network service, OD is responsible for handling the request. The OD service resolves all DNS requests, and through secondary processes resolves dynamic network service discovery information. Detailed information regarding DNS was covered in Lesson 6, "Network Configuration," and information regarding dynamic network service discovery was covered earlier in this lesson.

The second main OD function is to act as the primary authority for resource information. OD can provide information about a variety of resources, but the most common resource type is account information. The OD service resolves all account identification requests and through secondary processes coordinates account authentication and authorization services. The primary focus of this section is managing and troubleshooting directory services on Mac OS X as it relates to account identification, authentication, and authorization.

Open Directory

The "directory" in directory services and Open Directory refers to the fact that it provides a directory of information similar in many ways to an online phone book. The most commonly accessed directory resource is account information. With Mac OS X, all account information, including user and group information, is stored in a directory. OD handles all directory interaction for Mac OS X, making it the single source for providing account information to every Mac OS X application, command, or background service.

Common directory resources used by Mac OS X include:

▶ User Accounts—The primary resource used to identify a human user to the computer. Detailed information regarding user accounts was covered in Lesson 2, "User Accounts."

▶ User Groups—A collection of user accounts used to provide greater control over management and security settings. Detailed information regarding group accounts was also covered in Lesson 2.

▶ Computer Accounts—This is information used to identify a specific computer for purposes of applying management settings.

▶ Computer Groups—A collection of computer accounts used to facilitate efficient application management settings to many computers.

▶ Network File Mounts—Information used by Mac OS X's automatic network file mounting system. Automatic mounts are covered in Lesson 5, "Using File Services," of *Apple Training Series: Mac OS X 10.5 Server Essentials*.

▶ Management Settings—Information used to automatically apply specific user and computer preferences based on administrator controlled settings. Directory-based management settings are covered in Lesson 10, "Managing Accounts," of *Apple Training Series: Mac OS X 10.5 Server Essentials*.

▶ Collaboration Information—This includes any information used to facilitate collaboration services, including, iCal, iChat, and Wiki Services. Collaboration services are covered in Lesson 8, "Using Collaborative Services," of *Apple Training Series: Mac OS X 10.5 Server Essentials*.

Through OD, Mac OS X is able to easily access multiple directory services simultaneously. This ability allows Mac OS X to integrate into a mixed directory environment with little difficulty and few compromises. As a result, Mac OS X has become very popular among administrators who manage large networks with complicated directory service infrastructures.

Directory types supported by Mac OS X include:

▶ Local—OD maintains a local directory database with a series of XML-encoded files located in the /var/db/dslocal/nodes/Default/ folder. Any locally stored resource information, including local user account information, is saved to this directory. The local directory is consulted first for any requested resource information.

▶ Berkeley Software Distribution (BSD) Flat File and Network Information Systems (NIS)—Stand-alone UNIX systems typically use BSD flat files to store local directory information, or use the NIS protocol to access network directory information. Both are still supported by Mac OS X but disabled by default. If support is enabled, these systems will always be consulted second for any requested resource information.

▶ Lightweight Directory Access Protocol version 3 (LDAPv3)—LDAPv3 has emerged as one of the most popular network directory standards. In fact, Mac OS X Server's built-in directory service, appropriately dubbed Open Directory Server, uses the LDAPv3 protocol. Configuring Mac OS X to connect, or bind, to an LDAPv3 service is covered in the "Configuring Network Directory Services" section later in this lesson.

▶ Active Directory (AD)—This is Microsoft's implementation of the LDAPv3 protocol. Though it's based on LDAPv3, Microsoft made so many changes to meet their design goals that AD is considered a unique network directory protocol unto itself. Configuring Mac OS X to connect, or bind, to an AD service is covered in the "Configuring Network Directory Services" section.

Understanding Network Directory Services

Until now, you've only dealt with locally hosted directories, which contain resources and account information available to only a single Mac system. Even so, OD gives Mac OS X the ability to access resource and account information hosted by network-based directory services. So Mac OS X can simultaneously access accounts located in both local and network directories.

Mac OS X account location types include:

▶ Local account—Information is stored on the local Mac and is only available to that Mac.

▶ Network account—Information is stored on a network server that is providing a shared directory to any connected, or bound, network client. The Mac must be connected to the network directory in order for you to access a network account.

▶ Mobile account—Information is stored on a network server providing a shared directory, but the account information can also be cached to the Mac's local directory. Every time you log in using a mobile account, the account information will be cached to the Mac's local directory. As long as the cached information remains on the Mac, you'll still be able to access the mobile account if the Mac isn't connected to the network directory.

Implementing network directory services is certainly more complicated than simply using the default local directory service. However, the administrative benefits of using resource and account information hosted on a network directory far outweigh the extra time spent setting it up.

Advantages of using network directory services are:

▶ User accounts are no longer tied to individual Macs—Users with a network or mobile account can log in to any Mac connected to the network directory service. Because the directory service maintains the account information, their entire user environment can be accessed from any Mac they can log in to.

▶ The same user account information can be used for multiple network services—Devices providing network services can connect to the network directory service. You can use the same user name and password for any network service even if those services are hosted on multiple separate servers.

▶   You can use Kerberos to provide secure single-sign-on authentication—Kerberos also happens to be the most secure popular authentication service to date. Details regarding Kerberos are covered in the "Authentication Services" section later in this lesson.

▶   You can define user and computer settings from a centralized location—In addition to providing a single location for all account attributes, you can manage application and system settings from a single location. In other words, you can save client configuration information to a centralized network directory service, and any Mac connected, or bound, to the directory service will be automatically configured with those settings. Again, directory-based management settings are covered in Lesson 10, "Managing Accounts," of *Apple Training Series: Mac OS X 10.5 Server Essentials*.

Configuring Network Directory Services

The process of connecting Mac OS X to a network directory service is called *directory binding*. The term *bind* is used to describe this connection because, unlike other types of network connections that come and go, the connection between a client and a network directory service is persistent. Whenever directory service information is requested, the Mac will attempt to communicate with the network directories to which it's bound.

NOTE ▶ If your Mac has access to multiple directory services, OD will search for account information in local directories first, followed by network directories. If multiple network directory services are available, OD will search for account information based on service order. If a similarly named account exists in multiple directories, the first account OD locates is the one that's used.

The primary tool you'll use to configure directory services is the /Applications/Utilities/ Directory Utility application. When you first open Directory Utility, it will attempt to use the Bonjour protocol to discover any Mac OS X Servers on your network running the OD network directory service. Directory Utility will also attempt to discover LDAP binding information provided by the DHCP service. If a Mac OS X Server providing network directory services is discovered, the Directory Utility will automatically prompt you to set up a connection. With this method you will only have to enter a few administrator passwords and answer a few simple questions to complete the setup process.

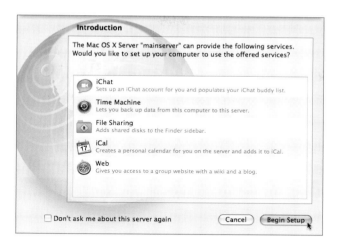

If Directory Utility doesn't automatically find a network directory service, you'll have to manually configure the settings. Directory Utility doesn't automatically connect to the most popular network directory service, Microsoft's AD; fortunately, Directory Utility features a simple-to-use basic configuration mode for both OD and AD services.

To manually bind Mac OS X to an Open Directory service:

1   Open /Applications/Utilities/Directory Utility, and then click the lock icon in the bottom-right corner to authenticate as an administrative user.

2   Click the small plus button at the bottom-left corner of the directory list.

    This will reveal a dialog allowing you to add a new network directory service. This dialog will default to the Open Directory service.

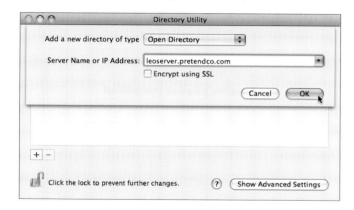

3 Enter the full domain name of the master OD server as provided by the network administrator, and then click the OK button to continue.

Directory Utility will establish an initial connection to the master OD server and download additional configuration information.

4 Depending on how the OD service is configured, you will experience one of two binding situations: if the OD service is configured to allow for anonymous binding, Directory Utility will complete the bind process automatically; or if the OD service is configured to require authenticated binding, you will have to enter the user name and password of a directory administrator account. You may also need to enter a new computer identifier if the given name is already being used by another computer bound to the OD service. Click the OK button to complete the bind process.

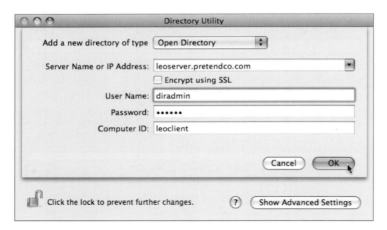

5 When binding is done, the OD server appears in the directory list.

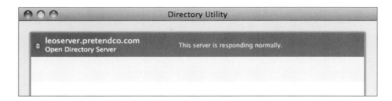

TIP ► If your Mac is bound to multiple network directory services, you can rearrange the search order in Directory Utility by clicking and dragging individual services in the directory list.

To manually bind Mac OS X to an Active Directory service:

1   Before you initiate the AD bind process, make sure the Mac is configured to access DNS services from the appropriate Windows domain server. Configuring DNS was covered previously in Lesson 6, "Network Configuration."

2   Open /Applications/Utilities/Directory Utility, and then click the lock icon in the bottom-right corner to authenticate as an administrative user.

3   Click the small plus button at the bottom-left corner of the directory list to reveal a dialog allowing you to add a new network directory service. From the directory type pop-up menu, choose Active Directory.

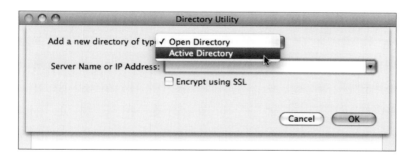

4   Enter the full domain name of the AD domain, and the user name and password of a directory administrator account.

You may also need to enter a new computer identifier if the given name is already being used by another computer bound to the AD service.

Click the OK button to initiate the bind process.

5 Once binding is done, the AD server appears in the directory list.

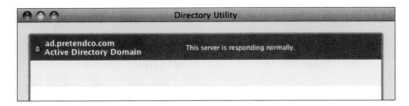

> **MORE INFO** ▶ Attempting to fully integrate Mac OS X into an AD system requires additional configuration. Find out more about Mac OS X AD integration at http://www.apple.com/itpro/articles/adintegration/.

Once you bind Mac OS X to a network directory service, OD will allow all local services to request information from those network directories. Most importantly, you will be able to log in and authenticate to the Mac with user accounts hosted on the network directory. You will also be able to directly browse or search for resource and account information hosted on a network directory using built-in applications like the /Applications/Address Book and /Applications/Utilities/Directory application.

Directory Utility also features an advanced configuration mode accessed by clicking the Show Advanced Settings button. Advanced mode gives you greater control over each directory service type, including the ability to enable and configure BSD Flat File and NIS directory services. You can also configure custom automatic network mounts and further adjust the directory search order.

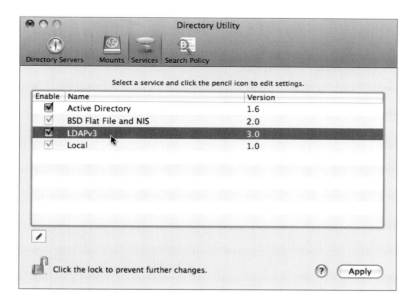

Authentication Services

The concept of authentication was introduced in Lesson 2, "User Accounts," but to reiterate, authentication is the process of proving your identity to the computer. More specifically, you are proving to the computer that you should be allowed to access an account because you know a secret about the account that only the account's holder should know. Mac OS X supports elaborate authentication systems that require special hardware to validate your identity, but alphanumeric passwords are still the most commonly used authentication secret.

Authorization is closely tied to authentication, but they are not the same things. Authentication is only used to prove your account identity to the system, but authorization defines which items or services the account is allowed to access. In other words, authentication is who you are, and authorization is what you can do.

Authentication and authorization are used throughout Mac OS X to ensure a safe computing environment. Open Directory (OD) coordinates authentication for Mac OS X, but authorization is handled by each service differently. For example, Lesson 2, "User Accounts," showed how each user account type has different levels of access to the system. The login window uses the OD service to identify and authenticate the user, but Mac OS X's system authorization services dictate which applications and services the user is authorized to access. A large part of Lesson 3, "File Systems," covered how access to files and folders is granted. Again here, OD provides identification and authorization services, but the file system uses ownership and permissions to determine which files and folders the user is authorized to access.

Authentication systems vary as widely as the services they help secure. Often legacy technologies use authentication techniques that are considered rudimentary and unsecured in today's world of Internet thieves and spyware. Local account authentication tends to be more relaxed, but as you come to rely more on network and Internet services the need to provide strong authentication becomes paramount. In general you can categorize an authentication service into one of four groups:

▶ Basic, or clear-text password—In this simplest form of authentication, passwords are pasted between client and service in standard text. Obviously, this provides no network security, as passwords could be easily recovered using common network diagnostic tools. The few services that still rely on basic password authentication do so to support the widest possible audience. Mac OS X avoids using this type of encryption at all costs, and so should you.

▶ Encrypted password—Many variations of this type of authentication exist, but they all involve sending password information between client and service in an encrypted format. This is a more secure technique than clear text, but it still involves passing secrets across the network, so a determined individual could possibly uncover your password. The likelihood of a nefarious person decrypting your password depends on the strength of encryption being used. Mac OS X uses encrypted passwords for local accounts, as do some generic LDAP directory services. In fact, most network services now rely on encrypted passwords if they don't already rely on the next two types of authentication.

▶ Kerberos—This advanced authentication system provides highly secure, single-sign-on authentication. Both Apple's OD and Microsoft's Active Directory (AD) rely on Kerberos to provide authentication for a variety of network and Internet services. Details on Kerberos are covered next in this lesson.

Understanding Kerberos Authentication

Kerberos is a secure authentication service that's popular with many universities and corporations. Both Apple and Microsoft have implemented Kerberos as their primary authentication mechanism for network directory services. Originally developed by the Massachusetts Institute of Technology (MIT), Kerberos provides ticket-based single-sign-on authentication services.

Single sign-on means that you have to enter your account password only once per session, often at the login window. As long as you remain logged in to the Mac or connected to the Kerberos system, it will use your previous credentials to satisfy the authentication for any other network service that supports Kerberos. A network service that supports Kerberos authentication is often called a *kerberized* service. Many primary network applications and services included with Mac OS X are kerberized, including Mail, iChat, iCal, Screen Sharing, SSH, AFP, SMB, and NFS.

Kerberos was designed with the idea that you can't trust network traffic to be secure. So, Kerberos ensures that account passwords are never transmitted across the network. This system also provides mutual authentication, where both the client and server can verify each other's identity. Kerberos provides these features by generating tickets that are used to validate the authenticity of each Kerberos participant.

The only downside to ticket-based authentication is its relative complexity when compared to other techniques. Kerberos authentication requires a special trusted service known as the Key Distribution Center (KDC). In the case of OD and AD, the server providing directory services is often also the primary KDC. With the introduction of Mac OS X 10.5, every Macintosh can also provide local KDC services. However, to keep things simple this lesson will focus on the authentication relationship between a Mac OS X client and a centralized KDC tied to a network directory service.

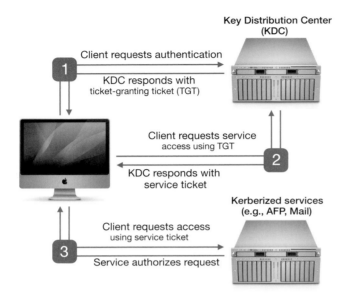

An example of the basic Kerberos authentication process:

1 Enter your user name and password at the login window.

The login window, via OD, negotiates a connection to the KDC. The KDC issues you an encrypted ticket-granting ticket (TGT). The TGT is encrypted in such a way that it can only be unlocked and used if you entered the correct password.

Think of the TGT as a "day pass" that can be used to access other services. TGTs are usually good for several hours, but if they expire before you log out, the Kerberos system will automatically generate a new one for you.

2 Upon attempting to connect to a kerberized network service, such as an AFP network volume or an email service, OD will use the TGT to request a service ticket from the KDC.

If the KDC trusts your TGT and trusts the service you're attempting to connect to, it issues you a ticket for that service.

3 OD uses the service ticket to authenticate your account to the requested network service. Assuming your service ticket is good, the Kerberized service will trust your identity and allow the connection.

Notice that you only had to enter your user name and password once at the login window. Further, at no point did your password ever travel across the network, nor did the requested network service have to communicate with the KDC to verify your authenticity.

> **MORE INFO ▶** The information presented here is merely an introduction to the Kerberos authentication system. For more, please visit MIT's Kerberos website at http://web.mit.edu/Kerberos/.

Finally, it is important to not confuse Kerberos' single-sign-on ability with the keychain systems' ability to save authentication information locally. Even though both services are used to automatically authenticate network services, they are quite different in architecture and scope. Kerberos can only be used to authenticate kerberized services, and is often managed on a networkwide scale. The keychain system can be used to save a wide variety of authentication information, but saved keychain information is only accessible to the local Mac. The keychain system is covered in detail in Lesson 2, "User Accounts."

Managing Kerberos Authentication

Kerberos is so well integrated in Mac OS X that it is possible to extensively use Kerberos without once having to manage its configuration. Assuming you have bound your Mac to an OD or AD service, Kerberos is already configured for you. Directory Utility configures the Kerberos settings automatically during the binding process. Users probably won't even know that they are using Kerberos because the login window and OD will automatically handle all future authentications. Apple even goes so far as to hide the Kerberos utility application in a rarely visited folder.

Despite this level of integration, you should be aware of some advanced Kerberos management features. The aforementioned hidden Kerberos utility application can be used to perform a variety of management tasks.

To manage Kerberos:

1   Open the Kerberos application located at /System/Library/CoreServices/Kerberos.

2   When the Kerberos utility opens, it will show you any currently active accounts.

To view active TGTs or service tickets, select an account from the Ticket Cache list. The TGT will appear first in the Tickets list followed by any service tickets.

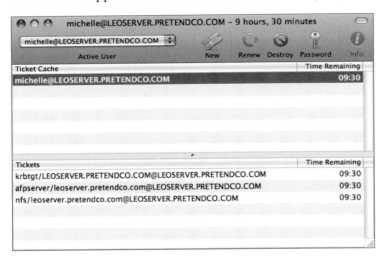

3   If you haven't yet obtained a TGT or you wish to obtain an additional TGT, click the New button in the Keychain utility's toolbar.

This will reveal the Authenticate to Kerberos dialog; enter your user name and password here. If your Mac is configured to access multiple KDCs, you can specify a particular KDC from the Realm pop-up menu. You can also save your authentication information to a local keychain. This is useful if you wish to automatically authenticate to multiple Kerberos accounts at login. Click the OK button to complete authentication.

TIP ▶ In the Authenticate to Kerberos dialog, you can also change the Kerberos account's password and access other ticket options by clicking the gear button at the bottom-left corner of the dialog.

The newly added Kerberos account should appear in the Ticket Cache list. Service tickets will only be generated for the active Kerberos user. You can change the active Kerberos user at any time from the pop-up menu in the Keychain utility's toolbar.

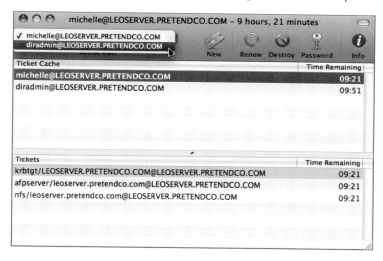

4   To manually renew a Kerberos account, select the account and then click the Renew button in the Kerberos utility's toolbar.

Renewing a Kerberos account will issue a new TGT and destroy any currently cached service tickets. It will not disconnect any currently connected network service that was authenticated with those tickets.

5   To change the password of a Kerberos account, select the account and then click the Password button in the Kerberos utility's toolbar.

This will reveal the Kerberos Change Password dialog; enter your old password once and your new password twice. When choosing a new Kerberos password, be sure to use a high-quality password. Open the Password Assistant by clicking the small lock icon to the right of the Password entry field to help qualify your master password choice.

Click the OK button to complete the password change.

6   Finally, to rid the Mac of your currently active Kerberos account and tickets, select the account and then click the Destroy button in the Kerberos utility's toolbar.

Again, destroying any cached service tickets will not disconnect any currently connected network service that was authenticated with those tickets.

Other advanced options are available from the Kerberos application preferences dialog (choose Kerberos > Preferences from the menu bar). Also, while you have the Kerberos application open do yourself a favor and permanently add the Kerberos application to the Dock for easy access. You can do this from the Kerberos application's Dock icon shortcut menu (which you access by right-clicking/Control-clicking on the Kerberos application's icon in the Dock). In fact, you'll see that the most-often-used Kerberos management commands are also located in the Kerberos application's Dock icon shortcut menu.

Troubleshooting Directory Services

Directory services and authentication services are tightly linked to each other. Also, Open Directory (OD) is responsible for both of these services in Mac OS X, so they share similar troubleshooting techniques. Almost all common OD issues are discovered because of a single symptom: a user is unable to access or authenticate to his or her account. Other symptoms might indicate an issue with OD, but an inability to authenticate is often the first and most significant issue a user will experience. After all, if the Mac has OD issues, then the user probably won't even make it past the login window.

> **NOTE ▶** Again, before digging too deep into troubleshooting a specific network service, take a few moments to check for general network issues as outlined earlier in this lesson.

Common troubleshooting techniques specific to directory services and authentication services include:

▶ Attempt to authenticate with another user account—Remember, Mac OS X supports multiple directory services, so first test another user account hosted from the same directory. Also, keep in mind that if a similarly named account exists in multiple directories, the first account OD locates is the one that's used. Otherwise, if the other account works properly, the problem lies only with the account record. Yet if you are unable to authenticate from multiple accounts, you are experiencing a problem with the directory service as a whole.

▶ Reset the account password—This approach often requires that you have administrative access to the directory hosting the account. Not only will this technique resolve any potential human errors, it will also reset the account's authentication information, which may have become compromised.

▶ Verify network directory service connectivity and configuration—As covered previously, Directory Utility shows you the current status of bound network directory services. If a service isn't responding properly, first check the advanced settings by clicking the Show Advanced Settings button and then the Services button in the Directory Utility's toolbar. You can also reset the network directory service configuration by unbinding and then rebinding to the service using the plus and minus buttons at the bottom of the directory list.

▶ Verify Kerberos authentication and configuration—As explained earlier, the Kerberos application will show you currently connected Kerberos accounts and tickets. First attempt a quick fix by destroying all current tickets and then re-authenticating. If multiple Kerberos KDCs or accounts are available, make sure the appropriate account is being used. Finally, Kerberos is a time-sensitive protocol, so verify that your Mac has the correct date and time set. Ideally, all Kerberos participants will be configured to use the Network Time Protocol (NTP) to ensure clock synchronization.

▶ Check directory service log files—If none of these techniques work, fall back on information collected by the OD log files. OD generates very thorough log information that can help pinpoint directory service and authentication service issues. From the /Application/Utilities/Console application, inspect three specific log files located in /Library/Logs: DirectoryService.server.log has OD general usage and configuration information; DirectoryService.error.log has all OD error messages; and SingleSignOnTools.log has all Kerberos configuration and error messages.

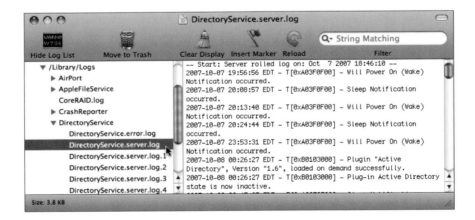

TIP ▶ As a last resort, you can completely reset OD to default settings by deleting the /Library/Preferences/DirectoryService folder and restarting the Mac.

What You've Learned

▶ Mac OS X includes built-in support for accessing a wide variety of network services, including Internet, network file, and remote control services.

▶ The Finder allows you to connect to and mount network file systems by either manually entering a server address or browsing the network for servers via dynamic network discovery services.

▶ Mac OS X includes Open Directory for resolving network and directory resource information. Open Directory supports several network directory services, including LDAP services and Microsoft's Active Directory service.

▶ Open Directory also coordinates account authentication via a variety of authentication protocols, including the popular Kerberos authentication system.

References

Check for new and updated Knowledge Base documents at http://www.apple.com/support.

General Network Services

106439, "'Well known' TCP and UDP ports used by Apple software products"

306304, "Bonjour: Frequently asked questions"

106964, "Mac OS X 10.2: About your computer's Bonjour name"

107174, "Mac OS X: About Multicast DNS"

25758, "Mac OS X: Configuring AFP to use OpenSSH exclusively"

306723, "Mac OS X 10.5: About Kerberos in Mac OS X 10.5 clients"

Network Applications

107657, "Safari quits unexpectedly"

42827, "Mac OS X Mail: About secure email communications (SSL)"

25748, "iChat: Frequently asked questions"

61709, "Frequently asked questions about iCal"

306687, "Mac OS X 10.5: iChat system requirements"

306688, "Mac OS X 10.5: Using iChat with a firewall or NAT router"

URLs

Apple's product guide: http://guide.apple.com

iCal shared calendar website: http://www.icalshare.com

Official CalDAV calendar collaboration resource website: http://ietf.osafoundation.org/caldav

Official Zeroconf dynamic network discovery service website: http://www.zeroconf.org

Apple Remote Desktop network client management software: http://www.apple.com/remotedesktop

Group Logic's ExtremeZ-IP AFP server for Windows: http://www.grouplogic.com

Apple's Active Directory integration website: http://www.apple.com/itpro/articles/adintegration

Official Kerberos authentication resource website: http://web.mit.edu/Kerberos

Review Quiz

1. What is the relationship between clients and servers as it relates to network service access?

2. What is the relationship between a network service and a network port?

3. What are three common troubleshooting techniques for issues involving failure to connect to network services?

4. What five network file services can you connect to from the Finder's Connect to Server dialog?

5. What three dynamic network service discovery protocols are supported by Mac OS X?

6. How does Mac OS X use dynamic network service discovery protocols to access network services?

7. How are items inside the Finder's Network folder populated?

8. What are some known issues that arise when connecting to network file services?

9. What is a directory as it relates to directory services?

10. What are seven common types of resources Mac OS X can access from a directory service?

11. What are the primary differences between local, network, and mobile accounts?

12. What are four advantages of using network directory services to store account information?

13. What four directory service protocols can be used in Mac OS X?

14. What is authentication? What is authorization?

15. What are three common authentication service types?

16. What is a Kerberos ticket? What is a Key Distribution Center (KDC)?

17. How do Kerberos and the keychain system differ for managing authentication services?

18. What are five common directory services and authentication services troubleshooting techniques?

Answers

1. Client software is used to access network services provided by server software. The connection is established using a common network protocol known by both the client and server software. Thus, the client and server software can be from different sources.

2. Network services are established using a common network protocol. The protocol specifies which TCP or UDP port number is used for communications.

3. Review the Network preferences, review the Network Utility statistics, and attempt to connect to different network services.

4. From the Finder's Connect to Server dialog, you can connect to Apple File Protocol (AFP), Server Message Blocks/Common Internet File System (SMB), Network File System (NFS), Web-Based Distributed Authoring and Versioning (WebDAV), and File Transfer Protocol (FTP) network file services.

5. Mac OS X supports Bonjour, AppleTalk, and Network Basic Input/Output and Windows Internet Naming Service (NetBIOS and WINS) dynamic network service discovery protocols.

6. Devices providing a network service advertise their availability via a dynamic network service discovery protocol. Clients that are looking for services request and receive this information to provide the user with a list of available network service choices.

7. The Finder populates the Network folder using information provided by the dynamic network services discovery protocols. Computers providing services appear as resources inside the Network folder, while service discovery zones or workgroups appear as folders. Any currently connected servers will also appear in the Network folder.

8. Forked files may cause problems for NFS or WebDAV network file systems. Also, avoid AFP 2 services as provided by Windows file servers.

9. A directory is a database of information that is optimized for frequent read access. The most commonly accessed directory resource is account information.

10. Common directory resources that Mac OS X can access include user accounts, user groups, computer accounts, computer groups, network file mounts, management settings, and collaboration information.

11. Local accounts are only available to a single Mac, network accounts are available to Mac connected to a network directory service, and mobile accounts are network accounts that are cached to the local Mac for offline use.

12. Four advantages of using network directory services to store account information are: 1) user accounts are no longer tied to individual Macs; 2) the same user account information can be used for multiple network services; 3) you can use Kerberos to provide secure single-sign-on authentication; and 4) you can define user and computer settings from a centralized location.

13. The directory service protocols that can be used in Mac OS X are Local, Berkeley Software Distribution (BSD) Flat File and Network Information Systems (NIS), Lightweight Directory Access Protocol version 3 (LDAPv3), and Active Directory (AD).

14. Authentication is the process of proving your identity to the computer; authorization defines which items or services you are allowed to access.

15. Three common authentication service types are basic or clear-text passwords, encrypted passwords, and Kerberos ticket-based authentication.

16. Kerberos tickets are used to validate an account's identity. Kerberos uses ticket-granting tickets (TGTs) and service tickets. Kerberos requires a special trusted service known as the KDC. In most cases the KDC service is running alongside the network directory service.

17. Kerberos can only be used to authenticate kerberized services, and is often managed on a networkwide scale. The keychain system can be used to save a wide variety of authentication information, but saved keychain information is only accessible to the local Mac.

18. Common directory services and authentication services troubleshooting techniques are: 1) attempting to authenticate with another user account; 2) resetting the account password; 3) verifying network directory service connectivity and configuration; 4) verifying Kerberos authentication and configuration; and 5) checking the directory service log files.

8

Time   This lesson takes approximately 2 hours to complete.

Goals   Configure Mac OS X client computers to provide network file
              sharing and web sharing services

              Provide and protect network sharing and client services

              Troubleshoot network shared service issues

Lesson 8
Providing Network Services

Perhaps one of Apple's best-kept secrets is that Mac OS X and Mac OS X Server are nearly identical operating systems. Many of the core technologies that make Mac OS X a stable and secure client operating system also make a great server operating system. In fact, Mac OS X can provide many of the same network services as Mac OS X Server. With the exception of Mac OS X Server supporting a few additional advanced network services and administration tools, the two systems even share the same software for providing most network services.

The majority of this network service functionality is a result of Mac OS X's UNIX foundation, which includes extensive use of open source software. Because of this diverse foundation, Mac OS X again shows its compatibility advantage by providing a range of popular network services. Consequently, any modern operating system should be able to access your Mac's shared resources.

In this lesson you will focus on how to properly configure Mac OS X's built-in network sharing services. In the first section, you will enable and control network file sharing and web sharing services. Next, you will enable a variety of network and client remote control services.

You will also configure the Mac's firewall to protect it from malicious network traffic. Finally, you will learn some common network service troubleshooting techniques.

This, the final of three network-focused lessons, expands on what you learned in both Lesson 6, "Network Configuration," and Lesson 7, "Accessing Network Services," to complete your understanding of Mac OS X's network infrastructure.

Providing Network File Services

OS X has built-in support for providing three popular file sharing services—AFP, FTP, and SMB—along with web sharing services via HTTP. When you enable any network service, always confirm proper configuration by testing access to the service from another computer. Detailed information about these network service protocols, including how to access them from Mac OS X, was covered in Lesson 7, "Accessing Network Services."

> **MORE INFO ▶** Mac OS X includes support for providing NFS services, though not via the graphical user interface (GUI). You can find out more about providing NFS services by reading the nfsd manual page from the command-line interface (CLI).

Mac OS X's network file sharing services are, for the most part, enabled and managed entirely from the Sharing preference (choose Apple menu > System Preferences and click the Sharing preference icon). Three primary steps are required to properly configure your Mac so other computers can access its shared file resources: setting your Mac's network identification, enabling the network file service, and defining access to file system resources.

> **NOTE ▶** Users will not be able to access services on a Mac in sleep mode. You can disable your Mac's automatic sleep activation from the Energy Saver preference.

Network Identification

Before you start providing network services, you must configure your Mac so that other network clients can easily reach it. At a minimum your Mac can be reached by its IP address, but IP addresses are hard to remember and can possibly change if your Mac is using DHCP. Thus, it is much more convenient for you and other network clients to locate your Mac using a network name and discovery service.

Mac OS X network identification methods include:

▶ IP address(es)—The primary network identifier for your Mac, and as such, can always be used to establish a network connection.

▶ DNS host name—This name is hosted by a DNS server. Many network clients don't have a DNS host name because of the administrative overhead required to host client DNS names.

▶ Bonjour name—Bonjour is Mac OS X's primary dynamic network discovery protocol. This name is set in the Sharing preference.

▶ AppleTalk name—AppleTalk is Apple's legacy dynamic network discovery protocol. This name is also set in the Sharing preference, but AppleTalk is turned off by default.

▶ NetBIOS/WINS name—These are Windows' primary dynamic network discovery protocols.

You may be unable to control your Mac's IP address or DNS host name; the network administrator usually controls these. But as long as the Mac has properly configured TCP/IP settings as outlined in Lesson 6, "Network Configuration," your configuration is complete for these two identifiers. If your Mac has multiple IP addresses or DNS host names properly configured, it will also accept connections from those.

For dynamic network discovery protocols, though, you can locally set the Mac's network identifier from the Sharing preference. Simply enter a name in the Computer Name field and the system will set the name for each available protocol. For example, if you enter a computer name of "My Mac," the Bonjour name will be "My-Mac.local," the AppleTalk name will be "My Mac," and the NetBIOS/WINS name will be "MY_MAC." If the name you chose is already taken by another device, the Mac will automatically append a number on the end of the name. The Bonjour service needs no additional configuration, but both AppleTalk and NetBIOS/WINS may require additional configuration, as covered in Lesson 6.

> **TIP** ▶ To register your Mac's identification for Wide-Area Bonjour, click the Edit
> button below the Computer Name field, and then select the "Use dynamic global
> hostname" checkbox to reveal the Wide-Area Bonjour settings.

Enable File Sharing Services

If your Mac's network identification is set up correctly, it's easy to enable AFP, FTP, and
SMB file sharing services with the default access settings.

To enable network file sharing:

1   Choose Apple menu > System Preferences, then click the Sharing icon.

2   Click the lock icon in the bottom-left corner and authenticate as an administrative
     user to unlock Sharing preferences.

3   Select the File Sharing checkbox to enable the AFP network file service.

    This is the only service that will be enabled by default when you select the File
    Sharing checkbox.

The launchd control process will now listen for AFP service requests on TCP port 548,
and automatically start the AppleFileServer process as necessary to handle any requests.

> **MORE INFO** ▶ Details regarding the launchd control process are covered in Lesson 10,
> "Startup Process."

4   To enable the FTP network file service, make sure File Sharing is selected in the Service list, and then click the Options button in the bottom-right corner of the Sharing preference.

Select the "Share files and folders using FTP" checkbox in the dialog.

The launchd control process will now listen for FTP service requests on TCP ports 20 and 21, and automatically start the ftpd process as necessary to handle any requests.

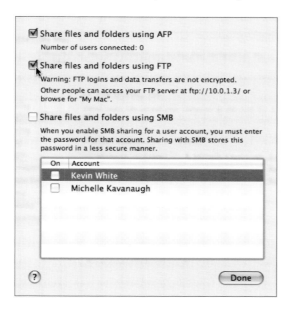

TIP ▶   From this dialog you can also choose to disable the AFP service if you intend to provide only FTP or SMB services. You can also view the number of connected AFP clients.

5   To enable the SMB network file service, make sure File Sharing is selected in the Service list, and then click Options.

Select the "Share files and folders using SMB" checkbox.

The launchd control process will now listen for SMB service requests on TCP port 139, and automatically start the smbd process as necessary to handle any requests.

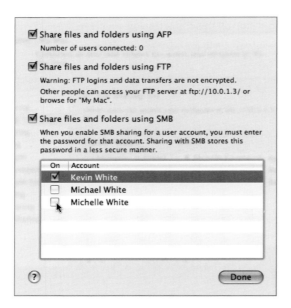

The SMB service uses a different style of password than the standard Mac OS X account password. Therefore, you will have to select the checkbox next to each account for which you wish to grant SMB access and reenter the password for that account.

MORE INFO ▶ Mac OS X uses the open source Samba software suite to provide SMB file services. To learn how to configure custom Samba service settings, visit http://www.samba.org/.

6   Click the Done button and then close the Sharing preference.

Once you enable a network file sharing service, if the Mac is up and running the service is actively listening for connections. Deactivating a service closes any current connections, and they remain deactivated until you reenable the service.

> **NOTE ▶** Deselecting the File Sharing checkbox deactivates all network file services. Further, reselecting the File Sharing checkbox will only re-enable the AFP service.

> **NOTE ▶** Deactivating a File Sharing service disconnects any currently active connections. Only the AFP service will remind you of this and allow you to warn currently connected users that the service will soon be unavailable.

The AFP service is limited to ten simultaneous connections. All other services remain limited only by your Mac's resources. For more simultaneous connections, look at Mac OS X Server. The unlimited-client edition of Mac OS X Server does not have this restriction.

While modern Macs are able to handle many simultaneous connections and multiple services, it's not a good idea to leave these services running all the time because they can be a security risk. This is especially true for portable Macs that often connect to public wireless networks, or any time you enable Guest access.

Be especially wary of the FTP service since all transactions are in clear text. Always be aware of exactly which files and folders you are allowing others to access. Next you will cover the default access configuration and how to change access settings to better fit your needs.

Configure File Sharing Access

Enabling a network file sharing service enables other users on the network to connect to your machine; however, they will still need to supply a username and password to make any changes to your files or to access files beyond your Public folder.

By default, both the AFP and SMB services allow others to authenticate to your Mac anonymously or as a guest user. For security reasons, anonymous FTP access is disabled by default on Mac OS X. Still, all three protocols also allow sharing, standard, and administrative users to authenticate to your Mac with their user account information. If you only want to grant known user accounts with the ability to access network file sharing resources on your Mac, you can easily disable guest access from the Accounts preference. Configuring user accounts was covered in Lesson 2, "User Accounts."

Once a user has been authenticated, the authorization services take over to control which files, folders, or volumes the user account is allowed to access on your Mac. File sharing access is controlled by these three authorization settings:

▶ Default Shared Items—AFP and SMB network file services will automatically grant default access to connect and mount specific folders or volumes based on the account type. The default shared items are covered in the next section.

▶ Custom Shared Items—For AFP and SMB, you can define custom folders or volumes as shared items, sometimes called share points, on your Mac. Making a folder or volume a shared item defines it as a location that other users can connect to and mount on their network client.

▶ Ownership and Permissions—Once users have mounted a shared item from your Mac, they will have access to files and folders inside the mounted file system based on your Mac's file system ownership and permissions settings.

Default File Sharing Access

To keep things simple, Mac OS X uses a predefined set of file sharing access rules for AFP and SMB services. You don't have to define a single shared item or configure any ownership and permissions settings to provide file sharing services on Mac OS X. You can simply enable file sharing and users will be able to access their items based on the default file sharing access settings. These default settings are based on user account types as defined in the Accounts preference:

▶ Guest User—The guest user, if enabled, is normally only allowed access to other standard and administrative users' Public folders.

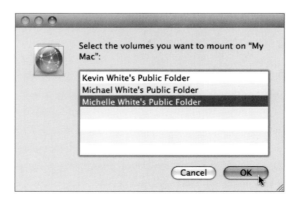

► Sharing User—By default, sharing users have the same access as the guest user, so you can disable anonymous access but still restrict certain users to Public folder access only.

► Standard User—Because standard users have local home folders, they will be allowed full access to their home folder contents as if they were using the Mac locally. Standard users also have access to other users' Public folders.

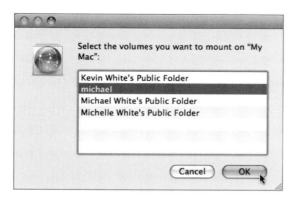

► Administrative User—Having full control over the Mac, administrative users can access every locally mounted volume on the shared Mac, including access to attached external drives and inserted optical media. Administrative users can also mount their home folder and other users' Public folders.

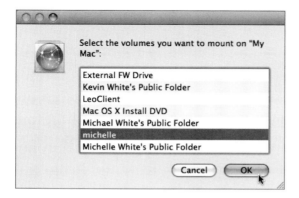

These default access settings will fulfill many users' file sharing needs, but for those Macs that are used as full-time network file sharing resources, these defaults are often not good enough. In the next section you will learn how to override these defaults and configure custom file sharing access.

Custom File Sharing Access

Previous versions of Mac OS X provided more flexibility for configuring custom file sharing access by allowing you to edit file system ownership and permissions settings from the Finder's Get Info window. However, you could not enable additional shared folders or volumes using the built-in interface tools. Mac OS X 10.5 introduced a revamped Sharing preference that allows you to easily edit ownership and permissions and also configure custom shared folders and volumes. You can use the Finder's Get Info window to set ownership and permissions, but you can also use the Get Info window to configure custom shared folders and volumes.

Before you begin configuring custom file sharing access, you should be aware of a few file sharing access rules. First, administrative users will always be allowed to remotely mount any volume, and both standard and administrative users will always be allowed to remotely mount their home folders. Second, as you create new standard and administrative users, their Public folders will be automatically set as a shared item. But you can easily disable the shared setting for each Public folder separately from the Sharing preference or the Finder's Get Info window.

Ultimately, all file sharing access is controlled by Mac OS X's file system ownership and permissions settings, so when you enable a folder or volume as a shared item, the file system ownership and permissions settings dictate which users can access the shared item. For example, the Public folders' Everyone permission setting is what grants all users, including guest and sharing-only users, with local and file sharing access to the Public folders contents. So, if you want to properly configure custom file sharing access, be familiar with the ownership and permissions architecture, as detailed in Lesson 3, "File Systems."

To configure custom file sharing settings from the Finder:

1   If you're setting up a new shared item, prepare the folder or volume to be shared. If you're sharing a new folder, create and name the folder with the Finder. If you're sharing a volume, be sure the volume is properly mounted and formatted as Mac OS Extended (Journeyed), as outlined in Lesson 3, "File Systems."

2   In the Finder, select the folder or volume for which you wish to configure the sharing settings, and then open the Get Info window (choose File > Get Info or press Command-I). You may have to click the General disclosure triangle to reveal the general information section.

3   Select the Shared Folder checkbox to share the selected folder or volume.

Deselecting this checkbox will stop sharing the item.

NOTE ▸ If you are a nonadministrative user, you'll have to authenticate with an administrative user account to enable or disable a shared item.

4   Click the Sharing & Permissions disclosure triangle.

You'll see the item's ownership and permissions settings. Click the small lock icon in the bottom-right corner of the Get Info window and authenticate as an administrative user to unlock the Sharing & Permissions section.

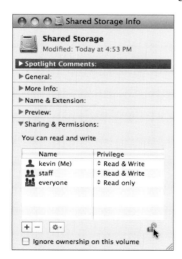

5 From the Sharing & Permissions area, you can configure custom file sharing access settings for any number of users or groups.

Only users or groups with read access will be able to mount the shared item. Always test newly shared items using multiple account types to ensure you have configured appropriate access settings.

To configure custom file sharing settings from the Sharing preference:

1 If you're setting up a new shared item, prepare the folder or volume to be shared.

2 Open the Sharing preference and authenticate as an administrative user to unlock its settings.

3 Select File Sharing from the Service list to access the network file sharing settings. The Shared Folder list will show currently shared items, including the Public folders that are shared by default.

4   To share a new folder or volume, click the small plus icon at the bottom of the Shared Folders list.

A file browser dialog appears. Select the folder or volume you wish to share, then click the Add button to start sharing that item.

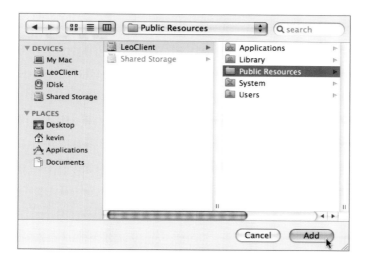

To stop sharing an item, select it from the Shared Folders list and click the small minus button at the bottom of the list.

5   Select a shared item to reveal its access settings in the Users list. The Users list is identical to the Sharing & Permissions area in the Finder's Get Info window.

Again, only users or groups with read access will be able to mount the shared item, and you should always thoroughly test newly shared items to ensure you have configured appropriate access settings.

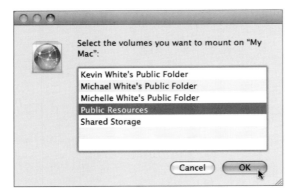

FTP File Sharing Access

Mac OS X's default FTP file sharing service configuration by default does not allow connections from guest or sharing-only users. The FTP service relies on file system ownership and permissions to dictate user access. With Mac OS X, when users connect to the FTP service, they start in their home folder but can access and navigate to any other items on the Mac for which they have the appropriate file system permissions.

Apple also disabled anonymous FTP access, because it is by far the least secure file sharing protocol available and is often exploited by malicious attackers. It's fair to say that authenticated FTP access poses an even greater security risk since users' passwords travel across the network in an unprotected form. If security is paramount, avoid FTP use entirely and instead use AFP or SMB services. Another secure alternative is the SFTP service, which is part of the SSH service covered later in the "Enable Remote Login" section.

MORE INFO ▶ Find out how to enable custom FTP service settings by reading the ftpd manual page from the CLI.

Web Sharing Service

Mac OS X also includes the Apache web server to allow users to share web pages and files from their own systems.

Enable Basic Web Service

Apple has preconfigured the web sharing service so that it can be enabled with literally a single click.

To enable basic web sharing:

1 Open Sharing preferences by choosing Apple menu > System Preferences and clicking the Sharing icon.

2 Click the lock icon in the bottom-left corner and authenticate as an administrative user.

3 Select the Web Sharing checkbox to enable the Apache 2 web service.

The launchd control process now listens for web service requests on TCP port 80, and automatically starts the httpd background process as necessary to handle any requests.

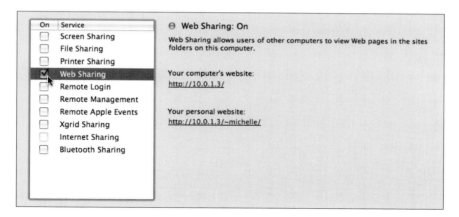

With the web sharing service enabled, other users can browse websites hosted from your Mac. This service is preconfigured with a main computer website and individual websites for each user who has a local home folder.

Computer Website

With web sharing enabled, you can browse to your Mac's primary computer website by entering http://<yourmac>/, where <yourmac> is your Mac's IP address, DNS host name, or Bonjour name. For example, if your Mac's IP address was 10.1.0.5 and its sharing name was My Mac, then you could enter http://10.1.0.5/ or http://My-Mac.local/. If you navigate to this website with the default configuration, you will see the Apache test page.

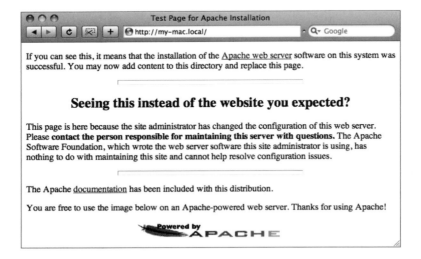

Configuring a custom website for your Mac is as simple as replacing the contents of your Mac's computer website folder (located at /Library/WebServer/Documents/). In this folder, you'll notice many index.html files that provide multilingual support for the Apache test page. To use your own custom website, replace this folder's contents with the website resources you created.

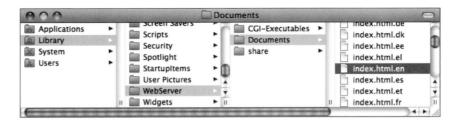

You can use any website creation tool that you like, such as iWeb or Pages, but you must keep in mind a few rules. First, the main page of your website must be named index.html. Second, you must ensure that ownership and permissions settings for your website files allow read access to Everyone. Finally, if you want to use advanced website features such as server-side scripts or secure transfers, you have to manually enable these services from the Apache 2 configuration files.

MORE INFO ▶ The Apache 2 web server has capabilities that go well beyond basic web sharing. To find out more, access the built-in locally hosted documentation at http://localhost/manual/, or visit the Apache web server project page at http://httpd.apache.org/.

User Websites

Mac OS X's web sharing service is also preconfigured to allow individual websites for each user with a local home folder on your Mac. You can browse to user websites by entering http://*<yourmac>*/~*<username>*/, where *<yourmac>* is your Mac's IP address, DNS host name, or Bonjour name, and *<username>* is the short name of the user account. For example, if your computer, with the sharing name of My Mac, has two user accounts with the short names of mike and debbie, then you could enter http://My-Mac.local/~mike/ or http://My-Mac.local/~debbie/. If you navigate to this website with the default configuration, you will see the Mac OS X user test page.

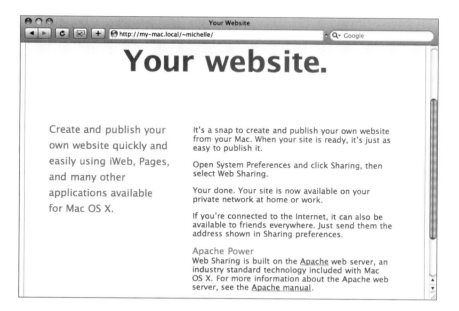

Each user's website is located inside the Sites folder within her home folder. To configure a custom website for the user, replace this folder's contents with the website resources you created. Again, you can use any website creation tools you like, and you must also follow the same website rules listed in the previous section.

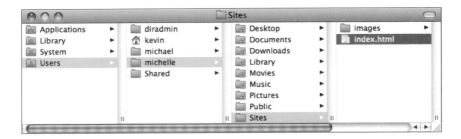

Providing and Protecting Network Services

Mac OS X includes an assortment of non-file-sharing network services, which you'll now see how to manage. These fall into two categories: client sharing services and Internet sharing services. Client sharing services vary in implementation and purpose, but they all allow users to remotely execute or control applications and processes on the Mac providing the service. Internet sharing services enable your Mac to share a single Internet connection to a network of devices. Related is the Mac's built-in, application-based network firewall, which protects your Mac (or any device connected to the Internet via your Mac's Internet sharing services) by blocking unwanted network communication.

MORE INFO ▶ Mac OS X can also provide Bluetooth and printer sharing services, as covered in Lesson 9, "Peripherals and Printing."

NOTE ▶ Users can't access services on a Mac in sleep mode. You can disable a Mac's sleep automatic mode from the Energy Saver preference.

Client Sharing Services

Each Mac OS X network client sharing service is designed to provide a specific remote management or application and process sharing need.

Mac OS X network client sharing services include:

▶ Screen Sharing—Allows remote control of your Mac's GUI.

▶ Remote Login—Allows remote control of your Mac's CLI via SSH.

▶ Remote Management—Augments the Screen Sharing service to allow remote administration of your Mac via the Apple Remote Desktop application.

▶ Remote Apple Events—Allows remote applications and AppleScripts to access resources on your Mac.

▶ Xgrid Sharing—Allows your Mac to remotely share its processing resources to help other users complete large computational tasks.

Recognize the security risk involved in providing a service that allows other users to control processes on your Mac. Obviously, if you're providing a service that allows remote control and execution of software, it's certainly possible for an attacker to cause trouble. Thus, it's paramount that when you enable these types of services you choose strong security settings. Using strong passwords is a good start, but you can also configure limited access to these services from the Sharing preference.

Enable Screen Sharing

Enabling this service, as its name implies, allows other users to view and control your Mac's GUI using the Virtual Network Computing (VNC) protocol. For many administrators this is an indispensable management feature that greatly enhances their ability to resolve technical issues. This is covered in more detail in Lesson 7, "Accessing Network Services."

To enable the Screen Sharing service:

1   Open the Sharing preference by choosing Apple menu > System Preferences, then clicking the Sharing icon.

2   Click the lock icon in the bottom-left corner and authenticate as an administrative user to unlock the Sharing preference.

3   Select the Screen Sharing checkbox in the Service list to enable the VNC Screen Sharing service.

The launchd control process will listen for Screen Sharing service requests on TCP and UDP port 5900, and automatically start the AppleVNCServer background process as necessary to handle any requests. By default, all nonguest user accounts will be allowed to access the service.

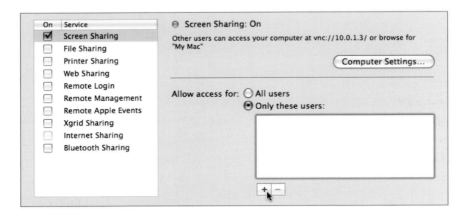

NOTE ▶ The Screen Sharing service is part of the Remote Management service. Thus, if Remote Management is enabled, the Screen Sharing checkbox will be inaccessible.

4 To limit screen sharing access, select the "Only these users" radio button, and then click the plus icon at the bottom of the users list.

In the dialog that appears, select the specific users or groups for whom you wish to grant screen sharing access. You can select existing users or groups, or create a new Sharing user account by clicking the New Person button or selecting a contact from your Address Book.

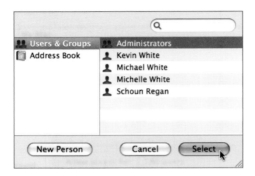

5   To allow a wider range of users to access your Mac's Screen Sharing service, click the Computer Settings button. Enable guest and VNC screen sharing access in the resulting dialog.

Select the top checkbox to allow anyone to ask permission to share the screen. When attempting to access your Mac's screen sharing, the currently logged-in GUI user must authorize the session.

Standard third-party VNC viewers cannot authenticate using standard user accounts, so you must set a password for VNC access.

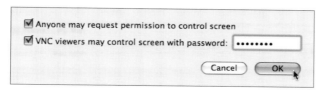

TIP ▸ You can use iChat to initiate ad hoc screen sharing sessions without enabling the Screen Sharing service. iChat screen sharing requires that both parties authorize the session, as covered in Lesson 7, "Accessing Network Services."

Enable Remote Login

Enabling this service allows other users to log in to your Mac's CLI using the SSH protocol. This is another great feature for advanced remote administration. For details, see Lesson 7, "Accessing Network Services."

To enable the Remote Login service:

1   Open the Sharing preference and authenticate as an administrative user to unlock the preference.

2   Select the Remote Login checkbox in the Service list to enable the SSH Remote Login service.

The launchd control process listens for remote login service requests on TCP 22 and starts the sshd background process as needed to handle any requests. By default, all standard and administrative user accounts will be allowed to access the service.

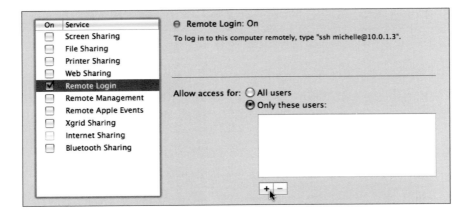

3   To limit remote login access, select "Only these users" and click the plus icon. In the resulting dialog, select the standard users, administrative users, or groups for whom you wish to grant access.

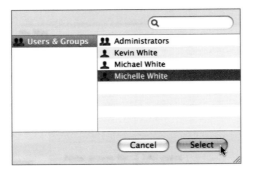

TIP Enabling the Remote Login service also enables the SFTP service, which is a secure, encrypted version of the FTP file sharing service.

Enable Remote Management

The Remote Management service is client-side software that allows the Apple Remote Desktop (ARD) administration tool to access your Mac. ARD is the ultimate remote management tool for Mac OS X computers. In addition to screen sharing, ARD allows administrators to remotely gather system information and usage statistics, change settings, add or remove files and software, and perform nearly any other management task you can think of. The real power of ARD is that you can execute all these tasks simultaneously on dozens of Macs with just a few clicks.

MORE INFO ▶ You can find out more about ARD at http://www.apple.com/ remotedesktop/.

To enable the ARD Remote Management service:

1   Open the Sharing preference and authenticate as an administrative user to unlock the preference.

2   Select the Remote Management checkbox in the Service list to enable VNC and the ARD client-side services.

    The launchd control process listens for Remote Management service requests on TCP and UDP ports 3283 and 5900 and starts the AppleVNCServer and ARDAgent background processes as needed to handle any requests.

    If this is the first time you have enabled remote management, you'll see a dialog that allows you to select the ARD options you wish to allow for all nonguest local users. You can individually select options, or you can hold down the Option key and then select any checkbox to enable all options. Click OK once you have made your selections.

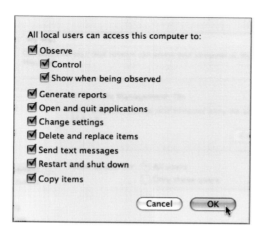

3 To limit ARD access, select "Only these users" and click the plus icon.

Then select a standard or administrative local user for whom you wish to grant ARD access. When you're done, another dialog appears, from which you select the ARD options this user can access.

You can edit a user's ARD options at any time by double-clicking that user's name in the user access list.

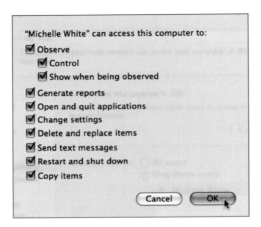

4 Additional ARD computer options are available by clicking the Computer Settings button. This opens a dialog that allows you to enable guest and VNC screen sharing access, enable the Remote Management menu bar item, and add information to help identify this particular Mac.

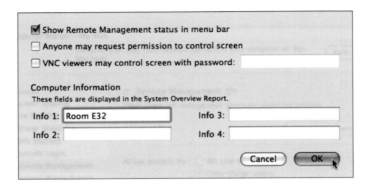

Enable Remote Apple Events

Remote Apple Events allows applications and Apple Scripts on another Mac to communicate with applications and services on your Mac. This service is most often used to facilitate automated Apple Script workflows between applications running on separate Macs.

MORE INFO ▶ You can find out more about AppleScript, Apple's English-like scripting technology, at http://www.apple.com/applescript/.

To enable the Remote Apple Events service:

1 Open Sharing preferences and authenticate as an administrative user to unlock the preferences.

2 Select the Remote Apple Events checkbox in the Service list.

The launchd control process listens for remote Apple Events requests on TCP and UDP port 3130 and starts the service_helper background process as needed to handle any requests. By default, all nonguest user accounts will be allowed to access the service.

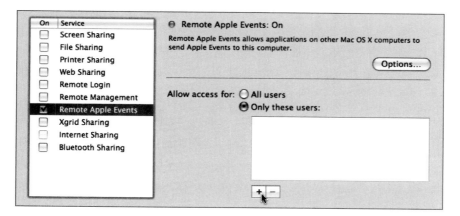

3 To limit Remote Apple Events access, select "Only these users" and click the plus icon.

In the resulting dialog, select the users or groups for whom you wish to grant Remote Apple Events access. Select existing users or groups, or create a new Sharing user account by clicking the New Person button or selecting a contact from your Address Book.

Enable Xgrid Sharing Service

Xgrid is Apple's distributed computing solution. It allows you turn a collection of networked Macs into a supercomputer. The Xgrid system can take a single computationally complex job and automatically split it into smaller pieces, then send those pieces to any Xgrid-enabled Mac for processing. If you have a building full of Macs that are used for everyday work, you can configure Xgrid to use these Macs during off hours to create an ad hoc supercomputer from your existing resources.

The Xgrid software built into Mac OS X only allows your Mac to become an agent of the Xgrid system. An Xgrid agent performs tasks at the behest of an Xgrid controller. Only Mac OS X Server includes the Xgrid controller software, so you cannot issue jobs from your Mac client. Further, though Xgrid is the easiest distributed computing solution to date, it is not designed for the casual user. You cannot just send any application process through the Xgrid system. At the very least, issuing jobs to Xgrid requires familiarity with the CLI or that you use software designed to take advantage of the Xgrid service.

MORE INFO ▶ You can find out more about Xgrid at http://www.apple.com/server/macosx/technology/xgrid.html.

To enable your Mac as an Xgrid agent:

1   Open the Sharing preferences and then authenticate as an administrative user to unlock the preferences.

2   Select the Xgrid Sharing item in the Service list, but do not select the Xgrid Sharing checkbox until you select an authentication method.

3   Choose an authentication method from the pop-up menu.

    The default selection is Password; if this is your choice, enter a password for your Mac. As an alternative, you can choose Single Sign On from the pop-up menu to use Kerberos as the authentication method. It is not recommended that you choose None as this will leave your Mac in an unsecured state. With authentication enabled, only Xgrid controllers with the proper authentication information will be allowed to use your Mac as an Xgrid agent.

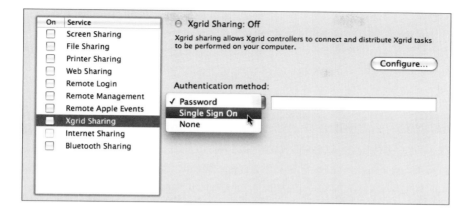

4   Click the Configure button and, in the resulting dialog, choose to tie your Mac to a specific Xgrid controller and adjust when your Mac will accept Xgrid jobs.

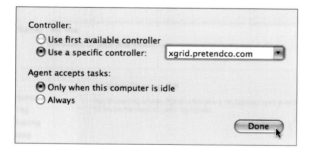

5   Select the Xgrid Sharing checkbox in the Service list to enable the Xgrid agent service.

The launchd control process listens for remote Xgrid service requests on TCP port 4111 and starts the xgridagentd background process as needed to handle any requests.

Network and Application Firewall

A network firewall protects your computer from unwanted network traffic by blocking unauthorized incoming network connections. Your Mac is already very secure because, by default, there are only a few essential services running that respond to external requests. Even once you start providing individual shared services, your Mac is designed to only respond to those services that are enabled. Still, users can open applications and services that could leave your Mac vulnerable to attack. To keep network services from allowing incoming connections to your Mac, you must enable the built-in network firewall; then you can completely block all nonessential incoming connections.

For the most part, blocking all nonessential connections won't prevent you from using most network and Internet applications, but it will completely block any shared network services that your Mac is providing and possibly hinder some network applications. For example, many iChat features won't work if the firewall blocks all incoming connections. So you can configure the firewall to block all but specifically allowed network connections.

To fix this, Mac OS X 10.5 introduces an easy-to-use adaptive firewall that lets you authorize individual applications and services to accept incoming network connections without having to know what network ports they use. For example, you can authorize iChat to accept any incoming connection without configuring all of the individual TCP and UDP ports used by the iChat application.

Mac OS X's firewall is built in as part of the core UNIX system software, so it's a secure and efficient firewall implementation that, when enabled, won't negatively affect network performance. Your Mac's network software is always inspecting every single network packet to determine which network application or process should receive the packet. Enabling the firewall service instructs the network system to simply disregard any unauthorized incoming network packets.

Enable and Configure the Firewall

1   Open Security preferences by choosing Apple menu > System Preferences, then clicking the Security icon.

2   Click the lock icon in the bottom-left corner and authenticate as an administrative user to unlock Sharing preferences.

3   Select the Firewall tab to reveal the firewall configuration interface.

    The default configuration is to allow all incoming connections. Without any additional configuration, currently enabled sharing services automatically appear in the list of allowed services.

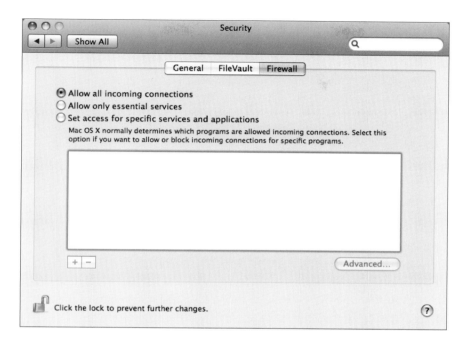

4   To disallow any nonessential network connection, select the "Allow only essential services" radio button.

The network firewall will block all nonessential incoming connections, but you will still be able to establish most outgoing connections. The list of essential services is covered in Apple Knowledge Base document 306938, "Mac OS X 10.5 Leopard: About the application firewall."

5   To disallow any incoming network connections except for essential services and authorized services and applications, select "Limit incoming connections to specific services and applications." Again, any currently enabled sharing services will be automatically authorized to allow incoming connections.

6   To add an authorized application, click the plus icon at the bottom of the authorized firewall list.

In the browser dialog that appears, select the application you wish to authorize, then click the Add button. The firewall service now allows incoming connections to that application, but only for the TCP or UDP ports that the application requires.

Or, click to the far right of the application's name to reveal a pop-up; then choose to allow or block incoming connections for the selected application.

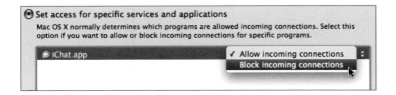

NOTE ▶ Once you configure the initial list of firewalled applications, the system will automatically help you track new network applications. As you open new network applications for the first time or update existing network applications, you will see a dialog where you can allow or deny the new network application.

7   Click the Advanced button in the bottom-right corner to open a dialog that allows you to manage advanced firewall options.

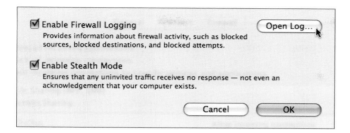

Here you can optionally select the Enable Stealth Mode checkbox to effectively hide your Mac's presence on the network. With this enabled, your Mac will not respond to any unauthorized network connections, including network diagnostic protocols like ping, traceroute, and port scan.

Firewall logging is always enabled, but you can disable it for instances where the log files grow too large. To see what your Mac's firewall is allowing or blocking, click the Open Log button to open the firewall log in the Console application. The firewall log is located at /var/log/appfirewall.log.

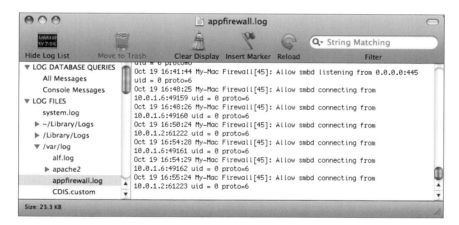

Internet Sharing Service

Mac OS X includes the Internet Sharing service, which can "re-share" a single network or Internet connection to any other network interface. Suppose you're traveling with a portable Mac that can obtain an Internet connection using a wireless broadband service, but your travel companions' computers have no such service. You can share your Mac's wireless broadband service via your Mac's AirPort and turn your Mac into a wireless access point for the other computers.

Traffic going through your machine, even to other systems, is still bound by your firewall rules. If you enable both the Internet Sharing and firewall services, any network clients taking advantage of your Mac's re-shared network connection will also be protected from unwanted network connections.

When you enable the Internet Sharing service, the launchd process starts several background processes to facilitate these additional network services:

▶ InternetSharing—Manages the Internet Sharing service as a whole.

▶ natd—Performs the Network Address Translation (NAT) service that allows multiple network clients to share a single network or Internet connection.

▶ bootpd—Provides the DHCP automatic network configuration service for the network devices connected via your Mac. When a network device connects to your Mac's shared network connection, it will automatically obtain an IP address in the 10.0.2.X range.

▶ named—Provides DNS services for network devices connected via your Mac. It's responsible for forwarding requests between these network devices and your Mac's primary DNS server.

To enable the Internet Sharing service:

1   Configure your Mac's primary network connection as outlined in Lesson 6, "Network Configuration."

    You need not configure the network settings for the interface that the other network devices will connect to, but you should connect any wired network interfaces at this point.

    NOTE ▶ You can only re-share a network or Internet connection to devices connected via your Mac's wired Ethernet, wireless Ethernet, or FireWire interfaces.

2   Select the Internet Sharing item in the Service list, but do not select the Internet Sharing checkbox until you configure the service settings.

3   Select the interface you wish to share from the pop-up menu. In most cases this will be your Mac's primary connection to the Internet. It can be any active network connection.

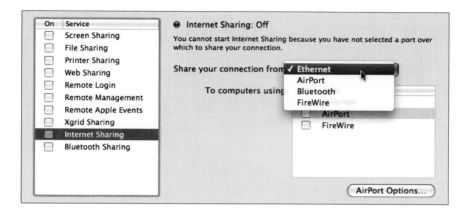

4   Select the checkboxes next to the network interfaces that other network devices will use to access your Mac's shared network.

Your Mac will provide DHCP services on the selected network interfaces, which can certainly cause problems on networks that are already configured to provide this service. So, don't provide the Internet Sharing service to an established network.

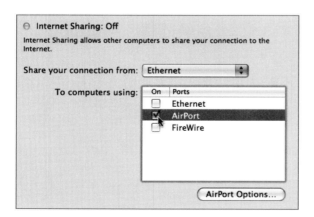

NOTE ▶ It's a bad idea to select the checkbox next to the same interface that you are sharing from—this means that your Mac will be re-sharing an interface back onto itself. Fortunately, the system will present you with a warning dialog if you attempt to choose this potentially bad configuration.

5   If you are sharing to an AirPort wireless Ethernet network, click the AirPort Options button to reveal these settings.

At a minimum you'll need to choose a network name so others know how to con-nect to your wireless service, but you should leave the wireless channel setting on Automatic for the best performance. It's also strongly recommended that you enable Wired Equivalent Privacy (WEP) encryption and set a password to protect your wireless Ethernet network. Further, choose 128-bit from the WEP Key Length pop-up menu—it's more secure, and nearly all wireless Ethernet cards support this higher standard.

Click OK after you have configured your wireless Ethernet network.

6   Once you have configured all the Internet Sharing settings, select the checkbox next to Internet Sharing in the Service list to enable the service.

You'll see a warning dialog reminding you of the potential issues that may arise should you improperly configure the Internet Sharing service.

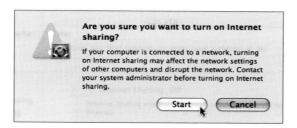

Click the Start button only if you're absolutely certain that you have properly configured the Internet sharing settings.

7   If you're re-sharing to your Mac's AirPort wireless interface, the AirPort menu item
changes appearance to indicate that you're sharing the interface.

8   Other wired Ethernet and FireWire network clients only have to physically connect to
your Mac's shared network interface. Other wireless clients must connect and authenticate to your Mac's shared wireless network as they would any with any other wireless access point.

Troubleshooting Shared Services

Once again, to effectively troubleshoot a network issue you must try to isolate the issue to
one of three categories; local, network, or service. You must also consider how established
the service is to determine where to focus your efforts. So, if your Mac has been reliably
providing a shared service for a while but now a single client computer has trouble accessing the service, troubleshoot the client computer before troubleshooting your shared Mac.
Troubleshooting client access is covered in Lesson 7, "Accessing Network Services."

Otherwise, if multiple clients cannot access your shared Mac, you may indeed have an issue with the sharing service. Nevertheless, you should always take a few moments to determine if this is a network-level issue by attempting to access services provided by a different network resource. From the client computers, try opening a web browser and navigating to a few local and Internet websites. If general network or Internet services aren't working, your problem most likely isn't due to the Mac providing the shared service. Troubleshooting general network issues is covered in Lesson 6, "Network Configuration."

After ruling out other potential local client and network issues, you can safely assume that the problem lies with the Mac providing shared services. If so, shared network service issues fall into two general categories: service communication or service access. Service communication issues are manifested by an inability to establish a connection to the shared service. However, service access issues generally result in failed authentication or authorization.

Network Service Communication Issues

If you are unable to establish a connection to the shared service, this may signal a network service communication issue. Keep in mind that, if you are presented with an authentication dialog, the client and server are establishing a proper connection and you should troubleshoot the issue as a service access issue.

To troubleshoot service communication issues:

▶ Double-check the shared Mac's network configuration—From the Network preference, make sure the Mac's network interfaces are active and configured with the appropriate TCP/IP settings. You can also use Network Utility to verify the network configuration. If a DNS server is providing a host name for your shared Mac, use the Lookup tool in Network Utility to verify the host name.

▶ Double-check the Mac's sharing service configuration—From the Sharing preference, verify the Mac's sharing name and ensure that the appropriate services are enabled and configured.

▶ Double-check the Mac's firewall configuration—From the Security preference, first temporarily allow all incoming network connections to see if disabling the firewall makes a difference. If you are able to establish a connection, adjust the list of allowed services and applications before you reenable the firewall.

▶ Check for basic network connectivity to the shared Mac—First, turn off the firewall's stealth mode, and then from another Mac use Network Utility's Ping tool to check for basic connectivity to the shared Mac. If you can't ping the shared Mac, you're probably having a network-level issue that goes beyond service troubleshooting.

▶ Check for network service port connectivity to the shared Mac—First, turn off the firewall's stealth mode, and then from another Mac use Network Utility's Port Scan tool to verify whether the expected network service ports are accessible. If the shared Mac is configured properly, the appropriate network service ports should register as open. If network routers exist between the network clients and the shared Mac, consider the possibility that a network administrator has decided to block access to those ports.

Network Service Access Issues

Failure to authenticate or be granted authorization to a shared service is considered a network service access issue. Try these troubleshooting suggestions, and also consider the directory service troubleshooting methodology covered in Lesson 7, "Accessing Network Services."

▶ Verify the local user account settings—When using local user accounts, make sure the correct authentication information is being used. You may find that the user is not using the correct information, and you may have to reset the account password. Troubleshooting user account issues was covered in Lesson 2, "User Accounts." Also, keep in mind that some services do not allow the use of guest and sharing-only user accounts. Further, the VNC, SMB, and Xgrid services use password information that is not directly linked to a user account.

▶ Double-check directory service settings—If you use a network directory service in your environment, verify that the Mac is properly communicating with the directory service by checking its status in the Directory Utility application. Even if you're only trying to use local accounts, any directory service issues can cause authentication problems. Also, keep in mind that some services, like remote management, do not allow you to authenticate with accounts hosted from network directories.

▶ Double-check shared service access settings—Several authenticated sharing services allow you to configure access lists. Use the Sharing preference to verify that the appropriate user accounts are allowed to access the shared service.

▶ Verify file system ownership and permissions—If you're able to authenticate or connect to file and web sharing services, but you're unable to access files and folders, then file system permissions are probably getting in the way. Use the Finder's Get Info window to inspect the file and folder permissions of the inaccessible items. Sometimes the easiest resolution is to simply create a new permission setting just for the user who is experiencing access issues. Mac OS X's adoption of file system ACLs allows you to make as many permission rules as you want. Also, remember that any files accessed by the web sharing service must be readable by Everyone. Detailed information about ownership and permissions, including troubleshooting access issues, is covered in Lesson 3, "File Systems."

What You've Learned

▶ Your Mac is accessible to other network clients via static network identifiers like its IP address(es) and DNS host name, or dynamic network service identifiers like Bonjour, AppleTalk, and NetBIOS/WINS.

▶ Mac OS X can provide AFP, SMB, and FTP file sharing services.

▶ Mac OS X also includes the Apache 2 web server, which is preconfigured to share a single computer website and individual websites for each user.

▶ Mac OS X can provide several types of client sharing services that allow others to remotely control or execute software on your Mac.

▶ Mac OS X's core network software lets you protect other network services by enabling adaptive firewall filtering, or share a network or Internet connection with others by acting as a network router.

References
Check for current Knowledge Base documents at http://www.apple.com/support.

Providing Network Services
106439, "'Well Known' TCP And UDP ports used by Apple software products"

306938, "Mac OS X 10.5 Leopard: About the application firewall"

306304, "Bonjour: Frequently asked questions"

106964, "Mac OS X 10.2: About your computer's Bonjour name"

107174, "Mac OS X: About Multicast DNS"

25758, "Mac OS X: Configuring AFP to use OpenSSH exclusively"

108058, "Choosing a Password for networks that use Wired Equivalent Privacy (WEP)"

108030, "Apple Remote Desktop: Configuring remotely via command line (kickstart)"

URLs

Official Samba SMB software suite resource website: http://www.samba.org/

Your Mac's locally hosted Apache 2 documentation: http://localhost/manual/

Official Apache web server software resource website: http://httpd.apache.org/

Apple Remote Desktop network client management software: http://www.apple.com/remotedesktop/

Apple Script resource website: http://www.apple.com/applescript/

Apple's Xgrid distributed computing solution resource website: http://www.apple.com/server/macosx/technology/xgrid.html

Review Quiz

1. How do you provide Mac OS X file sharing services so other computers can access them?

2. What items are shared by default to all users?

3. What shared items are accessible to an administrative user who connects via AFP or SMB? What about a standard user?

4. What shared items are accessible to any user who connects via FTP?

5. What password issues may arise related to the SMB service?

6. How do you provide Mac OS X web sharing services?

7. What files are associated with the computer's website? What about an individual user's website?

8. What client sharing services can Mac OS X provide?

9. What is the security risk of enabling client sharing services?

10. How is Xgrid implemented in Mac OS X?

11. How does Mac OS X's built-in firewall work? What advanced firewall settings are available?

12. What network services are provided by your Mac to facilitate Internet sharing? What options are available for Internet sharing via your Mac's AirPort wireless Ethernet interface?

Answers

1. To provide services to other network clients you first set your Mac's network identification, then enable the desired network file service, and finally define access to file system resources.

2. The items shared to all users by default are the local users' Public folders inside their home folders.

3. Administrators who connect to your Mac via AFP or SMB have access to any locally mounted volume. By default, standard users can only access their home folder and other users' Public folders.

4. Users who connect to your Mac via FTP have access based on the local file system ownership and permissions; by default they'll start in their home folders.

5. Passwords for the SMB service are not synced to users' normal account passwords. An administrative user will have to manually change the SMB passwords from the Sharing preference.

6. To enable the web sharing service select the checkbox next to Web Sharing in the Sharing preference.

7. The computer's website files are located in the /Library/WebServer/Documents folder. Each user's website files are located in the Sites folder inside their home folder.

8. Mac OS X's client sharing services are: Screen Sharing, Remote Login, Remote Management, Remote Apple Events, and Xgrid Sharing.

9. If a client sharing service is compromised, an unauthorized user can control your Mac and execute unwanted applications or processes.

10. Mac OS X includes the ability to share its computing resources as an Xgrid agent. A computer running Mac OS X Server is required to act as an Xgrid controller.

11. Mac OS X's built-in firewall inspects each incoming network connection to determine if it's allowed. You can choose to allow all incoming connections, deny all incoming

connections, or only allow incoming connections for services and applications you have specified. The advanced firewall settings allow you to investigate the firewall log file and enable stealth mode (which means your Mac will not respond to any unsolicited connections).

12. When Internet sharing is enabled, your Mac provides network routing NAT, DHCP, and DNS forwarding services for any network device connected to your Mac's shared network interfaces. When sharing a network or Internet connection to your Mac's AirPort wireless Ethernet interface, you can specify a wireless network name, channel, and WEP security settings.

9

Time   This lesson takes approximately 2 hours to complete.

Goals   Understand, manage, and troubleshoot peripheral connectivity from
both a hardware and a software perspective

Understand, manage, and troubleshoot printing and faxing systems

Lesson 9
Peripherals and Printing

Apple pioneered the concept of automatic peripheral support with the original Macintosh. This feature, commonly known as plug-and-play, is now supported with varying success in all modern operating systems. Peripheral hardware has also improved, as now the most common connectivity standards support hot-pluggable or even wireless connections. Mac OS X supports all popular modern peripheral standards, demonstrating Apple's continued commitment to making peripheral use as easy as possible. Nowhere is this commitment made clearer than by Apple's foray into the consumer electronics market with products like iPod, Apple TV, and iPhone.

Similarly, Apple and Adobe pioneered the desktop publishing revolution by introducing the first high-quality printing solution for personal computers. Although Adobe created the PostScript printing system, Apple was the first to include it in both the Macintosh operating system and the very first PostScript printer, the Apple LaserWriter. Apple has continued to pioneer advancements in printing software with Mac OS X by adopting a printing workflow based on Adobe's Portable Document Format (PDF) and the Common UNIX Printing System (CUPS).

At the start of this lesson, you'll learn how Mac OS X supports different peripheral technologies, and then you'll manage and troubleshoot peripherals connected to your Mac. Then you'll learn how Mac OS X supports different print and fax technologies, and how to manage and troubleshoot printers and faxes connected to your Mac.

Peripherals

For the purposes of this lesson, a peripheral is any non-networked device to which your computer system can be directly connected. A peripheral is directly connected to and controlled by the Mac, whereas network devices are shared.

Given the wide range of devices included in this definition, this lesson shows you how to categorize devices based on their connectivity type and device class. Understanding the available connection methods and device types is necessary to manage and troubleshoot peripherals, which is your ultimate goal in the first half of this lesson.

Understanding Peripheral Connectivity

Most peripherals communicate to the Mac system via a connection mechanism commonly known as a bus. Bus connections are the most common peripheral connection type because they allow multiple peripherals to connect to your Mac simultaneously. In fact, the only connection types that are not buses are those used for audio and video connectivity. Even then, your Mac is connected via a peripheral bus to intermediary hardware responsible for encoding or decoding the audio and video signals.

You can categorize peripheral connectivity into four types:

▶ Peripheral buses—General-purpose buses primarily used to connect an external device to your Mac

▶ Expansion buses—Designed to expand your Mac's hardware capabilities, often by adding extra connectivity options

▶ Storage buses—Only used for accessing storage devices

▶ Audio and video connectivity—Standard interfaces used to send audio or video signals from one device to another

Each connection is specialized for a particular type of communication, so a combination of technologies is often required to facilitate a peripheral. For example, your Mac's graphics hardware is obviously designed to output a standard video signal, but it communicates with the processor via an expansion bus. You'll see many examples of combined connection types as you explore various peripheral devices.

Given this, it's a good thing Mac OS X includes the System Profiler application to help you identify connected peripherals, including their connection types. Access the System Profiler by choosing Apple menu > About This Mac and clicking the More Info button in the resulting dialog. Once System Profiler is open, select a hardware interface from the Contents list to view its information. Using System Profiler for troubleshooting peripherals is covered in this lesson's "Troubleshooting Peripherals" section.

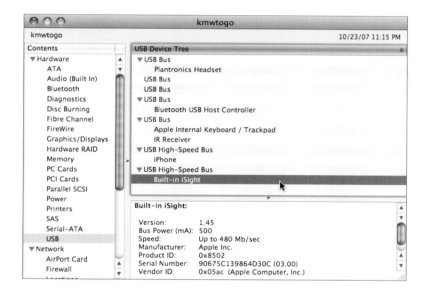

NOTE ▶ This lesson will only cover connection technologies included with Mac systems that support Mac OS X 10.5.

Peripheral Buses

Peripheral buses are the connection type most commonly associated with computer peripherals. Because they are designed to provide a general-purpose communications link between the computer and the peripheral, a variety of devices can use these connections.

There have been dozens of peripheral connectivity standards developed over the years, but in the last decade three peripheral standards have dominated the market: Universal Serial Bus (USB), FireWire, and Bluetooth.

Universal Serial Bus (USB) 1.1/2.0

Standard on every Mac that supports Mac OS X 10.5, USB is by far the most popular peripheral connection. In fact, it has become so popular that every single type of peripheral can be found in USB versions. You're probably already aware of the external USB ports on your Mac, but you may not know that Intel-based Macs also use USB for internal connectivity. For example, the MacBook's keyboard, trackpad, infrared receiver, iSight camera, and Bluetooth controller are all connected via internal USB connections.

USB was originally designed by Intel and is a hot-pluggable interface that allows the user to connect and disconnect devices while they are on, or "hot." USB is also a highly expandable connection platform that allows for daisy-chained connections. So, you can connect one USB device to your Mac, then connect another USB device to the first, and so on. With USB hubs, this allows for up to 127 simultaneous devices per host controller. Most Macs have at least two externally accessible USB host controllers.

The USB standard is also designed to provide up to 5 volts of power per host port. This is often enough to support low-power USB peripherals such as input devices, flash drives, and MP3 players. However, it is usually not enough to power USB hubs, multiple low-power USB devices from the same host port, or larger devices such as printers or scanners. These more power-hungry connections require a separate power source, from an electrical outlet. Peripherals that require a supplementary power source to operate via USB are often called self-powered USB devices.

At the time of this writing there are two primary USB versions: USB 1.1 and USB 2.0. USB 2.0 ports are backward-compatible with USB 1.1 cabling and devices. USB 1.1 supports low-speed connections at 1.5 megabits per second (Mbit/s) and full-speed connections at up to 12 Mbit/s. USB 2.0 supports high-speed connections up to a theoretical maximum of 480 Mbit/s. In practice, though, high-speed USB 2.0 connections fall short of the theoretical maximum. Then again, if you require a higher-performance peripheral connection bus, consider the next technology: FireWire.

MORE INFO ▶ You can find out more about USB at the official USB Implementer's Forum website: http://www.usb.org/.

FireWire

Also standard on every Mac that supports Mac OS X 10.5, FireWire is a high-speed, general-purpose peripheral connection originally developed by Apple. FireWire has been ratified as an Institute of Electrical and Electronics Engineers (IEEE) standard known as IEEE-1394, and has been adopted as a standard interface for digital video devices. Like USB, FireWire supports hot-pluggable and daisy-chained connections. Using hubs, each FireWire host controller can support up to 63 simultaneous devices.

FireWire has several advantages over USB. FireWire's primary advantage is that its host controllers work without placing a burden on your computer's main processor, allowing for higher overall performance compared with USB. These sophisticated FireWire host controllers also allow your Mac to be used in target disk mode without the need for a functional operating system, as covered in Lesson 3, "File Systems."

All Macs support FireWire 400 with a maximum transfer rate of up to 400 Mbit/s, and higher-end Macs also support FireWire 800 with a maximum transfer rate of up to 800 Mbit/s. These two FireWire standards use different port connections, but Macs with FireWire 800 ports can connect to FireWire 400 devices with the appropriate adapter. Because of the higher-performance components used to facilitate FireWire connections, FireWire 400 outperforms high-speed USB 2.0 even though it has a higher theoretical maximum throughput. This is mainly why FireWire has become a standard for digital video recording devices that require high-bandwidth connectivity.

Also, FireWire supports up to 30 volts of power per host port compared to USB's 5 volts. This increased power capacity makes FireWire ideal for use with external portable hard drives, as no additional power source is required to run the drive. But the additional cost and complexity of FireWire host controllers makes the technology overkill for many simple peripherals, such as mice, keyboards, and flash drives, that are well served by USB.

MORE INFO ▶ You can find out more about FireWire at Apple's official resource website: http://www.apple.com/firewire/.

Bluetooth

Bluetooth is a short-range wireless peripheral connection standard originally developed by Ericsson for cell phone headsets. Most Bluetooth devices have a range of only 1 to 10 meters, which is ideal for peripherals but inadequate for wireless networking. Further, it's not nearly as fast as wireless Ethernet; Bluetooth 1.2 has a maximum transfer speed of up to 721 kbit/s and Bluetooth 2.0 + Extended Data Rate (EDR) a maximum transfer speed of up to 3.0 Mbit/s. However, Bluetooth's primary advantage is that it works with low-power devices.

As Bluetooth increased in popularity, computer manufacturers adopted it for wireless peripherals as well. In addition to providing a wireless connection between your Mac and cell phone, Bluetooth allows your Mac to use wireless headsets, mice, keyboards, and printers. Many Macs include Bluetooth wireless, and for those that don't, you can easily add it with a USB-to-Bluetooth adapter. You can find out if your Mac has Bluetooth support by opening the System Preferences application and looking for the Bluetooth icon in the Hardware section.

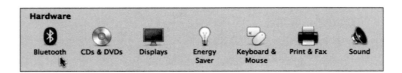

MORE INFO ▶ You can find out more about Bluetooth at the official Bluetooth Technology Information website: http://www.bluetooth.com/.

Because Bluetooth is a wireless technology, some configuration is required to connect your Mac to a Bluetooth peripheral. The process of connecting Bluetooth devices is known as *pairing*. Once two devices are paired, they will act as if they were directly connected to each other. Mac OS X 10.5 includes a revamped Bluetooth interface that makes the process of configuring peripherals even easier.

To configure and manage Bluetooth peripherals:

1   Open the Bluetooth preference by choosing Apple menu > System Preferences, then clicking the Bluetooth icon.

Make sure your Mac's Bluetooth power is enabled. You should also disable Discoverable mode, as leaving it enabled is a security risk.

NOTE ▶ Discoverable mode advertises your Mac as a Bluetooth resource, which in most cases leaves your Mac in a potentially unsecured state. The only time you should enable Discoverable mode is when you are having difficulty pairing your Mac to a Bluetooth peripheral; then you can try it the other way around and attempt to pair the peripheral to your Mac.

2   Enable Discoverable mode on the Bluetooth peripheral you're going to pair with your Mac.

Each device is different, so you may need to consult the device's user guide to enable Discoverable mode.

3   Click the Set Up New Device button to open the Bluetooth Setup Assistant, which walks you through the setup process.

4   Click the Continue button to move on from the Introduction screen, and then select the radio button next to the device type you are pairing. Click Continue to move on to the next step.

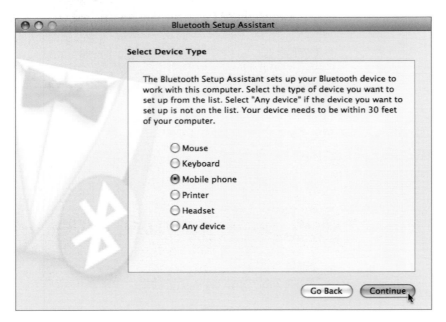

The Bluetooth Setup Assistant scans for any Bluetooth peripherals in range that are in Discoverable mode. It may take several moments for the device's name to appear; once it does, select it and click Continue.

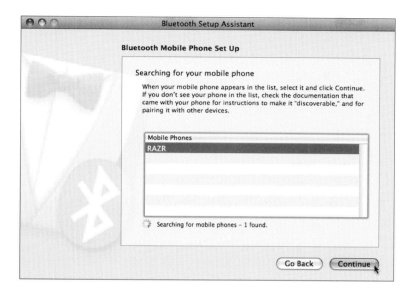

5 For most Bluetooth peripherals, you'll have to enter a passkey to authorize the pairing. Depending on the device, perform either of the following: On your Mac, enter a predefined passkey as given in the device's user guide and click Continue to authorize the pairing; or allow the Bluetooth Setup Assistant to create a random passkey that you then enter into the Bluetooth device to authorize the pairing.

TIP ▶ If you choose to set up iSync using the Bluetooth Setup Assistant, it automatically opens and configures the iSync application. For more, see "Peripherals That Synchronize" later in this lesson.

6   The Bluetooth Setup Assistant will automatically detect the capabilities of your Bluetooth peripheral and may present you with additional configuration screens. Continue through these screens until you complete the setup process.

7   Return to the Bluetooth preference to verify the pairing. You can further add, delete, or edit paired Bluetooth peripherals using the buttons at the bottom of the device list.

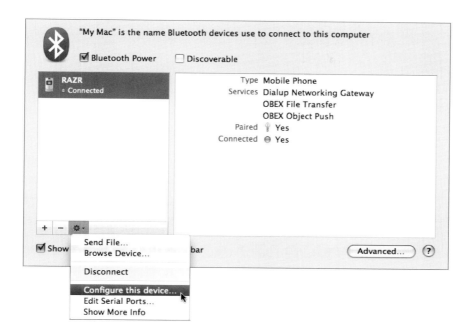

8   Once your Bluetooth peripheral is paired to your Mac, disable Discoverable mode on the device so that no one else can attempt to use it.

TIP   The Bluetooth menu item provides quick and easy access to most Bluetooth options, including the Bluetooth preference and Bluetooth Setup Assistant.

Expansion Buses

With expansion buses you can add additional hardware functionality to your Mac, usually in the form of a small computer board often called a *card*. Expansion buses are only found built into the main computer board inside your Mac. Though designed to allow for the addition of any type of technology, expansion buses are most often used to add support for another type of bus or connection. For example, most graphics cards are connected to your Mac via an expansion bus. Other common expansion cards add additional network ports, peripheral bus ports, storage bus connections, or audio and video input/output connections.

Even if you never add an expansion card to your Mac, several internal components are still connected via an expansion bus. Many Mac computers feature a space-saving design that accommodates most users' needs without additional expansion connections. Yet, for those who require hardware expansion, certain Mac computers have additional expansion bus connections: Power Mac, Mac Pro, PowerBook 15-inch and 17-inch, and MacBook Pro. The specific type of expansion ports varies by Mac model and age. As always, you can use the System Profiler application to identify your Mac's expansion bus capabilities.

Expansion buses supported in Mac hardware include:

► Advanced Graphics Port (AGP)—This type of expansion card is used specifically for graphics hardware, and supports a maximum connection bandwidth of up to 2 gigabytes per second (GB/s). Most PowerPC-based Macs use AGP-based graphics cards.

► Peripheral Component Interconnect (PCI)—This was the common desktop expansion card type for years, and supports a maximum connection bandwidth of up to 0.5 GB/s. Older Power Mac models feature PCI expansion ports.

► Peripheral Component Interconnect Extended (PCI-X)—This upgrade to the PCI standard supports a maximum connection bandwidth of up to 1 GB/s. Later Power Mac models have PCI-X expansion ports.

► PCI Express (PCIe)—This latest version of the PCI standard supports a maximum connection bandwidth of up to 4 GB/s. All Intel-based Macs use PCIe internally, and Mac Pro features PCIe expansion ports.

► PC Card—Also known as PCMCIA and CardBus, this expansion format is designed for portable computers and features a maximum connection bandwidth of up to 1 gigabit per second (Gbit/s). PowerBook 15-inch and 17-inch feature a single PC Card slot.

► ExpressCard 34—An extension of the PCIe technology, this expansion format is also designed for portable computers and features a maximum connection bandwidth of up to 2.5 Gbit/s. MacBook Pro models feature a single ExpressCard 34 slot.

Storage Buses

Storage buses are designed to connect your computer to disk or optical storage drives. The age and model of your Mac determines which storage bus technologies are used. But if your Mac features free expansion bus connections, you can generally add any storage bus connections you require via an expansion card.

Some storage buses are designed for internal use, and others can be used externally as well. It's important to know that external storage disk and optical drives connected via USB or FireWire are still using a dedicated storage bus inside the external drive case. So, every disk or optical drive is designed to use a specific storage bus, but those signals can also be retransmitted via a USB or FireWire connection. Therefore, you can purchase empty external drive enclosures that include hardware that bridges the storage bus connection to USB or FireWire, and then install your own internal drive in the case. This is extremely useful for recovering data from a Mac with a functional internal hard drive but otherwise inoperable hardware.

Storage buses supported in various Mac hardware include:

▶ Advanced Technology Attachment (ATA)—Sometimes called Parallel ATA, this storage bus was the most common standard for internal storage for many years, and supports a maximum connection bandwidth of up to 133 megabytes per second (MB/s). ATA host controllers are inexpensive because they support only two drives per controller. Most PowerPC-based Macs use ATA-based internal disk and optical drives.

▶ Serial ATA (SATA)—This improvement on ATA is now the most common storage bus for internal storage. It supports a maximum connection bandwidth of up to 384 MB/s, but no single drive is currently able to deliver that performance. SATA host controllers are also inexpensive, but they support only a single drive per controller. All Intel-based Macs use SATA-based internal disk and optical drives. External SATA connectivity can be added to your Mac via an expansion card.

▶ Small Computer System Interface (SCSI)—Sometimes also called Parallel SCSI, this was the original drive interface designed for personal computers. Over the years SCSI has evolved to become the most common storage bus for use in high-end or server computers, and though it supports internal storage, it's more often used for external storage. The latest SCSI supports a maximum connection bandwidth of up to 320 MB/s and up to 16 drives per controller. SCSI connectivity can be added to your Mac via an expansion card.

► Serial Attached SCSI (SAS)—This improvement on SCSI is becoming a popular storage bus for use in high-end or server computers. SAS also supports internal and external connections, but supports a maximum connection bandwidth of up to 384 MB/s and up to 16,384 devices through the use of expanders. The Intel-based Xserve supports internal SAS drives, but again you can add additional SAS connectivity to your Mac via an expansion card.

► Fibre Channel—This is the most advanced SCSI variant, and adds network-like features such as long-distance cabling and packet-based communication switching. Fibre Channel can offer speeds up to gigabytes per second. Fibre Channel host controllers are more complicated than other storage controllers, so they are also quite expensive and only available via an expansion card. Apple's Xserve RAID hardware and Xsan network storage technology are built around Fibre Channel.

Audio and Video Connectivity

Most audio and video connections are point-to-point and don't support multiple devices (like the previously covered bus connections). An audio or video signal is typically output from one device and directly connected to another single device designed to receive the signal.

All Macs, with this exception of some Xserve computers, have a variety of audio and video output connections. Most Macs also include audio input connections that allow you to record audio to digital files. Conversely, no Mac includes built-in support for direct video input. Nevertheless, there are a wide variety of video input options that allow you to capture video files to your Mac via USB, FireWire, or an expansion card.

Audio connections supported in various Macs include:

► Analog stereo audio—The standard stereo signal used by most consumer-grade audio equipment, which takes the form of either the 3.5 mm minijack or twin RCA connectors. Nearly every device made by Apple features built-in analog stereo output, and most Macs also feature analog stereo input.

► TOSLINK digital audio—This optical connection has become the most common digital audio connection for consumer-grade audio equipment. While both analog and digital audio connections support varying audio resolutions, digital audio connections do not suffer from electromagnetic interference. Thus, digital audio connections typically provide a much clearer audio signal. Most Intel-based Macs feature digital audio input and output. The Mac Pro uses standard TOSLINK ports, while all other Macs use special audio ports that support both analog stereo minijack and mini-TOSLINK connections.

Video connections supported in various Mac hardware include:

▶ Composite video—This RCA connection is the most common connection for analog standard-definition consumer-grade video. Most Mac OS X 10.5–compatible Macs can output a composite video signal using an Apple video adapter. However, composite video has an effective resolution of only 640 x 480 pixels, so it's not ideal for computer use.

▶ S-Video—This mini-DIN connection is also a common connection for analog standard-definition consumer-grade video, but it provides a slightly better picture than composite video. Most Mac OS X 10.5–compatible Macs can output an S-Video signal using an Apple video adapter. S-Video is also hindered by an effective resolution of 640 x 480 pixels.

▶ Video Graphics Array (VGA)—This is the most common connection used for analog computer video displays. Most Macs can output a VGA signal up to a resolution of 1600 x 1200 pixels, with some going as high as 2048 x 1536 pixels. Although older Macs feature built-in VGA ports, most Macs now require an Apple VGA adapter.

▶ Digital Video Interface (DVI)—This is the most common connection used for digital computer video displays and also high-definition televisions. DVI supports resolutions of up to 1920 x 1200 pixels. Many Macs feature built-in DVI ports, but some require an Apple DVI adapter.

▶ Dual-Link DVI (DVI-DL)—This is an extension to the DVI standard that supports resolutions of up to 2560 by 1600 pixels. Only newer high-end Macs support DVI-DL connections.

▶ High-Definition Multimedia Interface (HDMI)—This is fast becoming the standard connection for consumer-grade digital audio and high-definition video equipment. HDMI combines a DVI-based digital video signal with multichannel digital audio signals in a single, inexpensive copper connection. Although no Mac features built-in HDMI ports, you can convert any DVI connection to HDMI by using an inexpensive cable adapter.

Peripheral Device Classes

Peripherals are divided into device classes based on their primary function. Mac OS X includes built-in software drivers that allow your Mac to interact with peripherals from all device classes. While these built-in drivers may provide basic support, many third-party devices require device-specific drivers for full functionality. Detailed information about software drivers is covered in the next section.

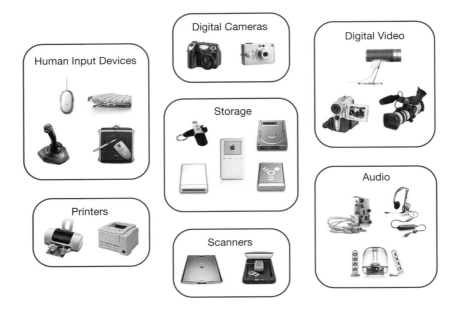

Device classes as defined in Mac OS X include:

▶ Human input devices (HID)—Peripherals that allow you to directly input information or control the Mac's interface. Examples are keyboards, mice, trackpads, game controllers, tablets, and even Braille interfaces.

▶ Storage devices—Disk drives, flash drives, optical drives, and even iPods and iPhones. Storage peripherals are covered in Lesson 3, "File Systems."

▶ Printers—Printers of all types, plotters, and even fax machines. Printing is covered later in this lesson.

▶ Scanners—Flatbed, negative, slide, and drum scanners. Mac OS X supports scanners via the Image Capture framework, which allows you to control scanners from /Applications/Image Capture or any other compatible third-party capture application, such as Photoshop.

TIP ▶ You can share scanners and digital cameras attached to your Mac via the network using Bonjour. In the Image Capture application, choose Devices > Browse Devices from the menu bar and then click the Sharing button.

▶ Digital cameras—These peripherals include both directly connected cameras and camera storage cards mounted to the Mac's file system. Recall that many digital cameras, when connected to a computer, simply extend their internal storage to the computer. In this case, Mac OS X accesses the camera's internal storage, or any directly attached camera storage cards, as it does any other storage device. Applications like iPhoto or Aperture then take over to essentially copy the picture files from the camera storage to the Mac's storage. Some cameras support a tethered capture mode in which they are directly controlled by the Mac and send the captured picture data directly to the Mac. Mac OS X supports this type of camera connection via the Image Capture framework, which again also allows you to use /Applications/Image Capture or other compatible third-party capture application.

TIP ▶ You can adjust which application automatically opens when you attach a digital camera from the Image Capture application preferences.

▶ Video devices—These peripherals include video cameras and video converters connected via USB, FireWire, or an expansion bus. Mac OS X supports these video devices via the QuickTime framework, which allows you to use /Applications/QuickTime Player or any other compatible video application, such as Final Cut Pro.

▶ Audio devices—These peripherals include external audio interfaces connected via USB, FireWire, or an expansion bus. Mac OS X supports these audio devices via the Core Audio framework, so you can use any compatible audio application, such as GarageBand or Logic Pro.

Peripheral Software Drivers

One of the primary responsibilities of the system software is to act as an intermediary between peripherals and applications. If an application supports a general device class, the operating system handles all the technical details of communicating with each model of peripheral in that class. Here's an example: For an application to print, it needs to submit a job to Mac OS X's printing system, but it doesn't need to know any details about how to print to your printer model because it's handled by the operating system. This separation of peripherals and applications by the operating system allows you to use nearly any combination of the two with few incompatibilities.

Mac OS X supports peripherals using device drivers, specialized pieces of software that allow peripherals to interoperate with Mac OS X. Some peripherals are supported via a generic driver, but many require a device driver created specifically for the peripheral. Although Mac OS X includes a decent selection of common device drivers, you may have to install third-party device drivers to support your peripherals. Nearly all device drivers are installed using an installer utility that places the driver software in the correct folder on your Mac. Device drivers are implemented in one of three ways: kernel extensions, framework plug-ins, or applications.

NOTE ▶ It's always best to check the peripheral manufacturer's website to obtain the latest version of the driver software.

Device driver implementations in Mac OS X include:

▶   Kernel extensions (KEXTs)—This is a special type of software created to add peripheral support at the lowest level of Mac OS X: the system kernel. KEXTs load and unload from the system automatically, so there's no need to manage them aside from making sure they are installed properly. While some KEXTs are hidden inside application bundles, most are located in the /System/Library/Extensions folder. Examples of peripherals that use KEXTs are human input devices, storage devices, audio and video devices, and other expansion cards.

▶   Framework plug-ins—This type of device driver adds support for a specific peripheral to an existing system framework. For example, support for additional scanners and digital cameras are facilitated via plug-ins to the Image Capture framework.

▶   Applications—In some cases a peripheral is best supported by an application written just for that peripheral. Examples are the iPod and iPhone, which are managed solely by the iTunes application.

Viewing Loaded Extensions

Even though the Mac OS X kernel is designed to manage KEXTs without user interaction, you may still need to verify that a specific KEXT is loaded. You can view currently loaded KEXTs from the System Profiler application (choose Apple menu > About This Mac, and click the More Info button in the resulting dialog). Once System Profiler is open, select the Extensions item in the Contents list; it may take a few moments for the system to scan all currently loaded KEXTs. Once the list appears, you can further inspect individual KEXTs by selecting them from this list. Using System Profiler for troubleshooting extension issues is covered in the "Troubleshooting Peripherals" section later in this lesson.

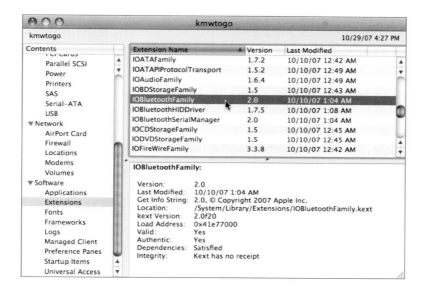

Peripherals That Synchronize

Some peripherals are sophisticated enough that they act as computers themselves, managing personal information such as contacts and calendar events. Examples include personal digital assistants (PDAs), Bluetooth-enabled cell phones, iPods, iPhones, and Apple TVs. As you use your Mac and the peripheral separately to make changes to this information, the two devices will invariably have conflicting information. Thus, synchronization software is required to consolidate any differences between your Mac and the peripheral.

Mac OS X features three synchronization methods, each supporting a specific type of peripheral or service: the iSync application, the iTunes application, and the .Mac service. Fortunately, these three separate methods all draw from the same personal information applications. For instance, no matter which methods are used, your Mac's Address Book application will always take part in the synchronization process to ensure that your contacts are properly updated.

NOTE ▶ Third-party personal information applications, like Entourage, tie into these synchronization systems with varying degrees of compatibility. Always read the application's documentation to be aware of any compatibility issues.

Synchronization methods in Mac OS X include:

▶ iSync application—Located at /Applications/iSync, this application allows you to sync Palm PDAs and Bluetooth-enabled cell phones. To enable Palm syncing, open iSync and then choose Devices > Enable Palm OS Syncing. You will have to install the Palm HotSync software and the iSync HotSync Conduit, but iSync will walk your through those steps. To enable Bluetooth cell phone syncing, pair your Mac to your cell phone as outlined previously in the "Bluetooth" section of this lesson.

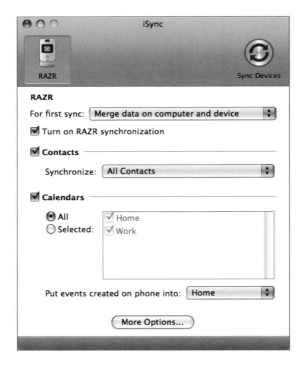

▶ iTunes application—This application, located at /Applications/iTunes, is responsible for managing and synchronizing iPods, iPhones, and Apple TVs. By default, iTunes automatically opens when you attach an iPod or iPhone to your Mac.

▶   .Mac service—Subscribers to the .Mac service can synchronize their personal information to their .Mac account for safekeeping. This also allows .Mac subscribers to
easily maintain the consistency of their personal information between separate Macs.
You can enable .Mac syncing from the .Mac preference in the System Preferences
application.

Troubleshooting Peripherals

Troubleshooting peripheral issues can be difficult because of the wide variety of devices out there, but there are some general troubleshooting techniques you can use that will help with many situations.

General peripheral troubleshooting techniques include:

▶ **Always check System Profiler first.** If you only remember one peripheral trouble-shooting technique, it should be this: connected peripherals appear in System Profiler regardless of functioning software drivers. In other words, if a connected peripheral does not show up in System Profiler, then you are almost certainly experiencing a hardware failure. If a connected peripheral appears as normal in System Profiler, you are probably experiencing a software driver issue. In that case, use System Profiler to validate whether the expected extensions are loaded.

▶ **Unplug and then reconnect the peripheral.** Doing this will reinitialize the peripheral connection and force Mac OS X to reload any peripheral-specific drivers.

▶ **Plug the peripheral into a different port or use a different cable.** This will help you rule out any bad hardware, including host ports, cables, and inoperable hubs.

▶ **Unplug other devices on the same bus.** There may be another device on the shared bus that is causing an issue.

▶ **Shut down and then restart the Mac.** This tried-and-true troubleshooting technique reinitializes all the peripheral connections and reloads all the software drivers.

▶ **Try the peripheral with another Mac.** This helps you determine whether the issue is with your Mac or the peripheral. If the device doesn't work with other computers, your Mac is not the source of the issue.

▶ **Check for system software and driver software updates.** Software bugs are always being fixed, so it's always a good time to check for software updates. You can use Mac OS X's built-in Software Update application, but you should also check the peripheral manufacturer's website for the latest driver updates.

▶ **Check for computer and peripheral firmware updates.** Like software updates, firm-ware updates may also be necessary to resolve your peripheral issue. This is especially true for more sophisticated devices like iPods and iPhones, which have their own internal firmware.

USB-Specific Issues

While general peripheral troubleshooting techniques certainly apply to USB, Mac OS X can also detect and report some USB-specific issues. For detailed information about these USB error messages, see Apple Knowledge Base article 43023, "USB: Troubleshooting error messages."

Here are the USB-specific error messages in Mac OS X:

▶ Not Enough Power to Function—The attached USB devices are not able to draw enough power, or a device that requires its own power source is not plugged into an electric outlet.

▶ Not Enough Power for All Functions—A USB device is not able to fully function because it is unable to draw enough power.

▶ The USB driver needs to be updated. Would you like to search for the update on the Internet?—Mac OS X has detected the currently installed driver for the peripheral, but it's out of date.

▶ No Driver Found—Mac OS X has not detected a currently installed driver for the peripheral, and the generic driver for the device class does not work either.

Printing and Faxing

Though printing may seem like a trivial task to most users, the software that facilitates it is complex enough to merit quite a bit of attention and will occupy a significant portion of this lesson. Mac OS X's printing system also handles faxing—after all, a fax is essentially a printer connected via modems communicating across the phone system.

Robust printing has always been an important part of the Mac operating system because of its popularity with graphic design users. Mac OS X 10.5 continues this tradition with an updated printing system featuring redesigned and simplified printing interfaces. In this second portion of the lesson, you will configure printers and faxes, as well as manage print jobs. You will also learn how to troubleshoot printing issues.

Print and Fax Technology Architecture

Mac OS X 10.5 uses the open source Common UNIX Printing System 1.3 (CUPS) to manage local printing and faxing. Originally an independent product, CUPS was recently purchased by Apple and remains an open source project. Architecturally, CUPS uses the

Internet Printing Protocol (IPP) standard as the basis for managing printing and faxing tasks, and uses PostScript Printer Description (PPD) files as the basis for printer drivers.

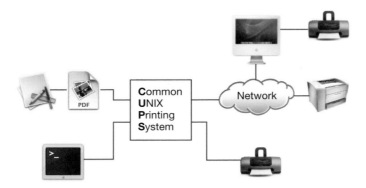

A print or fax job starts when a user prints from either the graphical user interface (GUI) or command-line interface (CLI). When you print from a GUI application, Mac OS X's Quartz graphics system generates a Portable Document Format (PDF) file. When you print from the CLI, a PostScript (PS) file is generated. In either case, the file created is called a spool file and is placed inside the /var/spool/cups folder. The CUPS background process, cupsd, then takes this spool file and passes it through a series of filter processes known as the print chain. These processes convert the spool file to a format that is understood by the destination printer or fax, and then ultimately communicate this information to the printer (or in the case of a fax, your Mac's modem).

MORE INFO ▶ CUPS provides capabilities beyond the scope of this text. To find out more visit, the official CUPS website at http://www.cups.org/.

Configuring Printing and Faxing

Before you can print or fax, you must configure printer or fax modem settings. Mac OS X includes printer drivers for thousands of printer models, among them Brother, Canon, Epson, EFI, Hewlett-Packard, Lexmark, Ricoh, Samsung, and Xerox. Most of these PPDs are preinstalled in the /Library/Printers folder. If you install additional drivers, they will also be placed in this folder. New with Mac OS X 10.5, the Software Update system can automatically download and install new PPDs for popular printer models.

If your Mac has the correct PPD for a directly attached USB or FireWire printer, the system automatically detects the appropriate settings and configures the new printer for you.

Network printer and all fax configurations have to be manually added by an administrative user. In the GUI you can start the process to add new printers or faxes from the Print & Fax preference or from an application's Print dialog. Either method opens the AddPrinter process, which displays a single dialog that allows you create any new printer or fax configuration. Once you've added the printer or fax configuration, a copy of the PPD with the name of the device is placed in the /etc/cups/ppd folder. The first time a user prints or accesses a printer or fax queue, the system will also create a printer or fax queue application, again with the name of the device, in the ~/Library/Printers folder in the user's home folder.

> **TIP** ▶ You can directly access the CUPS configuration by visiting the built-in CUPS management website at http://localhost:631/.

Adding a New Printer or Fax

To add a new printer or fax:

1 Open the Print & Fax preference by choosing Apple menu > System Preferences, then clicking the Print & Fax icon.

2 Click the lock icon in the bottom-left corner and authenticate as an administrative user to unlock the Print & Fax preference.

3 Click the small plus button at the bottom left of the Print & Fax preference to open the new printer configuration dialog.

   The top half of this dialog features several interfaces for selecting a printer or fax. Click one of the following buttons in the toolbar:

   ▶ Default—This browser lets you select network printers discovered using AppleTalk, Bonjour, FireWire, IPP, USB, shared, or network directory services.

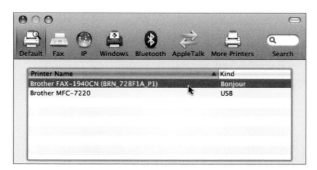

▶ Fax—This browser allows you to select the specific modem port that will be used for incoming and outgoing fax transmissions.

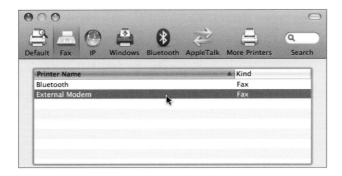

▶ IP—This dialog allows you to manually enter the IP address or DNS hostname of a Line Printer Daemon (LPD), IPP, or HP JetDirect printer. You must select the appropriate protocol from the pop-up menu and enter the printer's address. Entering a printer queue is optional.

▶ Windows—This browser lets you select printers shared via the SMB printer sharing protocol. Double-click on a SMB server and authenticate to access the server's shared printers.

▶   Bluetooth—This browser lets you select and pair Bluetooth wireless printers within range.

▶   AppleTalk—If you're having trouble with the Default printer browser, you can use this browser to select an AppleTalk printer.

▶   More Printers—Sometimes printer manufacturers will use a proprietary printer connection protocol. If you have such a printer, and the appropriate drivers are installed, you will select that printer using this dialog.

Once you have selected a printer or fax modem from the top half of the new printer configuration dialog, the system will complete the bottom half for you using information it has discovered. This includes automatically selecting the appropriate PPD if possible.

Often this information isn't ideal, and you can easily change it. The Name and Location fields are only there to help you identify the device, so you can set those to anything you like.

4   To specify another PPD file, choose "Select a driver to use" from the Print Using pop-up menu. You can manually scroll through the list of installed PPDs, but using the Spotlight field to narrow the search is much quicker.

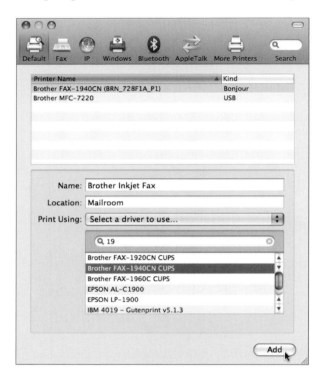

5   Once you have selected and configured the new printer or fax, click the Add button to finish.

Modify an Existing Printer or Fax

You may find it necessary to edit a printer or fax configuration after you set it up. From the Print & Fax preference, you can:

▶   Delete a printer or fax configuration—Select the item you wish to delete from the printer and fax list, and then click the small minus button at the bottom of the list.

▶   Set printing defaults—From the two pop-up menus at the bottom of the Print & Fax preference, select the default printer and paper size.

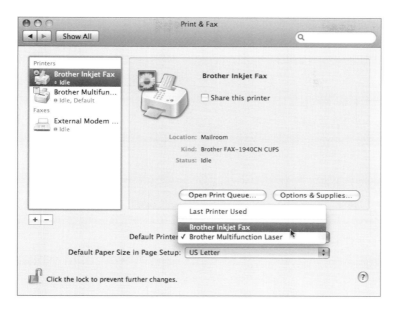

▶ Edit an existing configuration and check supply levels—Simply select the configuration from the printer and fax list and click the Options & Supplies button. In the resulting dialog, edit the printer's name and location on the General tab, and specify the PDD on the Driver tab.

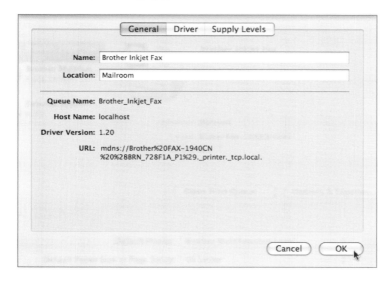

> **NOTE** ▶ The only way to edit a fax configuration is by clicking the Info button in the fax's queue application toolbar, as covered in the "Managing Print and Fax Jobs" later in this lesson.

Configure Your Mac to Receive Faxes

Creating a fax configuration is all that's required to prepare your Mac to send faxes. Still, a few more steps are required to configure your Mac to *receive* faxes. First you must create a fax configuration, as outlined previously in this lesson.

> **NOTE** ▶ Your Mac can't receive faxes in sleep mode. You can disable your Mac's automatic sleep activation from the Energy Saver preference.

To receive faxes on your Mac:

1   Open and unlock the Print & Fax preference.

2   Select a fax configuration from the printer and fax list, and if you haven't already entered the phone number for your Mac's fax, do so now.

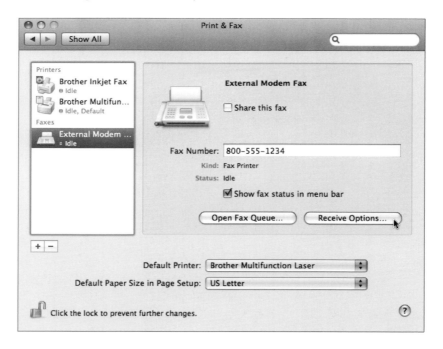

3   Click the Receive Options to reveal a dialog where you'll enable and configure your Mac to receive incoming faxes.

At the very least, you must select the "Receive faxes on this computer" checkbox. You can also define the number of rings before the fax will answer and the destination folder for the received fax documents, which are saved as PDF files. Optionally, you can have the Mac automatically print or email received fax documents.

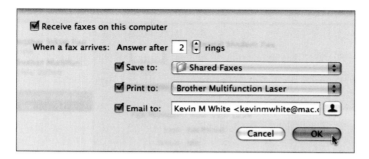

4   Click OK when you have completed your configuration options, and the Mac will wait patiently for incoming faxes.

> **TIP** ▶ Quickly view the status of your Mac's fax configuration by selecting "Show fax status in menu bar," which enables the fax status menu item on the far-right side of the menu bar near the time.

Sharing Printer and Fax Configurations

It's very easy to share printer and fax configurations with Mac OS X. Your Mac's shared print service is made available via the IPP and SMB printer sharing protocols. While Macs and Windows PCs technically support both printing protocols, Macs are more likely to use IPP, and Windows PCs are more likely to use SMB. Both protocols support automatic PPD configuration and installation, so when another user connects to your Mac's shared print service, his or her system will automatically select, and download if necessary, the appropriate PPD.

The CUPS shared print service also allows other network clients to easily locate your shared printer and fax configurations with Bonjour for IPP or NetBIOS/WINS for SMB. Again, Macs and Windows PCs support both discovery protocols, but Macs are more likely to use Bonjour, and Windows PCs are more likely to use NetBIOS/WINS. Or, network clients can manually enter your Mac's IP address or DNS hostname to access your Mac's shared print service. Configuring your Mac's identification for providing network services was covered in Lesson 8, "Providing Network Services."

NOTE ▶ Users will not be able to access shared print services on a Mac in sleep mode. You can disable your Mac's automatic sleep activation from the Energy Saver preference.

To share printers and faxes from your Mac:

1 Open and unlock the Print & Fax preference.

2 To share a printer configuration, select it from the printer and fax list, and select the "Share this printer" checkbox. This allows other network clients to send print jobs to your Mac's print spool for the selected printer.

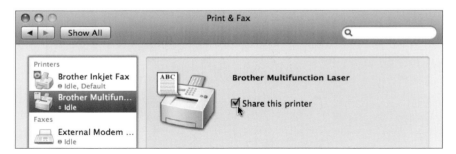

To share a fax configuration, select it from the list and then select the "Share this fax" checkbox. Now other network clients can send fax jobs via your Mac's selected modem port.

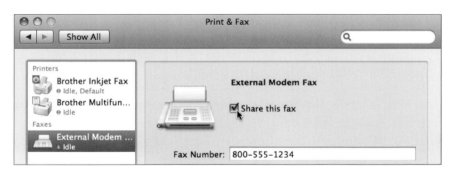

Selecting either shared print service option tells the launchd control process to listen for IPP print service requests on TCP port 631, and automatically start the cupsd background process as necessary to handle any requests.

NOTE ▶ It may be a bad idea to share network printers using your Mac's shared print services if network printers are already available on your network.

3   Verify your print sharing selections by opening the Sharing preference.

Click the Show All button to return to the main System Preferences view, and then click the Sharing icon to open the Sharing preference. Select Printer Sharing from the service list and you will notice that your shared devices should already be enabled. You can also configure print sharing from this section of the Sharing preference.

4   To enable print sharing via the SMB protocol, you must also enable file sharing via this protocol.

Select the checkbox next to File Sharing in the Service list, then click the Options button. In the resulting dialog, select the "Share files and folders using SMB" checkbox. Finally, you'll select and enter passwords for the user accounts you wish to allow to connect to your SMB shared resources. Click the Done button once you have made your selections.

The launchd control process will now listen for SMB service requests on TCP port 139, and automatically start the smbd background process as necessary to handle any requests.

Though covered briefly here you can find out more about the SMB file sharing service in Lesson 8, "Providing Network Services."

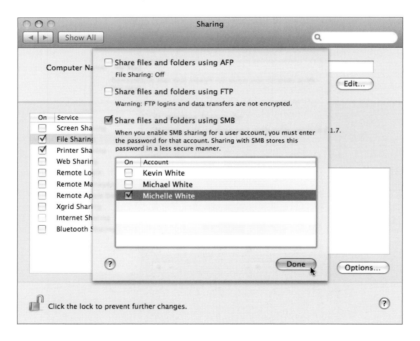

Printing to a Printer or Fax

Mac OS X 10.5 breaks from past tradition and features a new unified Print dialog that combines the previously separate Page Setup and Print dialogs. The Page Setup dialog typically contains document size, orientation, and scale settings, and the Print dialog has all other printer settings. For backwards compatibility, Mac OS X 10.5 allows older applications to continue to use separate Page Setup and Print dialogs, but older apps will still be able to use the new unified printing interface when you open a Print dialog. In other words, some older applications will have document settings in both the Page Setup and the Print dialogs.

The new unified Print dialog also features two modes: basic mode allows you to quickly start a print job based on print setting presets, and advanced mode allows you to specify any page or print option and save print setting presets.

> **NOTE ▶** Some applications, specifically graphic design and desktop publishing applications, use custom print dialogs that may look different from the standard Print dialog covered in this lesson.

Basic Printing

To start a print job based on print setting presets:

1   From an application, start a print job by choosing File > Print or by pressing Command-P.

> **NOTE ▶** Some applications will bypass the Print dialog and issue a print job to your default printer when you use Command-P.

The Print dialog appears. In some cases it will slide out of the application's window title bar (as in this screenshot from the Preview application); in other cases it will appear as its own dialog window.

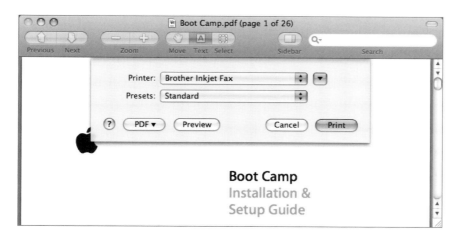

The default printer and print preset will be selected, but you can choose any other configured printer or preset from the associated pop-up menu.

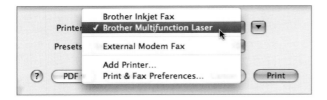

2   Click the Print button to start the print job.

Advanced Printing and Saving Print Presets

To start a print job based on custom print settings:

1   From an application open the Print dialog by choosing File > Print or by pressing Command-P.

2   The default printer and print preset will be selected, but you can choose any other configured printer or preset from the associated pop-up menu.

3   Click the small arrow button to the right of the selected printer, and the Print dialog will expand to its advanced mode.

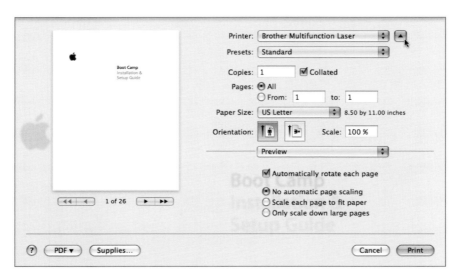

The arrow button will toggle the Print dialog between basic and advanced modes. The Print dialog also remembers which mode you were in last for each application. In other words, every application will start with a simple Print dialog the first time you print, but for subsequent print jobs, the Print dialog will open to the mode last used for each individual application.

4   On the left side of the advanced Print dialog, page through a preview of the print job. Any changes you make to the page layout settings are instantly reflected in the preview.

5   On the right side of the dialog, you can configure all possible print settings for most applications. The top half features basic page setup and print settings.

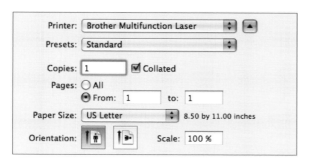

Settings on the bottom half vary based on the application you're printing from and your selected printer's PPD file. You can select a category of print settings to modify by choosing it from the pop-up menu that separates the print settings from top to bottom.

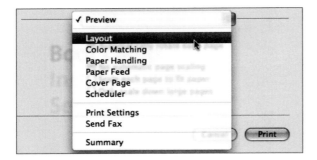

Explore each settings category and don't forget to review your settings from the print Summary category, again accessed via the pop-up menu.

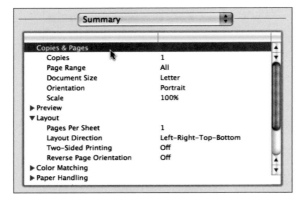

6   To save the current print settings as a preset, choose Save As from the Presets pop-up menu. Give the preset a name in the resulting dialog and click OK to save it.

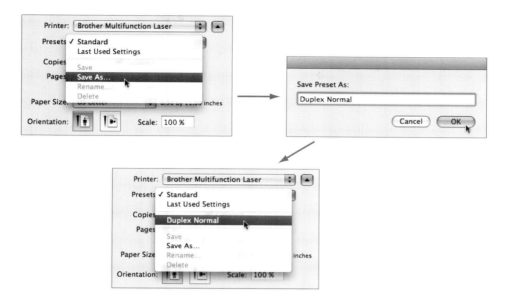

The preset will now be accessible from the Preset pop-up menu from both basic and advanced Print dialogs. The print presets are saved to the ~/Library/Preferences/com. apple.print.custompresets.plist file, so each user has his or her own custom print presets.

7 Click the Print button to start the print job based on your print settings.

Printing to a Fax

Using your Mac's modem to print to a fax machine via the telephone system is similar to normal printing, but you have to define a few destination fax settings. Before you can print to a fax, you must first configure your Mac's modem to send faxes, as outlined earlier in this lesson.

To start a print job destined for a fax:

1 From an application open the Print dialog and expand to advanced mode.

2 Again, the default printer and print preset will be selected, so you must choose your fax configuration from the Printer pop-up menu.

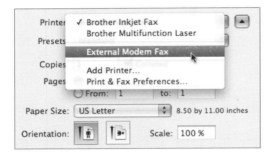

3   Once your fax configuration is selected, the bottom half of the printer settings changes to reveal the Fax Information settings.

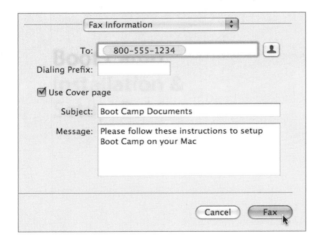

At a minimum you must enter the phone number for the destination fax in the To field, or you can click the user button to the right of this field and access your Address Book contacts. You can also configure a fax cover page.

TIP ▶ Adjust fax modem settings by choosing the Fax Modem category from the print settings pop-up menu.

4   Click the Fax button to start the fax job based on your settings.

The fax status menu item, enabled in the Print & Fax preference, shows fax progress and allows you to manage the fax preferences.

Using the PDF Workflow

Mac OS X includes a built-in PDF workflow. The full Adobe Acrobat suite has more advanced PDF features, but Mac OS X includes all the tools to create PDF documents or perform basic editing. Any application that can print can use Mac OS X's Quartz imaging system to generate high-quality PDFs. In any Print dialog, click the PDF button. You see a pop-up menu where you can choose a PDF workflow destination, including the ability to save a PDF to any location.

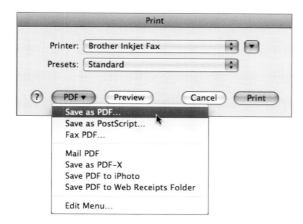

From the PDF pop-up menu you can also specify an AppleScript application designed to accept and automatically process PDF files. Some presets are built in, but you can add your own PDF workflow by choosing Edit Menu from the PDF pop-up menu. Use the /Applications/AppleScript/Script Editor application or the /Applications/Automator application to create an AppleScript application that automatically processes PDF files using nearly any workflow.

> **MORE INFO ▶** You can find out more about AppleScript, Apple's English-like automation technology, at http://www.apple.com/applescript/.

Mac OS X's /Applications/Preview application offers comprehensive PDF editing functionality—you can edit and adjust individual elements, reorder pages, crop the document, add annotations, and fill out form data. From Preview you can also convert PDF files to other formats or resave the PDF file using more appropriate settings.

Managing Print and Fax Jobs

As stated previously, when a print or fax job is started the spool file is placed inside the /var/spool/cups folder, and then CUPS takes over to process the file and send it to the printer or fax modem. When you print from the GUI, Mac OS X opens a print queue application to manage the print job. If a job completes quickly, the file will only be in the print or fax queue for a few moments and the print queue application will quit when done. However, printers always seem to be the most problematic of peripherals, so often your Mac will not be able to complete the print job. The printer or fax queue application will remain open until the print job finishes or you resolve the print issue.

> **NOTE ▶** If Mac OS X detects an error with the printer or fax modem, it will stop all print jobs to that device. You will still be able to issue print jobs to that device, but they will simply fill up in the device's queue.

To manage print and fax job queues:

1   You can access the print or fax queue application using one of the following methods. If a printer or fax queue is already open, simply click on it from the Dock. Or, you can manually open a fax or print queue from the Print & Fax preference by selecting the device from the printer and fax list, and then clicking the Open Print Queue or Open the Fax Queue button.

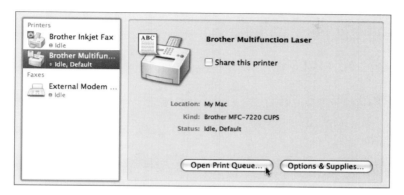

2   When the printer or fax queue opens, you will immediately see the current status of the printer and any current queued print jobs.

Here is a typical example print queue wherein the printer is offline, and the user has printed multiple versions of the same job because they incorrectly assumed this would fix the issue. Mac OS X will automatically detect when the printer becomes available again, assuming the queue isn't paused.

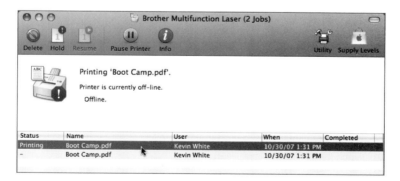

3   To pause or resume the printer queue, click the Pause Printer or Resume Printer button in the queue application toolbar.

4   To hold or resume a specific print job, select it from the job list and then click the Hold or Resume button in the queue application toolbar.

You can also delete a job by selecting it from the job list and then clicking the Delete button in the queue application toolbar.

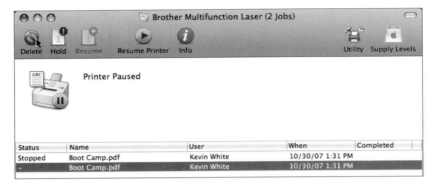

TIP ▶ From the printer or fax queue application's toolbar, edit the device's configuration by clicking the Info button or check a printer's device settings or supplies by clicking the Utility or Supply Levels buttons.

Once you are done managing a printer or fax queue, it's acceptable to leave the application running. You may find it useful to leave often-used print and fax queues in the Dock for direct access. Simply right-click or Control-click on the queue application's Dock icon and from the shortcut menu choose Keep in Dock. You can also provide quick access to all your print and fax queues by dragging the ~/Library/Printers folder to your Dock. Clicking on this folder in your Dock reveals all configured devices.

 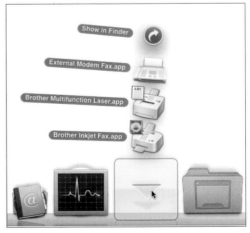

Printing from the Command-Line Interface

CUPS was originally designed for UNIX systems, so it provides comprehensive print management tools for the command-line interface (CLI). You'll learn a few basic printing commands in this lesson, but you can find out more about a command by reading its manual page.

> **TIP** If you are unfamiliar with using the CLI, you should thoroughly examine the CLI introduction in Lesson 3, "File Systems."

lpq. This command will let you view current jobs in print and fax queues. The syntax is lpq followed by any command options. In the following example, Michelle uses the lpq command with the –a option to view all jobs on all print devices:

```
MyMac:~ michelle$ lpq –a
Rank Owner  Job  File(s)     Total Size
1st  michelle 10  Boot Camp.pdf    444416 bytes
2nd  michelle 13  APSG Jan06.pdf    869376 bytes
```

lprm. This command lets you delete current print jobs in print and fax queues. The syntax is simply lprm, and if no more information is provided it deletes the first job on the default printer queue. Here, Michelle uses the lprm command to delete the first print job, then checks the queue with the lpq –a command. She enters the lprm command again to delete the final job, and then checks the queue one last time:

```
MyMac:~ michelle$ lprm
MyMac:~ michelle$ lpq –a
Rank Owner  Job  File(s)     Total Size
1st  michelle 13  APSG Jan06.pdf    869376 bytes
MyMac:~ michelle$ lpq –a
no entries
```

lpr. This command lets you print a file from the CLI. The syntax is simply lprm and then the path to a print-ready file. A print-ready file is any PDF or PS formatted document. In the following example, Michelle uses the lpr command to print the MyDoc.pdf file in her Desktop folder, and then she checks the print queue with the lpq –a command:

```
MyMac:~ michelle$ lpr Desktop/MyDoc.pdf
MyMac:~ michelle$ lpq –a
Rank Owner  Job  File(s)     Total Size
1st  michelle 13  MyDoc.pdf    235123 bytes
```

Troubleshooting the Printing System

You will probably experience more printing issues caused by hardware than by software. Fortunately, printing issues are usually easy to identify. The following is a series of general print system troubleshooting techniques. These techniques are based on information from Apple Knowledge Base document 106714, "Troubleshooting printing issues in Mac OS X":

▶ **Always check the printer queue application first.** The print and fax queue application will always show the first symptoms of an issue, and odds are you were made aware of the issue by the queue. The print queue will let you know if there is a printer connection issue, but you should also check to make sure the queue is not paused and that none of the jobs are on hold. Sometimes deleting old print jobs from the queue will help clear the problem.

▶ **Double-check page and print settings.** If the job is printing but doesn't print correctly, double-check page and print settings using the Print dialog's advanced mode.

▶ **Print from another application.** If you suspect the application is at the root of the problem, try printing from another application. You can also print a test page while in the printer queue application by choosing Printer > Print Test Page.

▶ **Check the printer hardware.** Many modern printers have diagnostic screens or printed reports that can help you identify a hardware issue. Also don't forget to double-check cables and connections. You may also be well served by contacting the printer manufacturer to diagnose printer hardware issues.

▶ **For fax issues, check phone line and phone settings.** As with any fax system issue, you need to check for modem and phone line problems. When sending faxes via the print system, you may encounter issues that are outside of your control because you are relying on the phone system and another user's fax hardware.

▶ **For directly connected printers, use peripheral troubleshooting techniques.** For printers connected via USB or FireWire, use the peripheral troubleshooting techniques outlined previously in this lesson.

▶ **For network printers, use network troubleshooting techniques.** For printers connected via a network connection, use the network troubleshooting techniques described in Lesson 6, "Network Configuration."

▶ **Delete and then reconfigure printers or faxes.** From the Print & Fax preference, delete and then reconfigure a troublesome printer or fax using the techniques outlined earlier in this lesson. This will reset the device's drivers and queue.

▶ **Reset the entire print system.** Sometimes it's necessary to reset the entire printing system. From the Print & Fax preference, right-click or Control-click anywhere in the printers and fax list and choose "Reset printing system" from the shortcut menu. Click OK in the verification dialog. Next you'll have to authenticate as an administrative user. This clears all configured devices, shared settings, custom presets, and queued print jobs.

▶ **Review CUPS log files.** Like other system services, CUPS writes all important activity to log files. You can access these logs while in any printer queue application by choosing Printer > Log & History. This opens the Console utility to the CUPS error_log file. While in the Console you can also check the CUPS access_log and page_log files.

▶ **Reinstall or update PPD files or printer drivers.** Again, software bugs are always being fixed, so it's always a good time to check for PPD and printer driver updates. You can use Mac OS X's built-in Software Update application to check for system updates and some printer updates. However, be sure to also check the printer manufacturer's website for the latest PPD and driver updates.

▶ **Repair installed software disk permissions.** Third-party installers tend to sometimes mess up system software permissions. Use Disk Utility's Repair Permissions feature to resolve permissions issues with PPD and other print system files (see Lesson 3, "File Systems.")

What You've Learned

▶ Mac OS X supports a wide variety of peripherals, expansion cards, storage devices, and audio/video connections.

▶ These devices are supported in groups of device classes, and Mac OS X includes a selection of generic software drivers.

▶ Built-in and third-party drivers are supported via kernel extensions, framework plug-ins, and stand-alone applications.

▶ Mac OS X uses CUPS to provide print and fax services for both local and shared users.

▶ A rich PDF workflow is also built into Mac OS X.

▶ You learned a variety of peripheral and printing troubleshooting techniques.

References
Check for current Knowledge Base documents at http://www.apple.com/support.

Peripherals

30650, "USB 1.1: FAQ (1 of 4)"

43023, "USB: Troubleshooting error messages"

58648, "Mac OS X: Do not connect USB printer to Apple Pro keyboard"

60985, "FireWire: Frequently Asked Questions"

51768, "What can you do with Bluetooth?"

106403, "Mac OS X: 'No driver for this platform' message"

Printing

106714, "Troubleshooting printing issues in Mac OS X"

25407, "Mac OS X: About third-party printer compatibility"

306684, "Mac OS X 10.5: Included printer drivers"

URLs

Official USB Implementer's Forum resource website: http://www.usb.org/

Apple's official FireWire resource website: http://www.apple.com/firewire/

Official Bluetooth Technology Information website: http://www.bluetooth.com/

Official CUPS print server resource website: http://www.cups.org/

Your Mac's local CUPS resource website: http://localhost:631/

AppleScript resource website: http://www.apple.com/applescript/

Review Quiz

1. Which peripheral, expansion, and storage buses are supported by Mac OS X?

2. What are some common USB issues and error messages?

3. What are the device classes used in Mac OS X to categorize peripherals? What are some example peripherals of each class?

4.   What is a device driver?

5.   What does iSync do?

6.   What does CUPS do?

7.   What are PPD files responsible for?

8.   How do you share printers to other Mac and Windows users?

Answers

1.   Mac OS X supports Universal Serial Bus (USB), FireWire, and Bluetooth peripheral buses; Advanced Graphics Port (AGP), Peripheral Component Interconnect (PCI), Peripheral Component Interconnect Extended (PCI-X), PCI Express (PCIe), PC Card, and ExpressCard 34 expansion buses; and Advanced Technology Attachment (ATA), Serial ATA (SATA), Small Computer System Interface (SCSI), Serial Attached SCSI (SAS), and Fibre Channel storage buses.

2.   Common USB issues and error messages are: "not enough power to function," "not enough power for all functions," "the USB driver needs to be updated," and "no driver found."

3.   Devices classes as defined by Mac OS X are: human input devices (HID) like keyboards and mice; storage devices like hard drives and optical drives; printers; scanners; digital cameras; video devices, including both input and output devices; and audio devices, including both input and output devices.

4.   A device driver is software specially designed to facilitate the communication between Mac OS X and a peripheral. They can be kernel extensions, framework plug-ins, or stand-alone applications.

5.   iSync allows you to synchronize personal information between Mac OS X applications and peripherals like Palm PDAs and Bluetooth-enabled cell phones.

6.   Common UNIX Printing System (CUPS) manages all printing and faxing for Mac OS X, including both local and shared printing.

7.   PostScript Printer Description (PPD) files are printer driver files that instruct the CUPS system on how to communicate with specific printer models.

8.   You can enable printer sharing for Mac clients from the Print & Fax or Sharing preference, but to share to Windows clients you must also enable SMB file sharing services from the Sharing preference.

10

Time   This lesson takes approximately 1 hour to complete.

Goals   Understand the Mac OS X startup process

Identify the essential files and processes required to successfully boot Mac OS X

Troubleshoot the startup and login processes

Lesson 10
Startup Process

System startup certainly isn't the most glamorous part of Mac OS X, but it's clearly important and technically quite impressive. Apple has improved startup and runtime processes with every revision of Mac OS X. When things work correctly, the startup process on Intel-based Macs is generally under 30 seconds. Obviously, users appreciate a quick startup, but most don't and shouldn't have to care what goes on during system startup because they expect their Macs to work properly.

However, when things do go wrong during system startup, users often fear the worst. Novice users may assume that if their Macs won't start up, they will lose their important documents. But the system startup process can fail due to many issues that probably won't result in any user data loss. So, it's important to properly diagnose startup issues so you can return the Mac to proper working order, or at least try to recover data.

This lesson focuses on the process that your Mac goes through from the moment you press the power button until you ultimately reach the Finder. First you will identify the essential files and processes required to successfully start up Mac OS X. This allows you to effectively troubleshoot startup and login issues covered in the remaining portion of this lesson.

Startup Process Overview

This section examines the four main stages of the Mac OS X system startup procedure. At each stage the Mac will present an audible or visual cue to help you validate startup progress. The startup cues discussed here are what you'll experience during a typical startup. Any deviation will be covered throughout this section as you learn more about the startup process. At the end of this section, you will also learn about system sleep modes and the logout and shutdown processes.

The four main Mac OS X system startup stages are, in order:

▶ Firmware—At this stage the Mac's hardware initializes and the booter is located and started. Successfully completing this stage results in an audible startup chime and a bright flash from the power-on light, and all displays show a light gray background.

▶ Booter—The booter's main job is to load the system kernel and essential kernel extensions (KEXTs) into main memory and then allow the kernel to take over the system. The booter stage is indicated by a dark gray Apple logo on the main display.

▶ Kernel—The kernel provides the system's foundation and loads additional drivers and the core BSD UNIX system. It is indicated by a dark gray spinning gear below the Apple logo on the main display.

▶ User environment—Once the core operating system is loaded, it starts the first process, launchd, which is responsible for loading the entire user environment. This stage is indicated by a bright blue background on all displays. Successful completion of this stage results in either the login screen or the Finder.

Firmware

Your Mac's firmware, also called BootROM, resides on flash memory chips built into your Mac's main computer board. This way, when you power on your Mac, even before it starts a "real" operating system, the firmware acts as a mini-operating system with just enough software to get things going. Specifically, your Mac's firmware tests and initializes the hardware, and then locates and starts the system software booter.

PowerPC-based Macs feature firmware based on Sun's Open Firmware technology, and Intel-based Macs feature firmware based on Intel's Extensible Firmware Interface (EFI) technology. Aside from supporting Intel's processor hardware, EFI is what allows your Mac to start up from Mac OS X, Windows, or any other Intel-compatible operating system.

MORE INFO ▶ EFI is an extremely flexible boot architecture, and is now managed by the Unified EFI Forum. In fact, EFI will soon be known as Unified Extensible Firmware Interface (UEFI). You can find out more at http://www.uefi.org/.

Power-On Self-Test

The first thing your Mac's firmware does at power on is the Power-On Self-Test (POST). The POST tests built-in hardware components such as processors, system memory, network interfaces, and peripheral interfaces. When your Mac passes the POST, you hear the startup chime and see a light gray background on all displays. After a successful POST, the firmware will go on to locate the booter file.

If your Mac fails the POST, the displays will remain blank or off, and you may get hardware error codes. Depending on the age and model of your Mac, these error codes may manifest as audible tones or a series of flashes from the external power-on light, or internal diagnostic lights may illuminate. You may even see a combination of these things. Regardless of which error code you experience, they all indicate a hardware problem exists outside of Mac OS X's control. You can visit Apple's support website at http://www.apple.com/support/ to identify your specific Mac's error code, or you can take your Mac to an Apple Authorized Service Provider.

Booter Selection

By default, the firmware will pick the system booter file that was last specified from the Startup Disk preference in Mac OS X or the Boot Camp control panel in Windows. The booter file's location is saved in your Mac's non-volatile RAM (NVRAM) so that it remains persistent across system restarts. If the booter file is found, EFI will start the booter process and Mac OS X will begin to start up. This is indicated by the dark gray Apple logo in the center of the main display.

If the firmware cannot locate a booter file, you will see a flashing folder icon with a question mark. Troubleshooting this issue will be covered in the second portion of this lesson. The following screen shot shows an Intel-based Mac; PowerPC-based Macs show a similar icon.

Startup Modifiers

Your Mac's firmware also supports many keyboard combinations, which, when pressed and held during initial power-on, allow you to modify the startup process. Some of these combinations modify the booter selection, while others modify how Mac OS X starts up. Alternate Mac OS X startup modes are covered later in the "Troubleshooting Startup" section.

NOTE ▶ Some hardware does not support startup modifier keyboard combinations, including third-party keyboards, keyboards connected via some USB hubs or keyboard-video-mouse (KVM) switches, and Bluetooth wireless keyboards on PowerPC-based Macs.

Mac startup modifiers include:

▶ C—Starts up from a bootable CD or DVD in the optical drive.

▶ D—Intel-based Macs only. Starts up from the Apple Hardware Test partition on the first restore DVD included with your Mac.

▶ N—Starts up from a compatible NetBoot server. The Mac will show a flashing globe icon in the center of the main display until it locates the NetBoot server, at which point it will show the dark gray Apple logo.

▶ T—Powers on the Mac in FireWire target disk mode, allowing other computers to access your Mac's internal drives. Target disk mode was covered in Lesson 3, "File Systems."

▶ Shift—Starts up Mac OS X in Safe Mode.

▶ Option—Starts up into the Startup Manager, which allows you to select any volume containing Mac OS X to start up from. This includes internal volumes, optical drive volumes, and some external volumes.

> **NOTE** ▶ Startup volumes selected with the Startup Manager are not saved to NVRAM, so this setting will not persist between system restarts.

▶ Option-N—Intel-based Macs only. Starts up from the NetBoot server using the default system image.

▶ Command-V—Starts up Mac OS X in verbose mode.

▶ Command-S—Starts up Mac OS X in single-user mode.

▶ Command-Option-P-R—Resets NVRAM settings and restarts the Mac.

▶ Command-Option-O-F—PowerPC-based Macs only. Starts up into Open Firmware command-line mode.

▶ Command-Option-Shift-Delete—PowerPC-based Macs only. Bypasses the default startup volume.

▶ Eject key, F12 key, mouse or trackpad button—Ejects any removable media, including optical discs.

Firmware Updates

Boot read-only memory, or boot ROM, refers to older versions of firmware technology that are not upgradable. Your Mac's firmware, however, is upgradable and on Intel-based Macs it's even replaceable if it has become damaged. Mac OS X's Software Update service may automatically update some Mac's firmware, but you can also check Apple's Knowledge Base for the latest list of Mac firmware updates. Specifically, document 86117, "Mac OS X: Available firmware updates," covers PowerPC-based Mac firmware updates, and document 303880, "Firmware updates for Intel-based Macs," covers Intel-based Mac firmware updates. You can also replace your Intel-based Mac's firmware using a firmware restoration CD as outlined in document 303469, "About the Firmware Restoration CD (Intel-based Macs)."

> **MORE INFO** ▶ You can easily extend your Intel-based Mac's EFI capabilities using the open source rEFIt toolkit available at http://refit.sourceforge.net/.

Booter

The booter process is launched by your Mac's firmware and is responsible for loading the Mac OS X kernel and enough essential KEXTs so the kernel can take over the system and continue the startup process. Your Mac's firmware also passes on any special startup mode instructions for the booter to handle, such as when the user is holding down the Shift key, indicating that Mac OS X should start up in Safe Mode.

Typically, the booter process itself resides in the /System/Library/CoreServices folder of the selected startup volume. PowerPC-based Macs start up using the BootX booter process, whereas Intel-based Macs start up using the boot.efi booter process. Both perform essentially the same actions, but each is optimized for their specific processor architecture.

To expedite the startup process, the booter will load cached files whenever possible. These cached files contain an optimized kernel and KEXTs that load much quicker than if the system had to load them from scratch. These caches are located at /System/Library/Caches/com.apple.kernelcaches and /System/Library/Extensions.mkext. If the system detects a problem or you start Mac OS X in Safe Mode, these caches will be discarded and the kernel-loading process will take much longer.

As covered previously, the booter process is indicated at startup by the dark gray Apple icon in the center of the main display. If the booter successfully loads the kernel, this will be indicated by a small, dark gray spinning gear icon below the Apple icon.

If your Mac is set to NetBoot and the firmware successfully locates the booter file on the NetBoot server, you will again see the dark gray Apple icon. However, in this case the booter and the cached kernel information must be downloaded from the NetBoot server. This process is indicated by a small, dark gray spinning earth icon below the Apple icon. The earth icon will be replaced by the standard spinning gear icon once the kernel has been successfully loaded from the NetBoot server.

Finally, if the booter is unable to load the kernel, a dark gray prohibitory icon will take the place of the Apple icon. Again, troubleshooting this issue will be covered in the second portion of this lesson.

Kernel

Once the booter has successfully loaded the kernel and essential KEXTs, the kernel itself takes over the startup process. The kernel has now loaded enough KEXTs to read the entire file system, allowing it to load any additional KEXTs and start the core BSD UNIX system. Finally, the kernel starts the first official user environment process, launchd, which is ultimately responsible for starting every other process. A bright blue background on all displays indicates that the kernel has successfully started the launchd process.

Again, in most cases the kernel is loaded by the booter from cached files. However, the kernel is also located on the system volume at /mach_kernel. This file is normally hidden from users in the graphical user interface (GUI), because they don't need access to it. Many other hidden files and folders at the root of the system volume are necessary for the BSD UNIX system, and again the average GUI user doesn't need access to these items. As covered in Lesson 9, "Peripherals and Printing," KEXTs mostly reside in /System/Library/Extensions.

User Environment

Once the kernel and the core BSD UNIX system is up and running, the user environment is ready to start running processes at the behest of the system user and eventually human users. It may seem odd to consider the system user, also known as root, as part of the "user environment." Still, Mac OS X considers any process outside of the kernel and the core BSD UNIX system to be part of the user environment. After all, the root user is tied to many background processes that human users also run.

The very first process started in the user environment is /sbin/launchd, which runs as root, and is given the process identification of 1. In UNIX terms, this first instance of launchd is the first parent process that spawns all other child processes, and those processes go on to spawn other child processes, and so on. Essentially, this first instance of launchd, also known as the parent launchd process in this text, will ultimately be responsible for starting all other system user and human user processes.

The /Applications/Utilities/System Profiler application lists all processes along with their identification numbers and parent/child relationships. In the System Profiler, you can sort the process list by clicking on the title of the Process ID column, and you can view a process's parent process by double-clicking on its name in the list. You will find it beneficial to open the System Profiler and examine the process listing as you learn about how Mac OS X starts up the user environment. Detailed information about using the System Profiler application was covered in Lesson 5, "Applications and Boot Camp."

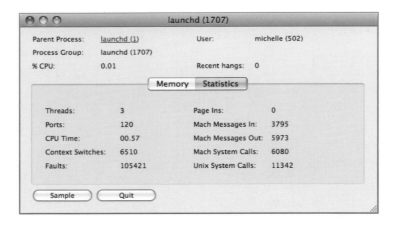

System Initialization

The first task for the parent launchd process is to complete the system initialization by starting all other system processes. Previous versions of Mac OS X show the "Welcome to Mac OS X" dialog with a progress bar to indicate system initialization status as the various system processes start up. However, with Mac OS X 10.5 the launchd process has been highly optimized, so the system initialization process takes only a few moments and is indicated by a bright blue background on all displays.

The parent launchd process is designed to expedite the system initialization by starting multiple system processes simultaneously whenever possible and by starting only essential system processes at system startup time. After startup, the parent launchd process automatically starts and stops additional system processes as needed. By dynamically managing system processes, launchd keeps your Mac responsive and running as efficiently as possible.

As covered in Lesson 4, "Data Management and Backup," launchd manages system processes as described by launchd preference files in the /System/Library/LaunchAgents and /System/Library/LaunchDaemons folders. Third-party processes can also be managed when described by launchd preference files in the /Library/LaunchAgents and /Library/LaunchDaemons folders.

Apple strongly encourages all developers to adopt the launchd system for all automatically started processes. But the parent launchd process also supports legacy startup routines. This includes support for running the traditional UNIX /etc/rc.local script during system initialization, though this script is not included on Mac OS X 10.5 by default. The parent launchd process also starts the /sbin/SystemStarter process, which manages system processes as described by legacy Mac OS X startup items. Mac OS X 10.5 no longer includes any built-in startup items, but SystemStarter will still look in the /System/Library/StartupItems and /Library/StartupItems folders for third-party startup items.

> **MORE INFO ▶** launchd is an extremely powerful open source system for managing services. Learn more about launchd at Apple's developer website: http://developer.apple.com/macosx/launchd.html.

Starting the User Session

Eventually, after enough system processes have started, the parent launchd process will open /System/Library/CoreServices/loginwindow.app as the final step of system initialization. The loginwindow process is unique in its ability to run as both a background process and a GUI application. The loginwindow coordinates the GUI login screen and, in coordination with Open Directory, authenticates the user. After authentication, it also sets up the GUI user session and, in coordination with launchd, continues to run as a background process to maintain the user session.

A user can authenticate manually using the login screen, or the loginwindow can be set to automatically authenticate a user at startup, which is the default when your Mac has only a single user account. The loginwindow settings are stored in the /Library/Preferences/ com.apple.loginwindow.plist preference file. As covered in Lesson 2, "User Accounts," you can configure loginwindow settings from the Accounts preference.

If no users are logged into the Mac, the loginwindow process is owned by the root user. Once a user successfully authenticates, the loginwindow process switches ownership to this user and then proceeds to set up the GUI user session with help from launchd. In fact, the parent launchd process starts another instance of launchd that is also owned by the authenticated user. All user processes and applications, even those that the user manually opens, will be started by this user-specific launchd process. If fast user switching is enabled, the parent launchd process will start additional loginwindow and launchd processes to set up and maintain each user's session.

The user's loginwindow process sets up the GUI user session by:

▶ Retrieving the user account information from Open Directory and applying any account settings

▶ Configuring the mouse, keyboard, and system sound using the user's preferences

▶ Loading the user's computing environment: preferences, environment variables, devices and file permissions, and keychain access

▶ Opening the Dock, Finder, and SystemUIServer

▶ Automatically opening the user's login items

Within the User Session

The system startup process is complete once the user has successfully logged into the session. This is indicated by observing the Dock, the Finder, or any user login items.

It's important to understand the difference between startup items and login items. Again, startup items are opened during system initialization by the parent launchd process on behalf of the root user. On the other hand, login items are opened at the end of the user session setup process by the user's specific launchd process. In other words, startup items affect the system as a whole, while login items affect only a single user. A user's login item list is stored in the ~/Library/Preferences/com.apple.loginitems.plist preference file. As covered previously in Lesson 2, "User Accounts," you can configure a user's login item list from the Accounts preference.

The user-owned launchd and loginwindow processes will continue to run as long as the user is logged in to the session. The user's launchd process will start all user processes and applications, while the user's loginwindow process will monitor and maintain the user session.

The user's loginwindow process monitors the user session by:

▶ Managing logout, restart, and shutdown procedures

▶ Managing the Force Quit Applications window, which includes monitoring the currently active applications and responding to user requests to forcibly quit applications

▶ Writing any standard-error output to the user's console.log file

While the user is logged in to the session, the user's loginwindow process will, via the user's launchd process, automatically restart any user application that should remain open, such as the Finder or the Dock. If the user's loginwindow process is ended, whether intentionally or unexpectedly, all the user's applications and processes will also immediately quit without saving changes. If this happens, the parent launchd process will then automatically restart the loginwindow process as if the Mac had just started up. In other words, the loginwindow will, depending on configuration, either display the login screen or automatically log in the specified user.

Sleep Modes, Logout, and Shutdown

At the other end of the spectrum, but still related, are the processes required to pause or end the user session. The main distinction is that your Mac's sleep function does not quit any open processes, whereas the user logout and system shutdown functions will quit open processes. In most cases, the user manually issues a sleep, logout, or shutdown command from the Apple menu or by pressing the Mac's power button.

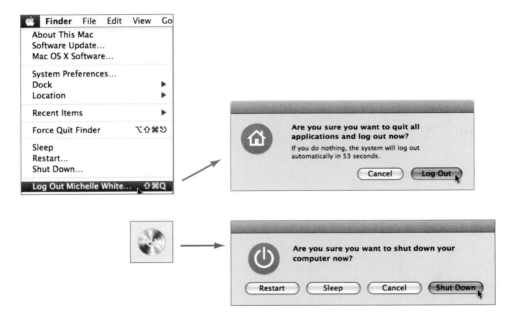

However, other processes and applications can also initiate sleep, logout, or shutdown commands. For instance, the Installer and Software Update applications can request a restart when the installation of new software requires it. Further, you can configure the Mac to automatically perform certain commands such as: put the system to sleep after inactivity with settings in the Energy Saver preference; set a schedule to sleep, shut down, or start up the Mac with settings in the Schedule dialog of the Energy Saver preference; automatically log out users after inactivity with settings in the Security preference; and automatically log out managed users with settings in the Parental Controls preference. Many of these settings can be managed remotely from Apple Remote Desktop or from managed client settings hosted on a network directory server.

Sleep Modes

Your Mac's sleep function is convenient because it does not quit any active processes or applications. Instead, the system kernel pauses all processes and then essentially shuts down all the hardware except for system memory and power to the USB and FireWire ports. This greatly reduces the amount of power used; as an example, portable Macs can remain in sleep mode for several days on a single battery charge. Waking your Mac from sleep mode restarts all hardware, and the kernel will resume all processes and applications from the point you left them.

Late-model PowerBook G4s and all Intel-based portable Macs also support a safe sleep mode. When these Macs go to sleep, they also copy the entire contents of system memory to an image file on the system volume. This way, if these Macs stay in sleep mode long enough to completely drain the battery, no data is lost when the system has to fully shut down. When you restart a Mac from safe sleep mode, the booter process will reload the saved memory image from the system volume instead of proceeding with the normal startup process. The booter process indicates the Mac is restarting from safe sleep mode by showing a light gray version of your Mac's screen when it was put to sleep and a small progress bar at the bottom of the main display. It should take only a few moments to reload system memory, and the kernel will resume all processes and applications.

Logout

Users can log out any time they want to end their GUI user session, but they also have to log out to shut down or restart the Mac. When the currently logged-in user chooses to log out, the user's loginwindow process manages all logout functions with help from the user's launchd process. Once the user authorizes the logout, the user's loginwindow process issues a Quit Application Apple event to all GUI applications. This gives GUI applications a chance to save any changes or ask the user if changes should be saved. If the GUI application fails to reply or quit itself after 45 seconds, the logout process will be stopped and loginwindow will display an error message.

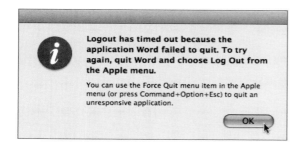

If all the user's GUI applications successfully quit, the user's loginwindow process will then forcibly quit any background user processes. Finally, the user's loginwindow process will close the user's GUI session, run any logout scripts, record the logout to the main system.log file, and reset device permissions and preferences to their defaults. If the user chose only to log out, as opposed to shutting down or restarting, the user's loginwindow and launchd processes will quit, the parent launchd process will restart a new loginwindow process owned by the root user, and the login screen will appear.

Shutdown

When a logged-in user chooses to shut down or restart the Mac, again the user's loginwindow process manages all logout functions with help from the parent launchd process. First the user's loginwindow process logs out the current user. If other users are logged in via fast user switching, the loginwindow process will ask for administrative user authentication and, if granted, will forcibly quit all other users' processes and applications, possibly losing user data.

After all user sessions are logged out, the user's loginwindow process tells the kernel to issue the quit command to all remaining system processes. Processes like loginwindow should quit promptly, but the kernel must wait for processes that remain responsive while they are going through the motions of quitting. If system processes don't respond after a few seconds, the kernel will forcibly quit those processes. Once all processes are quit, the kernel will stop the parent launchd process and then shut down the system. If the user chose to restart the Mac, the Mac's firmware will begin the system startup process once again.

Troubleshooting Startup

The most important part of troubleshooting system startup is fully understanding the startup process. Once you can identify the four stages—and know which processes and files are responsible for each—you are well on your way to diagnosing any startup issue. In the second portion of the lesson, you'll troubleshoot each of these stages as well as investigate logout and shutdown problems.

Here you will learn about the three primary Mac OS X diagnostic startup modes: verbose mode, Safe Mode, and single-user mode. These three modes are initiated at the firmware stage but can affect the remaining startup process at each stage. The ramifications of each diagnostic startup mode are covered with each stage throughout this section.

The Mac OS X diagnostic startup modes are:

▶ Verbose mode—This mode is initiated by holding down Command-V during system startup. In verbose mode, the system will not hide the startup progress from you with the light gray or blue screens. Instead, you will see a black background with white text showing all details of the startup process.

▶ Safe Boot/Safe Mode/Safe Login—This mode is initiated by holding down the Shift key during system startup and user login. Safe Boot occurs when the system is starting up; Safe Mode is when the system is actually running; and Safe Login is when the system starts up the user session. During Safe Boot, the system will more carefully test startup procedures and limit automatically launched processes during each stage.

▶ Single-user mode—This mode is initiated by holding down Command-S during system startup. When starting up in single-user mode, the system will only start core kernel and BSD UNIX functionality. You must be familiar with the command-line interface (CLI) to use single-user mode. CLI was introduced in Lesson 3, "File Systems."

Troubleshooting the Firmware

Issues at the firmware stage are indicated by an inability of your Mac to reach the light gray screen with the dark gray Apple icon. The key to troubleshooting at this point is to determine whether this issue is related to hardware or system volume.

Hardware Issues

If you don't hear the startup chime or see the power-on light flash, the Mac's hardware did not pass the POST. You may also hear a series of diagnostic tones or see a series of power-on flashes. If this is the case, your Mac has a fundamental hardware issue.

To troubleshoot hardware issues:

▶   Always check for simple things first. Is the Mac plugged into an electrical outlet? Are the keyboard and mouse working properly?

▶   Run the Apple Hardware Test (AHT) included on the first restore disc packaged with your Mac. Insert the disc in the optical drive, and on PowerPC-based Macs, start up holding down the Option key to use the Startup Manager to select the AHT volume. On Intel-based Macs, start up holding down the D key to automatically select the AHT volume.

▶   On Intel-based Macs, you can also attempt to reset your Mac's firmware by using a firmware restoration CD as outlined in Apple Knowledge Base document 303469, "About the firmware restoration CD (Intel-based Macs)."

▶   Ultimately, if this is a serious hardware issue, you will have to take your Mac to an Apple Authorized Service Provider.

System Volume Issues

If your Mac passes the POST but you are left with a flashing dark gray question mark folder icon, it means the firmware cannot locate a valid system volume or booter file. The Mac's main processor and components are probably working correctly, and you may only have a software issue. Hold down the Option key during startup and use the Startup Manager to locate system volumes.

To troubleshoot system volume issues:

▶   If the original system volume appears, select it to start up from. If your Mac starts up from the system on the volume, open the Startup Disk preference to reset the volume as the startup disk. You can attempt to define the startup disk when booted from another system volume like the Mac OS X Install DVD.

▶   If the original system volume appears but your Mac still cannot find a valid system or booter, you may need to reinstall Mac OS X on that volume. As always, back up any important data from that volume before you make significant changes.

▶ If your original system volume does not appear, the issue obviously lies with that storage device. Start up from another system, like the Mac OS X Install DVD, and use the storage troubleshooting techniques outlined in Lesson 3, "File Systems."

Troubleshooting the Booter

Issues at the booter stage are indicated by a flashing dark gray prohibitory icon—evidence of a failure to load the kernel.

To troubleshoot the booter:

▶ If you're starting up the Mac from a volume containing a system this Mac has never booted from, the prohibitory icon usually indicates that the version of Mac OS X on the volume is not compatible with your Mac's hardware.

▶ Start up the Mac while holding down the Shift key to initiate a Safe Boot. The booter will first verify and repair the startup volume; if repairs were necessary, the Mac will automatically restart before continuing. If this happens, continue to hold down the Shift key. The booter will verify the startup volume again, and if the volume appears to be working properly, the booter will attempt to load the kernel and essential KEXTs again. The booter uses the most judicial, and slowest, process to load these items. If successful, the booter will pass off the system to the kernel, which will continue to safe-boot.

▶ If the booter cannot find or load a valid kernel, you may need to reinstall Mac OS X on that volume.

Troubleshooting the Kernel

Issues at the kernel stage are indicated by an inability to reach the bright blue screen, as evidence of a failure to load all KEXTs, the core BSD UNIX system, and ultimately the parent launchd process. If this is the case, your Mac is stuck at the light gray screen with the dark gray spinning gear icon.

To troubleshoot the kernel:

▶ Start up the Mac while holding down the Shift key to initiate a Safe Boot. In addition to the Safe Boot procedures covered in the "Troubleshooting the Booter" section earlier, this will force the kernel to ignore all third-party KEXTs. If successful, the kernel will start the parent launchd process, which will continue to safe-boot. Completing the kernel startup stage via a Safe Boot indicates the issue may be a third-party KEXT, and you should start up in verbose mode to try to identify the problem KEXT.

▶ Start up the Mac while holding down Command-V to initiate verbose mode. The Mac will show you the startup process details as a continuous string of text. If the text stops, the startup process has probably also stopped, and you should examine the end of the text for troubleshooting clues. When you find a suspicious item, move it to a quarantine folder and then restart the Mac without Safe Boot, to see if the problem was resolved.

> **NOTE** ▶ If your troublesome Mac successfully starts up in Safe Boot mode and you're trying to find the issue, do not use Safe Boot and verbose mode at the same time. If the startup process succeeds, verbose mode will eventually be replaced by the standard startup interface and you will not have time to identify problematic items.

▶ If Safe Boot continues to fail or you have located a suspicious system item that you need to remove, start up the Mac while holding Command-S to initiate single-user mode. You'll see a minimum CLI that will allow you to move suspicious files to a quarantine folder. If you want to modify files and folders in single-user mode CLI, you will first have to run two commands: the /sbin/fsck –fy command will verify and repair the startup volume, and the /sbin/mount –uw / command will mount the startup volume as a read and write file system. Once you have made your changes, you can exit single-user mode and continue to start up the system by entering the exit command, or you can shut down the Mac by entering the shutdown –h now command.

> **TIP** ▶ While in single-user mode or the normal CLI, you can manually load and unload KEXTs using the kextload and kextunload commands. You can find out more about these commands by reading their manual pages.

▶ If the kernel cannot completely load while safe booting or you are unable to locate and repair the problematic items, you may need to reinstall Mac OS X on that volume.

Troubleshooting the User Environment

Issues at the user environment stage are indicated by an inability to reach the login screen or log in a user (evidence of a failure by the parent launchd process). The key is determining if the problem relates to the system initialization process or the GUI user session setup process.

System Initialization Issues

If the parent launchd process is not able to complete the system initialization, the loginwindow process will not start. Your Mac will be stuck at the bright blue screen.

To troubleshoot system initialization issues:

▶ Start up the Mac while holding down the Shift key to initiate a Safe Boot. In addition to the Safe Boot procedures covered earlier in the "Troubleshooting the Booter" and "Troubleshooting the Kernel" sections of this lesson, this will force the parent launchd process to ignore all third-party fonts, LaunchAgents, LaunchDaemons, and Startup Items. If successful, the parent launchd process will start the loginwindow. At this point the Mac system has fully started up and is now running in Safe Mode. Completing the system initialization process via Safe Boot indicates the issue may be a third-party system initialization item, and you should start up in verbose mode to try to identify the problematic item.

▶ Start up the Mac while holding down Command-V to initiate verbose mode. Again, if the text stops, examine the end of the text for troubleshooting clues; if you find a suspicious item, move it to a quarantine folder and then restart the Mac normally.

▶ At this point you might be able to successfully safe-boot into the Finder. If so, use the Finder's interface to quarantine suspicious items.

▶ You may also consider removing or renaming system cache and preference files, as they can be corrupted and cause startup issues. Begin by removing /Library/Caches because those files contain easily replaced information. As far as system preferences go, you can remove any setting stored in the /Library/Preferences folder you're comfortable with having to reconfigure. A much safer solution would be to simply rename individual system preference files or the /Library/Preference folder itself. Once you have moved or replaced these items, restart the Mac, and the system will automatically replace these items with clean versions.

▶ If Safe Boot continues to fail, you can again start up in single-user mode to quarantine suspicious system initialization items or remove system cache and preference files.

> **TIP** While in single-user mode or the normal CLI, you can manually control the launchd process using the interactive launchctl command. You can find out more about launchctl by reading its manual page.

▶ If the system initialization process cannot complete while safe-booting or you are unable to locate and repair the problematic items, you may need to reinstall Mac OS X on that volume.

User Session Issue

If the loginwindow process is not able to start the user session, the user will never be given control of the GUI. You may see the user's desktop background picture, but no applications will load, including the Dock or the Finder. Or, it may appear that the user session starts, but then the login screen will reappear. At this point you should first attempt a Safe Login, which is initiated by holding down the Shift key while you click the Log In button at the login screen. Safe Login is also part of the Safe Boot startup mode. In addition to the Safe Boot procedures covered previously in this lesson, the loginwindow displays the login screen with the words "Safe Boot" in bright red text under the Mac OS X logo.

With Safe Login enabled, the loginwindow process will not automatically open any user-defined login items, and the user's launchd process will not start any user-specific LaunchAgents. Obviously, if a Safe Login resolves your user session issue, you need to adjust this user's Login Items list from the Accounts preference or any items in the ~/Library/LaunchAgents folder.

If a Safe Login doesn't resolve your user session issue, there are other troubleshooting sections in this book you should refer to. Primarily, you should follow the troubleshooting steps outlined in Lesson 2, "User Accounts." Additionally, the loginwindow process relies heavily on Open Directory, so you may also be well served by the troubleshooting steps outlined in Lesson 7, "Accessing Network Services."

Troubleshoot Logout and Shutdown

An inability to log out or shut down is almost always the result of an application or process that refuses to quit. If you're unable to log out, as long as you still maintain control of the GUI, you can attempt to forcibly quit stubborn processes using the techniques outlined in Lesson 5, "Applications and Boot Camp." You may find the loginwindow process has closed your user session, but the Mac refuses to shut down. This is indicated by a small spinning gear icon on top of your desktop background or the bright blue screen after all your GUI applications are quit. You should let the system attempt to shut down naturally, but if it takes any longer than a few minutes, it means a system process is refusing to quit. You can force your Mac to shut down by holding down the power-on key until the Mac powers off, as indicated by a blank display.

> **NOTE ▸** When you restart the Mac, the firmware does not perform a full POST during the subsequent startup process. Thus, if you're troubleshooting hardware issues you should always shut down and then start up, never restart.

What You've Learned

▶ The Mac OS X startup process happens in four stages: firmware, booter, kernel, and user environment.

▶ At each stage there are audible or visual cues that help you recognize startup progress.

▶ Your Mac's firmware features a variety of startup modes that help you administer and troubleshoot the system.

▶ The launchd and loginwindow processes are primarily responsible for managing the user environment, including processes such as system initialization, GUI user session setup, and login, logout, and shutdown.

▶ Safe Mode, verbose mode, and single-user mode are the three primary Mac OS X startup diagnostic modes.

References

Check for current Knowledge Base documents at http://support.apple.com/support.

Firmware

58442, "Power on self-test beep definition"

303083, "Intel-based Mac Power-On Self-Test RAM error codes"

75459, "Mac OS X keyboard shortcuts"

303124, "Startup key combinations for Intel-based Macs"

106178, "Startup Manager: How to select a startup volume"

86117, "Mac OS X: Available firmware updates"

303880, "Firmware updates for Intel-based Macs"

303469, "About the firmware restoration CD (Intel-based Macs)"

42642, "'To continue booting, type 'mac-boot' and press return' Message"

General Startup

106805, "Mac OS X: 'Broken folder' icon, prohibitory sign, or kernel panic when computer starts"

303363, Intel-based Mac: Startup sequence and error codes, symbols"

107392, "What is Safe Boot, Safe Mode? (Mac OS X)"

302477, "Progress bar appears after waking from sleep"

25392, "Isolating issues in Mac OS X"

URLs

Official Unified Extensible Firmware Interface (UEFI) resource website: http://www.uefi.org/

rEFIt alternative EFI booter with advanced features website: http://refit.sourceforge.net/

Apple's official launchd developer documentation: http://developer.apple.com/macosx/launchd.html

Review Quiz

1. What are the four primary startup stages in Mac OS X, and in what order do they start?

2. What are the visual and/or audible cues of the stages of startup?

3. What does the firmware do? What is the POST?

4. What role does the launchd process serve during system startup?

5. What items are automatically started by launchd during the system initialization process?

6. What role does the loginwindow process serve in system startup?

7. What is the difference between startup items and login items?

8. What happens during user logout?

9. What happens during system shutdown?

10. What is the difference between Safe Boot, Safe Mode, and Safe Login?

11. Which items are not loaded when Mac OS X safe-boots?

12. What keyboard combination is used to safe-boot Mac OS X?

13. How do you further resolve an issue that disappears when the Mac successfully safe-boots?

Answers

1. The primary startup stages are: firmware, booter, kernel, and user environment (in that order).

2. Each stage is indicated by the following: firmware, startup chime or bright flash of the power-on light followed by a light gray screen on the primary display; booter, a dark gray Apple logo on the primary display; kernel, a small dark gray spinning gear or spinning earth icon below the Apple logo; and user environment, a bright blue screen on all displays followed by the login screen or user desktop.

3. The firmware initializes the Mac's hardware and locates the booter file on a system volume. The Power-On Self-Test (POST) checks for basic hardware functionality when your Mac powers on.

4. The launchd process is ultimately responsible for starting every other process and application. It also manages system initialization and starts the loginwindow process.

5. During system initialization the launchd process automatically starts LaunchAgents, LaunchDaemons, StartupItems, and the /etc/rc.local UNIX script.

6. The loginwindow process displays the login screen that allows the user to authenticate, and then sets up and manages the GUI user session.

7. Startup items are opened during system initialization by the parent launchd process on behalf of the root user. Login items are opened at the end of the user session setup process by the user's specific launchd process.

8. During user logout the user's loginwindow process does the following: requests that all user GUI applications quit; forcibly quits any user background processes; runs any logout scripts; records the logout to the main system.log file; resets device permissions and preferences to their defaults; and finally quits the user's loginwindow and launchd processes.

9. At system shutdown the loginwindow process logs all users out and then tells the kernel to quit all remaining system processes. Once the kernel quits all system processes, the Mac will shut down.

10. Safe Boot refers to when the system is starting up; Safe Mode is when the system is actually running; and Safe Login is when the system starts up the user session.

11. When Mac OS X safe-boots, it will not load third-party KEXTs, LaunchAgents, LaunchDaemons, StartupItems, fonts, user login items, or user-specific LaunchAgents.

12. A Safe Boot is initiated by holding down the Shift key during system startup.

13. If an issue disappears when the Mac successfully safe-boots, then you must find and remove or quarantine the third-party startup resource that caused the issue. The best way to isolate the problematic item is to start up the Mac in verbose mode and then observe where the startup process fails. Verbose mode is initiated by holding down Command-V during system startup.

General Apple Troubleshooting

Each lesson in this guide features troubleshooting information specific to the technologies covered in that lesson. This appendix serves as a supplementary quick reference to general Apple troubleshooting techniques.

Troubleshooting Workflow

Always remember that the two primary goals of troubleshooting are to fix the issue properly and to fix it quickly. Following a systematic troubleshooting process will let you consistently achieve both of these goals. Even if you or your organization already has a preferred troubleshooting process, you will still find the following workflow useful.

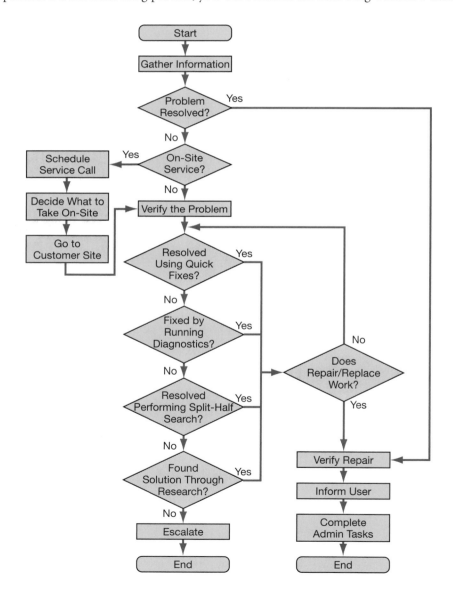

The AppleCare support group uses this workflow to ensure that all customer issues are properly handled. The beginning steps involve gathering information and verifying the problem. The end steps involve verifying the solution and informing the user, or escalating the problem to a higher support level. This appendix focuses on the four primary troubleshooting steps in the diagram: quick fixes, diagnostic tools, split-half search, and research resources.

Quick Fixes

The quick fixes applicable to troubleshooting Mac OS X are divided into three increasingly invasive strategies: innocuous fixes, less innocuous fixes, and invasive fixes.

Innocuous Fixes (Consider These First)

The following general troubleshooting steps have little impact on the computer and Mac OS X, and may fix transient issues:

▶ Shut down and then restart the Mac.

▶ Repair disk volumes with Disk Utility.

▶ Disconnect all external devices.

▶ Run Software Update to check for any uninstalled updates.

When you begin troubleshooting, you might try these innocuous tactics to assess the problem:

▶ Try the same task in another application if available.

▶ If you're experiencing a network issue, try connecting to another network service.

▶ Check with other Macs to see if they are experiencing the same problem, indicating a possible network issue.

▶ Inspect your Mac using System Profiler.

▶ Review logs using Console.

▶ Perform a safe boot by holding down the Shift key during startup until the words "Safe Boot" appear at the login screen; then you will be running Mac OS X in Safe Mode.

▶ Start in single-user mode by pressing Command-S during startup.

▶   Start in verbose mode by pressing Command-V during startup.

▶   Start from another known good system like the Mac OS X Install DVD.

Less Innocuous Fixes (Consider Next)

The following fixes have a moderate impact on the computer or the user environment. They are somewhat more time-consuming, so you should use caution and document your work:

▶   Choose Force Quit from the Apple menu if an application is not responding.

▶   Adjust user-specific settings using System Preferences.

▶   Log in with another user account or with an administrative user account.

▶   Delete cache files from the ~/Library/Caches and /Library/Caches folders.

▶   Move, rename, or delete suspect user preference files in ~/Library/Preferences.

▶   Try a different network interface or port.

▶   Verify network settings using the Network, Sharing, and Security preferences.

▶   Create a new test network location.

▶   Update peripheral and printer drivers.

▶   Try another known good peripheral.

▶   Check the settings in the Startup Disk preference.

▶   Fix permissions using Disk Utility.

▶   Check for firmware updates.

▶   Move, rename, or delete suspect system preference files in /Library/Preferences.

Invasive Fixes (Consider Last)

The following fixes have a more substantial impact on the system:

▶   Reinstall the suspect application.

▶   Reset Parameter Random Access Memory (PRAM) or nonvolatile RAM (NVRAM) by pressing Command-Option-P-R at startup until you hear the startup chime twice.

▶   Reset Power Manager (see the Knowledge Base for reset instructions for your computer).

▶   Remove non–Apple internal hardware upgrades from your computer, including memory or expansion cards.

▶ Perform an Upgrade installation of Mac OS X.

▶ Perform an Archive and Install installation of Mac OS X.

▶ Perform an Erase and Install installation of Mac OS X.

Diagnostic Tools

The following tools are often used for diagnostics on Mac OS X:

▶ Activity Monitor

▶ System Profiler

▶ Console

▶ Network Diagnostics accessed from the Network preferences

▶ Network Utility

▶ Directory Utility

▶ Disk Utility

▶ Apple Hardware Test, which is on your Mac's first software restore disc

▶ Apple Service Diagnostic, which is available to Apple Authorized Service Providers

▶ Display Utilities, which is available to Apple Authorized Service Providers

▶ MacTest Pro, which is available to Apple Authorized Service Providers

> **TIP** ▶ Several third-party utilities are useful for troubleshooting, including Tech Tool Deluxe, which is available with the purchase of an AppleCare Protection Plan.

Split-Half Search

When you cannot quickly isolate the cause of a problem, a technique known as a split-half search can be helpful. Split-half searches can take a considerable amount of time, so you should exhaust any quick-fix techniques before proceeding. The aim of a split-half search is to isolate an issue by systematically eliminating variables that could be its cause. You must temporarily remove half the variables, and then try to re-create the problem. When you discover which half contains the problem-causing item, you again halve the set of variables with the issue. Repeat to get successively smaller sets of variables. With each subsequent split you come closer to the source, ultimately narrowing down to the problematic item.

The following are common split-half search techniques:

- ▶ Start using safe boot by pressing Shift during startup.
- ▶ Start in single-user mode by pressing Command-S during startup.
- ▶ Forcibly quit processes in a systematic manner.
- ▶ Systematically remove potential problem files such as third-party system items, cache files, or preference files.
- ▶ Disconnect peripherals.
- ▶ Use Network Utility to evaluate connectivity to other devices and computers on a network.

Research Resources

The best problem-solving experts don't necessary know every answer; instead, they know where to *find* every answer.

Common resources to consult for troubleshooting Mac OS X issues are:

- ▶ User documentation
- ▶ Read Me files
- ▶ The Mac Help menu
- ▶ Command man pages viewable using the Terminal
- ▶ Log files viewable using Console
- ▶ The Apple support website: http://support.apple.com
- ▶ Internet support communities
- ▶ Results gathered from a well-queried Google search
- ▶ Apple's Service Source, which is available to Apple Authorized Service Providers

Index